DATE DUE

The Royal Navy at the windmill, November 1838

Three armed steamers under the command of Captain Williams Sandom, RN, bombard the windmill located in Edwardsburgh Township, near Prescott, Upper Canada. Their efforts proved totally ineffective and Sandom had to keep his distance lest his hastily converted civilian craft take a hit in their vulnerable machinery from the defenders' artillery. For five days in November 1838, Windmill Point was the scene of the bloodiest fighting of the undeclared war that raged along the Canadian border in 1837-1840.
(Painting by Peter Rindlisbacher, courtesy of the artist)

DONALD E. GRAVES

Guns Across the River

THE BATTLE OF THE WINDMILL, 1838

Additional research by
Arthur J. Robinson

Maps by
Christopher Johnson

Marine art by
Peter Rindlisbacher

Published by
THE FRIENDS OF WINDMILL POINT
Prescott

Produced and distributed by
ROBIN BRASS STUDIO
Toronto

Produced and distributed for
The Friends of Windmill Point
P.O. Box 775, Prescott, Ontario K0E 1T0, Canada
by Robin Brass Studio Inc.
10 Blantyre Avenue, Toronto, Ontario M1N 2R4, Canada
Fax: 416-698-2120 • e-mail: rbrass@total.net
www.rbstudiobooks.com

Distributed in the United States of America by
Midpoint Trade Books
27 West 20th St., Suite 1102, New York, NY 10011
Fax: 212-727-0195 • e-mail: midpointny@aol.com

Printed and bound in Canada by AGMV-Marquis, Cap-Saint-Ignace, Quebec

National Library of Canada Cataloguing in Publication Data

Graves, Donald E. (Donald Edward)
    Guns across the river : the battle of the Windmill, 1838

Includes bibliographical references and index.
ISBN 1-896941-21-4

1. Windmill, Battle of the, Ont., 1838. 2. Canada – History – Rebellions, 1837-1838. I. Title.

FC457.W55G72 2001   971.03'8   C2001-930488-9
F1032.G72 2001

Contents

This book is dedicated to the spirit, beliefs and personal sacrifices of those individuals whose fate drew them to Windmill Point in November of 1838. Whatever their motivation, their courage and personal commitment to their cause were exemplary. The result of their actions was one of the most colourful and tragic events in the history of the upper St. Lawrence River region.

THE FRIENDS OF WINDMILL POINT

THE FRIENDS OF WINDMILL POINT
GRATEFULLY ACKNOWLEDGE THE FINANCIAL ASSISTANCE
OF THE FOLLOWING INDIVIDUALS AND ORGANIZATIONS
WHOSE CONTRIBUTIONS MADE THIS BOOK POSSIBLE.

Parks Canada, Prescott, Ontario

George Drummond and Family, Spencerville, Ontario

Edwardsburgh Historians

3M Canada Company Brockville Site

South Edwardsburgh Recreation Association, Johnstown, Ontario

Grenville County Historical Society

René Schoemaker, Prescott, Ontario

Township of Edwardsburgh/Cardinal

Earl Connell, Spencerville, Ontario

DuPont Canada Maitland Site

Sandra Shouldice, Johnstown, Ontario

Rob Heuvel and Family, Cardinal, Ontario

Shell Brockville Lubricants Plant

Toronto Dominion Bank, Prescott, Ontario

Royal Bank of Canada, Prescott, Ontario

Foreword

The picturesque and historic windmill anchored on a bluff overlooking the St. Lawrence River in Edwardsburgh Township near Prescott, Canada, is a well-known landmark but the intriguing story of the 1838 battle fought on the site is regrettably a little-known episode. Although the windmill has been a National Historic Site since 1920, the only information that visitors could glean about this event was contained in the brief texts of plaques installed at the site from time to time.

In 1994 a group of concerned local citizens founded the Friends of Windmill Point, a non-profit organization whose objects are to increase both awareness about the Battle of the Windmill and visitors' enjoyment of the windmill historic site. In cooperation with Parks Canada, the Friends of Windmill Point developed public programs and educational exhibits and, staffed with volunteers, the windmill was opened to the public with an enthusiastic response in 1996.

In order to better comprehend the historic context of the battle and to make this information available beyond those visitors who happened to stop at the windmill, the Friends of Windmill Point also created a publication project. This venture has developed into an exciting partnership between the Friends and Donald E. Graves, one of Canada's foremost military historians, as well as Robin Brass Studio of Toronto, the designer and distributor of this book, noted marine artist Peter Rindlisbacher, and our main sponsor, Parks Canada. With the financial backing of those persons and organizations whose efforts we gratefully acknowledge on the opposite page, the result is *Guns Across the River: The Battle of the Windmill, 1838.*

Quite deliberately, the Friends of Windmill Point made a decision not to influence, in any way, Donald Graves's work. We feel, however, that his enthusiasm for this project has resulted in a study of the battle of windmill that, in its comprehensiveness and presentation, has exceeded our expectations. *Guns Across the River* is an exhaustive and entertaining analysis of a fascinating yet tragic episode in American and Canadian history that will be a valued addition to any library. The Friends of Windmill Point are also sure that it will prove a popular work that will help us achieve our objective of sharing this important but neglected event with the wider world.

THE FRIENDS OF WINDMILL POINT
Prescott, Canada
April 2001

Preface

When René Schoemaker buttonholed me on the main street of Brockville one fine autumn morning to insist I write a book about the battle of the windmill, I must confess I did have my doubts. In the first instance, this action was outside my normal grazing areas of 1793-1815 and 1939-1945 and, second, it was coupled in my mind with the Canadian Rebellions of 1837, a topic that I have never found particularly enthralling. However, since René wasn't going to let me get away without some kind of answer, I told him I would look into the matter and get back to him.

I am now glad that René caught me because, once I began to investigate the battle, I discovered it was a fascinating episode involving some very colourful characters. The battle of the windmill was also an event that had its humorous aspects, and if so many people had not lost their lives during those five awful days in November 1838, it would have made a delightful comic opera, but unfortunately it resulted in much death and suffering that was all the more tragic because it was needless. I also found that in the 162 years since the action was fought it had become thickly covered with mythological weeds that badly needed to be cut back.

Take, for example, the Upper Canada Rebellion of 1837, which in the minds of many people is connected with the battle of the windmill. Back in the days when history was still being taught in school, I was told that that rebellion was "a good thing," in Molesworth's immortal phrase, because "it led to the growth of responsible government." (You had to memorize that phrase, you see, to answer the inevitable question on the term test.) Now I am not so sure, at least not as far as William Lyon Mackenzie is concerned, because responsible government requires responsible leaders and Mackenzie was, if anything, an irresponsible man. As I explain below, he has much to answer for in the period that immediately followed his abortive attempt to overthrow the government of Upper Canada.

There is also that interesting man Nils von Schoultz, the leader of the American invaders at the windmill, who has become imbued with a distinctly romantic aura as a misguided hero who fought well for a bad cause. In the three decades that have passed since the last study of the windmill battle was published, we have discovered much about this man, including his true nationality. I learned that almost everything von Schoultz said about himself was untrue and that, far from being a tragic figure, he was really nothing more than a well-bred confidence trickster who, although personally brave, was not a particularly good soldier.

Next, there is the question of the nationality of the men who attacked Prescott in November 1838. There are still those in this country who believe that they numbered many Canadians in their ranks and that the invasion was an integral part of the political turmoil that had resulted in the Rebellion of 1837. In fact, there were only twenty-five British subjects in an invading force that may have numbered as many as three hundred and of those twenty-five men perhaps only seven or eight can be accurately described as Canadian rebels or Reformers, and one of those was mentally unstable. Most of the invaders (four of every five) were Americans, members of a terrorist (for want of a better word) organization, the Patriot Hunters, commanded and funded by Americans. The only serious connection that this organization had with the Canadian rebels was in the persons of William Lyon Mackenzie and Charles Duncombe, leaders of the 1837 uprising, who helped to create it.

Not all Americans were so ill-disposed toward their neighbours. Far from approving or tacitly supporting the efforts of the Patriot Hunters, as many Canadians thought at the time, the United States government did its best to prevent them carrying out their work of destruction but was hampered by simple lack of force. Without the efforts of American officers such as Major General Winfield Scott, Brigadier General Hugh Brady and Colonels John Wool and William J. Worth, however, the loss of life and property in Canada would have been much higher than it was in 1837-1840.

In the end, whatever its political origins, the battle of the windmill was a military problem and it was solved by military means. Canada was fortunate in 1838 that it was defended by the British army and navy, otherwise it might well have gone the way of Mexico, which, in the first twenty-seven years of its existence as an independent state, lost nearly a third of its national territory to the United States. The lesson for Canadian politicians is simple – it is not enough to proclaim sovereignty, you must be prepared to defend it – but it is doubtful, based on their record, that they will ever learn this lesson.

Enough talk of politicians, let me now render homage to those who helped with the research and writing of *Guns Across the River*. First, I must acknowledge the efforts made by the Friends of Windmill Point – Paul Fortier, Rob Heuvel, Elizabeth Pilon, René Schoemaker, Sandra Shouldice, Gordon Swoger, John Warren and Murray Workman – whose enthusiasm gave birth to this book.

All the Friends were helpful but I would be extremely remiss if I did not acknowledge the particular debt I owe to René Schoemaker. A lifelong student of the history of Prescott and area, René has been a tower of strength during this project and many times went far beyond the call of any required duty to help me, including crawling out on the snow-covered and treacherous ice of the St. Lawrence River in the middle of a Canadian winter to take a photograph of the International Bridge from just the right angle. Without René's vision and energy, this book might not have been started – and it would certainly not have been finished.

I am very grateful to Arthur J. Robinson of Victoria, British Columbia, for donating his specialized expertise on the Canadian militia who fought at the windmill which will be found in Appendix C.

I owe much to the five outside readers of *Guns Across the River* in manuscript. Dennis Carter-Edwards of Cornwall, Paul Fortier of Prescott, Pat Kavanagh of Buffalo, Robert Malcomson of St. Catharines and Brigadier General (Retd.) William Patterson of Kingston all gave good, positive and helpful advice and, if I ignored it, I did so at my peril.

My sincere appreciation goes to the professional staff of the following institutions for their help: the Brockville Museum;

Fort Wellington National Historic Site and the Grenville County Historical Society in Prescott; and Parks Canada collections staff in Cornwall.

I am indebted to the following American colleagues who, ignorant of what I was writing about their fellow citizens, cheerfully helped with my labours: Brian Dunnigan of the Clements Library, Ann Arbor, Michigan; Russell Grills of the Cazenovia State Historic Site, New York State; John Schedel of Buffalo, New York; Dr. Traer Van Allen of New York City; Professor Joseph Whitehorne of Lord Fairfax College, Virginia; and Dr. Robert K. Wright of the United States Army Center of Military History.

I also owe a particular debt to two good American friends and fellow historians, John Morris and Patrick Wilder. They are both proud sons of Jefferson County, New York, and in the last decade or so, on various pretexts, we have scoured that county from Redwood to Mannsville and from Cape Vincent to Antwerp, and must have looked at every structure built prior to 1850 – at least twice. Thanks also to Joan Morris and Katrina Wilder for not showing too much pleasure at our long absences.

At the Directorate of History and Heritage, Department of National Defence, Ottawa, I am grateful to Major Paul Lansey, Major Michael McNorgan, and Michael Whitby for helping out with many obscure and (to them) annoying questions.

On marine and naval matters I must thank Lieutenant Commander (Retd.), RCN, Pat Whitby of Ottawa, who loaned me his charts and his knowledge of the St. Lawrence; and Maurice Smith and the staff of the Marine Museum of the Great Lakes in Kingston, who let me loose in their library for a morning.

For providing illustrations, or taking photographs, I owe a debt to my old friend René Chartrand of Ottawa; Ron Ridley, Curator of Old Fort Henry, Kingston; and Major John Grodzinski of the same city.

This is the third book I have worked on with the production team of Robin Brass on design, Chris Johnson on maps, and Peter Rindlisbacher on cover and marine art. The boys get better every time and, again, the result has been splendid.

A number of personal friends have assisted in my labours. Dr. David Atack of Almonte helped me to comprehend the medical aspects of death by hanging, while Bruce Kingsley tried repeatedly, without success, to convert me to the political philosophy espoused by Prime Minister Mackenzie King. Lieutenant Colonel (Retd.) Brian Reid of Kemptville was helpful on matters of local history, while Doug Hendry of Merrickville became so excited to learn his beloved Argyll and Sutherland Highlanders fought at the windmill that he bought me a magnificent meal to hear more about it – a distressing experience for a thrifty Scotsman. I feel I should apologize to many local hostesses, particularly Sandy Atack and Noreen Young, for disrupting pleasant dinner parties with enthusiastic and detailed descriptions of the various methods of capital punishment. It is a funny thing, but I am rarely invited twice to the same house.

On the home front I have to curse those critical editors, Ned and George, who like to tear a draft to shreds as it comes off the printer but are otherwise unobjectionable cats. Finally, of course, there is the beautiful Dianne, who finds crucial books and documents that ran away and hid in the night, takes great photographs, compiles conscientious appendices and indexes, skips the country if the writing is going badly, ignores me if it is going well and who is, in a word, wonderful.

DONALD E. GRAVES
St. Patrick's Day
Wolf Grove, Upper Canada

NOTE TO THE READER

The modern nation of Canada did not exist during the time of the events described below although Americans often referred to the separate colonies of British North America as "Canada." In 1838, the correct term would have been "the Canadas" as there were two: Upper Canada (modern Ontario) and Lower Canada (modern Quebec). I have tried to use the period terms throughout this book.

Most readers will be familiar with the geography of the St. Lawrence River but for those who are not, this major waterway flows northeast ("uphill" on the map) from the Great Lakes to the Atlantic. On that part of the St. Lawrence featured in *Guns Across the River*, the right or southern bank is in the United States while the left or northern bank is in Canada. Down-river is to the east (actually the northeast) while up-river is west (actually southwest).

Although it is often called the Prescott Windmill, it should be noted that both the structure and Newport, the hamlet that surrounded it in 1838, were located in Edwardsburgh Township, Grenville County, Upper Canada.

As usual I spell the name of the village Sackets Harbor thus, except in quoted text, although I am aware that there are other permutations.

It was to be nearly another half century after the battle of the windmill before time zones were introduced and, therefore, the times given below are a consensus based on all available sources.

I have tried to keep discussion of military organization and technical matters to a minimum in the main text of *Guns Across the River* lest it distract from the narrative. The reader unfamiliar with these subjects, or who wishes to know more about them, should consult Appendix A.

D.E.G.

Windmill Point near Prescott, Canada

Friday, 1 July 1938

The organizers of the Prescott International Peace Centennial were worried. It had rained that morning, forcing them to cancel the historical pageant at Fort Wellington, and although the drizzle had tailed off by noon, overcast skies posed a threat to the memorial ceremony scheduled for the afternoon. This was troubling because the organizers had planned this ceremony to be the major public event of the Centennial and invited to it nearly every politician within reach on both sides of the border, including Prime Minister Mackenzie King of Canada, who had promised to try to make it if his public duties permitted.

The purpose of this ceremony was to commemorate the men who had fought in an obscure military action called the "Battle of the Windmill." Perhaps the most colourful event in the history of Prescott, it had taken place almost a century before, near the old stone lighthouse on Windmill Point, a mile or so east of town. As most people understood it, this battle was a prominent episode in the Upper Canada Rebellion of 1837 when reform-minded Canadians, led by William Lyon Mackenzie, took up arms against Britain to fight for responsible government and gain control of their political future. A group of these patriots, so the story went, joined by American and European volunteers sympathetic to their cause, and all under the leadership of an aristocratic Polish soldier of fortune, Nils von Schoultz, had occupied the lighthouse on Windmill Point in November 1838. For five days, they had held out bravely against superior British forces but their dream of freeing the oppressed Canadians ended when they were forced to surrender.

By the time the centennial of this battle approached in 1938, most Canadians had forgotten about it – but not the people of Prescott, who decided to hold a festival to celebrate the event and, incidentally, to promote tourism. "If you haven't visited Prescott, You've wasted other holidays," was the optimistic slogan dreamed up by the organizing committee of the International Peace Centennial to be held at the "Oasis for World-Weary Realists" during the first week of July 1938. It was to be a week filled with sports meets, band concerts, pageants, a carnival, boat races, fiddling competitions, street dances and fireworks – and a good time would be had by all, if only the weather would co-operate.[1]

Fortunately, the rain held off that Friday afternoon and the ceremony at Windmill Point went ahead as scheduled. One after another, politicians from Canada and the United States spoke about the struggle for responsible government in the late

1830s and how the spillover from that struggle caused an undeclared war to take place along the border. The speakers emphasized that, in 1938, such problems would never happen, and this optimistic message was reinforced by a representative from the League of Nations Society who assured his listeners that peaceful negotiation would solve the current international problems with Mr. Hitler in Europe and a militant Japan in Asia.[2]

This worthy but deluded man was followed by the Polish consul-general from Ottawa, who expressed pride that his countrymen, including that tragic figure Nils von Schoultz, had helped to achieve freedom in Canada. He then unveiled a plaque dedicated "To the Memory of the Polish Patriots who fought at the Battle of the Windmill" as a guard of honour, drawn from the Polish Legion, the Royal Canadian Mounted Police and the Stormont, Dundas and Glengarry Highlanders, a local militia regiment, stood at attention. To the organizers' great delight, the final speaker of the day was Prime Minister Mackenzie King, who managed to arrive just after the ceremony had begun.[3]

They need not have worried about the prime minister attending because, as it happened, he was extremely interested in the battle of the windmill. It was a family matter: King's maternal grandfather was William Lyon Mackenzie, that great Canadian who had begun the noble struggle to achieve independence from Britain that his grandson was determined to complete, while his paternal grandfather was Bombardier John King of the Royal Artillery, who had fought in the battle. It was unfortunate, if not tragic, that one forebear had tried hard to kill men who believed in the admirable cause of the other forebear, and that tragedy was something the prime minister was determined to address in his speech. Although 1 July 1938 was a very busy day for the prime minister, being the last sitting day of the current parliamentary session, he managed to leave Ottawa in time to speak in the closing minutes of the ceremony.[4]

When the clapping had died away, King delivered a speech he had researched and written himself. He talked of the 1837 uprisings in Canada, how the men who had led them, such as his mother's father, had been forced to take up arms against an intransigent British Crown and how they had been reviled in their time as rebels and traitors, but were now revered. He described how the American and European volunteers who had joined them had been severely punished as pirates and brigands for their belief in democracy. He spoke movingly of that Polish hero, Nils von Schoultz, who had sacrificed his life in the fight for liberty, and he stressed that Canadians should render "the honour that was due" this martyr as they now knew that his purpose "had been to serve a larger freedom."[5]

It was an emotional speech – quite "the best of the day" in Mackenzie King's modest opinion – but it was the truth as the prime minister saw it. And King thought that it was important that the truth be known about these matters because, even in enlightened modern Canada, there were those (many in the ranks of the opposition Conservative Party) who continued to speak ill of such heroes as Grandfather Mackenzie and Nils von Schoultz. King was proud to have set the historical record straight, and late that night, after he had biscuits with his little dog, Pat, in the library of Laurier House, his residence in Ottawa, he confided to his diary that the day "had been one of the best and most memorable of my life."[6]

Unfortunately, like many Canadian politicians, Mackenzie King was thoroughly ignorant of the history of his own country and his account of what had taken place at Prescott nearly a century before was not quite accurate. What follows is the story of that obscure action and that story begins a few miles north of Toronto in the early evening of 5 December 1837 ......

PART I

"The Amalekites are among us:" Troubled times in the Canadas

1837-1838

The march on Toronto, 5 December 1837

In the early evening, a group of poorly-armed men under the leadership of William Lyon Mackenzie splashed south down muddy Yonge Street toward the provincial capital of Toronto. Their object was to overthrow the established government of Upper Canada. (From C.W. Jefferys, *Portrait Gallery of Canadian History*)

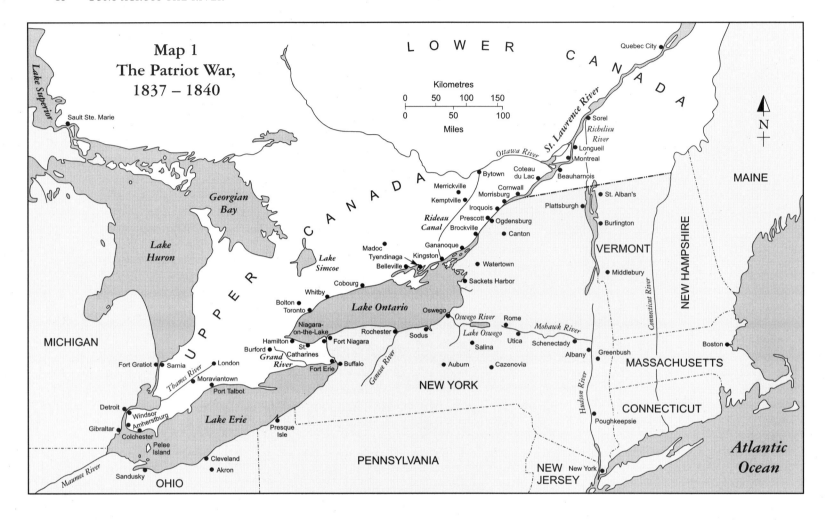

Map 1
The Patriot War,
1837 – 1840

CHAPTER ONE

"A brave stroke of liberty!"
The Canadian rebellions of 1837

Now that the rebellion's o'er
Let each true Briton sing
Long live the Queen in health and peace
And may each rebel swing.

But still for Mac there's one more step
To end his life of evil
Soon may he take the last long step
From gibbet to the d____l.[1]

The march began in the early evening. Although the men in the column tried to maintain a semblance of military order, no soldier would have mistaken them for other than what they were – a procession of about seven hundred civilians, mostly farmers wearing great or short coats, tall hats or caps, gaiters, boots or shoes. Almost all were carrying weapons or would-be weapons, including old military muskets, fowling pieces, twenty-foot pikes, axe handles, clubs and pitchforks, but some were armed with nothing more dangerous than slogans on hastily-lettered signs. Out in front, mounted on a white pony, rode the improbable figure of their leader, a small man sporting a sandy-haired wig whose wiry frame was swaddled in several bulky overcoats. His name was William Lyon Mackenzie and his purpose, and that of the men splashing behind him down muddy Yonge Street toward Toronto this early winter evening of 5 December 1837, was to overthrow the established government of the British province of Upper Canada.

The discontent that had brought these men to take up arms had been brewing for more than a decade. Its focus was a small but tightly-knit group known as the Family Compact which, most simply put, consisted of the leading members of the government of Upper Canada (modern Ontario). Connected by marriage, background and religion, the Compact was also united by a shared belief that the province was, and must remain, a British possession, a belief expressed in unwavering support for the established church (the Church of England) and a marked aversion to all things American, particularly republican political institutions. The men of the Compact abhorred the popular democracy practised in the United States – to them, elected legislators were only one (and certainly not the most important) part of government.[2]

They came by these views honestly. Drawn largely from the children of the original settlers of the province or early immigrants from Britain, as young men they had witnessed the havoc wrought in Upper Canada by American invasion during the War of 1812: the devastation and depopulation of the Niagara and western districts, the occupation of the capital, and the widespread disaffection among American-born residents incited and led by three members of the provincial Legislative Assembly. The men of the Compact were convinced that the province had only been preserved in 1812-1814 by their efforts, with a little help from Britain. They regarded the republic to the south as a perpetual threat and viewed any criticism of the established government, no matter how valid, as intolerable and were quick to suppress it. The Compact was able to do this because it controlled the machinery of government, particularly the executive and the judiciary.

Many Upper Canadians did not share these beliefs and in the 1820s an opposition coalition, commonly called the Reformers, began to demand change. The Reformers were drawn from religious congregations who resented the favouritism shown the Church of England; businessmen and merchants who wanted more effective economic programmes; American-born residents who disliked the government's restrictive alien policies; settlers in frontier areas who needed better roads and schools; and those who desired government positions and appointments. The Reformers' cry was "responsible government," government accountable to the elected Assembly, and their main targets were the Legislative Council, or upper house of the provincial parliament, and the Executive Council or cabinet, both of which were controlled by the Compact. In 1828 the Reformers gained a majority in the Assembly and by the early 1830s, guided by able men such as the father and son combination of William and Robert Baldwin, Marshal Spring Bidwell, Peter Perry and Egerton Ryerson, they had placed the Compact squarely on the defensive.

William Lyon Mackenzie (1795-1861)
At best erratic, at worst unstable, William Lyon Mackenzie was an arrogant puff-toad of a man on a personal mission to bring down the high and mighty. He led an uprising against the Crown in December 1837 and then fled to the United States, where he was instrumental in the creation of the American patriot movement which brought considerable suffering to his fellow countrymen. Mackenzie soon fell out with the American patriot leaders and moved to New York to do what he did best – publish a newspaper attacking every person or thing that attracted his ire, and there were many. He remains a controversial figure to this day. (Author's collection)

Ryerson, Bidwell and the Baldwins were respected community leaders but the same cannot be said of William Lyon Mackenzie, the Compact's most outspoken critic. An arrogant little puff-toad of a man on a personal mission to bring low all the high and mighty, Mackenzie had emigrated from Scotland to Upper Canada in 1820. Four years later, he began to publish the *Colonial Advocate*, a newspaper that took aim at the "sturdy beggars, parsons, priests, pensioners, army people, place-men, bank directors, and stock and land jobbers" of the Compact.[3] Although his criticisms were often warranted, Mackenzie frequently couched them in words that bordered on the scurrilous and the *Advocate* did not appeal to the more intelligent portion of the population. Its circulation had nearly withered by June 1826 when a gang, composed of the sons of Compact families, destroyed Mackenzie's press, thus not only saving him from his creditors but also transforming him into a martyr to the freedom of the press. Mackenzie won a suit for damages, purchased a better press, and continued to raise the fiery cross against any person or thing that incited his wrath – and there were many targets.[4]

In 1828 Mackenzie was elected to the Assembly but was expelled by the members on the basis that he had libelled the institution in print. He promptly ran in the by-election held to contest his vacated seat and was re-elected. He was expelled again and re-elected again – in fact Mackenzie was to suffer expulsion and enjoy re-election many times. In 1832, he took his complaints to London, where they were listened to with attention as Britain itself was in political turmoil caused by its own Reform movement, which was attempting to make the parliament at Westminster more accountable. Reinstated to a Legislative Assembly dominated by Reformers, Mackenzie chaired a committee to investigate the problems in Upper Canada and sent a lengthy report to London which alarmed the officials of the Colonial Office. They questioned Sir John Colborne, the lieutenant governor of the province, about its veracity, and when Colborne replied that the report was exaggerated, he was informed that he would shortly be replaced by Sir Francis Bond Head.

Armed with instructions to investigate the problems and to conciliate the opposing factions, Head arrived in Toronto in

The best soldier in North America: Sir John Colborne (1778-1863) Widely regarded, after the Duke of Wellington, as the best soldier in the British army, Colborne had an outstanding combat record in the Napoleonic Wars. He was less successful as the lieutenant governor of Upper Canada but performed extremely well as military commander in chief, British North America, 1837-1839. Calm, methodical, competent and decisive, Colborne provided professional leadership during the rebellions and the border crisis that followed. (Toronto Reference Library)

Not the Crown's best: Sir Francis Bond Head (1793-1875)
A former engineer officer and travel writer, Head was appointed lieutenant governor of Upper Canada in 1836. The reasons for this appointment are uncertain because he had no previous experience in colonial administration, but nonetheless he arrived in Toronto, armed with instructions to investigate and ameliorate the political tensions in the province. He managed to make a bad situation worse and was replaced in the spring of 1838 by the more competent Sir George Arthur. Head never again held public office but continued to entertain friends with his fancy trick rope work, a skill he had acquired in South America. (Toronto Reference Library)

early 1836. An engineer with no experience of colonial administration, he soon took a dislike to the Reformers. He did appoint some to his Executive Council but, since he rarely saw reason to consult it, when its six members, conservative as well as Reform, resigned in protest, he replaced them with men sympathetic to his views. This angered the Assembly, which refused to approve money bills, thus cutting off the salaries of many officials. In retaliation, Head refused assent to those money bills already passed and then dissolved the Assembly in May 1836, forcing an election.

As the lieutenant governor, it was not really proper for Head to participate in a political campaign, but nonetheless he stamped the hustings with a very simple but effective message – the choice was not between conservatives and Reformers, but between loyalty and disloyalty. This struck a responsive chord with the recent British immigrants, who were suspicious of the Reformers and disliked Mackenzie's stridency. A loose but effective alliance developed between elements of the Methodists, the Catholics, the Orange Lodge, business interests and conservatives which managed not only to get its adherents out to the polls in strength but also to hamper those who supported the Reformers. There were complaints about election irregularities but the result, an overwhelming defeat for the Reformers, was valid and marked a shift in opinion among Upper Canadians, who were becoming weary of political strife.

Mackenzie lost his seat in the conservative landslide but quickly returned to the fray. Having sold the *Advocate*, he launched a new paper, the *Constitution*, and was soon lambasting the "Pensioners! Placemen! Profligates! Orangemen! Churchmen!, Brokers! Gamblers!" and parasites whose feet were "on the people's necks."[5] He began to assert the virtues of a republic and there were some in the province prepared to listen to this radical view as Sir Francis Head had quickly thrown away the fruits of his electoral victory. Exultant at having defeated the Reformers at the polls, Head did not try to conciliate them but embarked on a reckless attempt to destroy them. The result was that, within six months of the election, he managed to alienate most of the people in the province, whatever their political views. Head also quarrelled with his superiors in London, and when he tendered his resignation in September 1837, it was quickly accepted. Head's buffoonery, coupled with a severe economic recession, led to an increasingly tense situation in Upper Canada,

Things were worse in the adjoining province of Lower Canada, where the most outspoken critic of the government was Louis-Joseph Papineau. A Montreal lawyer who had first been elected to the Legislative Assembly in 1808 at the age of twenty-two, Papineau and those who followed him agitated for an elected Legislative Council that would be responsible to the Legislative Assembly, and for greater control of government revenues, patronage and bureaucracy. These views were popular among both the English- and French-speaking populations of the province, but in the 1830s, when Papineau began to advocate not only control of the government by the French-speaking majority but also the establishment of a republic, he lost the support of many moderates. Papineau and his followers, known as the *Patriotes*, became increasingly isolated and by 1837 the political middle ground in Lower Canada had disappeared as the *Patriotes* and their extreme English-speaking counterparts organized paramilitary groups. This development worried the lieutenant governor, Lord Gosford, who had been sent from Britain with a mission of conciliation similar to that of Head, and Gosford found himself in an impossible situation when the Legislative Assembly, influenced by Papineau, refused to pass the supply bill, thus cutting off the government's funds. Tiring of the obstructionist tactics of the *Patriotes*, Gosford

The *Patriote*: Louis-Joseph Papineau (1786-1871)

The son of a distinguished family, Papineau was first elected to the legislative assembly in 1809 and became the leader of the *Patriotes*, the extreme element among the Lower Canada Reformers. By the late 1830s, his radical views had caused him and his followers to become isolated from most people in Lower Canada. When the *Patriotes*' opposition flared up into open revolt in November 1837, Papineau proved to be better with words than weapons, fled Lower Canada without experiencing any fighting and was replaced as *Patriote* leader by the more effective Robert Nelson. Granted amnesty in 1844, Papineau returned to Canada and resumed his political career, later becoming an advocate of annexation to the United States. (National Archives of Canada, C-5462)

Future rebels drilling, autumn 1837
In the autumn of 1837, deciding that they would never achieve their aims through peaceful means, the radical element of the Upper Canada Reform movement began to prepare for an armed uprising against the Crown. They had little support, as most Upper Canadians were either loyal or not prepared to take such extreme measures to settle their political grievances. (From C.W. Jefferys, *Portrait Gallery of Canadian History*)

announced in April 1837 that he would spend the required funds without approval from the Assembly – a move that cost him much sympathy among the French-speaking population. By the summer of 1837, Lower Canada was moving toward a crisis and the *Patriotes* were actively preparing for armed rebellion.[6]

Papineau maintained communication with Mackenzie, although he neither liked nor trusted the Scot. For his part, Mackenzie boasted in the pages of the *Constitution* that if an uprising occurred in the lower province, it would receive military assistance from the "tens of thousands of Englishmen, Scotchmen, and above all, Irishmen, now in the United States" who waited only for the republican standard to be planted in the Canadas "to throw their strength and numbers to the side of democracy."[7] He toured the settlements north of Toronto, which had a large number of American-born residents, addressing public meetings and urging the creation of "Vigilance Committees," or paramilitary groups. These committees were formed but they did little real military training, holding only one large drill in Bolton that was amateurish in nature – an eyewitness remembered that it consisted of three or four hundred men "marshalled or rather scattered in picturesque fashion hither and thither" wearing a great variety of uniform and poorly armed, some "having only a carving knife at the end of a fishing pole."[8]

Activity like this was reported to Sir Francis Head, but since the lieutenant governor possessed a low opinion of Mackenzie, he refused to take any precautions. In early October he sent the one regular British regiment in Upper Canada to Lower Canada and obstinately refused requests by militia officers to have their units called out. Neither did he pay any attention to the constitution for a "State of Upper Canada" the Scotsman published in his newspaper in November 1837.

Doctor Charles Duncombe (1792-1867)

A believer in utopian ideals, Duncombe was Mackenzie's counterpart in western Upper Canada. He played a major role in the patriot movement and the successor Hunters, conceiving the idea of an investment bank to fund their activities. Duncombe may have wished to improve the lot of mankind but the fact is that he made a major contribution to an organization that killed and wounded many Canadians. He never returned to Canada, dying in California in 1867. (Toronto Reference Library)

When this document appeared, Mackenzie had been ready to act for more than a month. In early October, after receiving a vague message from Papineau that the time for a "brave stroke of liberty" was at hand, he assembled his principal subordinates to plan a raid on the arms stored in Toronto city hall.[9] Faced with moving from rhetoric to action, they hesitated and it was finally decided the attack would be put off in favour of a general uprising. In late November, when he learned that serious fighting had broken out in Lower Canada, Mackenzie rode to Montgomery's Tavern a few miles north of Toronto, where his followers would assemble prior to marching on the capital. That march was to take place on 7 December 1837.

In Lower Canada, events came to a head in November when street fighting broke out between a *Patriote* paramilitary group and a similar English-speaking organization. British troops had to restore order, and when Papineau and the other *Patriote* leaders learned warrants had been issued for their arrest, they fled to the countryside. On 16 November, a *Patriote* force fired at loyal militia near Longueil on the south shore of the St. Lawrence and, in response, General Sir John Colborne, who had been appointed military commander-in-chief in North America, sent regular troops to the Richelieu Valley, the centre of anti-government sentiment. Seven days later, a force of British regulars was forced to retreat after a brisk skirmish at the village of St. Denis. This evoked a stronger response from Colborne and on 25 November his troops captured the insurgents' headquarters at St. Charles, north of St. Denis, after a two-hour fight. Papineau fled to Vermont with many of his followers and Colborne spent a couple of weeks pacifying the Richelieu area before moving on the second hotbed of *Patriote* sentiment, the Lac des Deux Montagnes area northwest of Montreal. After a four-hour battle fought on 14 December to evict the *Patriote* defenders from the village church at St. Eustache, seventy insurgents lay dead and the rebellion in Lower Canada had ended.[10]

Although he was aware of Papineau's failure in Lower Canada, Mackenzie was still determined to carry out some sort of political demonstration in the upper province, up to and including marching on the provincial capital. If this was done, he assured the men who assembled at Montgomery's Tavern on 4 December 1837, thousands of supporters would flock to their banner. At the same time, Mackenzie's associate, Doctor Charles Duncombe, a 45-year-old resident of Burford, would raise the western district of the province. For the most part, the 700 or 800 would-be revolutionaries who listened to these assertions about a rosy future were poorly armed and badly trained. Many had only come to take part in a political demonstration, and when they suspected that Mackenzie was set on armed rebellion, they went home in disgust.[11]

For Mackenzie, all hope of surprise was lost when a self-appointed government scout, Toronto alderman John Powell, rode up Yonge Street that evening to verify rumours that insurgents were gathering north of the city. He was personally captured by the rebel leader, who, believing the alderman's assurance he had no weapons, did not bother to search him. A few minutes later, Powell pulled out two pistols, used one to kill Anthony Anderson, the rebels' military leader, and pointed the other at Mackenzie's face. It misfired and Powell then galloped down Yonge Street to spread the alarm.

Sir Francis Head had stubbornly refused to believe that an uprising was imminent but Powell's information forced him to confront the truth. The capital was nearly defenceless but those Torontonians loyal to the government armed themselves from the weapons at City Hall and, somewhat nervously, prepared to put their political beliefs to the test. Buying time, Head dispatched a delegation to offer the rebels an amnesty if they laid down their arms. It consisted of two men the insurgents would trust: the Reform leader Robert Baldwin and Doctor John Rolph, a 45-year-old physician, who was actually one of Mackenzie's co-conspirators.

In the early afternoon of 5 December, Baldwin and Rolph encountered Mackenzie and his ragtag army about a mile north of Toronto. The unfortunate encounter with Powell had convinced Mackenzie to advance by two days his plans to seize the capital and he had moved his little force toward the city. He heard the envoys' terms and requested they be put in writing, but promised not to move until they returned. While he waited, the Scotsman amused himself by threatening to horsewhip a local housewife unless she cooked for his men and by burning down the residence of the director of the Bank of Upper Canada. Rolph and Baldwin arrived with the bad news that Head, having learned militia reinforcements were on their way, had withdrawn his offer. Rolph, however, took one of Mackenzie's lieutenants aside and urged an advance into the city as the rebels greatly outnumbered its defenders.

Shortly after 6 P.M., mounted on his white pony, Mackenzie led the march down Yonge Street. The rebel column had reached the outskirts of Toronto when they were fired on by loyalist militia. Mackenzie's chief subordinate, Samuel Lount, ordered the van of the insurgent column to return fire and the leading element opened up with their muskets and fowling pieces, before dropping to one knee to reload and give their comrades behind a clear field of fire. Unfortunately the men in the rear, hearing the noise of the volley and then seeing the sudden disappearance of the leading ranks, concluded their comrades had been killed, the contest lost, and it was time to go – within minutes, the rebel army had melted away. Mackenzie, however, was not yet ready to give up and with Lount's help managed to re-assemble about five hundred disheartened followers at Montgomery's Tavern.

That night, Colonel Allan MacNab, an energetic militia officer from Hamilton, arrived in Toronto by steamer with reinforcements, and other loyalist volunteers began to flood into the city from the outlying areas. On the following day, 6 December, there was an uneasy truce and Mackenzie, anxious to learn whether Duncombe's uprising had started, rode south to Dundas Street to intercept the western mail coach. He not only took the mail but, according to some, also relieved the passengers of their cash. Mackenzie later denied these charges but it was noted that he had "considerable money with him for the next few days even though he was usually short of cash."[12] At dusk, he returned to Montgomery's tavern to prepare for the battle sure to take place on the morrow.

MacNab and Lieutenant Colonel James Fitzgibbon, a prominent veteran of the War of 1812, spent the day organizing about twelve hundred volunteers into companies, appointing officers to command them, and arming them from the weapons stored in the City Hall. At noon on 7 December, accompanied by Lieutenant Governor Head, two brass bands and, perhaps more useful, two pieces of artillery, they marched north, urged on by enthusiastic cheers from the people in Toronto.

Encountering rebel riflemen in the woods on either side of Yonge Street, MacNab and Fitzgibbon extended skirmishers on both sides of the road and unlimbered their artillery. Under the supporting fire of the two guns, which terrified the insurgents, they herded the rebels north until they broke and disappeared into the countryside. Among those who escaped was Mackenzie, and Head promptly put a price on his head, offering £1,000 for the rebel leader, described as a short man, wearing "a sandy-coloured wig, has small twinkling eyes that can look no man in the face – he is about five feet four or five inches in height."[13] Avoiding posses keen to gaze on those "twinkling eyes," Mackenzie crossed the Niagara River into American territory on the night of 10 December. His rebellion was over.

Nor did the planned secondary uprising in the London District have better success. Charles Duncombe managed to as-

Defender of the Crown: Colonel Allan MacNab (1798-1862)
An energetic militia officer, MacNab arrived in Toronto with a force of militia in time to prevent Mackenzie's rebels from occupying the nearly defenceless capital. He was joint commander of the force that put Mackenzie's men to flight, and commanded the military expedition which dispersed a second uprising led by Charles Duncombe. In December 1837 and January 1838, MacNab commanded the troops deployed against the patriots on Navy Island and, along with Captain Andrew Drew of the Royal Navy, was responsible for the destruction of the *Caroline*. He was knighted for his services and later served as the premier of Canada, 1854-1856. (Toronto Reference Library)

semble a few hundred followers near Norwich but when he learned that the aggressive MacNab was marching toward him with a large force of loyal militia and volunteers, he wisely ordered them to disperse on 14 December. Duncombe then fled over the Detroit River to the United States.

The Upper Canada Rebellion of 1837 had failed. It had suffered from Mackenzie's hasty preparations and erratic leadership but the primary reason it did not succeed was that Mackenzie had misjudged the people of Upper Canada. The uprising was not a truly popular movement. Many people had grievances, and legitimate grievances, against the government but only a very small minority, perhaps fewer than a thousand in all from a population estimated in 1836 to be just under 400,000, were prepared to resort to arms to see those grievances settled.[14]

Unfortunately, many innocent people suffered in the reaction that followed. Initially, government measures were not as harsh as they might have been because the entire affair was finished in less than a week, but, in the tension caused by the border raids of January and February 1838, sterner measures were taken. It was later reported that 824 men were arrested, although the actual figure was possibly higher as many were detained without any record. Of these, 608 were found not guilty and released, or found guilty and released with a caution. Of the 216 who were convicted, only two, Samuel Lount and Peter Matthews, both prominent rebel leaders, were executed, despite a widespread and popular appeal for clemency. Of the remainder, 27 were transported to the Australian penal colonies, 18 were banished and no fewer than 14 escaped from custody.[15]

This was the official reaction but there was also considerable unofficial repression. Many Upper Canadians whose only sin was to be Reformers fell under suspicion and some were severely handled by loyalist militiamen and Orange Lodge gangs, who used the opportunity to settle personal scores. Some of these people fled immediately; others waited and then sold their property at a fraction of its value before emigrating, mainly to the United States. There are no exact figures but it has been calculated that as many as 25,000 people left the province in the wake of the rebellion, including such talented men as the Reform leaders Peter Perry and Marshal Spring Bidwell, former speaker of the Legislative Assembly. Since this figure

WANTED! WILLIAM LYON MACKENZIE! £1000 REWARD!

Wanted poster issued on 7 December 1837 by Lieutenant Governor Sir Francis Head for Mackenzie and the other leaders of the abortive Toronto uprising, the same day it failed. When his attempt to overthrow the government was crushed, William Mackenzie fled to the United States, where he was instrumental in creating the patriot movement which attacked the Canadas between 1837 and 1840. (Archives of Ontario)

PROCLAMATION.

BY His Excellency SIR FRANCIS BOND HEAD, Baronet, Lieutenant Governor of Upper Canada, &c. &c.

To the Queen's Faithful Subjects in Upper Canada.

In a time of profound peace, while every one was quietly following his occupations, feeling secure under the protection of our Laws, a band of Rebels, instigated by a few malignant and disloyal men, has had the wickedness and audacity to assemble with Arms, and to attack and Murder the Queen's Subjects on the Highway—to Burn and Destroy their Property—to Rob the Public Mails—and to threaten to Plunder the Banks—and to Fire the City of Toronto.

Brave and Loyal People of Upper Canada, we have been long suffering from the acts and endeavours of concealed Traitors, but this is the first time that Rebellion has dared to show itself openly in the land, in the absence of invasion by any Foreign Enemy.

Let every man do his duty now, and it will be the last time that we or our children shall see our lives or properties endangered, or the Authority of our Gracious Queen insulted by such treacherous and ungrateful men. MILITIA-MEN OF UPPER CANADA, no Country has ever shewn a finer example of Loyalty and Spirit than YOU have given upon this sudden call of Duty. Young and old of all ranks, are flocking to the Standard of their Country. What has taken place will enable our Queen to know Her Friends from Her Enemies—a public enemy is never so dangerous as a concealed Traitor—and now my friends let us complete well what is begun—let us not return to our rest till Treason and Traitors are revealed to the light of day, and rendered harmless throughout the land.

Be vigilant, patient and active—leave punishment to the Laws—our first object is, to arrest and secure all those who have been guilty of Rebellion, Murder and Robbery.—And to aid us in this, a Reward is hereby offered of

One Thousand Pounds,

to any one who will apprehend, and deliver up to Justice, WILLIAM LYON MACKENZIE; and FIVE HUNDRED POUNDS to any one who will apprehend, and deliver up to Justice, DAVID GIBSON—or SAMUEL LOUNT—or JESSE LLOYD—or SILAS FLETCHER—and the same reward and a free pardon will be given to any of their accomplices who will render this public service, except he or they shall have committed, in his own person, the crime of Murder or Arson.

And all, but the Leaders above-named, who have been seduced to join in this unnatural Rebellion, are hereby called to return to their duty to their Sovereign—to obey the Laws—and to live henceforward as good and faithful Subjects—and they will find the Government of their Queen as indulgent as it is just.

GOD SAVE THE QUEEN.

**Thursday, 3 o'clock, P. M.
7th Dec.**

☞ The Party of Rebels, under their Chief Leaders, is wholly dispersed, and flying before the Loyal Militia. The only thing that remains to be done, is to find them, and arrest them.

R. STANTON, Printer to the QUEEN'S Most Excellent Majesty.

represents about one in sixteen people in Upper Canada, it is an indication of just how narrow support was for the rebellion. Nonetheless, Upper Canada lost some very good citizens in this *diaspora* and the province was the poorer for their going.[16]

Unfortunately, if Upper Canadians thought the worst of their troubles had ended when the little man with the "twinkling eyes" crossed the Niagara River, they were mistaken. William Lyon Mackenzie was about to preside over the birth of a movement that would pose a more dangerous threat to British North America.

Guarding prisoners in Lower Canada, December 1837
The Lower Canada Rebellion, fuelled by enmity between the English- and French-speaking people of the province, was a far more serious affair than William Mackenzie's comic-opera uprising in Upper Canada, and there was much hard fighting and loss of life before it was crushed. In this drawing by M.J. Hayes, an escort from the 71st (Highland) Light Infantry Regiment guards rebel prisoners. Note the tartan trews and the diced band around the soldiers' shakos, which mark them as men from a Scots unit. (National Archives of Canada, C-3653)

CHAPTER TWO

"Sturdy fear-nothing boys:"
The rise of the Patriot movement

December 1837 to March 1838

The cannon's pealing roar was heard
At midnight hour, 'twas greatly fear'd
The Navy Island Patriots had
By long delay, grown raving mad;
And thus were preaching loud discourses,
To Queen Victoria's loyal forces;
Or tired of waiting for their calls,
Were all at once now giving balls,
Which well we know, was there a chance,
Would make full many a Red Coat dance.

Our Governor and General Scott
The warrior brave, were on the spot;
The hero of a war or two,
Knew exactly just what to do;
For nearly thirty years before
He'd stopped the British lions roar,
And made him drop his bristling mane
In battle over at Lundy's Lane;
And he had not the least idea
Of being now disposed to fear,
What Navy Island patriots few,
Or Canada herself could do.[1]

On the evening of 11 December 1837, a grey-haired man mounted the stage of the Coffee House, the largest public hall in Buffalo, to address an attentive audience. His name was Doctor Cyrenius Chapin and he was a pioneer settler of the area and a respected local figure, although "a too free use of ardent spirits … hindered his usefulness, both as a physician and citizen."[2] Drunk or sober, Cyrenius Chapin hated Britain and all things British. During the War of 1812 he had raised and led a small unit of mounted volunteers that had raided the Canadian side of the Niagara River and proved such enthusiastic looters that their regular American army counterparts christened them "Doctor Chapin and his Forty Thieves." Nonetheless, Chapin was a popular man in Buffalo and the audience became quiet as he began to speak.[3]

They had come that night in response to an appeal by a local lawyer, Thomas Jefferson Sutherland. A native of the village of Lancaster near Buffalo, Sutherland was known primarily as a "stilted pettifogging" legal counsel and his nickname was "Duke of Lancaster" or "Red Rose of Lancaster" because of his predilection for wearing a scarlet coat.[4] The events in Upper Canada had attracted much interest in Buffalo and when Sutherland advertised that John Rolph, Mackenzie's co-conspirator, would be present, the result was a packed house. Rolph did not appear but Sutherland made the announcement that the leader of the Upper Canada rebellion, William Lyon Mackenzie himself, was staying with Chapin and he then called the doctor to the stage to say a few words. What followed, according to one spectator, was a scene of "thrilling interest."[5]

Chapin began by making a fervent appeal for Americans to end British oppression in Upper Canada. This rhetoric found an appreciative audience as many in the United States were receptive to any declamation, no matter how ill-founded, against Britain and its despotic monarchy. In June 1837 there had been a flare-up of the longstanding Maine–New Brunswick controversy. The boundary between these two jurisdictions had never been properly settled and a crisis had occurred when New Brunswick authorities arrested a Maine official trying to carry out a census in an area claimed by both nations. A more serious cause for American resentment against Britain was the severe recession that had started that same month when a five-year economic boom, based on massive land speculation in frontier areas and boosted by canal and railway construction, had collapsed after nervous London money markets began to retrench. British banks called in their loans to their American counterparts, and since many American banks had been issuing paper notes based on land holdings, not gold, they suspended species payment, triggering a wave of business failures that led to widespread unemployment. Buffalo, a city of 25,000 and a manufacturing and communications centre, was particularly hard hit and its streets were thronged with jobless men looking for either work or amusement.[6]

The bad feeling against Britain generated by these events merged with a traditional American belief that Britain was the hereditary enemy. In the United States of 1837, veterans of the Revolutionary War still walked the land and would often appear on the Fourth of July to add proud memories of the struggle for independence to the jingoism of politicians. More fresh in memory was the War of 1812, particularly in northern New York, which had suffered numerous British incursions during the conflict. The fact that the United States had come perilously close to losing that war had been forgotten in the general satisfaction that at New Orleans in January 1815 Andrew Jackson had gained the final victory.

Jackson's military success catapulted him into the presidency in 1829 and his election marked a shift in American political focus from the Atlantic seaboard to the frontier states and territories in the south and west. Impelled by a rising birth rate and waves of immigration from Europe (the population of the United States increased by nearly a third between 1830 and 1840), driven by an inexhaustible thirst for land, and fuelled by the economic boom, America expanded steadily west throughout Jackson's term in office, which ended in 1836. Times were good and there was a widespread feeling in the republic that its ways were better than other ways and that Americans had a right to impose them on those unfortunates who were less blessed or able – including the aboriginal peoples and neighbouring nations. Americans were beginning to hold, one remarked, "a deep-seated conviction that liberty could be enjoyed under none other than republican institutions and that the same should be extended to the freedom-loving peoples wherever they might be found."[7]

In fact (although its proponents would not have chosen that term), what he was describing was old-fashioned imperialism cloaked in a respectable new fiction that the United States, possessing the incomparable virtues of republican democracy, was on a divine mission to dominate the continent. The shock troops of this crusade were the "Go Ahead" men. Aggressive, ambitious, violent, greedy, often lawless, they were usually (but not always) young males from the frontier states and territories who took their slogan from one of the more prominent of their number, Tennessee congressman David Crockett, whose somewhat inane motto, "Be sure you're right, then go ahead," could be used to justify any variety of acts. Another prominent "Go Ahead" man was James Bowie, a former slave dealer who had given his name to a weapon that had become popular in the United States during the 1830s – a large butcher knife with a concave, sharpened, indentation toward the tip of the blade. There were many others of the "Go Ahead" breed and throughout the 1830s they pushed steadily westward into the territory of the aboriginal peoples or neighbouring nations, engaging in filibustering or land piracy and counting on their government to bail them out if they got into more trouble than they could handle.[8]

President Jackson, himself a former frontiersman and duellist, was never particularly sensitive about the matter of international boundaries. As a military commander, he had twice attacked Spanish Florida without authorization in 1813 and 1818 and, as president, tried to purchase the vast territory of Texas from Mexico, only to meet with indignant refusal. Thwarted, Jackson watched with satisfaction as thousands of Americans, many of them of the "Go Ahead" variety, flooded into Texas until they outnumbered the Spanish-speaking population. When these Texians, Texicans or Texans declared independence from Mexico and proclaimed the establishment

Vol. I. "Go Ahead!" No. 3.

Davy Crockett's 18 ALMANACK, 37 OF WILD SPORTS IN THE WEST. Life in the Backwoods, & Sketches of Texas.

O KENTUCKY! THE HUNTERS OF KENTUCKY!!
Nashville, Tennessee. Published by the heirs of Col. Crockett.

King of the Wild Frontier: Davy Crockett
Crockett, a former congressman, died at the Alamo in 1836 and became a legend in the United States and a hero to many young Americans who joined the patriot movement in 1837-1838. Note the reference to the "Hunters of Kentucky" at the bottom of the page – this was the marching song of the men who attacked Prescott. (From *Davy Crockett's Almanack*, 1837, author's collection)

of republican institutions in the territory (including the institution of slavery), Jackson permitted armed volunteers to move freely across the border and dispatched troops to occupy Mexican territory.[9]

In February 1836, about two hundred Texas rebels, including Bowie and Crockett, managed to get themselves surrounded by a superior force of Mexican troops in an old mission hard by the little village of San Antonio de Bexar. Their commander, William Barret Travis, a 26-year-old refugee from a bad marriage and a host of creditors, sent out a message addressed to the "People of Texas & All Americans in the World," imploring them to come to the aid of their countrymen at the Alamo fighting "in the name of Liberty, of patriotism & everything dear to the American character."[10] This stirring appeal aroused public support for the Texas rebels, as did exaggerated accounts of the death of the defenders of the Alamo, including Crockett, who died "on his back, a frown on his brow, a smile of scorn on his lips – his knife in his hand," with a dead Mexican soldier across his body, "and twenty-two more lying pell-mell" before him.[11] The rebellion, which ended with the successful creation of the new republic of Texas, planted the dangerous concept in the minds of many Americans that their government would support (or, at the least, officially ignore) the invasion of a neighbouring state, provided, of course, such an invasion was carried out in the name of republican democracy.[12]

What went for one border would do just as well for another and there were those in the United States who felt their nation

He died with his boots on: The end of Colonel Crockett, 1836
One of many illustrations depicting the heroic last stand of David Crockett at the Alamo in 1836. There is actually some evidence that Crockett survived the battle only to be executed on the order of Generalissimo Santa Anna after the shooting had stopped. The Texas rebels of 1836 became heroes in the United States and many Americans in the patriot movement believed that their own struggle against British rule in the Canadas would have the same successful outcome. (From *Davy Crockett's Almanack*, 1837, author's collection)

should also be extended to the north "to preserve a safe balance of its growth to the south."[13] One American journalist asked why the Canadas should not be brought "into the union with us as another star or stars, in the bright American constellation of freedom's jewels, to increase our stripes?"[14]

Many who held these beliefs were present in the Coffee Mill that night to hear Cyrenius Chapin. "Every foot of the house, from the orchestra to the roof, was literally crammed with people," reported the newspapers, "the pit was full – the galleries were full – the lobbies were full – the street was full" and hundreds were turned away.[15] They listened to Chapin's declamation against perfidious Albion and enthusiastically applauded when he promised that Mackenzie, that priceless friend of liberty, would appear on the following evening. Having worked himself up, Chapin next vowed that any scoundrel who attempted to collect the British reward posted on Mackenzie's head would have to "walk over my dead body!"[16] At this, the old border raider flourished a Bowie knife of "very respectable dimensions" and was greeted by a storm of cheers. "The Amalekites are among us," Chapin thundered, "they thirst for the blood of this patriot," and he called for six brave young men, "as good sons of the Almighty has among us," to guard Mackenzie. "You may have a hundred!" was the loud response. "No!" said Chapin, only "six sturdy, fear-nothing boys. Who'll go?" A dozen men sprang on the stage.[17]

There was less drama the following night when Mackenzie harangued an audience estimated to be three thousand strong, one of the largest public gatherings in the history of Buffalo up to that time. Six days before, while still at Montgomery's Tavern, he had dispatched a letter to Buffalo asking for American assistance for the Canadian rebels, and he now expanded on this theme, stressing the parallel between the thirteen colonies in 1776 and the Canadas in 1837. He was followed by Thomas Sutherland, who announced his intention of organizing a force of American volunteers to liberate Upper Canada and appealed for men, money, weapons and ammunition. The response was overwhelming and immediate – that same night a gang broke into the small armoury in the Buffalo courthouse and removed two hundred stand of arms.[18] The next day, the newly-appointed "Brigadier General" Sutherland of the newly-formed "Patriot Army" marched with drummers and fifers through the streets, distributing handbills directing potential recruits to the Eagle Tavern, his designated headquarters.[19]

"Republicans" would be a more accurate description of those who joined the movement created by Mackenzie and Sutherland, but as they called themselves "patriots," this is the term that will be used throughout this book. The patriot movement was based on a very shaky foundation of belief, assumption and misinformation. Exaggerated tales of repression in the north country spread by such prominent figures as Duncombe, Mackenzie and Rolph, prompted many Americans to participate in what seemed to be a replay of their own struggle for independence. When they listened to stories told by worthy Canadians who had been forced to flee for their lives, one recalled, leaving property and families to the merciless "jackals of royalty," it was "impetus to the sympathy burning in American bosoms."[20] After all, as another patriot wrote, Americans and Canadians were "two peoples of the same race, in national feeling, in conviction and aspiration."[21]

These sentiments were buttressed by other convictions. There was the totally false but seemingly unshakeable belief that once the republican flag was raised in the north country, thousands of Canadians would flock to it and that all that was needed was good leadership and determination. That the Canadian rebellions had primarily failed because they lacked popular support was either unknown or ignored by the patriots. There was also the dangerous precedent of Texas. As Daniel Heustis, a patriot officer, put it, when "Texas rebelled … thousands of American citizens crossed the lines, and assisted in achieving her independence. They went and returned, as they pleased, without molestation from the government of the United States."[22] Heustis and his comrades were confident a similar sequence of events would unfold in Canada.

The basic credo of the patriot movement was summed up by one prominent member who felt that, notwithstanding the utter failure of Mackenzie's rebellion, the vast majority of Canadians were in favour of a republican form of government. All it would take was one successful battle and "a good stand maintained for a short time" by Americans, and then Canadians would do their own fighting. This being the case, he decided to join, in "hope of being instrumental in hastening a crisis so desirable to all the republican world," his personal "wish as a Northerner to see the chivalrous example of the South, in the case of Texas, emulated here," and because of his "innate detestation of tyranny and oppression wherever manifested."[23]

This was the philosophy of the idealists, but while rank and file patriots may have paid lip service to such ideas, they were probably attracted to the movement for more mundane reasons. Unemployment, coupled with promises of regular pay and free land in the Canadas to any man who volunteered, caused many to enter the Eagle Tavern and sign up. Although their ranks included sons of prominent families, most of the patriots seem to have been restless young men looking for money, work, land, adventure or an escape from the law, debts, wives or boredom. They flocked, not only to the Eagle, but to public meetings convened in American border communities from Vermont to Ohio in the last days of 1837. The interest, the support and the recruits were in place – all Mackenzie and the other patriot leaders had to do was take advantage of the situation.[24]

Late on 13 December, Mackenzie, Rolph and Sutherland met at the Eagle Tavern. At this time, they still believed that Duncombe and his followers were engaged in active rebellion in western Upper Canada and they decided to mount an operation that would distract Sir Francis Head and his military advisors by occupying Navy Island, a Canadian possession in the Niagara River about three miles above the great falls. Command of the expedition was offered to Rensselaer Van Rensselaer, son of the postmaster of Albany and a descendant of an old New York family, who claimed to have attended the military academy at West Point and fought in a South American revolution. Described as a "gin-sling, sottish looking genius of twenty-seven, but apparently much older from disease and dissipation," Van Rensselaer was commissioned a "general" in the patriot army and, the following day, he, Mackenzie and Sutherland led several hundred armed men, some clearly intoxicated, north down the American side of the Niagara.[25] When this lively swarm, preceded by a band and trailed by two pieces of artillery borrowed from the New York militia, reached a point opposite Navy Island, they boarded a waiting flotilla of small boats and crossed the Niagara River to occupy it.[26]

Navy Island was a good choice of position (see Map 2). Although closer to the Canadian than the American side of the Niagara, the current between it and the Canadian bank was strong while communication with the American bank was fairly easy. About a mile in length and half a mile in width, the island was wooded and its western side was formed by a steep bank nearly twenty feet higher than the Canadian shore opposite. In military terms, the island was easy to reach from the United States but difficult to attack from Canada.[27]

Once established, Mackenzie issued a proclamation announcing the creation of a provisional government for Upper Canada and appealing for brave men to overthrow the "blighting influence of military despots, strangers from Europe" who ruled by the "dictates of their arbitrary power."[28] Each volunteer would receive 300 acres from the ten million in the Canadas that would "be speedily" at the patriots' disposal. The proclamation bore the great seal of the new state, a new moon casting light through darkness, which had been designed by Mackenzie himself. Mackenzie sweetened the pot in a printed hand bill, issued a few days later, that offered $100 in silver to every recruit. Actually the newly-established government had no cash reserves, but, until it did, Mackenzie issued currency in $1 and $4 denominations redeemable at Toronto City Hall four months hence. Meanwhile, his long-suffering wife, who had joined him from Upper Canada, occupied herself sewing cartridges for artillery projectiles.[29]

There was only one house on the island, a rude log cabin, which served as both headquarters and the Mackenzies' residence. Provisions, arms and ammunition were shipped over from the United States. Among the weapons were no less than twenty pieces of artillery, most from a source patriots called Mister "SNY" (or Mister "State of New York") as they came from local militia units. The occupying force, which numbered about two hundred, managed to position six to eight of these weapons, mainly 6-pdr. guns, in entrenchments they constructed on the western side of the island and frequently fired at the Canadian militia on the other side of the river. Throughout the occupation, the American shore of the Niagara

swarmed with curious on-
lookers, well-wishers, journalists – and spies from
Canada. One of the latter
reported that in northern
New York the patriot cause
"daily gains adherents" and
the "very Women are inciting the Men to proceed to
the frontiers" while "Depots
of Men, Money, arms, &c.
are being formed in all the
small Towns in the interior
ready to move as occasion
may require – One woman
was seen casting bullets at
her own house from a
Mould that ran 60 at a
time."[30] On Christmas Day
1837, the patriots fired a
twenty-two gun salute, one
round for each state in the
union and two for the
Canadas, to mark the arrival
"of a very large body of gallant fellows from Rochester

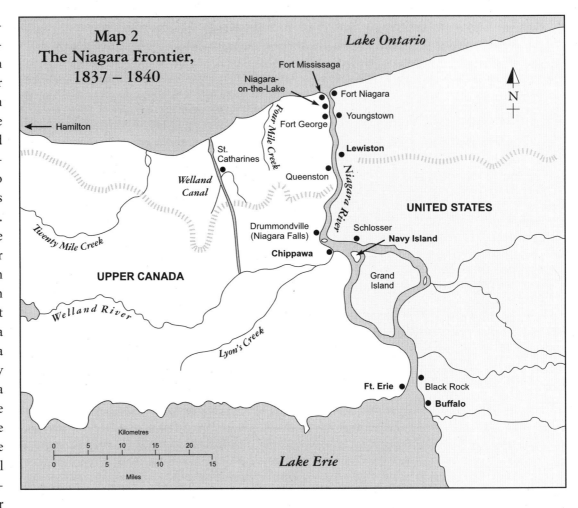

Map 2
The Niagara Frontier,
1837 – 1840

and its vicinity," every man "completely armed and equipped
for instant service."[31]

Despite the popular support, there were tensions among the
patriot leaders. Mackenzie did not trust Sutherland, and when
he learned that Duncombe had arrived in Detroit, he dispatched the lawyer to the west to co-ordinate patriot activities
in that quarter. Mackenzie also quarrelled with Van Rensselaer,
who spent much of his time drinking and talking to journalists,
and the two began to avoid one another, which was rather hard
to do in the tight confines of the island. Relations were also
strained between Mackenzie and John Rolph as Rolph, living in
nearby Lewiston, blamed the disaster at Toronto on Mackenzie.
Rolph made one brief trip to the island and thereafter dis-
associated himself from the patriots and all their works.[32]

PROCLAMATION

BY WILLIAM LYON MACKENZIE,

Chairman pro. tem. of the Provincial Government of the State of Upper Canada.

INHABITANTS OF UPPER CANADA!

For nearly fifty years has our country languished under the blighting influence of military despots, strangers from Europe, ru ing us, not according to laws of our choice, but by the capricious dictates of their arbitrary power.

They have taxed us at their pleasure, robbed our exchequer, and carried off the proceeds to other lands—they have bribed and corrupted ministers of the Gospel, with the wealth raised by our industry—they have, in place of religious liberty, given rectories and clergy reserves to a foreign priesthood, with spiritual power dangerous to our peace as a people—they have bestowed millions of our lands on a company of Europeans for a nominal consideration, and left them to fleece and impoverish our country—they have spurned our petitions, involved us in their wars, excited feelings of national and sectional animosity in counties, townships and neighbourhoods, and ruled us, as Ireland has been ruled, to the advantage of persons in other lands, and to the prostration of our energies as a people.

We are wearied of these oppressions, and resolved to throw off the yoke. Rise, Canadians, rise as one man, and the glorious object of our wishes is accomplished.

Our intentions have been clearly stated to the world in the Declaration of Independence, adopted at Toronto on the 31st of July last, printed in the Constitution, Correspondent and Advocate, and the Liberal, which important paper was drawn by Dr. John Rolph and myself, signed by the Central Committee, received the sanction of a large majority of the people of the Province, west of Port Hope and Cobourg, and is well known to be in accordance with the feelings and sentiments of nine tenths of the people of this state.

We have planted the Standard of Liberty in Canada, for the attainment of the following objects:

Perpetual Peace, founded on a government of equal rights to all, secured by a written constitution, sanctioned by yourselves in a convention to be called as early as circumstances will permit.

Civil and Religious Liberty, in its fullest extent, that in all laws made, or to be made, every person be bound alike—neither shall any tenure, estate, charter, birth, or place, confer any exemption from the ordinary course of legal proceedings and responsibilities whereunto others are subjected.

The abolition of hereditary honours, of the laws of entail and primogeniture, and of hosts of pensioners who devour our substance.

A Legislature composed of a Senate and Assembly chosen by the people.

An Executive to be composed of a Governor and other officers elected by the public voice.

A Judiciary to be chosen by the Governor and Senate, and composed of the most learned, honourable, and trustworthy of our citizens. The laws to be rendered cheap and expeditious.

A free trial by Jury—Sheriffs chosen by you, and not to hold office, as now, at the pleasure of our tyrants. The freedom of the Press. Alas for it, now! The free presses in the Canadas are trampled down by the hand of arditrary power.

The vote by ballot—free and peaceful township elections.

The people to elect their court of request commissioners and justices of the peace—and also their militia officers, in all cases whatsoever.

Freedom of Trade—every man to be allowed to buy at the cheapest market, and sell at the dearest.

No man to be compelled to give military service, unless it be his choice.

Ample funds to be reserved from the vast natural resources of our country to secure the blessings of Education to every citizen.

A frugal and economical government, in order that the people may be prosperous and free from difficulty.

An end forever to the wearisome prayers, supplications and mockeries attendant upon our connexion with the Lordlings of the Colonial Office, Downing St. London.

The opening of the St. Lawrence to the trade of the world, so that the largest ships might pass up to Lake Superior, and the distribution of the wild lands of the country to the industry, capital, skill, and enterprise of worthy men of all nations.

For the attainment of these important objects, the patriots now in arms under the standard of Liberty, on NAVY ISLAND, U. C. have established a Provisional Government of which the members are as follows, (with two other distingnished gentlemen, whose names there are powful reasons for withholding from public view,) viz:

WILLIAM L. MACKENZIE, Chairman, Pro Tem.

NELSON GORHAM,	ADAM GRAHAM,
SAMUEL LOUNT,	JOHN HAWK,
SILAS FLETCHER,	JACOB RYMALL,
JESSE LLOYD,	WILLIAM H. DOYLE,
THOMAS DARLING,	A. G. W. G. VAN EGMOND,

CHARLES DUNCOMBE.

We have procured the important aid of Gen. Van Rensselaer of Albany, of Colonel Sutherland, Colonel Van Egmond, and other military men of experience; and the citizens of Buffalo, to their eternal honour be it ever remembered, have proved to us the enduring principles of the revolution of 1776, by supplying us with provisions, money, arms ammunition, artillery and volunteers; and vast numbers are floating to the standard under which, heaven willing, emancipation will be speedily won for a new and gallant nation, hitherto held in Egyptian thraldom by the aristocracy of England.

BRAVE CANADIANS! Hasten to join that standard, and to make common cause with your fellow citizens now in arms in the Home, London and Western Districts. The opportunity of the absence of the hired red coats of Europe is favourable to our emancipation. And short sighted is that man who does not now see that although his apathy may protract the contest, it must end in INDEPENDENCE, freedom from European thraldom for ever!

Until Independence is won, trade and industry will be dormant, houses and lands will be unsaleable, merchants will be embarrassed, and farmers and mechanicks harrassed and troubled; that point once gained, the prospect is fair and cheering, a long day of prosperity may be ours.

The reverses in the Home District were owing, 1st, to accident, which revealed our design to our tyrants, and prevented a surprise, and 2dly, to the want of artillery. 3500 men came and went, but we had not arms for one in twelve of them, nor could we procure them in the country.

Three hundred acres of the best of the publick lands will be freely bestowed upon any volunteer, who shall assist personally in bringing to a conclusion the glorious struggle in which our youthful country is now engaged against the enemies of freedom all the world over.

Ten millions of these lands, fair and fertile, will, I trust, be speedily at our disposal, with the other vast resources of a country more extensive and rich in natural treasures than the United Kingdom or Old France.

Citizens! Soldiers of Liberty! Friends of Equal Rights, let no man suffer in his property, person or estate—let us pass through Canada, not to retaliate on others for our estates ravaged, our friends in dungeons, our homes burnt, our wheat and barns burnt, and our horses and cattle carried off; but let us show the praiseworthy example of protecting the houses, the homes, and the families of those who are in arms against their country and against the liberties of this continent. We will disclaim and severely punish all aggressions upon private property, and consider those as our enemies who may burn or destroy the smallest hut in Canada, unless necessity compel any one to do so in any cause for self defence.

Whereas, at a time when the King and Parliament of Great Britain had solemnly agreed to redress the grievances of the people, Sir Francis Bond Head was sent out to this country with promises of conciliation and justice—and whereas, the said Head hath violated his oath of office as a governor, trampled upon every vestige of our rights and privileges, bribed and corrupted the local legislature, interfered with the freedom of elections, intimidated the freeholders, declared our country not entitled to the blessings of British freedom, prostrated openly the right of trial by jury, placed in office the most obsequious, treacherous and unworthy of our population—and sought to rule Upper Canada by the mere force of his arbitrary power, imprisoned Dr. Morrison, Mr. Parker, and many others of our most respected citizens, banishing in the most cruel manner the highly respected speaker of our late House of Assembly, the Honorable Mr. Bidwell, and causing the expatriation of that universally beloved and well tried eminent patriot, Dr. John Rolph, because they had made common cause with our injured people, and setting a vast price on the heads of several, as if they were guilty persons—for which crimes and misdemeanors he is deserving of being put upon his trial before the country—I do therefore hereby offer a reward of FIVE HUNDRED POUNDS for his apprehension, so that he may be dealt with as may appertain to justice.

In Lower Canada, divine providence has blessed the arms of the Sons of Liberty—a whole people are there manfully struggling for that freedom without which property is but a phantom, and life scarce worth having a gift of. General Girard is at the head of 15,000 determined democrats.

The friends of freedom in Upper Canada, have continued to act in strong and regular concert with Mr. Papineau and the Lower Canada Patriots—and it is a pleasing reflection that between us and the ocean a population of 600,000 souls are now in arms, resolved to be free!

The tidings that worthy patriots are in arms is spreading through the Union, and the men who were oppressed in England, Ireland, Scotland and the continent are flocking to our standard.

We must be successful!

I had the honor to address nearly 3,000 of the citizens of Buffalo, two days ago, in the Theatre. The friendship and sympathy they expressed is honorable to the great and flourishing republic.

I am personally authorised to make known to you that from the moment that Sir Francis Head declined to state in writing the objects he had in view, in sending a flag of truce to our camp in Toronto, the message once declined, our esteemed fellow citizen Dr. John Rolph openly announced his concurrence in our measures, and now decidedly approves of the stand we are taking in behalf of our beloved country, which will never more be his until it be free and independent.

CANADIANS! my confidence in you is as strong and powerful, in this our day of trial and [...]ty, as when, many years ago, in the zeal and ardour of youth, I appeared among [...] humble advocate of your rights and liberties. I need not remind you of the sufferings [...]secutions I have endured for your sakes—the losses I have sustained—the risks I have [...] I ten lives I would cheerfully give them up to procure freedom to the country of my c[...] my early and disinterested choice. Let us act together; and warmed by the hope of [...] a patriotic course, be able to repeat in the language so often happily quoted by Irel[...]pions,

> The nations are fallen and thou still art young,
> Thy sun is but rising when others have set;
> And tho' Slavery's cloud o'er thy morning hath hung,
> The full tide of Freedom shall beam round thee yet.

Militia-men of 1812! Will ye again rally round the standard of our tyrants! [...]lieve it possible. Upper Canada Loyalists, what has been the recompense [...] and devoted attachment to England's Aristocracy? Obloquy, and contemp[...]

Verily we have learnt in the school of experience, and are prepared to [...] the past. Compare the great and flourishing nation of the United S[...] distracted land, and think what we also might have been, as brave, i[...] Leave then, Sir Francis Head's defence to the miserable serfs de[...] the last hour of your lives the proud remembrance will be yours [...]liverers of our country."

Navy Island, December, 13, 1837.

Mackenzie's proclamation, 13 January 1838

Dated at Navy Island, this proclamation appealed to Upper Canadians to end the "blighting influence of military despots, strangers from Europe" and adhere to the Declaration of Independence Mackenzie had published six months before, a declaration he claimed had "received the sanction of a large majority of the people of the Province, west of Port Hope and Cobourg." Actually, very few people in Upper Canada were prepared to follow Mackenzie – with good reason because he always talked a better game than he played. (Author's collection)

The occupation of Navy Island took Sir Francis Head by surprise. The lieutenant governor had thought that the unrest in Upper Canada had ended when MacNab pacified the London District and all that remained was to seek out and arrest the ringleaders. Head ordered MacNab to take command in the Niagara area, and within a week that officer had assembled a large force of militia on Captain Edgeworth Ussher's farm, directly opposite Navy Island. One of the first units to arrive was a company of black volunteers from St. Catharines under the command of James Sears, a member of the Reform faction in the Legislative Assembly. Composed of men who had escaped from slavery in the United States or their sons, this company had better reason than most to fight, and throughout the border troubles of the next two years black Canadians would prove to be some of the most loyal and dependable defenders of the province. A force of 250 aboriginal warriors, the Crown's traditional allies, showed up from the Grand River, as did ordinary militiamen in great numbers – one American reported that volunteers were "swarming to the Niagara River to oppose Mackenzie in any demonstration he may be disposed to make."[33] By the last week of December, MacNab commanded nearly 2,500 men.[34]

He set them to work building entrenchments to provide cover from the patriot artillery. MacNab was eager to attack the island but was restrained by the lieutenant governor, who was reluctant to risk a defeat which might "be the signal for a general rush into the province."[35] Head felt it wiser to let the occupiers stay where they were and "let *them* undertake the dangerous course of attacking *us*." Sir John Colborne agreed with the strategy of containment and, as the rebellion in Lower Canada had ended by this time, he dispatched three battalions of regulars to the upper province. MacNab chafed at Head's decision, particularly after the patriots began to bombard his position

with hot shot, killing three militiamen and wounding others. He and his men were particularly angered on the evening of 28 December when they saw the small steamer *Caroline*, which had been engaged by the patriots to transport men and supplies, arrive on the far side of the island.[36]

MacNab resolved to do something about this flagrant violation of Canadian sovereignty. He ordered Captain Andrew Drew, a half-pay officer of the Royal Navy, to organize a cutting-out expedition consisting of about sixty men which embarked in small boats and made a difficult nighttime passage to the far side of Navy Island. Drew expected to find the *Caroline* at anchor there but instead discovered the vessel tied up at a dock in Schlosser on the American side of the river. Drew crossed the river, boarded the vessel and, after a fight in which one American was killed and several wounded, captured the steamer. When they were unable to get the vessel under way, Drew's men set the *Caroline* alight, towed her out into the current and cut her adrift. In flames from stem to stern, the steamer drifted down the Niagara River before grounding near the eastern bank, where she was consumed. Triumphant, Drew's party returned to Chippawa.[37]

It was an understandable act but the simple fact was that Drew had destroyed an American vessel in American territorial waters. Newspapers across the United States printed exaggerated reports of the incident, claiming as many as a dozen Americans had died in this act of piracy. In fact only one man, Amos Durfee, had been killed and his corpse was proudly displayed on the front steps of the Buffalo City Hall before being given a splendid public funeral. There was a frantic exchange of diplomatic notes, and although the British minister in Washington, Henry S. Fox, emphasized that the steamer had been supplying armed insurgents on Canadian soil, in violation of American neutrality laws such as they were, the furore refused to die down. Most Americans viewed the destruction of the *Caroline* as "a national insult, of the grossest kind," constituting an armed invasion of their territory.[38]

Sympathy for the patriots, already strong in the border states, now increased. One American reported that excitement was "running to quite a high pitch along the whole frontier and extending backward to a considerable distance to the interior" with numerous meetings at which "Resolutions and speeches, glowing with patriotism and valor, were read, spoken and published."[39] More money, weapons and men were forthcoming and Van Rensselaer recorded that his strength trebled in the first week of January 1838 to nearly a thousand with the 450-man garrison of Navy Island organized in four

infantry companies and a rifle company. There was even a band with five fifers, four drummers, two buglers and a bass player.[40]

The *Caroline* incident forced President Martin Van Buren to take action before the tension on the frontier escalated into outright war. Federal and state officials who had tried to curb the patriots were hampered because they were not backed up by reliable force, the only troops in the area being state militia, many of whom were sympathetic to the patriots. There were also loopholes in the American neutrality legislation, which provided fines and imprisonment for offenders who

The destruction of the *Caroline*, December 1837
On the night of 29 December 1837, a group of Canadian militia crossed into U.S. territory and destroyed the American steamer *Caroline*, which had been transporting supplies to the patriots on Navy Island. This irresponsible, if understandable, act infuriated Americans, who began to actively support the patriots in their mission to wrest the Canadas away from Britain by force. Within days, arms, funds and recruits were pouring into the patriot camps on the Niagara frontier. In fact the *Caroline* did not go over Niagara Falls, as depicted here, but ran aground and burned on the American bank of the river. (National Archives of Canada, C-4788)

Border hero: Major General Winfield Scott, United States Army (1786-1866)

A hero of the War of 1812 and a national icon in the United States, Scott was sent north in December 1837 by President Van Buren to restore order on the frontier. Although there were almost no regular soldiers available, Scott accomplished his task with the assistance of capable subordinates such as Brigadier General Hugh Brady and Lieutenant Colonel William J. Worth. (From *United States Military Magazine*, 1840)

invaded neighbouring foreign states only *after* they had done so and had been apprehended; it did not apply to those who made preparations to do so. Nathaniel Garrow, the federal marshal for northern New York who had to police an area from Lake Champlain to the Ohio border with only a few deputy marshals, arrived in Buffalo on 22 December to find the frontier "in a state of commotion."[41] New York Governor William Marcy sent a senior militia officer to Buffalo to recover the weapons taken from state arsenals but this emissary's demands were either ignored or met with the polite response from the patriots that the arms would be returned in good order when they were no longer needed. The situation had potential for great danger and on 5 January 1839 Van Buren ordered Major General Winfield Scott to restore order on the northern border.[42]

A distinguished veteran of the War of 1812 and a national idol, the six-foot five-inch Winfield Scott looked the complete military hero. He would be assisted by three other competent officers, all veterans of the northern campaigns of the earlier war: Brigadier General Hugh Brady, Colonel John Wool and Lieutenant Colonel William Jenkins Worth. Worth was to accompany Scott to the Niagara while Brady went to the Detroit area and Wool to the Lake Champlain area. Unfortunately, distinguished officers were about all the United States had to spare in the way of military force. The United States Army, which had an authorized strength of only 7,958 all ranks and an actual strength of about 5,000, was largely deployed in Florida waging a bitter war against the Seminoles and on the western frontier, and the military posts in the north, at Sackets Harbor, Fort Niagara and Fort Gratiot near Detroit, had been more or less abandoned. Scott was not daunted but ordered all available regulars, amounting to a few hundred recent recruits, to be sent north as soon as possible.[43]

Accompanied by Governor Marcy, Scott arrived on the frontier in early January 1838, determined his nation would not be plunged into war "by our borderers, wrong end foremost."[44] Although he was authorized to call out militia to preserve order, providing they were "exempt from the state of excitement," Scott wisely decided to use only regular troops and a force of dependable volunteers, the Buffalo City Guards, which he organized.[45] He made himself as prominent as possible, wearing full dress uniform to speak to public gatherings wherever he found them and his message to the patriots was clear: "I tell you, then except it be over my body, you shall *not* pass this line – you shall *not* embark.[46]

Scott told Van Rensselaer bluntly that his men did not stand a chance if the British made a determined assault on his position, he harried federal and state officials into doing their job, and he cautioned the militia against providing the patriots any assistance lest the United States become "little better than a na-

tion of pirates."[47] Learning the patriots were planning to charter another vessel to replace the *Caroline*, he forestalled them by hiring it for the American government. Scott's position became stronger when Worth arrived at Buffalo with 110 regular soldiers.[48]

By now, it was clear to the patriot leaders that the occupation could no longer serve a useful purpose. If there were any doubts about the matter, they were laid to rest on 12 January when MacNab, who had assembled 4,000 regulars and militia, opened fire on the occupiers of Navy Island with eleven pieces of artillery, including heavy mortars. MacNab's gunners fired 203 rounds that day and added another 130 for good measure on the next, 13 January. That night Mackenzie and Van Rensselaer began to evacuate, and although American law officers tried to disarm the patriots as they landed, the majority were able to retain their personal weapons, although their artillery

Her Majesty's Guards in winter
During the crises of 1837-1840, British troop strength in North America rose to its highest level since the War of 1812. By early 1839 there were 12,000 regulars in the Canadas, including two battalions of the Guards, who were rooted out of comfortable barracks amid the fleshpots of London and sent to experience the doubtful pleasures of a Canadian winter. Note the fur hat, mittens and overshoes worn by the corporal on the left. (Watercolour by James Hope, National Archives of Canada, C-40295)

was impounded by a militia officer on Scott's order. That was no matter, however, because two days later it was released by another militia officer and soon back in patriot hands. A few days later, British and Canadian troops landed on Navy Island to find only abandoned entrenchments, primitive shelter huts, rotting provisions, empty bottles, garbage, dirty clothing and temperance literature.[49]

For the patriots, the occupation of Navy Island had been a military draw but a political success. It had come perilously close to causing outright hostilities between Britain and the United States and any such hostilities could only be to the movement's benefit. The question was what to do next, and on 16 January Mackenzie and Van Rensselaer met to plan strategy. They were joined by a newcomer, William Johnston. Popularly known as the "Pirate of the Thousand Islands," the 54-year-old Johnston was a Canadian who had fled to the United States during the War of 1812 after he had come under suspicion as a traitor. Johnston, who operated a tavern and a profitable smuggling operation at French Creek (modern Clayton, New York), was promptly appointed "Commodore of the Patriot Navy in the East."[50]

The leaders agreed it was useless to continue operations in the Niagara as not only were large British and Canadian forces assembled in the area but "the authorities of the United States were making great exertions to thwart our plans."[51] It was decided the next moves would be made on the Detroit and St. Lawrence frontiers. Sutherland had already been sent west and he was followed by most of the men from Navy Island under the command of "Brigadier General" Donald Mcleod. They were to attack western Upper Canada and distract British attention from the St. Lawrence, where Johnston, Mackenzie and Van Rensselaer would mount a major new operation.[52]

Although they enjoyed considerable sympathy and support, the patriots' winter offensive on the Detroit frontier was a series of disasters. In late December, several well-attended public meetings had been held in Detroit to incite support for the rebels in Upper Canada and on 1 January 1838 the "Patriot Army of the North West" was formally organized with "General"

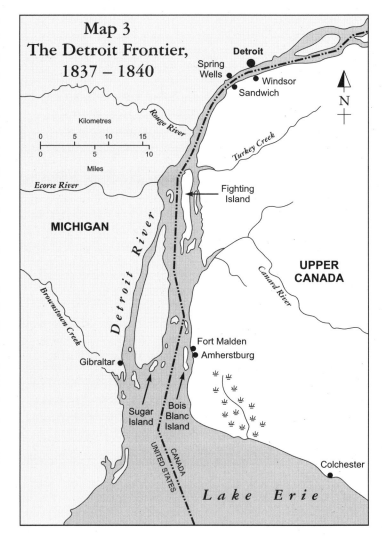

Map 3
The Detroit Frontier,
1837 – 1840

Henry S. Handy in command and "Brigadier General" Edward Theller appointed to lead "the first Brigade of French and Irish troops to be raised in Canada."[53] Little is known about Handy but Theller, a native of Ireland, was a fiercely anti-British resident of Detroit who made a living as an apothecary, grocer and whisky trader. On 7 January, Handy and Theller assembled about 200 men, armed with weapons stolen from the Detroit city jail, in the little village of Gibraltar, thirty miles south of the city (see Map 3). Their intention was to cross to Bois Blanc island opposite Amherstburg, Upper Canada, in a motley squadron of seized and chartered small watercraft. Brigadier General Hugh Brady, the American army commander in the area, became aware of this plan but he commanded fewer than one hundred regulars to guard a hundred miles of border; even so, Brady managed to seize one patriot vessel and briefly detain Handy.[54]

The attack on Bois Blanc was an utter fiasco. Just as the invaders were preparing to set out, "General" Thomas Jefferson Sutherland arrived to inform Theller that Mackenzie had appointed him to lead operations in the Detroit area. After some discussion, the two "generals" sorted out the command structure and crossed over to Sugar Island, near Bois Blanc but still in American territory. The next day, 9 January, Sutherland and sixty men landed on Bois Blanc, where Sutherland, despite the island having been evacuated by the civilian lighthouse keeper and his wife, insisted on reading aloud a proclamation urging Canadians to rally "around the standard of Liberty and victory."[55]

Theller, meanwhile, cruised along the Canadian bank of the Detroit River in the small schooner *Anne*, exchanging shots with Canadian militia who had assembled to counter any landing. When he attempted to return to Bois Blanc, the *Anne* ran aground near the Canadian shore and the watching militia captured the vessel, Theller and twenty patriots, 300

muskets and three pieces of artillery. On seeing Theller's plight, Sutherland, who had meanwhile been marching about on Bois Blanc Island with banners and martial music, panicked and withdrew to Sugar Island and finally to the American mainland. This was the good "General" Sutherland's one and only operation, as a few weeks later, while on a scouting mission on the frozen river, he was spotted and arrested by delighted Canadian militia.[56]

All was quiet until late February 1838 when the patriots tried again. This time it was the turn of "General" Donald McLeod, a 59-year-old school teacher and former militia officer from Prescott. McLeod had led several hundred men from the Navy Island occupation force to the west but his march had been beset by problems. The alert Lieutenant Colonel William Worth had followed his progress in a steamer and had impounded most of his men's weapons, and when McLeod sent his senior subordinate officer ahead to find new arms, the man disappeared without a trace except a pile of unpaid tavern bills. The result was that, on 24 February, when McLeod reached the jumping-off point for the attack, the Rising Sun Tavern in Spring Wells south of Detroit, he was broke and his 150 men were all but unarmed. Just to complete his disagreeables, McLeod learned that Brady was on his way to arrest him. Unable to go back, McLeod decided to go forward and led his little force, armed with fifty hastily procured muskets, across the frozen Detroit River to Fighting Island, a low strip of marshy ground near the Canadian bank.[57]

They did not stay long. Brady had warned his counterpart in Upper Canada of the invaders' plans and a strong force of British regulars (who by now had arrived in the western part of the province) and militia had assembled in Sandwich under the command of Lieutenant Colonel John Maitland of the 32nd Foot. Soon after dawn on 25 February, Maitland advanced across the ice towards McLeod's position, under the covering fire of a Royal Artillery 6-pdr. field gun. The patriots returned fire with a small 3-pdr. gun they had scrounged from somewhere but it was hard work as this weapon had no carriage and its gunners had neither implements nor proper ammunition. Undaunted, they extemporized a carriage out of fence rails and, as McLeod proudly recorded, did their best:

> they broke open a keg of rifle powder, and loaded her in the following manner: Colonel Bacon held the muzzle up between his legs; Jones poured in the powder with his hands and rammed the wad home with a piece of broken rail, and in lieu of a ball filled her up with boiler puncheons [pieces], Colonel McKinney firing her off.[58]

Fortunately for this rather high-ranking gun detachment, the battle did not last long. When Maitland's regulars reached Fighting Island, they formed a beating line that drove the patriots at the point of the bayonet back to the American bank, where Brady's waiting regulars arrested them. Donald McLeod managed to elude capture but this was his last attempt to invade his former country.[59]

Bois Blanc and Fighting Island were comic opera affairs but a more serious incursion took place on 26 February when a force of about 400 patriots crossed the frozen surface of Lake Erie and seized Pelee Island, about thirty-five miles east of Amherstburg and twenty miles from the Canadian shore. Their presence became known to Lieutenant Colonel Maitland at Amherstburg on 1 March and he dispatched an officer to make a reconnaissance of the invaders' position. This officer returned about noon the following day with the information that, although it would be a cold and difficult journey, it was possible for troops to move across the frozen surface of the lake to the island. Maitland assembled five companies of the 32nd Foot, a troop of militia cavalry, a company of militia infantry and a Royal Artillery detachment with two 6-pdr. guns. Just as the sun was setting, they left Amherstburg on a convoy of sleighs and, guided by aboriginal warriors, moved south to the lake shore and then along it to the village of Colchester. Here they rested until the early hours of 3 March before setting out on the final twenty-mile leg to the island.[60]

Maitland had intended to be in position to attack by first light but blowing snow, which obscured the track to the island, hampered his progress. Following a lantern on the leading sleigh, his column did not come in sight of Pelee Island until daylight and the patriots, forewarned, were ready for him.

The British commander split his command into two parts. He dispatched Captain George Browne with two companies of regulars and the militia cavalry along the shore of the island to take up a position on its southern tip that would block the invaders' escape route. Meanwhile, Maitland deployed his remaining regulars, the militia infantry and his artillery to scour the island from north to south.

The patriot commander, "Major" Lester Hoadley, who seems to have had more military skill than most patriot officers, perceived the trap and decided to concentrate against Browne's smaller force. Hoadley had also taken the trouble to train his men during their occupation of the island and the results of this preparation were apparent when, after advancing in a column toward Browne's two companies drawn up in line to receive them, the patriots, about 400 strong, deployed into line and threw out flanking parties of riflemen as skirmishers. For his part, Browne extended the interval between each of his men to three times normal distance so that his fire would cover the wider front of the opposing force and the two sides then exchanged volleys for about twenty minutes. The British got the worst of it because many of the patriots were armed with rifles, which were more accurate and had longer range than the smooth-bore muskets in the hands of Browne's regulars. Seeing this unequal contest could only end badly, Browne ordered his men to fix bayonets and charge. The British line moved forward but to Browne's surprise the patriots stood long enough to fire a last devastating volley before fleeing in all directions, most eventually reaching the safety of the United States. The invaders are believed to have lost 11 killed (including Hoadley), 11 taken prisoner, 18 wounded and one man drowned when he fell through the ice of the lake while trying to escape. Browne's casualties were heavy: 30 killed or wounded, nearly a third of his force, and, unfortunately, among the British casualties has to be included Lieutenant Colonel Maitland, who caught a cold during the attack and later died from it.[61]

William Lyon Mackenzie, meanwhile, accompanied Rensselaer Van Rensselaer and Bill Johnston to the St. Lawrence area. He was now a fugitive from American as well as British law, as he had been arrested before he left Buffalo on a charge of violating U.S. neutrality laws but had been released on $5000 bail put up by willing Americans. When he arrived at Watertown, across the border from Kingston, his host was Daniel Heustis, a 27-year-old salesman who had joined him at Navy Island, and Heustis, with the willing connivance of local law officers, had no problem sheltering Mackenzie, whose presence in Watertown was an open secret. Mackenzie generally kept out of sight until 18 February 1838 when he addressed a well-attended gathering in Ogdensburg, on the St. Lawrence River across from Prescott in Upper Canada. The response was enthusiastic, in fact so enthusiastic that "a cannon was fired several times with a view of honoring the speaker, but with the

For Queen and country, hearth and family: Militiaman, Upper Canada, 1838

During the time of Rensselaer Van Rensselaer's threatened raid on Kingston in February 1838, the sedentary militia along the St. Lawrence River, basically every able-bodied male between the ages of sixteen and sixty, were called out in great numbers. They were armed but not uniformed by the Crown, and since their enemy was also in civilian clothing, tied white cloth strips around their sleeves or hats as a recognition symbol. Throughout the border crisis of 1838-1840, the Canadian militia served willingly to defend their homes and farms against foreign invasion. (Painting by Douglas Anderson, courtesy Parks Canada) effect of assembling crowds of excited citizens."[62] When a delegation of Canadians from Prescott crossed the river to find out what the commotion was about, they were briefly detained by the Ogdensburg patriots.[63]

Heustis, Johnston and Van Rensselaer began to plan an operation against Kingston with the object of seizing Fort Henry near that town as a base for further operations. They commenced by distributing a printed circular appealing for money, supplies and provisions and establishing a central rendezvous at Watertown to store materiel and enlist volunteers. As usual, the local militia proved helpful and on the night of 17 February the conspirators obtained 700 muskets from the state arsenal in Watertown; the guards happily handed them out to waiting patriots, who loaded them onto wagons for transport to French Creek on the St. Lawrence, the assembly point for the forthcoming attack. In addition, militia artillery companies loaned field pieces and, by the evening of 21 February 1838, about 600 well-armed men had gathered at French Creek ready to invade Upper Canada.[64]

The British commander at Kingston, Lieutenant Colonel Richard Bonnycastle, Royal Engineers, was aware of the invaders' plans and had done his best to put the St. Lawrence area in the best state of defence. As most of the British regulars had moved to the west to deal with disturbances on the Niagara and Detroit frontiers, Bonnycastle called out nearly 2,000 militia, who were joined by Mohawk warriors from their settlement at nearby Tyendinaga. The greater part of this force garrisoned Kingston but pickets and dragoon vedettes were established from Prescott to Belleville. Bonnycastle placed Fort Henry in an active state of defence and even sent men to cut holes in the ice near Wolfe Island, off Kingston, to prevent sleighs crossing the frozen surface of the lake. Most of the militia had no uniforms and were instructed to tie strips of white around their hats as a recognition symbol but, as one participant (himself armed only with a dull and rusty sword) later wrote, this badge was "superfluous; since the paleness of the lengthened visages beneath it would have fairly borne the palm from the whitest linen that was ever bleached."[65] By these efforts, Bonnycastle made Kingston as ready as it could be, and although the townfolk were a little shaky, a local paper thundered defiance: "If Brother Jonathan wants a Battle, we are ready, aye ready."[66]

The Hunters had hoped to launch their attack on 22 February, Washington's birthday. According to Van Rensselaer, his purpose was not only to take Fort Henry but also to cause extensive property damage because he believed that if "he plundered and destroyed in the Canadas it would provoke retaliation from the loyalists, at which the American government would take umbrage" that would eventually lead to war and, ultimately, a patriot victory.[67] The invaders' first objective was Hickory Island, a Canadian possession in the St. Lawrence not far from French Creek, and during the bitterly cold evening of 21 February and the following morning, Van Rensselaer and Heustis led about 300 men onto barren and windswept Hickory. Their ardour, however, dropped with the temperature – throughout the daylight hours, men drifted away until by nightfall fewer than a hundred were still under arms. Bill Johnston showed up, took a quick look and departed. Heustis offered to lead an attack on Kingston if only ninety-nine men would accompany him but this proposal was turned down as it promised "nothing but inevitable defeat and destruction." With feelings of "deep mortification," Heustis remembered, the attack was called off and the few men remaining recrossed to the United States.[68]

While this farce was being played out, Mackenzie was meeting in Plattsburgh with the *Patriote* leaders who were planning an invasion of Lower Canada. He was beginning to have doubts about the strategy of border raids, particularly when he learned of Van Rensselaer's objective of inciting a larger war – a purpose he publicly denounced in the pages of the Watertown *Jeffersonian.* The two had never been on the best of terms, and when Van Rensselaer threatened to shoot the fiery-tempered Scot or hand him "over to the authorities in Canada" because he was "an injury" to the cause, Mackenzie wisely began to distance himself from the patriot movement.[69] In May 1838 he moved to New York to do what he did best, publish a newspaper to "expose the view of the patriots in Canada and their friends in the United States" and wage his battles in print, but the evil that he had helped to create – an armed movement devoted to overthrowing British rule in the Canadas – was far from spent.[70]

His Lower Canadian counterpart, Louis-Joseph Papineau, shared Mackenzie's doubts about border raids. On 2 January 1838, the *Patriote* leaders in Vermont convened a meeting at Middlebury to discuss plans and a rift developed between a conservative faction, including Papineau, who wanted nothing to do with cross-border attacks, and a more radical element in favour of such operations. The radicals won the day and Papineau departed for Albany, turning over effective leadership of the *Patriotes* to Robert Nelson, a 38-year-old doctor from Montreal. Nelson's plan was to occupy a piece of Lower Canada long enough to claim international status as a *bona fide* belligerent and ultimately to provoke war between the United States and Britain. Throughout January and February 1838, he and his followers in northern Vermont prepared for this operation and, as usual, received widespread support from American sympathizers and the state militia. Nelson was also heartened by secret overtures made to him by Governor Edward Kent of Maine, who hoped that any rupture in British-American relations would result in an adjustment in the Maine–New Brunswick border in favour of his state. Much less encouraging was Colonel John Wool of the United States Army, who told Nelson plain that although, under existing law, he could not legally prevent his followers from arming themselves and invading Lower Canada, he would be waiting at the border to arrest them if they tried to re-enter the United States.[71]

Despite this warning, Nelson decided to go ahead. By 28 February, he had assembled nearly 700 men, American and Canadian, and amassed 1,500 stand of arms, most procured from a raid on the Vermont state arsenal at Elizabethtown. That night, they crossed into Canada and occupied a farm about a mile inside the border, where Nelson issued a proclamation declaring Lower Canada to be a republic with himself both president of this new entity and commander-in-chief of its army. That is about all Nelson did because the following morning he discovered that his American volunteers had faded away and the army of his new republic consisted of less than 200 men. When word arrived that the Canadian militia were marching against him, he issued his first order – withdraw to the United States. As the *Patriotes* straggled back across the line they were greeted by Wool and a small detachment of American regulars, who arrested the man who would be president and disarmed his followers.[72]

Although the border appeared to have returned to a state of relative peace by March 1838, British military leaders remained concerned about the patriot threat. Sir John Colborne, the commander-in-chief, and Sir George Arthur, who that month replaced the detested Head as lieutenant governor of Upper Canada, received a steady stream of reports from agents in the United States and took appropriate measures of defence.

Land and water defences were strengthened as British troops flooded into North America. In June 1836 the strength of the regular establishment on the continent was 4,465 officers and

At the helm during the crisis: Lieutenant Governor Sir George Arthur (1784-1854)

In the spring of 1838, Arthur replaced the incompetent Sir Francis Bond Head as lieutenant governor of Upper Canada. His previous appointment had been as the governor of the penal colony of Van Diemen's Land (Tasmania), where he had been an efficient if somewhat tyrannical administrator. Although regarded by many as a conservative, Arthur was in reality a moderate and agonized over the capital punishment of the Hunters convicted for the attack on Prescott. (Toronto Reference Library)

men; by the end of November 1838 it would rise to 10,380, including two battalions of the august Guards which were rooted out of their comfortable barracks amid the fleshpots of London and sent to the less certain delights of Quebec City. The militia of both provinces were placed on a war footing. In Upper Canada six regiments of incorporated (or long-service) militia were created in January 1838 to serve for six months to replace the less reliable sedentary units basically composed of every male of military age, and, as well, there were many small volunteer companies in service. To guard the water approaches, a Royal Navy officer, Captain Williams Sandom, was sent to Kingston in April with orders to revive the moribund naval establishment on the Great Lakes.[73]

Legal measures were also taken to strengthen the hand of the authorities when dealing with raids across the border. In January 1838, the Legislative Assembly of Upper Canada passed an act to "protect the Inhabitants of this Province against Lawless Aggression from Subjects of Foreign Countries at Peace with her Majesty." Aimed squarely at the patriots, it decreed that foreign nationals or British subjects apprehended while committing acts of hostility against Upper Canada would be tried by courts martial – and if found guilty, would suffer death.[74]

As the winter of 1837, so fraught with tension, turned to the spring of 1838, the people of the Canadas were guardedly optimistic. The rebellions were over although the aftermath – crowded jails, treason trials, suspicion and enmity, economic and social disruption – were still with them. But many Canadians took heart when they learned the British government was sending a special envoy, Lord Durham, to investigate the recent unrest and find solutions that would be acceptable to the people of both provinces. In Upper Canada, Sir George Arthur, a professional administrator who proved to be more capable than Head, adopted a moderate policy toward those involved in the recent uprising. Arthur did not intervene to save the lives of Lount and Matthews, two of Mackenzie's co-conspirators, who were hanged at Toronto in early April, but these were the only death sentences meted out to those who taken part in the rebellion. Twenty-seven of the worst offenders were transported to the penal colony of Van Diemen's Land (Tasmania) but the rest of those arrested for participating in the uprising were eventually released.[75]

The events of the winter, however, had left a residue of bitterness in the Canadas toward the United States. It seemed the American government was powerless to prevent the patriot incursions and some even suspected that Van Buren's administration was quietly encouraging them. Canadians resented the widespread belief in the United States that they wished to sever their connection with Britain. As one journalist put it, Canadians had never asked for American aid

> to detach us from the mother country, to take from us the British Constitution, and to institute for it a republic; we tell you, and we say it advisedly, that nine-tenths of our population prefer the form of government we have to yours; we tell you that we are not an ill-governed or oppressed people, we are almost wholly free from taxation, we enjoy full, free and perfect liberty.[76]

Such feelings were clearly evident in the market square of Kingston one March evening when a large crowd watched the leaders of the rebellions being burned in effigy. Prominent beside the stuffed straw figures of Mackenzie and Papineau was a tall, gaunt Uncle Sam in a white hat and a green coat adorned with black crepe and placards reading "Authorized Sympathy," "Sham Neutrality" and "Vile Conduct." It was all good fun, but in the months to come Canadians would have more reason to fear their neighbours to the south.[77]

The fixer: Lord Durham (1792-1840)

John Lambton, Lord Durham, a Reform peer known as "Radical Jack," was appointed governor general of British North America in the spring of 1838, with the mission of investigating and reporting on the reasons for the recent rebellions in Upper and Lower Canada. He resigned six months later but in January 1839 submitted a report that made recommendations for the future political structure of the Canadas. The British government implemented some of these recommendations and, gradually, the North American colonies gained control of their own political future. (Toronto Reference Library)

Scenic Kingston, Upper Canada, c. 1839-1841

A town of 4,500 souls at the eastern end of Lake Ontario, Kingston served as the major British military and naval base for the St. Lawrence area in 1838. It was the station of many of the regular troops who fought at Prescott and also the venue for the legal process against the Hunters captured in the action. In this print by W.H. Bartlett, Fort Henry can be seen in the upper left corner while, across Navy Bay, is Point Frederick and the buildings of Captain Williams Sandom's naval station. The town itself, with its church spires, is in the background while the long bridge over the Cataraqui River is in the right middle ground. The Hunters captured at Prescott were marched across this bridge during the night of 17 November on their way to imprisonment at Fort Henry. The soldiers in this illustration appear to be men of the 93rd (Highland) Regiment of Foot, a unit which fought at the windmill. (J. Ross Robertson Collection, Toronto Reference Library)

CHAPTER THREE

"Do you snuff and chew?"
The coming of the Hunters

March to September 1838

Ye gentlemen and ladies fair
Who grace this famous city,
Just listen, if you've time to spare,
While I rehearse a ditty;
And for the opportunity,
Conceive yourselves quite lucky,
For 'tis not often here you see
A hunter from Kentucky.

> *Oh, Kentucky,*
> > *The Hunters of Kentucky,*
> *Oh, Kentucky,*
> > *The Hunters of Kentucky.*

We are a hardy, free-born race,
No men to fear a stranger,
Whate'er the game we join in chase,
Despising toil and danger.
And if a daring foe annoys,
Whate'er his strength or forces,
We'll show them that Kentucky boys
Are alligator-horses

> *Oh, Kentucky, etc.*[1]

In the months that followed the immolation of Uncle Sam in Kingston, it appeared to American and British military commanders that the border troubles had been brought under control. Noting with approval Wool's swift and efficient disarming of Nelson's followers, Sir John Colborne wryly concluded that the American government must "be anxious to avoid a war" and he could afford to be a little complacent as he had just learned that more reinforcements were on their way to his command.[2] His confidence was shared by his American counterparts. From Detroit, Brigadier General Hugh Brady reported that "perfect tranquillity" pervaded that frontier and he could not "discover any preparations making to disturb it."[3] At Buffalo, Lieutenant Colonel William Worth was certain that the patriots' "bubble has burst" and the United States Army had "given the coup de grace to the miserable adventurers in this quarter."[4] In March, feeling the crisis had ended, President Van Buren ordered Winfield Scott back to Washington.[5]

The calm was deceptive as the patriot movement had not subsided; it was undergoing a process of change. This transformation was necessary because, although the movement enjoyed widespread public support in the American border states, not one of the armed incursions it had mounted against the

Canadas had met with success, and most had been outright disasters. The closest the patriots had come to a victory was at Pelee Island, where they had inflicted heavy casualties on British regulars, but even that operation had ended in a retreat to American territory. The Navy Island occupation and the destruction of the *Caroline* had drawn attention to their cause and had certainly heightened international tension, but it had also prompted the American government to take steps to curtail their activities. New legislation passed in March 1838 gave American federal authorities the power to seize weapons and munitions of war on American soil if they had reason to believe they were to be used against a neighbouring state.[6]

It was clear to the patriot leaders that their biggest problem was security. British agents had found it easy to penetrate an organization which, complacent about public and newspaper support, operated in plain view. The leaders themselves had no discretion, boasting openly of their intentions, with the result that American, British and Canadian authorities quickly became aware of their plans. If it was to succeed, the patriot movement would have to go underground.

Robert Nelson was the first leader to come to this realization. Soon after his failed invasion of February 1838, he took steps to reorganize the *Patriotes* into a new entity, the *Frères Chasseurs* ("Hunter Brothers" or "Hunting Brotherhood"). He modelled the *Frères* on the secret revolutionary societies of Europe and adopted some of the outward trappings of the Masonic order with a hierarchy of degrees or ranks, each having its own distinct passwords and recognition signs. The headquarters of the *Frères* was at St. Albans, Vermont, but the new society was also active in Lower Canada, particularly in Montreal and the Richelieu Valley. Within a few weeks of their inception, the *Frères* were enlisting volunteers, receiving funds, stockpiling weapons and building a network of spies and sympathizers.[7]

Nelson's innovations transformed the patriots. After he visited Vermont in April 1838, Donald McLeod broadcast them throughout the movement and, during the spring and summer, the new secret society spread west as lodges sprang up like mushrooms along the American border from Maine to Ohio. The members of these lodges called themselves "Hunters" or "Patriot Hunters" and it has been claimed that this name derived from one of Mackenzie's followers, a Doctor James Hunter from Whitby, but it is more likely that it came from the translation of *Frères Chasseurs* combined with the name of the predecessor movement. Gradually the French and English terms became synonymous as a clandestine underground army, based on local lodges and dedicated to the overthrow of British rule in the Canadas, took form across the northern United States. Superior or grand lodges were created at St. Albans, Montreal,

The man who conceived the idea:
Doctor Robert Nelson (1794-1872)
Nelson succeeded Papineau as the leader of the Lower Canada *Patriotes*. He proved to be a more practical and effective leader and transformed his somewhat heterogeneous organization into a clandestine army, the Hunter Brotherhood. The idea was imitated by the American patriots, and in the spring of 1838 the Patriot Hunters, a secret and powerful organization dedicated to the overthrow of British rule in North America, spread like a brushfire across the American border states. (National Archives of Canada, C-31343)

Rochester, Buffalo, Detroit and Cleveland to disburse funds and direct the activities of hundreds of smaller local lodges. By September 1838, an American federal official in Oswego, New York, reported there was not "a city, town or port on the lake frontier in which [Hunter] associations are not found" and most were actively "collecting money, arms, and munitions of war."[8]

The Hunters were a much more dangerous threat than their hapless predecessors. They were stronger – one New York newspaper claimed there were 283 Hunter lodges in that state alone – and estimates of their overall membership range from 20,000 to 200,000 although the lower figure is more likely as many new recruits only attended one meeting. They were powerful enough to form a constituency that American politicians could only ignore at their peril, and the Hunters began to back candidates in federal and state elections they believed sympathetic to their cause. They also infiltrated the lower ranks of the federal and state bureaucracy – there were many customs and tax collectors, postmasters, militia officers, district attorneys and sheriffs in their ranks.

Perhaps most important, the Hunters were better funded as they created their own private financial institution, "The Republican Bank of Canada," which was basically a limited stock company in which Hunters and sympathizers bought shares that would be redeemed when the Canadas were free, the "whole wealth, revenue, and resources of the patriot dominions" that they held, or hoped to hold, being pledged for repayment. The shares were $50 each but they could be acquired on a regular purchase plan of small amounts. The bank's bills were to be decorated with the "heads of the late martyrs to the cause of liberty in Canada; the head of Matthews on the left end of the bill, the head of Lount in the centre, with the words in a semi-circle over it, *The Murdered; Death or Victory*, on the margins of the bills will be the words *Liberty, Equality, Fraternity*."[9] This institu-

tion was the brainchild of Charles Duncombe, who became an active Hunter just as his former compatriots, Mackenzie and Papineau, faded from the patriot movement.[10]

The Hunters enjoyed great success in the United States. Americans (possibly more so than Canadians) are "joiners" and in the 1830s they were enthusiastic participants in fraternal societies such as the Masons or Elks, social reform groups such as the abolitionist and temperance movements, and new religions such as the Church of Mormon. The Hunters offered not only fraternal, social and religious elements but the added attraction of being a secret elite dedicated to the Spirit of '76, which made them all the more exciting, particularly in small rural communities where entertainment was usually at a premium.

The only criterion for enlistment seems to have been that a Hunter or someone friendly to the cause vouched that a candidate was not a spy. Once this was established, the recruit went through an initiation ceremony for induction into the Snowshoe or lowest degree. Blindfolded, he knelt in front of the master of the lodge and swore the Hunter oath, said to be the work of Charles Duncombe, promising before God not to reveal the secrets of the movement, to "aid the cause of liberty, equality, and fraternity whenever," to assist brother Hunters in time of danger, and to attend the lodge when summoned.[11] At this, the new man was invited "to behold the light" and his blindfold was pulled away to reveal a sword pointed at his chest and pistols brandished at his head while the master solemnly intoned: "As you see light, so you also see death, presented to you in the most awful shape and form, from which no earthly power can save you, the moment you attempt to reveal any of the secrets or signs which have, or may be revealed to you."[12]

The secrets and signs were many and various, according to whether a member was a lowly "Snowshoe," a middling "Beaver" or "Grand Hunter," or a fully-fledged and exalted "Patriot

Hunter." Meetings in public places between brother Hunters involved much brushing of the coat (up or down depending on rank), pinching and twisting of coat buttons, biting of thumbs and rubbing of chins, all done while gravely exchanging apparently innocent conversation on the day of the week, the qualities of the beaver and the current state of "the great hunt in the north woods." In this respect, the Grand Hunters were the worst. If two of these worthies chanced to meet, an elaborate mating dance ensued which began with one asking the other: "Do you snuff and chew?" The only correct response was "I do," accompanied by the "drawing of a snuff or tobacco box from the pocket and scratching three times on the lid."[13]

The lodge meeting was the main event in the life of the Patriot Hunters. In the United States, they met openly in halls, churches, hotels, and taverns and other public places but they were much more circumspect on Canadian soil, gathering in private residences or farm buildings. Meetings were held in the various degrees. If, for example, they were called in the lowest Snowshoe degree, then all members were required to attend; if called in the higher degrees, only the appropriate ranks were present. A typical American meeting of the Snowshoe degree involved the initiation of new members, a call for all members to recruit new men, appeals for money, arms and supplies for the cause, and the broadcasting of announcements from the grand lodges. There were also long-winded speeches, particularly if the lodge could produce a veteran of the Revolutionary War who would hark back to the winter of Valley Forge when he was young, or an authentic Canadian refugee with a tale of royalist tyranny in the north country. Meetings often ended with singing, particularly Andrew Jackson's political campaign song, "Hunters of Kentucky," celebrating the president's famous victory at New Orleans, which the movement took as its own.[14]

Food and drink were usually provided at Hunter gatherings,

an added attraction for the unemployed or less enthusiastic. Detroit Hunters usually met at Heath's Tavern, where the proprietor would "freely spread his well-loaded table to his Hunter brethren, receiving only what they were willing and able to pay, and who thus spent a handsome fortune in his devotion to the cause."[15] The 1830s were a hard-drinking time – the average annual consumption of alcohol *per capita* in the United States was between seven and ten gallons – and although there were many temperance men in the lodges, there were also others who liked a taste of that good-old-republican-virtue-in-a-jug, particularly when time came to belt out "Hunters of Kentucky."[16]

As might be expected, many Hunters came from the fringes of society: the unemployed, the drinkers, the wastrels, fugitives from the law, adventurers, dreamers, thrill-seekers, the lazy and the crazy. But there were solid citizens in their ranks for the movement was genuinely popular. One Hunter in New York "was surprised to see the respectability of the people who attended … and the large amounts of money they subscribed and paid."[17] Among the more prominent recruits were Orrin Scott, the nephew of General Winfield Scott, and Charles Brown, nephew of General Jacob Brown, former commanding general of the American army. There were rumours, unsubstantiated and possibly spread by the Hunters themselves, that many politicians were secret members, including Governors William Marcy of New York, Edward Kent of Maine and Steven T. Mason of Michigan, Senator Henry Clay of Kentucky and Vice-President Richard M. Johnson. It was even claimed that President Van Buren was a sympathizer and certainly the Hunters were active in the American capital. In November 1838, while the British minister to the United States, Henry S. Fox, was complaining to Van Buren's administration about their activities, Edward Theller, who had escaped from British custody after having been taken prisoner at Bois Blanc Island, was addressing the organizational meeting of the Washington Hunter's Lodge at Carusi's Saloon, a few blocks from the White House.[18]

Despite all the elaborate passwords and various twiddlings, brushings and scratchings – and despite the many tales told about the fate of traitors who died grim deaths or simply disappeared – the Hunters were considerably less successful when it came to security and it was not long before Colborne and Arthur knew of their existence. British and Canadian agents found it relatively easy to penetrate the movement and a British spy, John McManman, was actually an early recruit to one of the first lodges established in Ohio, while another, William Kent, rose to become a lodge master. The Hunters attempted to foil such men by changing signs and passwords: Snowshoe members were directed to recognize each other by having one jingle pocket change while saying "Times are easier," which was to elicit nothing from the other Snowshoe but the response "Truly."[19]

Even though they were receiving intelligence about the Patriot Hunters, Colborne and Arthur found it difficult to take steps to counter their incursions. The basic problem was that, through the spring and summer of 1838, Hunter operations were often hastily conceived and carried out by individual lodges without the knowledge or blessing of senior leaders. An agent would not know about a planned operation unless he was the member of the lodge involved and, if he was a member, he often did not have time to get a seasonable warning to the Canadas.

In terms of private ventures, one of the worst offenders was Bill Johnston. An independent-minded man who waged his personal struggle against the Crown where, when and how he saw fit, Johnston had been arrested, along with Van Rensselaer, for the Hickory Island episode of February 1838 but was acquitted by a local jury. In late May 1838, he was thirsty for revenge and also anxious to make a little profit on the side (possibly to pay his legal bills). He therefore made plans to hijack the Canadian passenger steamer *Sir Robert Peel* during one of her regular voyages from Prescott to Kingston. He may have thought the vessel a legitimate target as she was partly owned by Judge Jonas Jones of Brockville, a member of the Family Compact, but Johnston's real purpose was probably robbery as the *Peel* often carried wealthy passengers.

It happened on the night of 29 May 1838 when the *Peel* made a stop for wood at Wells Island (near the modern Ivy Lea International Bridge). Johnston and a well armed gang, "dressed in Indian costume," rushed on board with "hideous yells and violent threats," and chased the crew and passengers, including ten ladies "in their night clothes," ashore after robbing them of their money, jewellery, watches and other valuables.[20] The press was to make great play of the fact that Johnston and his men offered "insults" to "defenceless females" although none of the ladies was harmed in any way. The gang tried to get the *Peel* under way into the St. Lawrence but ran her aground, so they set fire to the vessel and disappeared into the night.[21]

The destruction of the *Peel* provoked outrage in Britain and the Canadas similar to that caused in the United States by the *Caroline* incident. Lord Durham, who had just arrived from Britain to undertake his mission of investigation and conciliation, posted an award of £1000 for information leading to the arrest and conviction of the perpetrators. Governor Marcy of New York, not to be outdone, offered $500 for Johnston and $250 each for his three principal subordinates. Johnston eluded his pursuers but twelve of his followers were eventually apprehended, although only one was tried and he was acquitted. Tempers were particularly hot on the Canadian side of the St. Lawrence – three days after the incident, the Brockville militia fired at a passing American steamer. Sir George Arthur subsequently visited the area to appeal for calm, but also took the step of cautioning masters of Canadian vessels bound for American ports that they might find themselves "in the power of lawless banditti" although supposedly "within the protection of a friendly government."[22]

Both nations recognized that Johnston's deed was a criminal act that had occurred in United States territory and should therefore be punished by the American authorities. Nonetheless, Durham sent a personal envoy, Lieutenant Colonel Charles Grey, to Washington to inform the American government in no uncertain terms that he expected the perpetrators of the crime to be brought to justice and Van Buren's government to take steps for "the prevention in future of such crimes" as the Canadian frontier could not be exposed to "perpetual attacks and continual irritation."[23] On his return, Grey reported that there "was but one language used" in the republic to the south,

and that most hostile to England. This feeling, however, certainly does not extend to the higher Classes and is otherwise confined to the frontier Provinces, but there it exists to a degree that, as the President himself told me, makes it impossible for them to call out the Militia with any security – and we know how little power the General [American] Government possess of restraining their People.[24]

Van Buren did his best. He informed Congress that the burning of the *Peel* had caused "the most painful anxiety" to his government but that he was determined to frustrate "designs apparently formed" to involve the United States in a war with Britain.[25] The president dispatched General Alexander Macomb, the senior general of the United States Army, north with orders to take all measures to "detect unlawful combinations against the peace of a neighbouring and friendly power,

and to prevent and repress any outrage that may be meditated or attempted."[26] Van Buren also authorized the creation of a new unit, the Eighth Infantry Regiment, specifically for service on the northern frontier. It was to be stationed at the re-activated post at Sackets Harbor at the eastern end of Lake Ontario under command of the newly promoted Colonel William J. Worth, but such was the shortage of officers that fourteen recent graduates of the military academy at West Point, all artillerymen, were temporarily assigned to it. Worth co-operated with his British opposite numbers in Kingston to institute joint patrols of the St. Lawrence, and his regulars discovered Johnston's

William Johnston, pirate scourge of the Thousand Islands (1782-1870)

A former resident of Kingston, Johnston fled to the United States in 1812 because he was suspected of treason. He later blamed most of his problems in this respect on a bad marriage to an American girl from Jefferson County, New York. Johnston acted as a pilot for the American army that tried to take Montreal by moving down the St. Lawrence in the autumn of 1813 and after the war settled in the area of Clayton, New York, where he became a professional smuggler. Johnston hated Britain and was an early recruit to the Patriot movement. In May 1838, his robbery and destruction of the Canadian steamer *Sir Robert Peel* created an international incident. Armed with a Cochran multi-shot musket, a Bowie knife and two pistols, Johnston led the naval component of the attack on Prescott in November 1838. He was often accompanied, even to prison, by his beautiful daughter, Kate. (Lossing, *Pictorial Field Book of the War of 1812*) hiding place near French Creek but Johnston and his men were long gone. On the British side, volunteer companies were formed in all the river communities from Cornwall to Gananoque, and Captain Williams Sandom, RN, the British naval commander at Kingston, started regular patrols of the Thousand Islands area.[27]

The cause of all this activity, Bill Johnston, was not at all dismayed by the efforts of two nations to apprehend him. Learning that Durham had put a price on his head, Johnston sent the governor general a personal note complete with somewhat erratic spelling and references to Colonel Allan MacNab and Captain Andrew Drew, the men responsible for the destruction of the *Caroline*. "Durham!" he addressed the governor general of British North America,

How do you like to have your steamboat burnt?

Drew or McNab will get a Bowie in their damnd hart when they think of such a thing.

> God dam the Queen.
> Bill Johnston forever.[28]

Claiming to "hold a Commission in the Patriot Service of Upper Canada, as Commander-in-Chief of naval forces and flotilla," Johnston then issued his own *pronunciamento* on the *Peel* affair. He boasted about being the leader of the party that had destroyed the steamer, a party composed of men who were "nearly all natural born English subjects," and whose purpose was to achieve the independence of the Canadas.[29] Johnston also kept busy. Less than a week after the *Peel* incident, he raided Amherst Island, near Kingston and plundered several farmhouses, wounding one Canadian farmer who attempted to defend his property. A few days later he was reported near Brockville and throughout the summer of 1838 he was the

cause of frenzy on both sides of the St. Lawrence. At Prescott the local commander, Lieutenant Colonel Plomer Young, reported that "excitement" was "rather strong in this neighbourhood, as we scarcely know what to expect, and we have no means of defence along this frontier" and his concerns were echoed by his military counterparts from Cornwall to Kingston.[30] As a subject of public interest, Johnston was all the more fascinating because one of his chief lieutenants was his attractive 19-year-old daughter, Kate, who was promptly dubbed the "Queen of the Isles."[31]

The destruction of the *Sir Robert Peel* gave a tremendous boost to the patriots. From Detroit, Hugh Brady reported it had "caused much excitement on both sides of the Line" that would "require the utmost vigilance of the authorities both Civil & Military, to keep in check the disturbers of peace and good order."[32] Brady was right – during June 1838 several raids were carried out on the Sarnia area of Upper Canada although these seem to have been simple acts of armed robbery and it is uncertain whether the men involved were actually Hunters. A more serious incursion took place that month in the Niagara when a small party, not more than twenty-five strong, partly Hunters and partly drawn from the Canadian Refugee Association, a competing organization, raided the Short Hills area south of St. Catharines. This group crossed into Canadian territory on 10 June and wandered about for ten days before being rounded up. They were tried by a court martial under the act to protect Upper Canada "against Lawless Aggression from Subjects of Foreign Countries," and most were found guilty. Their leader, James Morreau, a 35-year-old Pennsylvanian, was hanged at Niagara-on-the-Lake on 29 July and fourteen of his men were transported to a penal colony.[33]

The most active centre of Hunter activity was Cleveland, Ohio, where Charles Duncombe had made his home and where

LIBERTY OR DEATH!

REGULATIONS AND PAY

OF THE NORTH WESTERN ARMY, ON PATRIOT SERVICE IN UPPER CANADA.

COMMANDER IN-CHIEF—Pay, $100 per month ; 16 Rations ; $300 per year for Equipage ; 4 Aid-de-Camps, Col's. Rank ; 2 Secretaries, do. ; 8 Servants.
ADJUTANT GENERAL—Pay, $100 per month ; 8 Rations ; 2 Assistants, Major's Rank ; 1 Clerk, do. ; 4 Servants ; $300 per year for Equipage.
QUARTER MASTER GENERAL—Pay, do. ; Rations, do. ; Equipage, do. ; Assistants, do. ; Clerk, do. ; Rank, do.
COMMISSARY GENERAL—Pay, do. ; Rations, do. ; Equipage, do. ; Assistants, do. ; Clerk, do. ; Rank, do.
PAY MASTER GENERAL—Pay, do. ; Rations, do. ; Equipage, do. ; Assistants, do. ; Clerk, do. ; Rank, do.
SURGEON GENERAL—Pay, do. ; Rations, do. ; Equipage, do. ; Assistants, do. ; Clerk, do. ; Rank, do.
JUDGE ADVOCATE GENERAL—Pay, do. ; Rations, do. ; Equipage, do. ; Assistants, do. ; Clerk, do. ; Rank, do.
AUDITOR GENERAL and SECRETARY OF DOMESTIC AND FOREIGN RELATIONS—Pay, do. ; Rations, do. ; Equipage, do. ; Assistants, do. ; Clerk, do. ; Rank, do.
MAJOR GENERALS *in Command of Divisions*, 8—Pay, $100 per month ; 8 Rations ; $300 per year for Equipage ; 2 Aid-de-Camps, Majors Rank ; 1 Clerk ; 6 Servants.
BRIGADIER GENERALS—Pay, $90 per month ; 4 Rations ; $250 per year for Equipage ; 1 Aid-de Camp, Captains Rank ; 3 Servants.
COLONELS, 64—Pay, $80 per month ; 3 Rations ; $200 per year for Equipage ; 2 Servants.
LIEUT. COLONELS, 64—Pay, $75 do. do. do. do.
MAJORS, 64—Pay, $70, do. do. do.
CAPTAINS, 256—Pay, $65 per month ; 2 Rations ; 1 Servant.
LIEUTENANTS, 512—Pay, $60 do. ; do.
NON-COMMISSIONED OFFICERS—1st, $18 ; 2d, $17 ; 3d, $16 ; 4th, $15 ; 5th, $14 ; 6th, $13 ; 7d, $12 ; 8th, $11 per month ; and Equipage and Clothing furnished.
SOLDIERS—$10 per month ; Equipage and Clothing furnished.

Each Soldier that shall serve to the end of the War shall receive as a bounty 200 acres of land—and each Officer that shall be enrolled, and serve to the end of the War, shall receive lands in the same ratio in proportion to their pay and rank.
All Officers and Soldiers that shall serve as Volunteers, for six months and upwards, shall receive the same pay and bounty in proportion to the time they serve.

NAVY DEPARTMENT.

COMMODORES, 2— Pay, $100 per month ; 8 Rations ; $200 per year for Equipage ; 2 Aid-de-Camps ; 4 Servants.
NAVY COMMISSIONERS, 3— do. do. do. do. do.
POST CAPTAINS, 16—Pay, $80 per month ; 3 Rations ; $100 per year for Equipage ; 3 Servants.
MASTER COMMANDANTS, 8—Pay, $75 per month ; 3 Rations ; $100 per year for Equipage ; 2 Servants.
LIEUTENANTS, 32—Pay, $65 per month ; 3 Rations ; $100 per year for Equipage ; 1 Servant.
Two BRIGADIER GENERALS OF MARINES—Pay, $90 per month ; 4 Rations ; $250 per year for Equipage ; 1 Aid-de Camp, Captains Rank ; 3 Servants.
COLONELS OF MARINES, 8—Pay, $80 per month ; 3 Rations ; $200 per year for Equipage ; 2 Servants.
LIEUT. COLONELS, 8—Pay, $75 per month ; do. do. do.
MAJORS, 8—Pay, $70 per month ; do. do. do.
CAPTAINS, 40—Pay, $65 per month ; 2 Rations ; $100 per year for puiqage ; 1 Servant.
LIEUTENANTS, 80—Pay, $60 per month ; 2 Rations ; 1 Servant.
NON-COMMISSIONED OFFICERS (of the Navy & Marine Service)—From $20 to $14 per month, equiped & furnished.
SAILORS—Pay, $15 per month, equiped and furnished.
MARINES—Pay, $12 do. do. do.

All Sailors and Marines enrolled, who shall serve to the end of the War, shall receive 400 acres of land. The Officers of the Naval and Marine Corps to receive the same bounty of lands as Officers of the Line, in proportion to their pay and rank.
The Engineer and Topographical Bureau, and Ordnance Department, to be taken from the Line.

JOHN MONTGOMERY,
President,
Of the Grand Eagle Chapter of Upper Canada, on Patriot Executive duty.

Head Quarters, Windsor, U. C.

ROBERT ROBERTSON, SECRETARY.

---

the Hunter bank was located. Duncombe and the other Ohio leaders had hoped to mount a major attack on Upper Canada on the Fourth of July but they were not ready in time. Throughout the summer of 1838 they worked hard to organize the Hunters across North America to undertake a major offensive in the autumn, and in mid-September 160 delegates representing most of the major lodges made their way to Cleveland to attend a "Patriot Congress" to prepare for this operation. Prominent Hunters from across North America were present including Duncombe, Bill Johnston (disguised as an aboriginal war chief) and Donald McLeod but not Robert Nelson, who sent representatives in his place. Significantly, William Lyon Mackenzie was not invited.[34]

The first item on the agenda was the creation of a provisional republican government for Upper Canada. A.D. Smith, a Canadian refugee, was elected

Even a secret army gets paid: Ranks and pay of the Patriot Hunters, September 1838

In September 1838 the incurably optimistic Hunters issued an elaborate schedule of ranks and pay, including provision for two "brigadier generals of marines." It is dated at Windsor, Upper Canada, as were most of the officers' commissions issued by the Hunter leaders and this is curious since the only troops in Windsor at that time were in the pay of Queen Victoria. The triumphant republican eagle clutching a distraught British lion in its claws was a popular Hunter symbol but, as events would show, it was the lion that prevailed. (National Archives of Canada, MG 24, B97) president with Nathan Williams, an Ohio militia officer, as vice president. Much time was spent over military matters. Donald McLeod became secretary of war while Lucius V. Bierce, an attorney from Akron, Ohio, and a brigadier general in the state militia, was appointed commander-in-chief of the "Patriot Army in the West," while operations in the east would be controlled by "President" Nelson of the previously established "Republic of Lower Canada." Under these senior officers were subordinate "generals": C.G. Bryant (a former Texas rebel) would command an English-speaking division in Vermont and Edouard Malhiotte would have a French-speaking division, while John Ward Birge would lead an independent division on the St. Lawrence frontier. Maritime forces were not neglected: Johnston was confirmed as commodore of the navy on the St. Lawrence and Lake Ontario while Gilman Appleby, former captain of the *Caroline*, was appointed commodore and commander of the navy on Lake Erie.[35]

These important matters having been decided, no doubt to the accompaniment of much cigar smoke, the Hunter leaders then got down to the serious business of overthrowing the established government of the Canadas. It was decided that Bierce, with the divisions from the west and New York, would mount a major offensive across the Detroit, while Nelson would undertake a simultaneous foray from Vermont into Lower Canada. The date set for these operations was 1 November, less than two months away, but the Hunter leaders knew that any further delay would be harmful as the British garrison in the Canadas was being reinforced and the Canadian militia put on a more effective footing, although Duncombe confidently assured everyone that Canadians would never turn out in numbers to resist a republican invasion. As well, despite all their failures and setbacks, enthusiasm for the patriot cause remained high and the men, weapons and funds (supposedly between $150,000 and $300,000) were at hand – any deferral of the liberation of the Canadas would damage the morale of the rank and file. These decisions taken, the delegates dispersed to their areas to prepare for the great day.[36]

It says much about the optimism of the Hunters that they created, on paper at least, an elaborate military and naval organization to carry out their mission. Ranks and pay in the Hunter armed forces ranged from a major general, who was paid $100 per month plus $300 *per annum* for equipage and allowed two aides-de-camp of the rank of major, down to buck privates who received only $10 per month. Hunters who served at sea ranged from commodores, who got the same pay as major generals but only $200 per annum for equipage, down to sailors who received $15 per month. Provision was even made for a Hunter marine corps, with an establishment that included two brigadier generals. Enlisted men were to receive 400 acres of land in Canada after six months service, while officers would "receive lands in the same ratio in proportion to their pay and rank." As an inducement to potential recruits, these details were promulgated in a broadsheet (supposedly printed at Windsor, Upper Canada, but actually somewhere in Ohio) embellished with a republican eagle, a British lion firmly fixed in its talons, winging across a sky adorned with twin stars and a maple leaf.[37]

In the Canadas, the summer and early autumn of 1838 were a period of cautious hope. The purpose of Lord Durham's mission was widely known and Reformers in both provinces approved of the selection of the 44-year-old peer, whose liberal political record in Britain had earned him the nickname of "Radical Jack," to investigate the grievances that had led to the uprisings of 1837. Durham made a quick tour of Upper and Lower Canada and proved sympathetic to the views expressed by Reformers, who urged that a form of responsible government be granted to both provinces, and incorporated many of these opinions in his formal report to the British government which he submitted in February 1839. By that time, however, Durham was no longer governor general as he resigned in October 1838 after a disagreement with the British government over his treatment of the leaders of the Lower Canada rebellion. With his departure, Sir John Colborne resumed the leadership of British North America.[38]

Colborne and Arthur continued to receive a steady stream of information about Hunter plans and intentions and took steps to improve the defences of the Canadas. Reinforcements continued to arrive; by the late autumn of 1838 there were 10,688 regulars in the two provinces, stationed, by Colborne's command, away from the border to discourage desertion. They were backed up by 21,000 provincial troops – volunteers trained, armed, uniformed and equipped as regulars, and enlisted for long periods of service. In Upper Canada alone, Arthur raised four battalions of incorporated militia to serve for eighteen months service and nine provisional battalions for six months.[39]

Of particular concern to British military leaders was the vulnerability of the St. Lawrence River and the Rideau Canal, the waterborne lifelines of Upper Canada. Van Rensselaer's abor-

tive operation in February, Johnston's destruction of the *Robert Peel* in May, and intelligence in early July that the patriots were planning to blow up locks on the canal, caused them to take steps to strengthen defences in the area. In June Colborne made an inspection tour of the St. Lawrence and the result was the creation of volunteer companies at "revolt stations," towns and villages along the Canadian side of the river between Kingston and Cornwall, backed up by six longservice militia battalions, "to preserve order and insure protextion"[40] Work also started on the reconstruction of Fort Wellington, a defence work at Prescott dating back to the War of 1812, which had been allowed to deteriorate in the intervening years.[41]

As events would demonstrate, these were wise steps.

LOYALISTS TO YOUR DUTY.

Queens Royal Borderers.

COMMANDED BY LIEUT. COLONEL GOWAN.

Wanted 100 Loyal Volunteers, for the above Corps, for six months service only.

Each man will get 8 dollars bounty, a new suit of clothes, and a great Coat & pair of Boots, also a free Gift of seven days pay when discharged at the end of the six months. Their pay will be one Shilling Sterling Money, per DAY, and free Rations.

Let no Man pretending to LOYALTY HANG BACK, at this time. FORWARD LADS, FORWARD.

APPLY TO LIEUTENANT COLONEL GOWAN, AT BROCKVILLE.

GOD SAVE THE QUEEN.

Queen Victoria Wants You! Recruiting notice for the 9th Provisional Battalion, Royal Borderers, raised by Ogle Gowan in Leeds and Grenville Counties in the autumn of 1838. In addition to the sedentary militia of Upper Canada (basically almost every male in the province from sixteen to sixty), four incorporated and twelve provisional militia battalions, nearly 12,000 men, were raised to serve for periods varying between six and eighteen months. Uniformed, armed and equipped as regular troops, they eventually proved very good soldiers. (Courtesy Friends of Windmill Point)

CHAPTER FOUR

"Brothers from a land of liberty:"
The New York Hunters and their plans

September to November 1838

I 'spose you've read it in the prints,
How Pakenham attempted
To make Old Hickory Jackson wince,
But soon his scheme repented;
For we with rifles ready cock'd,
Thought such occasion lucky,
And soon around the general flock'd
The Hunters of Kentucky.

> *Oh, Kentucky,*
> > *The Hunters of Kentucky,*
> *Oh, Kentucky,*
> > *The Hunters of Kentucky.*

Now Jackson he was wide awake,
And wasn't scared at trifles,
For well he knew what aim we take
With our Kentucky rifles.
So he led us up to a Cypress swamp,
The ground was low and mucky,
There stood John Bull in martial pomp,
And here was old Kentucky

> *Oh, Kentucky, etc.*

The decisions made by the Hunter convention at Cleveland did not please "General" John Ward Birge, commanding the Hunter division in northeastern New York. A pharmacist, grocer and state militia officer from Cazenovia in Madison County, Birge resented being relegated to second fiddle behind Lucius Bierce, a westerner. Nor did they suit the independent-minded Bill Johnston, who disliked operating far from the St. Lawrence. Determined not to take a back seat to a bunch of rubes from the midwest, the New Yorkers wanted their own operation, led and manned by men from the Empire State, and throughout October, according to Daniel Heustis, they discussed the possibility of mounting a separate offensive in the St. Lawrence area. They had the strength – Heustis estimated that 5,000 Hunters who "had pledged themselves to be ready for this movement" were under arms in the northeastern counties of the state.[1]

With this force at their disposal, the New York Hunters felt it only right they should have a greater share of the forthcoming glory. At a meeting in Watertown sometime in early October they decided (apparently at the urging of "General" Estes, a shadowy figure from French Creek about whom little is known) that, instead of co-operating with Beirce, they would seize Fort Wellington at Prescott and arm the thousands of Canadians, known to be "anxious to join us, and [who] would do so as soon as an opportunity should be offered them."[2] Birge and Johnston would command while the manpower would be drawn from the Hunter lodges in Jefferson, Madison, Oneida, Onondaga, Oswego and St. Lawrence counties near the Canadian border. Preparations were immediately put in hand for this operation but the New York leaders did not bother to inform either "President" Smith or "Commander in Chief" Bierce of their intentions.[3]

Of these northern counties, Jefferson was the jewel in the New York Hunters' crown. Located at the eastern end of Lake Ontario, Jefferson had always enjoyed a close social and commercial connection with the Canadian St. Lawrence communities. With a population of between 55,000 and 60,000 souls it was a large and fairly prosperous community with a mixed economy based on agriculture, transportation, cotton and woollen mills and tanneries fuelled by the power of the swift-running Black River. The economic recession of 1837, however, had hit Jefferson hard: money dried up, factories closed, prices fell and hundreds were out of work. Many in Jefferson blamed their economic woes on Britain and anti-British sentiment was exacerbated by the exaggerated stories of royalist oppression spread by the refugees who came over the border in the wake of the rebellion in Upper Canada, tales that were picked up and published, with further embellishment, by the newspapers of the county.[4]

Given this feeling it is not surprising that, from the outset of the border troubles, Jefferson County was a hotbed of patriot sympathies or that it became a Hunter stronghold. According to Heustis, the first lodge was organized in Watertown, the county seat, in May 1838 by a "Mr. Estabrook," who was said to be from Cleveland but was actually an Upper Canadian from Madoc, and he was assisted in his work by another Canadian, a man known as either Prendergast or Pendergast.[5]

The gospel was farther spread by John Birge, assisted by the ubiquitous Bill Johnston; the mysterious Estes from French Creek; Daniel Heustis, salesman turned liberator; John B. Kimball, a militia officer and factory owner from Dexter; Dorephus Abbey, a 47-year-old former newspaper publisher who farmed near Pamelia; and Daniel George, a 27-year-old teacher from Lyme. These men and the various businessmen, lawyers, state officials, tavern keepers, militia officers, stage drivers and boatmen who assisted them in their work, created a network of lodges in villages across the county (see Map 4), including Adams Center, Alexandria, Brownville, Cape Vincent, French Creek, Henderson Harbor, Sackets Harbor and many smaller communities. So successful were their efforts that Heustis claimed the Watertown lodge alone had 1900 members and, if this statement was true (and it probably wasn't), then almost every adult male in that town was a Hunter. A more accurate strength calculation was provided in November 1838 by a British agent who estimated there were 1,500 armed Hunters across Jefferson, a lesser figure but still one that represented about 14 per cent of the white males between sixteen and fifty years of age in the county.[6]

Another hotbed of Hunter activity was Onondaga County to the south, where Erasmus Stone, the postmaster at Salina (part of modern Syracuse), was the prime driving force. Stone recruited Martin Woodruff, the 40-year-old county sheriff, and Woodruff, occupying a position of influence, enlisted many new members. Stone (an employee of the American federal government, it should be noted) also enlisted Christopher Buckley, the 25-year-old owner of a salt manufactory, the major industry in Salina, and Buckley convinced many of his workers to join. Stone recruited actively among the large population of Europeans in the area, many of them veterans of the wave of uprisings that had convulsed Europe in 1830 when, encouraged by the success of the French who finally got rid of the Bourbons, the Belgians, Germans, Italians and Poles had risen in revolt. The longest and bloodiest of these struggles took place in Poland (then known as the Grand Duchy of Warsaw) in 1830-1831 when the Polish people came close to overthrowing Russian control. While moving among the Onondaga German community in the late summer of 1838, Stone met an intriguing man who claimed to have been a Polish freedom fighter.[7]

His name was Nils Szoltevki (sometimes Scholtewskii, Sholtesky, Schobtewskii, Czoltecky and many other variations) Von Schoultz. A 31-year-old chemist employed in a Salina saltwork, Von Schoultz was liked by the Onondaga Germans, who informed Stone that the handsome foreigner with the manners of a gentleman was actually an aristocratic Polish cavalry officer whose noble family had suffered dreadfully during the recent troubles in his homeland, his father, who was a general, and an officer brother having been killed fighting the Czar's troops, while his mother and sister were languishing in some frozen Siberian wasteland. Von Schoultz himself had been taken prisoner when the uprising collapsed but had managed to escape across Europe to enlist in the French Foreign Legion and fight in North Africa. Disgusted by the French atrocities he witnessed against the Arabs, he had deserted and, after further adventures, washed up on the shores of America — specifically Salina, Onondaga County, New York State.[8]

As became a veteran revolutionary "gashed and scarred with wounds, but covered with imperishable glory," Von Schoultz was reluctant to talk about his past but did occasionally drop a few pointed remarks. According to an American friend, the exiled nobleman was

The "famous Polish general:" Nils Gustaf von Schoultz (1807-1838) An artillery officer in the Swedish army, von Schoultz resigned his commission in late 1830, probably because of debts. He bragged of having served with the Polish insurgents of 1830-1831 and the French Foreign Legion but there is no concrete evidence to substantiate these claims. In 1836, he abandoned his young wife and two infant daughters in Sweden to emigrate to the United States, where he settled near Syracuse, New York. Posing as a Polish aristocrat, he was enthusiastically recruited by the New York Hunter leaders and led the attack on Prescott. A charming rogue who possessed physical but not moral courage, von Schoultz impressed all who met him, including several young ladies and a future prime minister of Canada. (Archives of Ontario)

extremely modest in his pretensions, I have seldom heard him revert to personal achievements incidental to events so memorable, and then only under circumstances of the highest excitement. But I have learnt from these occasional departures from self-reserve, incontestably from other sources, that the important part he enacted was brilliant with heroic adventures and hair-breadth escapes, the bare recital of which is calculated to enchain and captivate the most casual listener.[9]

Stone, Birge and the other New York Hunter leaders were fascinated with this European veteran, a professional officer with an extensive combat record, who was just the type of man they needed. Although Von Schoultz spoke English poorly, they asked him to become an officer in their organization, and the modest hero, "his sympathetic soul" on fire at "again being permitted to strike for freedom," promptly signed up.[10]

The New York Hunters were buying a pig in a poke. The impressive new recruit was not a Pole but a Swedish national, one Nils Gustaf von Schoultz born in 1807 and a former artillery officer in the Swedish army who had resigned his commission in late 1830, probably because of debts. He may have fought in the Polish rebellion of 1830-1831 but there is only his personal testimony that he did so because no concrete evidence has come to light confirming his participation in that event. It is very unlikely, however, that he saw action in North Africa with the French Foreign Legion as that famous corps, only created in the summer of 1831, was not deployed to Africa until November of that year. The Legion saw its first real action in April 1832 in the defence of a blockhouse near Algiers, at that time the only French enclave in Arab territory, and would not experience sustained combat until 1833, by which time von Schoultz was in Italy.[11]*

What is known for certain is that, after leaving Swedish service in early 1831, von Schoultz disappeared from view until 1833 when he joined his mother, brother and sister in Florence, Italy. In March 1834, he married a young woman from Scotland, Ann Campbell, but when the couple returned to Sweden that year, von Schoultz was hounded by creditors, who were, for a time, fended off by his wife's money. Various unsuccessful commercial ventures occupied his time until the summer of 1836, when he abandoned his wife and two infant daughters and sailed for the United States. With technical training provided by his military background, he successfully established himself in the saltworks at Salina and in May 1837 applied for naturalization as an American citizen, giving his name as Nils Scholtewskii von Schoultz from Sweden. Although rumours that he was not what he claimed followed him around the United States, von Schoultz was popular with the unsophisticated Onondaga Germans, who accepted him at face value.[12]

Birge and Stone believed von Schoultz's story. They also believed him when he gave hope of recruiting hundreds of his "fellow countrymen" to fight with the Hunters and in October they funded the Swede on a recruiting trip to the Polish refugee community in New York City. Von Schoultz established a recruiting office at 380 Pearl Street but, since he could speak very little Polish, met with limited success. In fact the Poles of New York, noting his Russian accent when he tried to speak Polish, suspected him of being a czarist *agent provocateur* and treated him "with contempt."[13] This farce should have alerted Birge and his fellow leaders that all was not right with their bright new star but they overlooked it and spread the word around the lodges that a Polish general who "promised the assistance of all the Poles in the country who had fought for him in Warsaw" had joined the cause.[14] Heustis, who was privy to the senior counsels of the New York Hunters, recorded that "500

Polanders" from the city of New York were going to join the attack on Fort Wellington.[15]

The question on the mind of every Hunter in northeastern New York was, when would the great day come? Many were ready and eager to start for the north country. They were mostly young men (the average age of those who would take part in the forthcoming invasion was 26.8 years) and many (about 40 per cent) were unemployed labourers; among those (about 25 per cent) who had a trade were blacksmiths, cabinet-makers, carpenters, wheelwrights, cobblers, coopers, weavers, hatters and stonemasons, occupations susceptible to economic fluctuations. There were few farmers in their ranks, nor, apart from the officers, were there many business or professional men. Most did not own property. Give their somewhat shaky economic status and their youth, there is a temptation to agree with Richard Bonnycastle's somewhat harsh assessment that the Hunters were "chiefly those restless frequenters of tavern bars who began smoking cigars and drinking spirits before nature has developed their perceptions of right and wrong."[16]

Nelson Truax, a 20-year-old harnessmaker from Watertown,

was a typical Hunter. Truax became "fired with the desire to relieve the oppressed" after listening at lodge meetings to false tales of British oppression in the Canadas.[17] For his part, 22-year-old William Gates, a labourer from Cape Vincent, remembered that his comrades were certain of victory because, "with the numbers that would flock about the triumphant standard of liberty" they would raise in Upper Canada, they could "put at defiance whatever force Britain might send against us."[18] For those who sought more concrete incentives, Birge promised $10 a month wages to each man on active service, a bonus of $80 dollars the moment he landed on foreign soil, a "license to plunder" while there, and 160 acres of Canadian land when it was all over. Finally, the Hunter organization pledged to look after the families of those men who did not return from the great hunt in the north woods.[19]

All this was welcome news to the young bucks in the lodges – not only would they be freedom fighters just like Jim Bowie and Davy Crockett in a northern version of the Texas rebellion, but they would be amply compensated for their efforts. They were assured that there would be no danger – not a shot would

The cult of the big knife

During the 1830s, large butcher knives became popular with American males and one of the most common versions was named after Alamo hero Jim Bowie, its supposed inventor. Many of the Hunters who fought at the windmill were armed with these articles, which their British and Canadian opponents, unfamiliar with such weapons, described as "dirks" or "cutlasses," an indication of their size. This photograph, taken twenty-three years later, shows the Chitwood brothers of Resaca, Georgia – from left to right, Daniel (age 17), John (20) and Pleasant (22) – about to set out for the Civil War. The young men who joined the Hunters would have looked much the same. (Courtesy, Georgia Department of History and Archives)

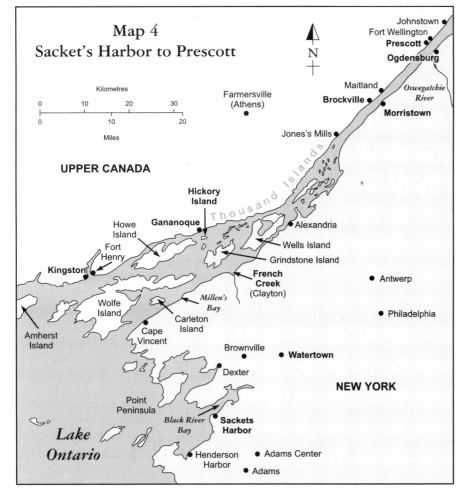

Map 4
Sacket's Harbor to Prescott

N

Kilometres
0   10   20   30

0   10   20

Miles

UPPER CANADA

Thousand Islands

Johnstown •
Fort Wellington •
Prescott •
Ogdensburg •

Maitland •   *Oswegatchie*
Brockville •   *River*

Morristown •

Farmersville
(Athens)
•

Jones's Mills •

**Hickory
Island**

Howe   **Gananoque**   • Alexandria
Island
Fort   Wells Island
Henry   Grindstone Island
Kingston •
                  **French
                  Creek**   • Antwerp
Wolfe   *Millen's* (Clayton)
Island   *Bay*
                Carleton
             Cape Island   • Philadelphia
Amherst   Vincent
Island
             Brownville
                            • **Watertown**
                • Dexter
Point   **NEW YORK**
Peninsula
          Black River **Sackets
          Bay*   Harbor**
*Lake
Ontario*
          • Henderson   • Adams Center
            Harbor
                  • Adams

tion and it included at least eight pieces of artillery of 3, 4, 6, 12 and 18-pdr. calibre, taken from state arsenals, complete with carriages and ammunition. With ready cash provided by backers, their agents had purchased or otherwise acquired military muskets and bayonets, naval cutlasses and boarding pikes, many bearing "US" or "SNY" markings as well as provisions, in containers also bearing state or federal markings. Particular attention had been paid to the acquisition of the most modern long-arms, many of the military muskets being percussion conversions, far superior to the flintlocks in service with the British army and Canadian militia. The Hunters had also acquired a number of the latest multi-round rifles, manufactured by makers such as Colt, Wurfflinger and Knox, which were issued free of charge or sold at cost to Hunter riflemen. It was somewhat ironic that, when purchasing weapons from American sources, the Hunters competed against agents working on behalf of the British government, who were trying to arm the newly-raised provincial units in the Canadas.[21]

By the last week of October 1838, all was ready. The final plan was complicated as it depended on a number of separate land and water movements that would end in Prescott (see Map 4). The men from the

be fired – and the operation would, one way or the other, "be the making of our fortunes."[20] Inspired by the famous last stand at the Alamo, already celebrated in song and story though it had taken place less than three years before, many procured themselves Bowie knives with which to cut royalist throats.

These were not their only weapons. The New York Hunters had amassed an impressive arsenal for the forthcoming opera- southern lodges were to assemble at Oswego and Sackets Harbor, as would the strong Watertown contingent, but the other Jefferson County men would proceed to Cape Vincent, Millen's Bay, French Creek and Alexandria, small ports on the St. Lawrence, or to Ogdensburg. Part of the arms and ammunition would be brought from the south by boat along the Mohawk Canal to Oswego, where they would be transferred to two small schooners owned by Hunter sympathizers, both named *Charlotte*, one from Oswego, the other from Toronto. The schooners would pick up any men already at Oswego and proceed to an anchorage at Millen's Bay, where the Hunters from that place and Cape Vincent would board with the remainder of the arms, ammunition and provisions.[22]

The *Charlottes* would only carry the advance guard and the heavy weapons. The main force would move on the civilian steamer *United States*, which operated a regular schedule between Oswego and Ogdensburg. The Hunters would board her at Oswego and Sackets Harbor on 8 November and hijack the vessel at some point between the latter place and Prescott. Joining the two *Charlottes* on the way, they would then land and seize Fort Wellington. Once this was accomplished, all three vessels would ferry reinforcements from Ogdensburg, across the St. Lawrence, where the Hunters from St. Lawrence County would be waiting with those from the eastern reaches of Jefferson County. John W. Birge would command the expedition while Bill Johnston would be waiting at Ogdensburg to control water movements. The date for the operation, Friday, 9 November 1838, was carefully chosen because state elections were scheduled for the previous Wednesday and it was thought that travel to and from the polls would provide a reasonable excuse for the appearance of numerous strangers in the border villages.[23]

Birge made the great announcement at a lodge meeting in the Amsterdam Hotel in Watertown. After "Colonel" Martin Woodruff had drilled the Hunters, Birge delivered a fiery speech in which he claimed that between 20,000 and 40,000 men would invade Upper Canada just after election day and, once on the soil of that province, they would be supported by nine of every ten Canadian citizens and three-quarters of the troops in garrison. When he was finished, Sampson Wiley and Phares Miller, the lodge drummers, "beat the long roll in the centre of the hall while Birge flourished his sword and called for volunteers for the liberation of Canada."[24] Like any good revolutionary, Birge had spent much time preparing the requisite manifesto proclaiming the justness of his cause. Addressed to the "Brother Patriots of Canada," this overwrought document is worth quoting in full:

We have come to your rescue; we have heard the groans of your distress; and have seen tears of anguish, burning on the cheeks of your exiled companions. They have besought us to aid them and you in the great work of reform, and to establish on your own native soil, EQUAL RIGHTS and EQUAL PRIVILEGES. We come not to invade your country as robbers and plunderers, but we come as brothers from a land of liberty, as free men PLEDGED to your cause, and have sworn by the sacred name of liberty not to desert you. RALLY then to our standard; it floats high above your soil, as a beacon to assert your rights. We must triumph. Shouts of VICTORY are already sounding in your ears. The cause is the cause of justice and humanity. Thousands of our countrymen are ready, with arms in their hands, to aid you. They have pledged to your exiled brethren, their lives, their property, and their sacred honour, not to desert the cause of LIBERTY. Let not your brother patriots, who are men struggling against their oppressors, be disappointed in you. They have raised their standard and will maintain it. They have gained victory after victory and they expect you to AROUSE to the conflict and join in the great work. Your homes, your firesides, and your sacred altars shall not be violated. Come on then, be men, be free men, and your liberties are secured! In behalf of the American and Canadian patriots.

J. Ward Birge
Brigadier-General Commanding Eastern Division[25]

Inspired, no doubt, by such extravagant rhetoric, many stepped forward that night to volunteer for the great hunt.

Similar scenes took place at other lodges across the northern counties of New York as men got their kit together, made their weapons ready and said their farewells. The rank and file Hunters were not told much about the operation, just to appear at the rendezvous points to wait for further orders. As Stephen Wright, a 25-year-old carpenter from Denmark in Jefferson County, remembered, his comrades "knew not where we were to land, or to what particular point we were bound."[26]

In Salina, Nils von Schoultz got a better send-off than most, being the guest of honour at a banquet held by his many friends, who presented him with a handsome engraved and silver-mounted sword. The Swede also received a flag made by Hunter ladies of Onondaga County to be given to Birge for use on the great day. Descriptions of this flag vary but it was apparently of white silk with a dark blue border and a central device consisting of a republican eagle with wings outstretched and one or two "radiant" stars, beneath which was an embroidered scroll bearing the words, "Liberated by the Onondaga Hunters" or "Canada Liberated."[27]

Von Schoultz thanked those present for these splendid gifts and "the friendship they had given a foreigner, who now bade them remember him as an unfortunate man they had comforted, a homeless man they had cherished as a kinsman." He is then said to have sung a love song of his own composition, addressed to a young woman from "whom he now parts with a heavy heart," begging her to forgive him. If this is true, the Swede had reason to be contrite. Not only had he abandoned his wife of four years, he was also romantically linked with two Salina women with the same first name: Emeline Pech, a German girl, and Emeline Field, a wealthy young widow – but then the ladies often have a soft spot for a smooth-mannered rogue.[28]

It was inevitable that Arthur and Colborne would receive intelligence of the plans and preparations of Birge and his cohorts. In fact, there so many rumours of an impending attack along the St. Lawrence in the autumn of 1838 that Arthur complained he could not discover "from what quarter all this evil is to come – and I do believe that there is a Class of Persons who are making a Market of the times, by originating these Stories."[29] By late October, the rumour mill had worked itself into a frenzy: Hunter attacks, launched from hijacked passenger steamers, were projected at various points along the river, with Prescott being the most favoured target. In response, Colborne warned the local commanders along the St. Lawrence to be on the alert and ordered Royal Navy gunboats and armed steamers to patrol the river until the end of the navigation season. The militia were called out at some of the river towns, particularly Prescott, where the local commander, Lieutenant Colonel Plomer Young, was authorized to raise as large a force as needed.[30]

In early November, however, events in Lower Canada distracted British commanders. On the third day of the month, in accordance with the decision taken at Cleveland in September, Robert Nelson launched his second attempt to conquer Lower Canada. It took the form of an uprising in Montreal and the Richelieu Valley assisted by military force from the *Patriotes* in Vermont. Although he had organized and armed hundreds of supporters within and without the province, Nelson was foiled by the prompt action of military and police authorities who, learning the details of his plans from agents and traitors, arrested the insurgent leaders and deployed troops to the threatened areas. After a week of fighting, British regulars and Canadian militia had dispersed the insurgents, captured many of their leaders and utterly crushed the invasion. Robert Nelson again escaped across the border to the United States – he would never return to Canada.[31]

The people of Kingston followed the events in the lower province in the local newspapers, which also carried stories about threatened raids against the St. Lawrence area. Kingstonians were not worried. Unlike the previous winter when there had been no regular troops in the town, there were now six companies of the 83rd Foot and a field brigade or battery of Royal Artillery, a total of 26 officers and 515 men in garrison, and there was also the comforting presence of the grey stone mass of Fort Henry, the strongest fortification in the Canadas west of Quebec, on its headland across from the town. Everyone was confident, a mood summed by the Kingston *Chronicle and Gazette* when describing a mock battle staged by the regulars on the glacis of the fort on 1 November. Such fine troops, boasted the *Gazette*, would be "able to annihilate ten thousand of the raggamuffins who are now threatening to invade us."[32]

A varied assortment of guests: The Union Hotel, Sackets Harbor
In the week preceding the attack on Prescott in November 1838, many of the Hunter leaders stayed in this hotel. They had to be very careful, as among the other guests were the officers of the Eighth United States Infantry stationed at nearby Madison Barracks. The building is currently being restored as a heritage site. (Photograph by Dianne Graves)

In the first week of November 1838, those ragamuffins began to congregate at the appointed places along the border. When questioned by the curious, they replied they were travelling to some distant poll to vote or were going on a lengthy hunting expedition, responses that fooled no one. As many as 500 Hunters marched into the little village of Sackets Harbor. The rank and file were accommodated in taverns and storehouses owned by sympathizers but Birge and the officers got rooms at the comfortable Union Hotel, although they had to watch their step since this establishment also served as quarters for the officers of Colonel William Worth's Eighth Infantry stationed at Madison Barracks just outside the village. Worth, of course, was too intelligent not to be aware that something was going on, but since the Hunters were not armed and kept to themselves as much as possible, he had no legal pretext to interfere with them. According to Anthony Flood, a British agent

in the Hunter organization, Worth at one point became suspicious when he noted a large number of young males on the wharf waiting to board the steamer *Oneida* for Ogdensburg. He peremptorily ordered her captain to depart from the Harbor without picking up any passengers and called out one of his companies to patrol the wharf area with their side-arms to ensure that this order was obeyed.[33]

As the great day neared, the Hunters were tense but on Thursday, 8 November, Birge learned that engine trouble had

Officers' Row, Madison Barracks, Sackets Harbor
During the War of 1812, the little village of Sackets Harbor was the major American naval and military base in the north. By 1838, the army post, Madison Barracks, was abandoned but it was reactivated that year to become the home station of the Eighth United States Infantry, a unit specially raised to maintain order on the northern frontier during the border troubles. (Photograph by Dianne Graves)

forced the captain of the *United States* to postpone sailing. The steamer would remain in Oswego until repairs were completed and was not expected to resume her regular schedule until Sunday, 11 November. Birge asked his men to wait for those few days, but most, beginning to have sober second thoughts about the wisdom of this invasion business, dispersed to their homes. Similar scenes occurred at the other rendezvous points – Oswego, Cape Vincent, Dexter, Millen's Bay and Ogdensburg – and the result was a fiasco, Heustis estimating that five or six

hundred men were lost by what he called "bad management at the outset."[34] Some remained, however, and others arrived late so that by Saturday, 10 November, Birge had perhaps as many as a thousand men along the St. Lawrence ready to embark.[35]

Two of the men who had joined the great hunt in the north wood were not disappointed when it was delayed because they were British agents. One was Anthony Flood, an ex-British army sergeant who had drifted into the United States in early 1838 to find work. Flood had been hired at the Dexter factory owned by the Hunter officer John B. Kimball, and Kimball had recruited him into the Hunters. Acting on the instructions of Judge John S. Cartwright of Kingston, Flood played along and had marched to Sackets Harbor on 7 November, but when the attack was delayed, he began to look for a chance to get away to Kingston to raise the alarm. He accompanied a party of Hunters who made their way to Millen's Bay, eating and drinking free at Hunter taverns along the way. They arrived there at midday on 9 November, but Flood's hope of escaping across the St. Lawrence was frustrated by the sentries posted around the Hunter camp to prevent desertion. Flood, a very intelligent man, bided his time.[36]

The other agent was Hely Chamberlain, a storekeeper from Onondaga County, who had also been engaged by Judge Cartwright. Chamberlain had been present when Birge made the announcement at the Watertown lodge and had travelled to Kingston to warn Cartwright that an attack was imminent but had been unable to give details as to time and place, and at Cartwright's request he had gone to Ogdensburg to get more information. Learning on Thursday, 8 November, that the operation had been postponed until the following Sunday, Chamberlain left Ogdensburg by steamer the next day, telling his comrades he was going to Sackets Harbor to meet the *United States*, but in fact on his way to Kingston.[37]

On Saturday, 10 November, onlookers at Oswego noted that two small schooners, which had been in the harbour some time, were being loaded by work gangs with heavy cargo transferred from boats that had travelled up the Mohawk Canal from Syracuse. This done, the *Charlotte of Toronto* and the *Charlotte of Oswego* left port and set sail in a northerly direction. It was all very mysterious, if not downright suspicious, but no one asked any questions, even when "about a hundred fine fellows, strangers" appeared in the town "who seemed to have no occupation, but who behaved with propriety, and gave cause for complaint to no one." It was an open secret that these men were Patriot Hunters bound for an attack on Canada somewhere along the St. Lawrence. Two days after that attack had actually commenced, an Oswego newspaper reported that on the evening of 10 November a stranger had arrived in town. He was "a handsome military looking man of about 35, who,

from several indications was thought by all to be their leader. He was a Pole and had witnessed the affair at Warsaw."[38]

There was no more curiosity at Oswego the next day, 11 November, when Captain James Van Cleve, master of the *United States*, got up steam in preparation for making his last trip of the season to Ogdensburg. As they made ready to sail, Van Cleve and his first officer, William Williams, watched as about 150 male passengers suddenly came on board, with little baggage except small valises and a few trunks. One man dropped and split a heavy nail keg by accident, and it was seen to be "filled with lead bullets, which rolled over the deck."[39] Neither Van Cleve nor Williams made any comment. Nor did Hiram Denio, a banker from Utica and a partner in the company that owned the steamer, feel anything was amiss. Denio thought the numerous male passengers were some of the foreign immigrants who were "constantly passing in considerable

To war in style: The steamer *United States*
The largest and most comfortable American passenger vessel on Lake Ontario, the *United States* unwittingly served as the Hunters' main troop transport during the attack on Prescott. On Monday, 12 November, they hijacked the steamer at Ogdensburg and, under the command of a temporary and drunk Hunter captain, the *United States* fought a naval engagement with Her Majesty's Steam Vessel *Experiment* in the middle of the St. Lawrence River. (Toronto Reference Library)

numbers; and being myself in the cabin while they were on the deck, I took but little notice of them."[40] At 9 A.M., the *United States*, pride of the Ontario and St. Lawrence Steam Boat Company and the largest and most comfortable American passenger vessel on Lake Ontario, cast off and steamed for Sackets Harbor.[41]

There had been heavy gales during the previous few days but the lake was calm that Sunday morning and Van Cleve made good progress. Shortly after 1 P.M., the *United States*, her high twin funnels belching smoke and her side-paddles splashing steadily, was sighted coming up Black River Bay west of the Harbor. Van Cleve, an experienced lake sailer, reversed engines to slow his progress around the headland of Navy Point and sometime between 1 and 2 P.M. tied up at the public wharf near the Union Hotel. While his stokers refuelled from the large wood pile nearby and his deck crew loaded cargo, Van Cleve watched as many waiting passengers – again, all males with little or no luggage – boarded his vessel. This time Worth was not around to interfere because he had left the previous day on the chartered steamer *Telegraph* to make an inspection tour of the American side of the St. Lawrence.[42]

In about forty-five minutes, the *United States* cast off and rounded Navy Point again to make for her next scheduled stop, the village of Cape Vincent on the American bank of the St. Lawrence near its confluence with Lake Ontario. Daniel Heustis, who had assumed command at Sackets Harbor after Birge had decided to go ahead to Ogdensburg, was one of those who had just boarded. He sought out Martin Woodruff, the senior Hunter officer from Onondaga, and asked him about the "500 Polanders from New York" promised by Birge, von Schoultz and others as they were clearly not on the *United States*. "Only six of them had come" was the somewhat lame response and, worse yet, Woodruff himself had brought only 160 men from the southern counties instead of the hundreds, if not thousands, expected. With this strength, the two men knew that the invasion would probably fail, but they did not contemplate calling it off. Woodruff summed up their situation: "I can't back out, neither can you. We must go and do our best. I had rather be shot than to back out now." As the *United States* chugged steadily northward on her appointed round, Heustis responded that, "whatever might be the issue," both would meet it as men "fighting in a good cause."[43]

PART II

The great hunt in the north woods

11-17 November 1838

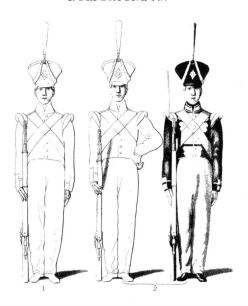

Fix bayonets!

A plate from the period British manual shows the movements for fixing bayonets. The enlisted British soldier was a firm believer that seventeen inches of cold steel with an attitude behind it would solve most tactical problems and he put this belief into practice most effectively at Prescott in November 1838. (From *Manual and Platoon Exercises*, 1828)

Natural wonder: The Thousand Islands of the St. Lawrence River

Located between Kingston and Brockville, the Thousand Islands present some of the most splendid natural scenery in North America. In the 1830s this area was the haunt of Bill Johnston, smuggler, pirate and commodore of the Hunter navy, and both the Prescott invaders and those who fought against them in 1838 passed through this beautiful part of the river. Twenty-five years earlier, during the War of 1812, an American army attempting to capture Montreal had passed down the same stretch of the St. Lawrence in a flotilla of 300 small boats. (Lithograph after painting by Augustus Köllner, J. Ross Robertson Collection, Toronto Reference Library)

CHAPTER FIVE

"Repel the midnight assassins"

Sunday, 11 November, to Monday, 12 November 1838, 6 A.M.

The cry of war is o'er the land! its wild voice on the blast,
And the beacon-fire, from height to height, is spreading fierce
*   and fast*
The battle trumpet sounds the call, our monarch's standard flies
Now children of the men of old! for life, for home, arise!

The foemen of our name are nigh, beyond yon lake's blue tide,
With boastings on their lying lips, with threats of taunting pride,
But the words they speak, the arms they wield, the Briton
*   laughs to scorn,*
As the howlings of a factious race, in empty strength upborne.

They brav'd the Lion in his sleep! they came in swarms of old,
To taint our careless forest breeze with their pirate banner's fold,
Our foemen gather'd for the fray, and mocked their dastard
*   flight,*
When the shout of victory swept along on Queenston's
*   glorious height!*[1]

Few people were abroad that morning in Kingston to see a somewhat bedraggled passenger disembark from a boat at the public wharf and make his way purposefully along Front Street. It was Sunday, 11 November, and the proper citizens of this scenic town on the shore of Lake Ontario were getting ready for church, and the not-so-proper were lying low to recover from the previous night's exertions. Ignoring the town dogs and hogs engaged in their perpetual and noisy battles in the streets and alleys, the man arrived at the Tête de Pont Barracks, station of Her Majesty's 83rd Regiment of Foot, just as the redcoated companies were falling in for church parade. Talking his way past the sentry at the gate, he gained admittance to the orderly room and, in reply to the questions of the sergeant on duty, gave his name as Anthony Flood, stated that he was a former NCO in the British army, and asked to see Lieutenant Colonel Henry Dundas, the commander of the garrison, as soon as possible.[2]

This was a highly unusual request for an unknown civilian to be making on a quiet Sunday in barracks and the orderly sergeant probably bristled when he heard it. Like all sergeants in all armies, he disliked disruption to established routine because, if not rigorously checked, such disruption might cause confusion which would in turn lead to chaos and ultimately to the collapse of civilization as we know it. Something in the stranger's bearing must have impressed the NCO as he did not dismiss the unwanted visitor with a few well-chosen (and long-polished) phrases but instead bucked the matter upstairs by sending for the orderly officer. As it was the traditional day of rest in garrison, this was probably the most junior officer in the 83rd but he in turn was impressed by the stranger and within minutes Anthony Flood was on his way under escort to see Dundas.

Explaining that he was a British agent who had been employed by Judge John S. Cartwright to spy on the Patriot Hunters, Flood told Dundas that the Hunters were about to launch a major attack on the village of Prescott, sixty miles down the St. Lawrence. He stressed that this information was fresh as he had only escaped the previous day from the Hunter camp at Millen's Bay on the American side of the river where hundreds of invaders were waiting to board two schooners, heavily laden with arms, including artillery, anchored offshore.[3]

If Anthony Flood expected Dundas to move quickly, he was to be disappointed as Lieutenant Colonel, the Honourable Henry Dundas was a slow and deliberate man. The scion of an aristocratic family (hence the appellation "honourable," as he was the eldest son of a viscount) Dundas came by this trait honestly as he was the son and grandson of senior government officials, his father having been First Lord of the Admiralty for sixteen years while his grandfather had served as a somewhat controversial secretary of war during the Napoleonic wars. It was not that Dundas disbelieved Flood, but he wanted his information made part of the official record and directed the agent to go first to Judge Cartwright and swear a legal deposition as to its veracity. Flood left immediately but unfortunately Cartwright was not at home. The agent then sought Sheriff Allan

Soldiers of the Queen: Light company, British infantry, 1838
Each British infantry battalion possessed a company of light infantry – trained skirmishers who covered the advance and withdrawal of the unit in action. The light company of the 83rd Foot fought at Prescott and their tactical skills were admired by their American army counterparts, who watched them in action from their side of the St. Lawrence. The artist has depicted these men in full dress uniform, including the awkward bell-top shako; the regulars were considerably less resplendent in the field. (Painting by P.W. Reynolds, Courtesy Department of National Defence, Canada)

Macdonell of Kingston, but that worthy too was absent, probably attending church along with the judge. It was now early afternoon and, possibly getting a little desperate, Flood went to the residence of Magistrate George Baker, who was not only at home but entertaining Captain Williams Sandom, RN, the British naval commander on Lake Ontario.[4]

The 53-year-old Sandom was a believer in swift action. A veteran officer said to have been under enemy fire more than sixty times during his forty-year career, Sandom had been ordered to Kingston in April 1838 to re-activate the moribund naval establishment on Lake Ontario. He had arrived to find the ribs of the warships of the once proud War of 1812 squadron rotting in the mud off Point Frederick but their ordnance, tackle, and equipment perfectly preserved in the "magnificent" Stone Frigate building near the old naval dockyard. A hard charger by any standard, Sandom set out to extemporize a naval presence on the Great Lakes and St. Lawrence, using veteran gunboats from the old squadron and hastily converted civilian steamers. He was an ideal choice for this assignment as he had gained experience with small boat warfare in Maine in 1814 and had recently spent a long period at civilian dockyards supervising the fitting of the new-fangled steam engines to sailing men-of-war. It did not take him long to create a squadron of three steam vessels, a schooner and three gunboats powered by sail and oar, manned by 267 officers, sailors and marines.[5]

Flood recalled that the naval officer "questioned him closely."[6] Sandom had good reason to do so because he had already heard a similar story from another agent. This was Hely Chamberlain, who had crossed the river to warn that an attack was planned on Prescott on 11 November. Sandom had not

been entirely convinced by Chamberlain, perhaps because the man was an American or perhaps because, as Sandom later wrote, he could not believe that Prescott was important enough to be a target. His doubts were not assuaged when Chamberlain suggested that the Hunters' real objective was Toronto. Unlike Flood, Chamberlain had not been at Sackets Harbor or Millen's Bay and could give no concrete details of enemy numbers or armament. All he could say was that a force of Hunters was planning a descent on Prescott – or maybe Toronto. It was all rather tenuous and Sandom did not immediately react, possibly

The Stone Frigate, Kingston, Upper Canada

During the War of 1812, the Royal Navy constructed a squadron of powerful warships on Lake Ontario, including a ship of the line larger than Nelson's *Victory*. After the conflict had ended, most of these warships were sunk in Kingston harbour or rotted away at the naval yard on Point Frederick. Their guns, tackle and other equipment were kept for possible future use and stored in the Stone Frigate, a building specially constructed for the purpose, and that is where Captain Williams Sandom found them when he reactivated a British naval presence on Lake Ontario in the spring of 1838. Today the Stone Frigate is part of the Royal Military College of Canada. (Photograph by John Grodzinski)

Tête de Pont Barracks, Kingston, Canada
This was the barracks of the 83rd Regiment of Foot, which fought at the battle of the windmill. Shortly after midnight, Saturday, 17 November 1838, the prisoners captured at Prescott were marched past it on their way to imprisonment at Fort Henry. An excited crowd, which included some wives of the soldiers, showered them with insults and worse things. Later renamed Fort Frontenac, the barracks are today the Canadian Forces Staff School. (National Archives of Canada, C-22938)

because he already had a vessel on station at Brockville, the small steamer *Experiment*, which could keep an eye on the St. Lawrence.[7]

The detailed intelligence brought by Flood, however, prompted Sandom to take more decisive steps. Flood not only confirmed Prescott as the object of the attack but also provided details on how it would be carried out – by a force of Hunters who would descend the river on the *United States* and two schooners. Sandom immediately issued orders for his squadron to make ready to sail (or steam as the case might be). Unfortunately, as he did so, he knew he had a major problem on his hands. Having not fully believed Chamberlain's story, he had granted his men liberty the previous night and they were now dispersed in taverns and alehouses across Kingston, a city "where Spirits and other intoxicating fluids are abundantly found at the cheapest rates" making it very difficult "to preserve sobriety and correctness of conduct with Seamen and Marines on shore."[8] Before Sandom could do anything, he would have to collect his men and sober them up, a process that would take time.[9]

According to Hiram Denio, there were no spirits flowing on board the steamer *United States* after it left Sackets Harbor in the early afternoon of 11 November. The Utica banker recorded that the many mysterious young male passengers "were very quiet – said little, drank nothing that I observed, and apparently were without arms."[10] A former circuit court judge, Denio was a keen observer and, after listening to their voices, changed his mind about the identity of these men. They were not foreign immigrants as he had earlier surmised, most appeared to be Americans, with a sprinkling of English, French and Canadians among them. He decided that, although the enigmatic passengers "were without arms," they were patriots making their way to Lower Canada to join Robert Nelson's followers. This suspicion was confirmed when, just opposite Point Peninsula eleven miles northwest of the Harbor, the *United States* met the steamer *Telegraph* on an opposite heading, and the *Telegraph* was plainly on government business because American troops were visible on her decks. When the two vessels passed, the crew of the *United States* heard some of the

Bastion of Upper Canada: Fort Henry

The strongest defence work in Upper Canada, the grey stone mass of Fort Henry on its headland east of the town ensured the security of Kingston during the rebellions and border troubles. It saw use as a prison for political prisoners, including Canadian rebels some of whom, in the early summer of 1838, made a daring escape. By the time the Hunters captured at Prescott arrived in the fort, security had been tightened. In this winter photograph, the fort is seen across frozen Navy Bay. (Photograph by Dianne Graves)

mysterious passengers urging others to get below and stay out of sight.[11]

Shortly after this incident, Denio went to his cabin as it was a cold day and a stiff breeze was blowing from the west. The *United States* continued on her voyage, stopping for thirty minutes at Cape Vincent to deliver freight and pick up passengers, including more young males without luggage, and then steamed down the south channel of the St. Lawrence. The ship was now passing through the Thousand Islands, some of the most beautiful scenery in North America, but most of those on board were not thinking about the wonders of nature. At the foot of Wolfe Island, near the mouth of Millen's Bay, Captain James Van Cleve spotted two small schooners ahead in the river. A "respectable looking passenger" (actually the Hunter officer Daniel George) informed Van Cleve that the vessels belonged to him and asked if they could be taken in tow as they were freighted for Ogdensburg.[12] This was a common practice among steamer captains so Van Cleve was amenable to the request, and George paid him $100 cash for the service, getting a

proper receipt in return. The steamer stopped, the *Charlotte of Oswego* and the *Charlotte of Toronto* were lashed to either side, and the *United States* proceeded on her way.[13]

Just after the steamer left French Creek, where she picked up still more male passengers with little luggage, Hiram Denio emerged from his cabin to see the two strange vessels alongside. Puzzled, he sought out Van Cleve, who informed him of the transaction with George and added that he was comfortable with the arrangement because he had begun to suspect his mysterious passengers and the schooner crews "might assist in a problem."[14] That Van Cleve did have "a problem" soon became evident when many of his passengers began to arm themselves with swords, pistols and rifles taken from crates in the hold that had been shipped as freight. Next, Denio saw young men "of a similar character with those already on the boat," emerge from below the decks of the two schooners alongside and climb onto the *United States*. Puzzled, he watched them move back and forth between the three vessels, cheerfully transferring heavy crates at the direction of a man with a cloak and a sword. It was only when he saw them gather in admiration around a flag decorated with an eagle and the motto "Liberated by the Onondaga Hunters" that it hit Denio that these tough-looking individuals were not on their way to Lower Canada but "contemplated a descent" somewhere along the St. Lawrence. That was bad enough but what was worse was that they seemed bent on using the *United States*, a considerable financial asset of Denio's bank, to carry out their plans.[15]

Once they had finished their tasks, the Hunters headed for shelter as the wind made the open decks very cold. It was therefore not difficult for Denio, Van Cleve and one of the other owners of the *United States* who was also on board, to hold a conference about their best course of action. Resistance was clearly impossible and it was decided to proceed to Morristown, the next port of call, where a message could be sent to Federal Marshal Nathaniel Garrow at Ogdensburg, and also across the river to Brockville in Canada. The *United States* would steam no farther after Morristown as her engine room crew would immobilize their machinery.[16]

It was about 10.30 P.M. when the *United States* neared Morristown. Suddenly, to Van Cleve and Denio's surprise, many of the Hunters on board transferred to the schooners, an action not done without much argument and shouting as many men refused to leave the steamer. Nonetheless, there were far fewer armed men on board when the two schooners cast off and disappeared into the darkness astern. About thirty minutes later, Van Cleve anchored at the Morristown wharf and Denio and the other owner rooted the local lawman out of bed to send the messages. It was nearly 1 A.M. on Monday, 12 November, when Denio returned to the *United States* to learn that Van Cleve, feeling his vessel was "free" of most of the Hunters, had decided to continue his voyage. Although he had some doubts, Denio accepted this decision and the *United States* departed for

Ogdensburg, where she arrived, after a quiet voyage without incident, at about 3 A.M.. Tired after his rather nervewracking experience, the banker decided not to sleep on board but instead took a hotel room ashore.[17]

During the voyage down the river, Daniel Heustis managed to recover his spirits. He was pleased when Martin Woodruff introduced him to Nils von Schoultz, whom Heustis thought "a gentleman of fine appearance and pleasing address."[18] He was even more pleased when Van Cleve picked up the two *Charlottes* as with this reinforcement he calculated the Hunter strength on board the three vessels as being over five hundred men – and more were waiting at Ogdensburg. He was pleasantly distracted by the task of directing working parties who brought up crates containing muskets, rifles, boarding pikes and cutlasses from the holds and distributed them. When the Hunters had armed themselves, they admired the flag of the ladies of the Onondaga Hunters, which von Schoultz displayed. After that, all Heustis and his comrades could do was wait and, as the night was cold, most took shelter in the public compartments of the steamer and its fireroom.[19]

In the meantime, the officers – Dorephus Abbey, Daniel George, Heustis, John Kimball, von Schoultz, Woodruff and others – finalized their plans for the landing at Prescott. After the men on the steamer had transferred to the *Charlottes*, they would proceed to the objective, and just before reaching the village the schooners would be lashed together and allowed to drift down on the current of the river to a wharf. When they had been made fast, von Schoultz, with 100 picked men (including Heustis), would land and move through Prescott to secure Fort Wellington while the schooners would move down the river to a point below (or east of) the fort and land the main body and the heavy weapons. Both groups would meet at the fort, raise the standard of liberty, and prepare to arm the thousands of Canadians expected to rally round once news of the invasion had spread.[20]

This plan immediately started to go awry when the officers ordered the men on the steamer to transfer to the schooners for the final leg of the voyage. Many refused to do so and Heustis stated that at this point "we were deserted by a large portion of the men" – he estimated as many as half the force.[21] In the end, despite threats and entreaties from the officers, only about 200 stalwarts transferred to the *Charlottes,* where they made themselves comfortable on hay spread on the bottom of small holds already crammed with weapons, ammunition and provisions. When the last willing man had transferred, the schooners cast off from the *United States,* raised sail and, impelled by the strong breeze from the west, moved quietly down the dark St. Lawrence.[22]

Fortunately for the Hunters' cause, the two *Charlottes* were not seen by Lieutenant William N. Fowell and the crew of Her Majesty's Steam Vessel *Experiment*, which was lying at anchor off Brockville across the river. Fowell had taken up this station

the previous night and during the day had heard rumours that there were armed vessels at Goose Creek, near Millen's Bay on the American side of the river. He had therefore kept a close watch on the river traffic all that Sunday but no armed vessel or vessels had appeared. When darkness fell, he extinguished his lights, and for this reason the *Experiment* was not seen by those on board the brightly-lit *United States* when it approached Morristown at about 10.30 P.M. Fowell had also heard rumours that the *United States* was transporting Hunters and visually inspected the vessel carefully as it passed but everything appeared normal. It was a dark night and so cold that a thick mist lay heavy on the river and none of the lookouts on the *Experiment* spotted the two small schooners that passed their position at about 11 P.M., headed for Prescott, twelve miles downstream.[23]

Prescott was ready for them. Located at the point in the St. Lawrence where cargo was shifted from large lake vessels to smaller craft to run the five rapids downstream, Prescott was (and still is) a workaday kind of place. Practical, not pretty, it

Small but feisty: Her Majesty's Steam Vessel *Experiment*, 1838
In the spring of 1838, Captain Williams Sandom, RN, was sent to Kingston to reactivate the British naval squadron on the Great Lakes using chartered civilian craft and some old veteran gunboats from the War of 1812. He purchased the little steamer *Experiment*, displacing 100 tons and powered by a 30 horsepower steam engine, armed her with two 3-pdr. pop guns and an 18-pdr. carronade, and commissioned her as HMSV *Experiment*. Under the command of Lieutenant William Fowell, RN, the *Experiment* played a major role in foiling the Hunter invasion at Prescott. (Toronto Reference Library)

The point of attack: Prescott, Canada, 1830

Located at the point on the St. Lawrence where freight was either transferred to smaller vessels to run the rapids down-river or to larger vessels for movement up the river and into the Great Lakes, Prescott was a bustling little port in 1838, and its main thoroughfare, Water Street, was lined with taverns and other establishments that catered to the needs of the riverboat men. Prescott and attendant Fort Wellington were the objectives of the New York Hunters' attack, and before it was over nearly every male of military age in the village would see service. (Painting by Thomas Burrowes, Archives of Ontario)

lacked the style of Brockville, its more scenic neighbour up river, whose citizens tended to look down their noses at its hard working residents – an antipathy the people of Prescott cheerfully reciprocated (and still do). In November 1838 this bustling river port boasted 2,000 citizens, three to four hundred dwelling places, four churches, a foundry, a distillery, a tannery, a slaughter house and at least a dozen "good houses of entertainment."[24] Most of these establishments were located on muddy Water Street near the river, a busy and somewhat notorious thoroughfare that was crowded day and night with sailors from the riverboats, lumberjacks from the timber rafts that ran the St. Lawrence rapids, travellers, businessmen – and those who catered to their needs.

Prescott's defences were under the command of 41-year-old Plomer Young, a British regular officer. First commissioned in 1805, Young had served until 1832 when he went on half pay as a major. He had been called back to active service with the rank of acting lieutenant colonel when Sir John Colborne had requested that a number of field grade regular officers be sent to the Canadas "on particular service" to assist in the defence of the border areas. Assigned to Prescott, Young had arrived there in April 1838. He had no doubts about the loyalty of the people of Prescott and the surrounding counties of Leeds and Grenville, as only a few ripples from the recent political turmoil had disturbed the tranquillity of the area: there had been trouble in Leeds and Grenville during the 1836 election, and William B. Wells, one of the twin counties' Legislative Assembly members, had fled after the abortive uprising but, during the government crackdown that followed, only eleven persons had been arrested in the area and they had later been released for lack of evidence.[25]

During the previous winter, Prescott had looked to its own defences. When Van Rensselaer had threatened Kingston in February 1838, Hamilton D. Jessup, a 32-year-old local doctor, had formed a volunteer company which stood guard at decrepit Fort Wellington. This company had been demobilized in the late spring but the rising tension along the St. Lawrence in the aftermath of the destruction of the *Robert Peel* had caused it to be raised again. In early July, Canadian James Philips, already wanted by the authorities, was rumoured to be intent on the destruction of the Rideau Canal locks, and local militia apprehended one of his men, John Thomas, but the magistrates let him go for lack of evidence. Thomas, along with John Berry, Ezra Brockway, the Chipman brothers and James Phillips, all from Leeds or Grenville, were about to return home on the two *Charlottes*.[26]

Young had dispatched an agent to the American side of the river "to collect in a quiet and systematic Manner all the information in his power" and this step paid dividends in the autumn of 1838.[27] When Colborne and Arthur learned that the Hunters were planning a major attack somewhere on the Canadian side of the St. Lawrence, Young received authority to call out such numbers of the local militia as he thought necessary to meet it. From mid-October onward, select companies from the Leeds, Grenville and Dundas County regiments had been mobilized for short periods and permission was also given to raise a longservice militia unit, the 9th Provisional Battalion, that would serve for a period of six months.[28]

On the night of 11 November, however, Young had only about a hundred militiamen on duty in Prescott, comprising Hamilton Jessup's company and Captain George Macdonell's company of Lancaster Glengarry Highlanders, a longservice unit raised the previous spring. Young had received positive information that Prescott would be attacked that night but, fearing a panic, this news "was not generally spread."[29] Instead, he doubled the sentries at all approaches to the village and attendant Fort Wellington.[30]

About 2 A.M., the men posted on the wharf owned by the forwarding company Hooker and Henderson (on the Prescott waterfront between Sophia and Anne streets) spotted suspicious sails coming down the river "unusually close to shore."[31] They alerted Young, who caused the alarm bell to be rung, and in the words of Alpheus Jones, the village postmaster, "a general *muster* was made of all who could procure arms, pitchforks, or anything which would repel the *midnight assassins*."[32] Young and Jones ran down to the wharf in time to see two small schooners, lashed together, bearing directly at them. The vessels made no response to Young's hail but, as they came closer, their pilot realized that he could not dock because the wharf was torn up for repairs and he therefore bore off for Fraser's wharf at the foot of St. Lawrence Street, a short distance downstream. Young, Jones and "a few straggling townsmen, with arms, who were on the alert," followed on land and saw a man leap from one of the vessels and attempt to make a line fast to Fraser's wharf.[33]

This was Hunter John Cronkhite who had volunteered for this hazardous duty. A "man of few words but ever ready in action," Cronkhite timed his jump nicely and, ignoring warning shots fired in the air by the two sentries on the wharf, secured the two *Charlottes*.[34] As the rope was frozen and stiff, this proved difficult but Cronkhite finally accomplished his task and jumped back on board. Unfortunately, the line broke from the strain of the current and the weight of the two schooners, and they moved past Fraser's wharf toward McMillan's, the next anchorage.[35]

Young, Jones and their men arrived at Fraser's just as their prey moved down the river. Again, Young hailed but again got no response so his party followed the mysterious vessels down to McMillan's wharf, where Cronkhite tried to repeat his feat. Exasperated, Young shouted that he would open fire unless the two vessels identified themselves and this threat brought the response "Charlotte of Toronto, George, master," but that was all because, failing in their third attempt to dock, the two schooners separated and made for the American side of the river, disappearing in the darkness and mist.[36]

Certain that he had frustrated an attack by the Patriot Hunters, Young immediately sent dispatch riders to inform Dundas at Kingston and alert the Canadian side of the St. Lawrence between that place and Prescott. It was now well past 3 A.M. and the ordinary citizens of Prescott, roused by the alarm bell, the shots, shouts, the sound of men running in the streets – all of which, of course, set the village dogs to howling – were wide awake and fearful. Most of the menfolk were in the streets by now and, it being a cold night and defending the Crown always thirsty work, one hopes the tavern keepers on Water Street did their patriotic duty by opening early or that John Buckley, purveyor of fine groceries on the same thoroughfare, allowed the village's gallant defenders to avail themselves of the keg of beer with its attendant chained wooden mug that stood square in the centre of his store. No one, it seemed, knew what the morrow would bring – as one resident later recorded, the "intense anxiety for daylight" was "not to be described."[37]

Everyone cheered up, however, when the Royal Navy, in the form of Lieutenant Fowell and HMSV *Experiment*, arrived thirty minutes before dawn. After he had seen the *United States* go, Fowell had maintained station before Brockville until past 3 A.M. when he learned that information had come over from Morristown warning that two schooners full of heavily-armed men had gone down the river intending to attack Prescott. Fowell set out to follow and was at Prescott when the dawn of Monday, 12 November 1838, revealed to anxious Canadian eyes the two unusual nighttime visitors anchored in the middle of the St. Lawrence, surrounded by small boats.[38]

Facing page

Strange sail on the river, 12 November 1838
During the early morning of Monday, 12 November, militia sentries on the Prescott wharves, peering through the heavy mist on the St. Lawrence, sighted two unknown vessels, lashed together, coming down the river. They raised the alarm and the quick response of the local commander, Lieutenant Colonel Plomer Young, and his troops prevented the Hunters in the *Charlotte of Toronto* and the *Charlotte of Oswego* from landing as planned in the village. (Oil sketch by Peter Rindlisbacher, courtesy of the artist)

CHAPTER SIX

"A dose of John Bull's powders"

Monday, 12 November 1838, 6 A.M. to midnight

Hark to the bugle's warlike notes
Which calls us forth to glory –
And see old England's banner floats
O'er troops renowned in story
  For Patriot *bands from other lands,*
  By force would try to bend her,
  But we will shout, to their rabble rout,
  Our watchword – "No Surrender!!"
For Briton's cause and Britain's laws,
We never will surrender.

The Patriot rebels lead the van
Well back'd by sympathizers.
We'll face them tho' but one to ten
And teach them how to fly, Sirs,
  The treach'rous brood of Yankee blood,
  No noble deeds could render,
  When Britain's men with echoing guns,
  Proclaim their "No Surrender!!"
For Britain's cause and Britain's laws,
We never will surrender.[1]

In fact, the *Charlotte of Oswego* and the *Charlotte of Toronto* were not at anchor – they had run aground on a mud bank deposited by the Oswegatchie River, which joins the St. Lawrence at Ogdensburg (see Map 5). To make things worse, the two vessels had got afoul of each other and were somewhat tangled up. For the Hunters on board, the only good news was that they were in American waters and therefore safe from Fowell's *Experiment,* which, as dawn broke, they could see at Prescott.[2]

At daybreak, Hunters in boats put out from Ogdensburg – among them swashbuckling Bill Johnston, armed to the teeth with a Cochran twelve-shot musket, a Bowie knife and two pistols. Johnston was a skilled river pilot and with his expert guidance the two luckless *Charlottes* were soon disentangled though still grounded. At this point, John W. Birge, wearing a uniform resplendent with "tasseled epaulets, bright buttons, and the glittering bald eagle and twin stars of the Patriot insignia," which he had probably designed himself, appeared in a boat.[3] Birge declined to come on board either schooner but shouted to the officers on the two vessels that they "must go ashore, and get the cannon ashore as quick as possible."[4] Having said this, Daniel Heustis later

"A dose of John Bull's powders"

Monday, 12 November 1838, 6 A.M. to midnight

Hark to the bugle's warlike notes
Which calls us forth to glory –
And see old England's banner floats
O'er troops renowned in story
    For Patriot *bands from other lands,*
    By force would try to bend her,
    But we will shout, to their rabble rout,
    Our watchword – "No Surrender!!"
For Briton's cause and Britain's laws,
We never will surrender.

The Patriot rebels lead the van
Well back'd by sympathizers.
We'll face them tho' but one to ten
And teach them how to fly, Sirs,
    The treach'rous brood of Yankee blood,
    No noble deeds could render,
    When Britain's men with echoing guns,
    Proclaim their "No Surrender!!"
For Britain's cause and Britain's laws,
We never will surrender.[1]

In fact, the *Charlotte of Oswego* and the *Charlotte of Toronto* were not at anchor – they had run aground on a mud bank deposited by the Oswegatchie River, which joins the St. Lawrence at Ogdensburg (see Map 5). To make things worse, the two vessels had got afoul of each other and were somewhat tangled up. For the Hunters on board, the only good news was that they were in American waters and therefore safe from Fowell's *Experiment*, which, as dawn broke, they could see at Prescott.[2]

At daybreak, Hunters in boats put out from Ogdensburg – among them swashbuckling Bill Johnston, armed to the teeth with a Cochran twelve-shot musket, a Bowie knife and two pistols. Johnston was a skilled river pilot and with his expert guidance the two luckless *Charlottes* were soon disentangled though still grounded. At this point, John W. Birge, wearing a uniform resplendent with "tasseled epaulets, bright buttons, and the glittering bald eagle and twin stars of the Patriot insignia," which he had probably designed himself, appeared in a boat.[3] Birge declined to come on board either schooner but shouted to the officers on the two vessels that they "must go ashore, and get the cannon ashore as quick as possible."[4] Having said this, Daniel Heustis later

wrote, Birge "pulled for Ogdensburgh, and I have never seen the coward since."[5]

After some discussion, the officers decided that the *Charlottes* would drop down the river about a mile and disembark their men on the Canadian bank at a small headland crowned by a tall stone windmill. As the shallow water in this area would make it impossible to get the schooners in close enough to land

The best of neighbours: Prescott, seen from Ogdensburg, c. 1840
Relations between the two communities on opposite sides of the St. Lawrence River had been close until the troubles of the 1830s. It took a long time for the people of Prescott to forgive their American neighbours for supporting the Hunters and lining the banks of the river to cheer them on during the battle of 13 November 1838. (Print by W.H. Bartlett, author's collection)

the artillery, Johnston went back to Ogdensburg to find a suitable craft. He returned some time later with a small scow – and a brass 6-pdr. field gun "borrowed" from the Ogdensburg militia artillery company – and began the lengthy process of transferring the artillery and other heavy material from the schooners. It proved easier to shift weapons than it did men as, again, many Hunters whose enthusiasm had evaporated with daylight took Birge's lead and crossed to Ogdensburg in the small boats that crowded around the *Charlottes*. One of those who stayed, Stephen Wright, bitterly complained that these miscreants were soon to be seen "talking (with their *extinguished* officers) bravely and gallantly" in the streets of that village, 900 yards away.[6]

Johnston unloaded the *Charlotte of Toronto* first and she was soon off the mud bank and floating free but he had no luck with the *Charlotte of Oswego*. He therefore sent to Ogdensburg for a steam-powered vessel and, in response, John Ward Birge made what was possibly his sole positive contribution to the invasion – he hijacked the *United States*.

Both Lieutenant Colonel Plomer Young in Prescott and Lieutenant Fowell on the *Experiment* watched the activity around the two schooners. Conscious of the controversy caused by the *Caroline* incident, Fowell dared not touch the Hunter craft as long as they remained on the American side of the international line, and any doubts he may have had on this score disappeared when the *Paul Pry*, a small steam vessel used as a ferry between Ogdensburg and Prescott, came over with a message from the Ogdensburg magistrates, asking him not to fire into American territorial waters. Also on the *Paul Pry* were three Canadians who told Young and Fowell that Ogdensburg was in the hands of an armed mob which had "overpowered

the authorities" and commandeered the *United States*.[7] The two officers were incredulous that the American authorities were powerless to prevent the hijacking of a large passenger vessel and that a village of some 2,000 souls could be under the control of pirates and brigands. Nonetheless, just after 9 A.M., they saw the *United States* leave Ogdensburg and move in the direction of the stranded *Charlotte of Oswego*.[8]

The information about Ogdensburg was unfortunately true as on Monday, 12 November 1838, it ceased to be a peaceable village in upstate New York and instead became the capital of the Patriot Hunters, a transition accomplished by the simple fact that it was overrun by men armed to the teeth. There were no troops to oppose them: the closest regular garrison was at Sackets Harbor, sixty miles away, and the state militia were either sympathetic to the Hunters or lying low until the whole thing blew over. If he had been present, Marshal Nathaniel Garrow might have prevented the takeover by sheer force of personality as he was a respected law officer, but Garrow, alas, was not at Ogdensburg. On Saturday, he had departed on the *Telegraph*, at Worth's request, to arrest the Hunters whom Worth had seen gathering at Sackets Harbor. In fact, the marshal and Worth had passed their prey when they had crossed with the *United States* travelling in the opposite direction. That left only two other representatives of the United States government in Ogdensburg to deal with the invasion – Smith Stilwell, the collector of customs, and Preston King, the postmaster – and they were overwhelmed. The best they could do was to send an express message to Worth at Sackets Harbor, appealing for assistance.[9]

Reactions to the takeover varied. With their streets crowded with heavily-armed strangers, and Prescott on the other side of

the river "alive with the bustle of preparations to resist the movement which were in progress against them," many in Ogdensburg abandoned their property and fled into the surrounding countryside.[10] Some openly or covertly assisted the Hunters, while others who

> looked upon the proceeding as tending to nothing but ruin, and as calling upon the patriotism of every good citizen, to lend his aid in discouraging the prosecution of the enterprise, and in protecting the national honour and the interests of the village. Such, however, was the influence of the armed strangers in the streets, that this sentiment could scarcely be found to operate in efficient exertions.[11]

One resident thought the whole thing delightful: Albert Tyler, editor and publisher of the *Ogdensburg Times and Advertizer*. Tyler was living a newspaperman's dream. Instead of having to chase the news, it had come to him.[12]

Hiram Denio, on the other hand, was not at all amused. Early that morning, the banker was dressing himself in his hotel room when he heard shouting outside and, looking out, saw the streets full of Hunters. Fearing the worst, he hurried to the docks just in time to see the *United States* pulling away and his inquiries produced the information that about a hundred armed men under the command of Birge had boarded the vessel and, with the assistance of volunteers from her crew, were on a mission to rescue the *Charlotte of Oswego*. Smith Stillwell, the collector, had tried to stop them but the Hunters had simply brushed by him. Helpless, Denio was forced to watch as his bank's valuable asset again sailed in harm's way and, what was worse, bystanders cheerfully informed him that her new captain, who was clearly intoxicated, was a certain Oliver B. Pierce, known locally as "an itinerant lecturer on grammar and phrenology."[13]

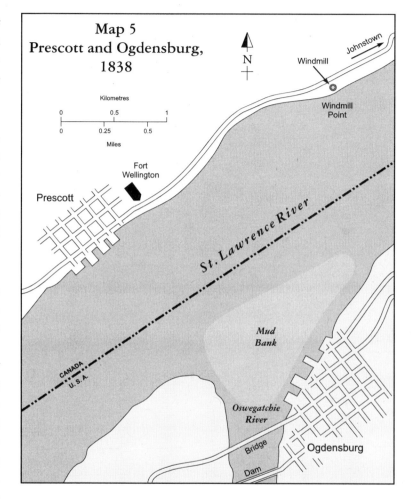

Map 5
Prescott and Ogdensburg, 1838

Because of the mud bank, the *United States* was not able to get near the *Charlotte of Oswego*. A shouted conference took place between Johnston on the scow, the Hunter officers on the schooners, and Birge and Pierce on the steamer. At Birge's urging, the *Charlotte of Toronto* and the scow moved down to the chosen landing place while the *United States* returned to Ogdensburg for a longer tow rope to pull the other schooner

off the mud bar. This was procured but when the steamer moved back out to the middle of the river she gave the mud bank a wide berth and came up on the northern side of the *Charlotte of Oswego*. In doing so, the *United States* crossed the international line into Canadian waters.[14]

Lieutenant Fowell had been waiting for just such a movement. HMSV *Experiment*, her thirty-horsepower engine straining and her White Ensign streaming, immediately moved on a course that would bring her alongside the trespasser. As his gun crews made ready the 18-pdr. carronade on the *Experiment's* foredeck, they could see Hunters on the upper decks of the *United States*, who began to cheer madly and fire rifles and muskets as the British vessel came near. When he was within good range, Fowell gave the order and his mate, David Wright, pulled the lanyard of the carronade to give the enemy "a dose of John Bull's powders" – in this case an 18 pdr. roundshot which hit the steamer's hull.[15] Wright's gun crew reloaded

Facing page

"A dose of John Bull's powders:" Naval action at Prescott, 12 November 1838
During the morning of Monday, 12 November 1838, HMSV *Experiment* fought one of the stranger battles in the long history of the Royal Navy when the steamer *United States*, four times its displacement and under the command of a drunken phrenologist, tried to ram the smaller vessel. Lieutenant William Fowell, captain of the *Experiment*, replied with a "dose of John Bull's powders," several rounds of 3- and 18-pdr. grapeshot, one of which decapitated the pilot of the Hunter vessel, bringing the business to a swift end. (Oil sketch by Peter Rindlisbacher, courtesy of the artist)

quickly and he was able to get off another round before the faster *Experiment* had passed by its target. Although both shots clearly hit the *United States*, as did some from the small 3-pdr. guns on the British vessel, the steamer did not slow but continued down the river toward Windmill Point, where the *Charlotte of Toronto* and the scow were unloading men and stores.[16].

Fowell was now in a dilemma. It was his information that the *United States* was carrying five or six hundred men and five pieces of artillery, and that the objective of the Hunters was to land them at Prescott. This being the case, he decided, about halfway to Windmill Point, that the Hunters were trying to lure him downriver and he came about to resume his station off the village. As he did, he saw that the Ogdensburg steam ferry, the *Paul Pry*, had taken advantage of his absence to go to the rescue of the *Charlotte of Oswego* and had managed to get her off the mudbank. Both vessels were moving through Canadian waters.[17]

This made it legal for Fowell. Closing to within ten yards, he fired grape and canister at the intruders. Inaccurate return fire came from a small artillery piece on board the *Charlotte* but the crew of the *Experiment* also heard men shouting that they wished to surrender. At this point, the *Paul Pry* abandoned her tow and headed for Ogdensburg. Fowell turned to capture the schooner, but by the time he got around, the *Charlotte of Oswego* had regained the safety of American waters and the naval officer let her go. Besides, there was a more pressing matter at hand – the *United States* was steaming at full speed up the river directly toward him.[18]

Oliver B. Pierce, student of phrenology and captain of the *United States*, still had some Dutch courage in him. After disembarking men and stores at Windmill Point, he apparently decided that his best course of action was to ram the *Experiment*. As the *United States* displaced 450 tons to the British vessel's 100 tons, this was a logical, if somewhat foolhardy, decision but Pierce possibly reasoned that, if he could not sink the *Experiment*, he might damage her enough to keep her out of the way, and on his orders the steamer's pilot, Solomon Foster, steered directly for the little British steamer. As the *United States* came up the river, the militia in Prescott fired at her but the Hunters on her decks, perhaps as intoxicated as her captain, jeered when the rounds fell short.[19]

They also jeered when Fowell, on an opposing course that brought him within ten yards of his enemy opened fire on the *United States* with his carronade and two 3-pdr. guns. Again, shots were seen to strike with no apparent effect. Fowell had no problems avoiding Pierce's clumsy attempt to ram and fired a second time as the steamer passed by. This time the results were positive. A 12-year-old boy on shore, Thomas Bog, saw wood splinter on the side of the steamer's wheelhouse as a 3-pdr. round went through it, removing most of pilot Foster's head in the process, while an 18-pdr. shot knocked out the steamer's starboard engine. The Hunters abruptly stopped cheering and Pierce's courage, in Denio's words, "evaporated with the effects of the liquor he had drunk."[20] One of the crew managed to steer the wounded vessel back to Ogdensburg while the *Charlotte of Toronto*, which had followed her progress up the river, seeing her fate, veered into American waters and came to anchor beside the *Charlotte of Oswego*, about a hundred yards off the Ogdensburg docks.[21]

Lieutenant William Newton Fowell and Her Majesty's Steam Vessel *Experiment*, having fought one of the stranger engagements in the long and illustrious history of the Royal Navy, resumed station off Prescott.

The naval action had been witnessed by spellbound crowds on both sides of the river. In Ogdensburg, newspaperman Albert Tyler boasted that his office window had been the best vantage point to watch "the skipping of the shot as they glanced along the surface of the water."[22] Understandably, Hiram Denio was considerably less entranced and, as soon as the *United States* had docked, he went on board with other owners and Smith Stillwell to recover possession of the bank's property. Foster's body was wrapped in a sheet and taken ashore and the rest of the Hunters were only too willing to leave except for Birge, who had locked himself in a cabin during the engagement with the *Experiment*. Birge claimed that he was too sick to move but, after preparations were made to carry him ashore, Denio recollected that the Hunter "found the use of his limbs" and "the muscular energy" he "exerted getting down the gangway, produced an impression" that Birge lacked a "quality generally esteemed essential in such enterprises as that in which he had embarked" – that is to say, courage.[23]

The owners had just rid themselves of Birge and Pierce, the latter disappearing into the crowd on the dock never to be heard from again, when Bill Johnston arrived and tried without success to get the Hunters still on board to cross the river with him. They refused and finally, when all the unwanted guests were gone, Denio and the other owners supervised the partial dismantling of the vessel's engine to immobilize her.[24]

In Prescott, meanwhile, Lieutenant Colonel Plomer Young had observed the enemy landing at Windmill Point. There was not much he could do, as he did not have the force to prevent it, and he was also distracted by news of a second incursion. Early that morning a force of marauders had crossed from the United States and landed near the mouth of Honeywell (now Bradley's) Creek, a mile up the river. They had captured two dragoon messengers and torn up the planks of the bridge that

Sentry of the St. Lawrence: Fort Wellington, Prescott, 1830

Constructed during the War of 1812, this defence work was a near ruin at the time the border troubles began in 1838. Its reconstruction had just started when Prescott was attacked. Fort Wellington was the main objective of the Hunters, who hoped to seize it and use it as a base to foment rebellion in Upper Canada. It has been reconstructed to its appearance in 1840 and today is open to the public as an historic site. (Painting by Thomas Burrowes, Archives of Ontario)

What Plomer Young saw: Windmill Point from Fort Wellington

From his headquarters at Fort Wellington, Lieutenant Colonel Plomer Young had a clear view of the Hunter landing at Windmill Point in neighbouring Edwardsburgh Township, which, as is shown in this photograph, was about a mile east or down-river of the fort. In the background can be seen the International Bridge across the St. Lawrence, completed in 1960. (Photograph by Dianne Graves) spanned the creek before returning to American territory. Fearing he might soon be attacked from two directions, Young opted to keep the greater part of his force, Macdonell's Highlanders, the village militia companies and half of Jessup's Volunteer Company, at Prescott and Fort Wellington. He did, however, send some of Jessup's men to a position north of the mill with orders to observe the Hunters there but to keep out of sight. Other than that, there was not much else he could do until reinforcements arrived.[25]

Help was on the way. It took Captain Williams Sandom most of Sunday afternoon, 11 November, to haul his sailors and marines out of the taverns of Kingston and herd them back to their vessels, and it was midnight before the armed steamer *Cobourg*, with the light company of the 83rd Foot on board as marines, headed for Sackets Harbor to inform Colonel William Worth that "250 miscreants and marauders" were at Millen's Bay, intending to attack Toronto.[26] Clearly, Sandom had not believed either Chamberlain or Flood's assertions that the invaders' target was Prescott. At 4 A.M., 12 November, Sandom sailed on the armed steamer *Queen Victoria* with Anthony Flood and a detachment of Royal Marines, to a point in the river near Millen's Bay to ensure that the Hunters at that place did not escape before American forces arrived.[27]

For his part, Lieutenant Colonel Henry Dundas did nothing. He may have believed that the Hunters were going to attack Toronto, which was not his responsibility, although it is curious that neither he nor Sandom asked the logical question why an invading force, intending to attack the provincial capital, would concentrate at Millen's Bay, 130 miles to the east, and not at Rochester or Oswego directly across Lake Ontario. Dundas may have decided to wait until he had better intelligence about the enemy objective or he may simply not have had any transport. The steamer *Brockville*, which had run aground in the St. Lawrence a few days earlier, was expected in Kingston late Monday night and possibly Dundas was waiting for her to arrive until he made his move.[28]

The *Cobourg* reached Sackets Harbor at about 3 A.M. on 12 November with Sandom's message for Worth. The American commander responded that he had received similar information and had brought Federal Marshal Garrow back from Ogdensburg to arrest the culprits. Ironically, Worth and Garrow had passed their prey, heading for Ogdensburg on the *United States*, the previous afternoon. Worth decided to proceed Millen's Bay to arrest the invaders and, about an hour after the *Cobourg* left the Harbor, he followed in the steamer

The good soldier: Colonel William Jenkins Worth, United States Army (1749-1894)

A veteran of the War of 1812, Worth was sent to the northern border in December 1837 to restore order. He proved effective in foiling the patriots in the Niagara and Detroit areas and was later shifted to the St. Lawrence frontier with his headquarters at Sackets Harbor. During the attack on Prescott in November 1838, he restored order in Ogdensburg and prevented reinforcements crossing the river, thus dooming the Hunters at the windmill. Worth is shown here in the uniform of a brigadier general. (Author's collection)

Telegraph with Marshal Garrow, two companies of the Eighth Infantry and a 6-pdr. field gun.[29]

Just after dawn Worth encountered Sandom in the *Victoria* near Carleton Island. After some discussion, the two commanders went their separate ways. Worth headed for Millen's Bay only to find his prey gone and continued on to French Creek, arriving about 10 A.M. To the delight of his officers, Kate Johnston, the pirate's daughter and beautiful "Queen of the Isles," was in the village but, more to the matter at hand, Worth also learned that the two vessels he was seeking had been towed down the St. Lawrence by the *United States* on the previous night.[30] He decided to continue down-river to Ogdensburg, checking all the possible anchorages on the American side during the voyage.[31]

Sandom, meanwhile, proceeded down the Canadian side of the river with the *Victoria* and *Cobourg*. He stopped briefly at Gananoque for wood and then steamed to Brockville, where he arrived at 8 P.M., only to learn from the steamer *Brockville*, which had just come up the river, that the enemy had attacked, not Toronto but Prescott. Sandom immediately prepared for action, but as his two vessels were full of civilian stores, it took his men four frantic hours to land these useless articles and it was after midnight before the *Cobourg* and *Victoria* steamed for Prescott.[32]

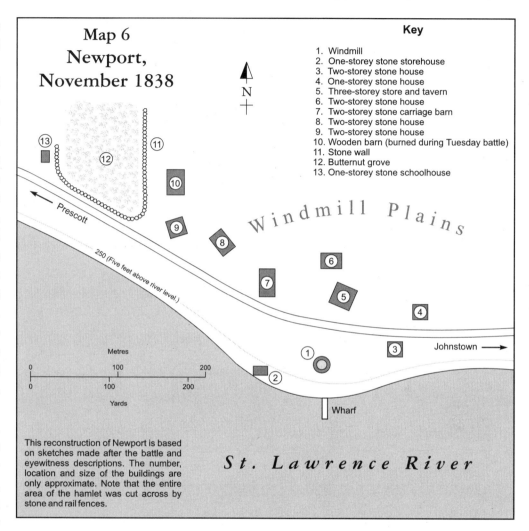

Map 6
Newport,
November 1838

Key

1. Windmill
2. One-storey stone storehouse
3. Two-storey stone house
4. One-storey stone house
5. Three-storey store and tavern
6. Two-storey stone house
7. Two-storey stone carriage barn
8. Two-storey stone house
9. Two-storey stone house
10. Wooden barn (burned during Tuesday battle)
11. Stone wall
12. Butternut grove
13. One-storey stone schoolhouse

Windmill Plains

Prescott

250 (Five feet above river level.)

Johnstown →

Wharf

St. Lawrence River

Metres
0   100   200
0   100   200
Yards

This reconstruction of Newport is based on sketches made after the battle and eyewitness descriptions. The number, location and size of the buildings are only approximate. Note that the entire area of the hamlet was cut across by stone and rail fences.

The first Hunters to land at Windmill Point came ashore some time after 10 A.M. on Monday, 12 November 1838. This was a small party led by von Schoultz who, using a boat from the *Charlotte of Toronto*, docked at the small wharf just below the stone mill and climbed up the steep bank, some thirty feet high, to the top of the headland. Here they found

The windmill, Edwardsburgh Township, Upper Canada

Three views of the windmill, from the east looking up-river (left), from the shore (below left) and from the north looking across the river towards Ogdensburg. This solidly-built structure with rubble stone walls about 3 feet thick is 25 feet in diameter at its base and about 60 feet high. In 1838, interior stairs led from the ground to the second floor but access to the upper floors was only possible by climbing an exterior ladder to a wooden gallery around the outside of the third floor, from which two doors, one in the north and one in the south face, opened to the interior. One of the first things the Hunters did was to build a stone wall about six feet high in front of the door to provide protection for the interior. (Photographs by René Schoemaker)

themselves in the middle of a straggling little hamlet called Newport (and less commonly, New Jerusalem), consisting of about a dozen stone and wood buildings clustered around the grist mill (see Map 6). This edifice, solidly constructed of rubble stone between 1822 and 1832, was an imposing structure twenty-five feet in diameter at the base, six floors and sixty feet high, with windows on each floor facing east or west, down or up the river. Interior stairs led from the ground to the second floor but access to the upper levels was only gained by climbing an exterior ladder to a wooden gallery positioned around the outside of the third floor from which two doors, one in the north and one in the south face, opened to the interior. Owned by the McQueen brothers of Prescott, the mill was not in operation in 1838 although its machinery was still in place.[33]

What the Hunters saw: The view from the top of the windmill

The Hunter sentries posted at the top of the mill had excellent observation in every direction. Looking west (first photo) they could see Prescott (marked by the water tower on the horizon, see arrow) and the river road from the village to the mill. The railway is a later 19th century construction; in 1838 the river road did not turn but continued straight along the shoreline to Prescott. The house in the middle ground is the only structure on the point besides the mill that dates to the time of the battle. The butternut grove was located about where the road makes a sharp turn to the right. Looking north (second photo) the sentries could see the flat area that locals called the Windmill Plains, which in 1838 was cut across by stone and wooden fences. On the morning of 13 November, Colonel Richard D. Fraser's column circled north of the high ground (near the tree line on the ridge) to attack Newport from the east. (Photographs by René Schoemaker)

Up to this point, the Hunter attack on Prescott had been a series of mishaps but things now began to turn in their favour. A quick inspection of the area was enough to tell a trained officer like von Schoultz that he was in a strong position. Windmill Point commanded the river; the upper levels of the mill provided good observation in all directions; and the building itself was a stronghold with walls three and a half feet thick at the base that would be impervious to all but the heaviest artillery. The river secured the rear and any attack would have to come from the landward side, which, beyond the hamlet around the mill, consisted of an area of flat, open fields the locals called the "Windmill Plains." These fields were cut across by stone walls and spit-rail fences that would provide cover for the Hunters, who, if forced back from them, could withdraw to the solid stone houses of Newport and, finally, to the mill itself.[34]

It was a good position, and while they waited for Birge and the main body to arrive, von Schoultz and the other officers set out to improve it. As more men landed from the *Charlotte of Toronto* and the boats that crossed the river throughout the day, they were put to work building a rubble stone wall some six feet high in front of the north door of the mill to provide protection from artillery and small-arms fire. Another defensive position with embrasures or firing ports was constructed near the west side of the stronghold for the three artillery pieces Johnston had offloaded from his scow. The three guns – a brass 6-pdr., an iron 4-pdr. and a brass 3-pdr. – were dragged up the bank with much difficulty and positioned west of the windmill aimed up river. The invaders occupied the houses and barns of Newport, and strong pickets were posted on the roads leading to Prescott to the west and Johnstown to the east.[35]

The men at the mill watched the morning naval action between the *United States* and *Experiment* with great interest. At least one piece of artillery was in position at that time as they opened fire on the British vessel when it came briefly within range. The result of the battle, however, was not so pleasing because the materiel on the *Charlotte of Oswego*, which comprised about two-thirds of their provisions, the bulk of their artillery ammunition, five artillery pieces, 176 rifles and 400 to 500 muskets, was now lost to them. Reinforcements continued to arrive, however, in small boats and, from an initial force of about 100 men, by nightfall there were nearly 250 well-armed Hunters ashore in Canada with enough ammunition to last four or five days. By then, everyone was confident they would either be victorious or evacuated to safety. Some daring soul scaled the mill and nailed the flag of the Onondaga Hunters to one of its wings and, as 20-year-old Justus Merriam remarked, "we made ourselves as comfortable as we could."[36]

Most of the residents of Newport were in their homes when the invaders arrived. Some ran away but the Hunters assured those who remained that their property would be respected, and von Schoultz issued clear orders that the men "were not to take anything without paying for it, and in all cases to protect women and children."[37] Daniel Heustis and three comrades, hungry after their long journey, entered one of the nearby houses and asked a Canadian farmwife to make them a meal, which she did, refusing payment for her effort. Another Canadian housewife, whose husband was absent, hid in the nearby woods with her children but returned after von Schoultz sent a man to assure her that she and her family would be protected. As the woman still wished to leave, friendly Hunters helped her to load her valuables and possessions in a cart and off she drove.[38]

Adonisah Bass, a resident of Newport, was returning from the mill at nearby Johnstown when heavily armed men surrounded his wagon. He was brought before von Schoultz, who questioned him but allowed him to go after extracting Bass's promise he would not take up arms against the invaders. Von Schoultz

Windmill Point and Prescott, c. 1840

A watercolour by William Bainbridge, made a few years after the battle, shows the windmill in relation to Prescott. Note the flag which marks the location of Fort Wellington and the smoke from a steamer on the river. (National Archives of Canada, C-11863)

wanted to keep Bass's horses to pull his artillery but the Canadian pleaded that his livelihood would be injured and he was allowed to take them to his house a few hundred yards away.[39]

Bass's neighbour, Henry Mosher, had also gone to the Johnstown mill early that morning and was on his way home about noon when he was stopped by a Canadian militia picket on the river road to Newport. Their commander, Captain Simon Fraser (a former fur trader and explorer who would give his name both to a river and a university in British Columbia), told Mosher that his home was now occupied by pirates and cautioned him against proceeding farther. Mosher, anxious about his family, insisted on being let through and Fraser let him go. At the edge of the hamlet, the Canadian was surrounded by armed men and Mosher recognized a Canadian, Ezra Brockway, who at one time had owned a store in Prescott. Mosher was brought before von Schoultz, who questioned him and then sent him with a guard to look for his wife and children. He found them unharmed and the Mosher family was then placed, with many of their neighbours, in the large house of a Mr. Smith, northwest of the mill. This high, stone three-storey building seems to have functioned as both as a store and tavern and the Hunter guards promptly helped themselves to the liquor behind the bar, although they behaved properly to their prisoners.[40]

Neither the farm wives, Adonisah Bass, Henry Mosher nor any of the Canadians in Newport showed any enthusiasm to join the glorious struggle to liberate Canada from British oppression. This puzzled the rank and file Hunters, who had been assured by their leaders that thousands of Canadians would flock to the Hunter flag as soon as it was planted on their soil, and they discussed it with their officers. Von Schoultz advised them not to judge Canadians by the residents of Newport as it was obvious they were just simple farm folk, peasants really, who could not be expected to comprehend the great events about to unfold in their obscure little hamlet.[41]

Throughout what must have been very long day, Plomer Young waited for help to arrive. To Young and Lieutenant Fowell on the *Experiment*, Prescott, not Windmill Point, was their focus of concern and they concentrated on defending the village from further attack. The *Experiment* anchored off the wharves and the British commander deployed the greater part of his militia on Water Street, the main thoroughfare and, as a mixture of rain and sleet began to fall late in the afternoon, it is likely some occasionally nipped into one of the dozen or so taverns which lined it, or Buckley's store, to fortify themselves against both the enemy and the cold. The men of Jessup's company on watch near the windmill did not have this advantage. Jessup, however, had not forgotten them and at 4 P.M. he arrived with provisions and the bad news that they would have to spend the night in their uncomfortable position.[42]

At about the same time, reinforcements began to reach Prescott in response to appeals sent early that morning. Among the first to arrive, probably late in the afternoon, were four infantry companies and a cavalry troop of the 1st Grenville Regiment of sedentary militia under the command of Lieutenant Colonel Hugh Munro and a company of the 1st Dundas Regiment of sedentary militia under Colonel John Crysler. These were followed by Colonel Richard Duncan Fraser with a company of the 2nd Grenville Regiment and two hastily assembled volunteer augmentation companies. Just after dark, Lieutenant Colonel Ogle Gowan marched in from Brockville with a company of his 9th Provisional Battalion and the Brockville Independent Company. He had been alerted at 10 A.M. when Reverend Robert Blakey of Prescott, who lived near Honeywell Creek, rode into Brockville to tell him that persons unknown had damaged the bridge. Gowan got on the road about 1 P.M., but it had taken him nearly five hours to cover the twelve miles from Brockville because, not knowing what the situation was at Prescott, he had decided to move tactically by extending flank and advance parties. This was a wise precaution but it made progress slow along the muddy highway that paralleled the river, and there was a further delay at Honeywell Creek, where his men had to replace the planks on the bridge. More militia were reported to be on the way: two companies of the 2nd Dundas Regiment under Colonel George Merkeley, another company of Munro's 1st Grenville and elements of nine companies of the 4th Glengarry Regiment. When all these units arrived, Young would command about 1,000 militia officers and men.[43]

If the Hunters had known anything about this point of Upper Canada, they would not have been surprised at the willing response of the local militia. The area had largely been settled by Loyalists and there were still men and women alive who had suffered during the American Revolution because of their allegiance to the Crown. Also moving toward the Hunters were men who had turned out before in 1812 to 1814 to defend their homes and families against American invasion. Almost twenty-five years to the day before, a major battle had taken place near Colonel John Crysler's property on the banks of the St. Lawrence, and Crysler, himself a 68-year-old veteran of the Revolutionary War, had fought that day as had his fellow militia colonels Fraser, Merkeley and Munro. As soon as he received news of the landing, Crysler had assembled as many men as he could gather, including two of his sons, and marched for Prescott.[44]

Merkeley's two companies of Dundas militia had been on duty at Mariatown near Morrisburg, thirty-five miles down river from Prescott, and were able to move off quickly. In their ranks were Allan and Lewis MacIntosh, whose family farm at Dundela, back of Iroquois Point, was the envy of their neighbours because a wild apple tree grew on it which produced a fruit none had ever seen before, with a dark red skin and a crisp and delicious white centre. Father John MacIntosh had care-

True Blue and Orange: Lieutenant Colonel Ogle Gowan (1803-1876)
The leader of the Orange Lodge in Upper Canada, Gowan was staunchly loyal to the Crown and had waged many political battles against the Reform movement. As a lieutenant colonel in the militia, Gowan was in the process of recruiting a longservice battalion when Prescott was attacked on 12 November. Hastily assembling two companies, he marched from Brockville that day and played a leading role in the battle on Tuesday, 13 November 1838. It was Gowan's first time in combat, and although his troops fought well, he suffered an embarrassing wound accidentally inflicted by one of his own men. (Toronto Reference Library)

fully nurtured the original tree and the family had ambitious plans to make some profit by selling cuttings from this wonderful discovery.[45]

Private Allan MacIntosh, a devout Methodist who was more interested in religion than money, remembered that his company was at drill when they got the order to march. He and Private Jerimiah Bouck (or Bouch), a friend who shared his deep faith, wished to make their peace with the Lord before setting out so they went into a nearby farm garden and, with "soft snow falling on their heads," knelt and prayed for a few moments. All too soon, their devotions were interrupted by rude shouts from their sergeant to fall in.[46]

The invaders at Windmill Point were blissfully unaware of the forces massing against them. Throughout the afternoon and early evening of Monday, boats crossed the river and as many as 300 Hunters may have stepped onto Canadian soil. But the boats also took men away. Despite threats from some of the officers, notably Dorephus Abbey, that deserters would be shot, there was a slow but steady haemorrhage of men so that by nightfall probably not more than 250 remained.[47]

By now it was clear that Birge was not coming over to assume command, and after some discussion the Hunters elected Nils von Schoultz as their leader. He was clearly the best qualified for the task, as had been evident during the day when he directed the efforts to strengthen their position. John Kimball, the factory owner from Dexter, was elected second-in-command but, as Heustis later wrote, Kimball disappeared in the darkness to return to Jefferson County, where he "arrived in safety, with no damage except tired legs."[48] The other officers – Dorephus Abbey, Charles Brown, Christopher Buckley, Daniel George, Heustis, James Philips and Martin Woodruff – were confirmed in their appointments.[49]

The Swede, with his military bearing and smooth manners,

Brockville the beautiful, c. 1840.
The citizens of scenic Brockville, twelve miles up the St. Lawrence, tended to look down their noses at practical, hardworking Prescott, an attitude that was cheerfully reciprocated (and still is). Nonetheless, when Prescott was attacked on Monday, 12 November 1838, the men of Brockville were quick to come to its aid. (Watercolour by F.H. Holloway, 1841, J. Ross Robertson Collection, Toronto Reference Library)

was much admired by his young followers. William Gates remembered that his commander "was of commanding appearance – was six feet in height – well proportioned – of good features, and a dark, piercing eye."[50] Stephen Wright thought no man "was ever more beloved by his companions in arms, or possessed more the power of fascinating his enemies."[51] Von Schoultz later stated that the men begged him to take command in order to lead them back to the United States and he only accepted in order to do so. However, he did not order an evacuation, which might have been possible as there was still communication with the opposite shore. Von Schoultz may have believed the assurances of Bill Johnston and the ever-mysterious Estes, who came over early in the evening with provisions, that 500 men would cross in the morning. In Abbey's words, von Schoultz and the other leaders decided to "fight as long as they could, or until they got off."[52]

About 9 P.M., communication with Ogdensburg suddenly ceased and the Hunters settled down for the night but, as Heustis later wrote, it was a night during "which no eye slept" as he and his comrades were in a situation of extreme peril:

> In regard to the number expected to join us, we had been woefully disappointed, and of those who started with us, a large majority had ignobly deserted. Our leaders had proved traitors and cowards. We had lost much of our ammunition. Our position was exposed to attack, both by land and water, by a force vastly larger than we could muster.[53]

Despite their problems, Heustis proudly recorded, there was "no wavering, no flinching" because a "braver company never shouldered muskets."

Crossing the river, Monday, 12 November 1838
Throughout Monday there was a continuous traffic of small boats from the United States transporting men to the windmill or taking them away. It ceased in the evening after Colonel William J. Worth of the U.S. Army arrived in Ogdensburg with the steamer *Telegraph* and two companies of regular infantry. These modern re-enactors are manning a classic river bateau, a useful craft for navigating the shallow water around Windmill Point. (Photograph by René Schoemaker)

Invading Upper Canada: Initial landing, 12 November 1838
Re-enactors dressed as Hunters for a recent film recreate the landing near the mill during the morning of 12 November 1838 on the actual ground in Edwardsburgh Township. Note the rocky shore and bushes. (Photograph by René Schoemaker)

Citadel of the Republic of Upper Canada: The McQueen brothers' mill in Edwardsburgh Township, Upper Canada

This watercolour, painted shortly after the battle by Thomas Ainslie, portrays the windmill as it would have appeared during the action with its wings tattered but still in place. Note the ruins of Newport and the wooden ladder to the exterior gallery, the only way to reach the upper levels of the structure. The tall, chimney-like structure to the right of the mill is a bake oven. In the background is Mile Point in the United States, where American spectators watched the battle of 13 November and cheered on the Hunters whenever it appeared that they had an advantage. (Watercolour by Thomas Ainslie, National Archives of Canada, C-130815)

CHAPTER SEVEN

"The rifle fire of the enemy was particularly true and steady"

Tuesday, 13 November 1838, midnight to 5 P.M.

On Tuesday morning we marched out,
In command of Colonel Fraser,
With swords and bay'nets of polished steel,
As keen as any razor.
Unto the Windmill plains we went,
We gave them three loud cheers,
To let them know, that day, below.
We're the Prescott Volunteers.

> *Oh, we're the boys that feared no noise*
> *When the cannons loud did roar;*
> *We cut the rebels left and right*
> *When they landed on our shore.*

Brave Macdonell nobly led
His men into the field;
They did not flinch, no not an inch,
'Til the rebels had to yield.
He swung his sword right round his head,
Saying, "Glengarrys, follow me,
We'll gain the day without delay,
And that you'll plainly see."

> *Oh, we're the boys that feared no noise, etc.*[1]

Communication with the American shore had ceased for two reasons. A heavy wind during the night made it difficult for boats to cross the river and, more importantly, at about 9 P.M. Colonel William J. Worth and Federal Marshal Nathaniel Garrow arrived in Ogdensburg on board the *Telegraph* and, briefed by Smith Stillwell and Preston King, moved quickly to restore order. Arrest warrants were issued for Birge, Johnston and Pierce, and Worth seized the *United States,* the *Paul Pry* and the two schooners – of which the *Charlotte of Oswego* was found to be "laden with rifles, muskets, pistols, cutlasses" and several artillery pieces, "two of them mounted, loaded & primed."[2] Worth ordered Sailing Master William C. Vaughan, USN, who had taken command of the *Telegraph* from her civilian master, to stop any traffic from the American shore to the windmill and the steamer spent the rest of the night cruising on the river – one soldier on board "observed several musket shots on the Canada shore, doubtless made by those squanderers of powder, militia sentinels."[3]

If Lieutenant Colonel Plomer Young's militiamen were somewhat nervous, it was understandable. In any case, they cheered up shortly after 2 A.M., Tuesday, 13 November 1838, when Captain Williams Sandom arrived with the *Cobourg* and

The view from America: Windmill Point from the south shore
Taken from Mile Point near Ogdensburg, this photograph shows
Windmill Point in Edwardsburgh Township as it appeared from the
American side of the river. Mile Point is where American spectators
watched the battle of 13 November. (Photograph by Dianne Graves)

Queen Victoria, carrying detachments of the 83rd Foot and
Royal Marines. The naval officer went ashore to find Young,
who reported that although his militia force "was not well
organized, and armed," he suspected that the invaders were in
even worse condition.[4] If Sandom would assist, Young proposed to attack Windmill Point.[5]

Sandom agreed and the two regular officers devised a plan.
While Sandom bombarded the mill from the *Cobourg*, *Experiment* and *Victoria* to distract the enemy and hopefully blow a
breach in the structure through which the troops could enter,
Young would attack Windmill Point from two directions (see
Map 7). Colonel Richard D. Fraser would command the left or
eastern force to be made up of the Royal Marine detachment,
Macdonell's company of Glengarry Highlanders, and elements
drawn from 1st Dundas and 1st and 2nd Grenville Militia regiments. This force of about 300 men would circle around the
high ground north of Newport and move on the hamlet from
the east. At the same time, Lieutenant Colonel Ogle Gowan
would lead the right or western force comprising the detachment of the 83rd Foot, a company of his own 9th Provisional
Battalion, the Brockville Independent Company and elements
of the Brockville Light Dragoons and Jessup's Volunteers,
about 250 men, directly along the river road from Fort Wellington to the objective. Young would be in overall command but
would accompany Gowan's force, probably because Gowan had
no combat experience. The combined weight of the two forces
converging on the windmill under the cover of Sandom's bombardment would, it was hoped, bring an end to the invasion.[6]

Dawn was only a few short hours away and there was a flurry
of activity. For a second night running, nobody got any sleep in
Prescott, if for no other reason than the village dogs thought the
sounds and smells of strangers marching in the streets worthy of
their loudest howls. Lieutenant William Stratford Johnson's

detachment of the 83rd Foot and Lieutenant Charles Parker's detachment of Royal Marines disembarked from the *Cobourg* and *Queen Victoria* and clumped in their boots along the wooden wharves "in a steady, fearless and determined manner."[7] The regulars were in heavy marching order, their load-carrying equipment strapped over their grey greatcoats and their leather bell-topped shakos covered with protective oilskins. The marines would have recovered from their Saturday night liberty in Kingston by now but as the column splashed along muddy Water Street to Fort Wellington, some of the hard cases may have cast a wistful eye at the welcoming portals of the Black Bull, Duffy's, the Dog and Duck and similar establishments. Once at the fort, the regulars removed their greatcoats, checked flint and priming, loosened bayonets in scabbards and probably exchanged caustic comments as to how many of the pasty-faced militiamen forming up nearby with the help of lanterns would still be in the ranks after the first hot round was fired.[8]

The redcoats' cynical assessment of the Canadian militia, well justified by previous experience, would this day prove to be wrong. Most of the militia assembling at the ramshackle old fort were farmers who had heard that every American invader was to get 160 acres of good land as part of his spoils, and each took it as a personal threat. A man might not fight that bravely for Queen and Country, or such other patriotic motives, but tell a hardscrabble farmer from Leeds, Grenville or Dundas County that the Yankees had crossed the river to steal his property and livelihood and he would fight like the devil. John Smith, 24 years old and newly wed, who farmed back of Prescott, did not hesitate to grab his musket and cartridge box and fall in with Captain Dunham Jones's Company of the 1st Grenville and such was his enthusiasm that Jones promptly promoted him sergeant. Smith remembered Prescott that night was all "excitement and confusion" and there was even talk of

removing the womenfolk and children "to the rear while, while the men remained to guard their hearthstones."[9] The militiamen were enthusiastic, and even men not required to serve volunteered to fight. Gowan actually enlisted one man, Christopher Leeson, into his provisional battalion a few hours before the attack commenced, and Leeson, aged 55 with a wife and four children, had no business shouldering a musket. Another volunteer was Harris Russell of Brockville, who rode through the night to Prescott determined to get at the enemy.[10]

It must be said that not all Canadians were anxious to fight. Newly-promoted Sergeant Smith wryly recollected that some of his neighbours, on learning of the landing at Windmill Point, remembered "that their woodpiles needed replenishing, and at once betook themselves to the rear of their farms, and were not seen again until the danger was past."[11] At Kemptville, where the local militia was put on alert, there were a number of men who sympathized with Mackenzie and the Hunter cause. When they were ordered out, they were "either sick, had a sore foot or made some plausible excuse for not joining" their regiment, but were encouraged at the point of the bayonet to do their little bit for Queen and country.[12] For years afterward, these laggards were marked men in Kemptville and one of them, a tailor named Martin, was tormented on patriotic occasions such as the Sovereign's birthday by the village boys, who would throw lighted firecrackers at his feet and pretend to limp, all the while shouting, "Oh! My leg! Oh! My leg!"[13]

Shortly before dawn, all was ready and Fraser, whose command had the longest distance to march, moved out. Circling around the high ground about a mile north of Newport, he reached the river bank east of the mill and formed under the cover of a grove of woods. As he was coming into position, Fraser met Lieutenant Colonel George Merkeley with the two companies of the 2nd Dundas Regiment, totalling about 100 officers and men, that had set out the previous afternoon from Mariatown. They had marched through the night to Iroquois, where they had been met by a column of farm wagons that transported them in fine style as far as Johnstown, two miles east of the mill. The Dundas boys had not eaten for twelve hours, and in that respect the news was not good – as a hungry Private Allan MacIntosh remembered: "No breakfast, at Sunrise, ordered to face the foe."[14] When he heard the sound of artillery fire coming from the river, Fraser ordered his men to advance through the woods.[15]

In contrast to the wretched weather of the previous night, Tuesday, 13 November 1838, dawned clear and bright. Von Schoultz tried to improve morale by suggesting that this was a "good omen of the glorious sun-burst of Canadian liberty," but there was no sign of Bill Johnston and his promised reinforcements.[16] As visibility improved, the Hunters could see the reason – the *Telegraph* steaming back and forth on the mist-shrouded river, armed soldiers visible on her upper decks. The sight infuriated them as they had hoped, despite considerable evidence to the contrary, that the American government would support, or at least ignore, their activities, as it had in Texas in 1836. Frankly, as William Gates commented, it just wasn't right:

Had Canada been the province of some imbecile power, our government would never have made that hot haste to construe the

laws in aid of royalty's schemes. But England was powerful, and our rulers wished to curry her favor! When Texas revolted from a sister republic, our men were permitted to … depart armed for the scene of the conflict, or if noticed, merely winked at. Mexico was weak – torn by intestine factions. She refused the black curse of slavery a home on her soil. Texas was determined to sustain negro servitude, and revolted, …… But here the Canadians were groaning under

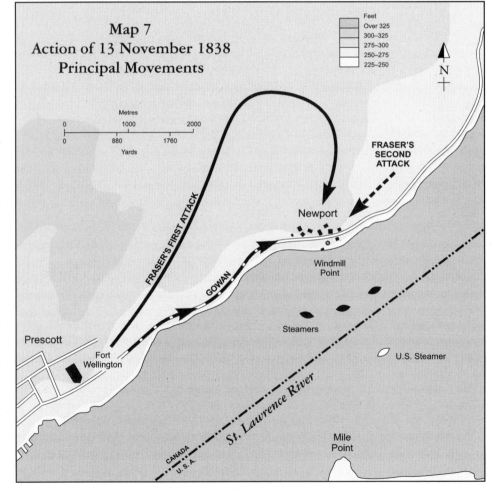

Map 7
Action of 13 November 1838
Principal Movements

grievances that had been refused redress. ...... Some of our citizens become fired with enthusiasm and strive to give a helping hand. But [the American] government interposes and commands them to stay at home and suppress their sympathies as unlawful, and then takes active and stringent measures to force obedience. Is there justice in the two cases?[17]

"It was now evident" that the Hunters at Windmill Point would "have to rely upon our resources which were feeble enough."[18] Gates later estimated that there were 250 men at the windmill on the morning of 13 October; other Hunters provide lower figures ranging from 170 to 225. It is difficult if not impossible, given the paucity of reliable evidence, to be more accurate and perhaps the best estimate is that there were 250 Hunters in Canada that morning, of whom between 170 and 200 were willing to fight. In addition, although von Schoultz had command of the invasion force, he did not have control – men had already drifted away from the ranks and they would continue to do so through the days that followed.[19]

At this point, however, Nils von Schoultz had a golden opportunity to bring the business to an end before blood was spilled. The sight of the *Telegraph* in the river and Sandom's three steamers at Prescott made it clear that he could expect neither rein-

forcement nor evacuation. Worse still, as the visibility improved with the sun, Hunter lookouts posted in the upper windows of the mill reported troops massing at Fort Wellington – evidence that the enemy were planning to attack. His tactical position was a good one but the Swede was intelligent enough to know that he would have to succumb to the superior forces that would inevitably be brought against him. If he surrendered now, the chances were good that his men would be treated leniently as no British or Canadian lives had been lost and there had been no major property damage. Such a decision, however, required moral courage, and unfortunately although Nils von Schoultz possessed considerable physical courage, he was somewhat lacking in the moral variety. He decided to fight.[20]

The Hunter commander did have the decency to let most of the residents of Newport get to safety before the shooting started. The Taylor family made for Prescott, Belden Taylor carrying his baby son in his arms while his wife took their teenage daughter by the hand. Adonisah Bass's family also left although Bass, his neighbour Henry Mosher and other men were retained under guard at Smith's house, possibly because they were able-bodied males.

This act of kindness had just been completed at about 7.00 A.M. when the lookouts on the upper levels of the mill shouted that armed British steamers were coming down the river.

Armed steamer *Cobourg*, 1838
Launched in 1833 and displacing 440 tons, the *Cobourg* was one of the hastily armed civilian steamers serving in Captain Williams Sandom's Royal Navy squadron based at Kingston. Armed with four 18-pdr. carronades, she played a major role during the week of operations at Prescott in November 1838. (Author's collection)

Sandom's objective, he later reported, was to create a diversion and "batter" the mill.[21] Unfortunately, he lacked the proper means to bring down the invaders' stronghold as his three vessels, the *Cobourg*, *Experiment* and *Queen Victoria*, were armed with carronades, really giant shotguns useful at close range but unsuitable for long-range fire or for destroying structures. The *Cobourg* mounted four 18-pdr. weapons of this type, the *Victoria* had two, while the little *Experiment* had just one. What was needed were heavy calibre guns, high velocity ordnance, but only the *Victoria* was armed with such a weapon and that was but a medium 12-pdr., too small to be effective against the soundly built mill. As for the little 3-pdr. brass guns mounted on the *Experiment*, they were probably not even fired that morning.[22]

The irony was that there were plenty of heavy 18-pdr. and 24-pdr. guns available in the Stone Frigate, the naval stores building in Kingston, but because of diplomatic sensitivity, Sandom had decided not to use them. The 1817 Rush-Bagot Treaty between Britain and the United States, which had demilitarized the Great Lakes, permitted each nation only one warship armed with a single 18-pdr. gun on those waters, and Sandom, obeying the spirit at least of this restriction, had decided to arm his somewhat motley squadron of steamers and gunboats with carronades. Since he probably anticipated that any possible engagements would be at close range, this was a logical decision, but now he found himself in a tactical situation that required long-range weapons.[23]

Sandom's gun crews did their best but their work was basically distraction, not destruction. They were also hindered because the naval carriages of their carronades were not designed for high-angle fire and, despite using maximum elevation, had difficulty clearing the river bank and hitting the buildings behind. Any 18-pdr. round shot that actually struck the McQueen mill bounced harmlessly off in a puff of stone chips and dust, to the great delight of the Hunters, who returned the fire with their two smaller guns (there being little ammunition for the 6-pdr.). Von Schoultz supervised the work of the gun detachments, which were drawn mainly from the Europeans in their ranks, most of whom had previous military experience. Banker Denio, watching from the deck of the *United States* anchored at Ogdensburg, "could see with perfect unhindrance the flashing of their guns and the smoke" and thought the Hunter gunners fought "with great spirit."[24] To a Canadian witness, however, they seemed "afraid to expose themselves in loading and firing" and he noted that not one round came within sixty yards of the British vessels.[25] Nonetheless, Sandom stayed at extreme range as he was reluctant to risk the vulnerable boilers and engine machinery of his civilian craft to a lucky shot and Worth, observing from the *Telegraph*, noted that the Hunter artillery did cause the British steamers to "frequently change position."[26]

This exchange of fire, more or less harmless to both sides, went on for several hours and it was about 9 A.M. when the Hunter sentries posted at the north side of the hamlet reported that the British were advancing against them. Running in that direction, the Swede saw Fraser's men debouching from the woods east of the mill while at the same time Gowan's men were approaching from the west along the river road. Hunter William Gates, "who had never seen so large a company of soldiers drawn up for fighting," was awed by the sight of fields and woods "alive with redcoats."[27] There were actually only about one hundred men sporting the traditional British uniform colour (Johnson's detachment of the 83rd Foot, Parker's marines and Macdonell's Lancaster Glengarry Highlanders) among the troops moving against the Hunters as most of the militia were in their civilian clothes. Still the invaders were impressed –

Smoke, noise and confusion: The attack, 13 November 1838
A Hunter officer, Daniel Heustis, had this sketch drawn for his memoir published in 1847. Note the flag on the windmill, the steamers in the river and the two opposing lines to the northwest of Newport, indicated by clouds of gunsmoke. After hard fighting, the British and Canadian attack was repulsed with heavy casualties. (From Daniel Heustis, *Narrative of the Adventures and Suffering...*, 1847)

Hunter Daniel Heustis calculated that his enemy numbered 1700 men, nearly three times their actual strength.[28]

For their part, the British regulars and Canadian militia could see the Hunters dressed in their "regular Yankee garb" of "long-tailed surtouts and cloaks, with a rifle in their hands, … running from one building to another."[29] This was a reference to an outer garment that seems to have been unpopular with Canadians but common among Americans, particularly those of the "Slouch-hatted, monkey-tail-coated backwoodsmen" variety, as one British officer termed them.[30] Most of the Hunter officers were wearing epaulettes as a mark of their rank and had armed themselves with swords rather than long-arms. The British and Canadians were somewhat puzzled by the Onondaga Hunter flag flying from the mill; it being mostly white, they thought it signified the invaders wished to surrender – they changed their minds when the shooting started.[31]

Von Schoultz made ready to meet Fraser by ordering his men to cross over the stone walls and rail fences that bordered the northern edge of the hamlet and move into the rocky open fields beyond. Here he formed them into a thin line, each man two to three yards from his neighbour, so that they equalled the wider front of their more numerous opponents who were about 400 yards distant. The Swede told them to hold their fire until the last minute and make every shot count. There is reason to question this deployment as it gave up the invaders' main advantage – the fact that many were armed with rifles that had more range and accuracy than the smooth-bore India Pattern .75 calibre muskets carried by the British and Canadians. By leaving the cover of the buildings and walls of the hamlet, where his men could offset their weakness in numbers with accurate fire, von Schoultz was actually placing them in peril. But, it will be remembered, the Swede's military background was in the artillery, not the infantry, and there is no concrete evidence that he had ever seen action before this day.[32]

Tragically, the first person to be killed that Tuesday was Mrs. Belden Taylor of Newport. Leaving the hamlet, holding her teenage daughter's hand, she ran down the river road toward Prescott but also, unfortunately, straight into the advance element of Gowan's force. Probably composed of men from the 9th Provisional Battalion, nervous in their first action, they fired at the two women, killing the mother instantly and severely wounding the daughter in the jaw. This incident was witnessed by the Hunters, who were appalled by this "unprovoked and barbarous act of cruelty" that "would have disgraced a band of savages," although none reflected that if they had not invaded Upper Canada, Mrs. Taylor would still be alive.[33]

The main land action commenced shortly after 9 A.M. and it started on the British and Canadian left flank. After clearing the woods, Fraser formed in a line of two ranks and ordered an advance. At between 200 and 300 yards range, the Hunter riflemen opened fire, concentrating on Macdonell's Glengarry Highlanders and Lieutenant Charles Parker's Royal Marines on Fraser's right flank, as these were the only opponents in red uniforms. These two units began to take casualties, including Parker, who was hit in the right arm but stayed with his marines. When his men were within extreme musket range, about 150 yards, Fraser ordered them to open fire and, from the left, his individual companies let loose a series of volleys.[34]

According to onlookers, "a line of fire blazed along the summit of the hill" to the rear of the mill "and the crack of the rifle and the musket made a continuous roar."[35] The fire of Fraser's men, which caused "a great deal of smoke, without a corresponding execution," remembered William Gates, was returned more accurately by the Hunter riflemen.[36] Lieutenant John Dulmage of the 1st Grenville Regiment was killed, as was Private Jerimiah Bouck of the 2nd Dundas, who died instantly when he was hit in the forehead by a rifle ball. Bouck's partner in prayer, Private Allan MacIntosh, was also struck in the head but not killed – pulling off his cap, MacIntosh saw that there "was a bullet hole in front … with a bullet sticking in the button."[37] He had been hit by a spent musket ball that did no harm. Sergeant John Smith of 1st Grenville also had a close call – he was biting off a cartridge when his musket was knocked out of his hands by an enemy round.[38]

As men went down, Hunter Gates remembered that, "finding our work too hot for comfort," his opponents began to falter and draw back.[39] Deciding that he had to get to grips with his enemy to offset their advantage in range, Fraser ordered his men to fix bayonets and charge. In response, there was a series of metallic click-clacks down the British and Canadian line as the men fastened their 17-inch bayonets onto their musket muzzles and then, moving slowly in order to maintain their dressing, advanced toward their enemy.[40]

This was too much for von Schoultz's men, who preferred war at long range, and they broke for the cover of a stone wall some distance to the rear, where they attempted to make a stand. To a watching Ogle Gowan, it was "Three British cheers, and a few paces of 'double quick,' with the *cold steel* in front" which soon resulted in "long-legged Yankees and gave our gallant boys possession of the ground."[41] When Fraser's regulars and militia saw their enemy running, they began to pick up the pace and, ignoring the shouts of their officers to maintain their ranks, raced after them, leaping over the wall and getting in among the invaders with the bayonet. The well-trained marines were most effective at this kind of work – lunge, recover, stance, parry; lunge, recover, stance, parry – until the opposing (and probably very desperate) Hunter, who often did not have a bayonet but tried to fend off the relentless attack with

The battle of the windmill, 13 November 1838

A print c. 1880 depicts the British and Canadian attack on the windmill on Tuesday, 13 November 1838. Note the smoke, burning buildings and the three Royal Navy vessels in the river. The viewer's position is Mile Point on the American side of the river where, during the action, an estimated 1000-1500 Americans cheered on the Hunters. This print is based on a painting by Ogdensburg artist Salathiel Ellis, who witnessed the battle. Ellis completed a six foot by four foot painting in February 1839 and exhibited it at the Ogdensburg Town Hall, charging 25 cents to view it. (Toronto Reference Library) a rifle or musket or Bowie knife, made a mistake and left an opening. A quick thrust to the abdomen (avoiding the rib cage where the point might get trapped) followed and then it was on to the next.[42]

Lance Corporal Thomas Hunn of the Royal Marines, 20 years old, jumped the wall on the extreme left of the Hunter position and

found himself in contact with six or seven of them, who were separated from their main body by another wall running perpendicular to that which covered their front. These men were either loading or in the act of firing at the advancing Marines when Hunn leaped the wall, and were so intent on their occupation that they did not notice Hunn until he was on them; so that he was able to close with them, and was seen by his commanding officer to bayonet three one after the other before they had time to load their pieces and fire. A fourth man, whose piece was loaded, turned and fired, and his ball struck the swell of Hunn's musket, where it was grasped by the left hand, which it passed through, destroying the second finger; while at the same time the musket was driven so violently against his stomach, as for a moment to suspend the breath. Recovering himself, however, Hunn fired effectively at the enemy, now in full retreat; but his disabled hand prevented his again loading, and he was most unwillingly obliged to give up any further share in the glory of the day, after having thus accounted for four of the enemy.[43]

Private Edward Landers of Macdonell's company, a blacksmith with great strength, pulled off his bayonet and "with the butt end of his Musket throwing himself upon the enemy, was observed to knock down great numbers of them in a manner which is almost incredible."[44]

Their attempt to stand proving futile, the Hunters ran for the next stone wall, a hundred yards distant, with blacksmith Landers hard on their heels, followed by the rest of the pack. Trying to emulate Hunn's feat, Landers was alone when he leaped the second wall and found himself surrounded by Hunters, trying to ward off "Bayonets, bowie knives & butts of Rifles" only to receive a knife thrust in the throat. Landers fell and was battered by repeated blows to the head so vicious that, by the time his horrified comrades had come up, he was a bloody mess on the ground.[45] The Canadians, if not as practised, proved just as ferocious as the regulars – one officer who fought in the action of 13 November saw a militiamen bayonet an opponent with the triumphant shout: "You [damned] scoundrel, you wanted to rob me of my farm, did you?"[46]

The second Hunter try at a stand was broken up and the invaders ran again, this time for the buildings around the mill, some passing on the way through a wooden barn in which they had torn holes in the walls for just such an eventuality. Reaching the safety of the solid stone buildings near the mill, they barricaded the doors and riflemen took post in the windows to bring fire against Fraser's oncoming men, who, in a red killing rage, ignored the commands of their officers to stop and reform.[47]

Meanwhile, Gowan on the right had attacked at about the same time. His orders were to advance along the river road and the beach and "drive the enemy from the stone houses" around the mill.[48] A 38-year-old native of Wexford in Ireland, Gowan had emigrated to the Brockville area nine years before and, as leader of the Orange Lodge of Upper Canada, had played a prominent role in the political turmoil that had marked the 1836 election in Leeds County. Gowan's men moved in column until contact was made at the western edge of Newport. Here von Schoultz had posted his firing line behind a stone wall that encircled a grove of butternut trees (see Map 6) and, in Gowan's words, the invaders opened "a most galling fire" on his men, inflicting heavy casualties, including middle-aged Private Christopher Leeson, who had so enthusiastically enlisted that morning.[49] Leeson took a rifle ball in the shoulder blade which passed through his body and lodged in his right arm. The Hunters also fired at least one of their artillery pieces at Gowan's column as Sergeant John Munro of the 83rd was crossing a plank over a small rivulet when a round-shot struck it, throwing him to the ground. Fortunately, he was unharmed.[50]

A place to make a stand (1): The butternut grove

This picture, taken by Prescott photographer R.A. Nunn about 1900, shows the river road as it approaches the windmill from the west, and the stone wall that surrounded the butternut grove where the Hunters attempted to make a stand against Gowan's column. Gowan's troops took the grove with the bayonet and then cleared the invaders from a barn and two houses immediately to the east of the grove, but were prevented from advancing further by sustained and accurate rifle fire from Hunters positioned in the buildings near the mill. Note the condition of the road; it would not have been any better sixty years before. (Courtesy of the Grenville County Historical Society)

Gowan, coming to the same tactical decision as Fraser, ordered his men to deploy into line and charge with the bayonets. Behind the stone wall at the butternut grove, Hunter Nelson Truax watched the British and Canadians, with the redcoats of the 83rd in the van, moving steadily towards him and decided it was time to depart. Many of his comrades got the same idea at the same time – "you should have seen us Yankees run," was Truax's remark on the matter – and they scrambled for the shelter of a rail fence about forty-five yards behind their position.[51]

Some of the invaders, however, tried to hold their position – in Gowan's words, "they stood the charge to the last" – and there was some confused fighting around the butternut grove.[52] Bran-

"A Life on the Ocean Wave:" Royal Marines and Royal Marine Artillery, 1838

From left to right: drummer, private and sergeant of the Royal Marines, officer and gunner of the Royal Marine Artillery. In 1838, the uniforms of Royal Marines, who were classified as light infantry, were similar to those of the army, while those of the Royal Marine Artillery were blue. Note the surtout and soft cap worn by the RMA officer; this was the normal dress for officers in the field in 1838. After the First World War, the Royal Marine Artillery was amalgamated with the Royal Marine Light Infantry to form the modern Royal Marines, who wear dress uniforms of dark blue. (Author's collection)

Usually first ashore: Royal Marine junior officers, 1838

The Royal Marines were no strangers to the inland waters, having served with distinction on the Great Lakes in 1813-1814. The marines had a reputation as well-disciplined, well-trained and resolute troops. Lieutenant Charles Parker's detachment, which fought during the battle of 13 November 1838, suffered 50 per cent casualties and Parker himself was wounded but refused to leave the field. (Author's collection) dishing his sword, Gowan leaped the wall around the grove to find himself surrounded by Hunters. He retrograded fast, so fast that he impaled himself on the bayonet of one of his men close behind him. The wound was not serious but it was in an embarrassing location that Gowan modestly described as his "left hip" – in fact he had been stabbed in the buttock.[53]

It was not long before the Hunters in the grove ran for the shelter of the buildings near the mill, their opponents in hot pursuit, firing as they came. Truax had just crossed the rail fence when he was hit in the right leg and fell to the ground. A Canadian was about to bayonet him when, fortunately for the 20-year-old, "up came a British regular, who pushed the militia man away and claimed me as his prisoner."[54] Truax was hustled, limping, back to Fort Wellington with a number of other prisoners while Gowan's men paused to reform for the final push.

At the western edge of the hamlet, Lieutenant William Stratford Johnson of the 83rd could see one of the Hunter artillery pieces on the road about a hundred yards west of the mill. This may have been the same gun that earlier fired on his men, although the Hunters later claimed that it was out of ammunition and had deliberately been abandoned in its exposed position to serve as a decoy to lure their opponents. Whatever the truth of the matter, Johnson decided to make a try for it, in keeping with his family motto "I hope." Born in County Wicklow, Ireland, Johnson had joined the army as an ensign in the 98th Foot in 1815 but had spent five years on half pay after his unit was disbanded in 1818. He had fortunately gained an ensigncy in the 83rd in 1823 and had seen service in Ceylon before coming to North America in 1828. Johnson was not a wealthy man – all his commissions and promotions had been without purchase – and as an aging 39-year-old lieutenant who had served thirteen years in that junior rank, he may have been anxious to distinguish himself.[55]

A place to make a stand (2): Good defensive position near the mill
This photograph, which appears to have been taken in the 1920s or 1930s from a ruined house northeast of the mill, shows the solid construction of the buildings of Newport. The Hunters blocked up the doors and ground floor windows of most of these buildings, converting them into miniature fortresses from which their riflemen were able to stop the advance of their British and Canadian opponents, who were armed only with smooth-bore muskets. Note the thickness of the wall – it required heavy artillery to get the invaders out of strongpoints like these. (Courtesy of the Grenville County Historical Society)

Redcoats in grey: British infantry

Modern re-enactors uniformed and armed as British regulars of 1838 pose at the windmill during the making of a recent film about the battle. The thick, grey coats were needed during the five days the invasion lasted as the weather was often abysmal, but they were put aside when time came for the regulars to go to work. Ironically, the Hunters were better armed than their opponents, having multi-round and percussion rifles against the regulars' smooth-bore muskets. (Photo by René Schoemaker)

He led his regulars up the road toward the gun, past the western houses of Newport (probably Buildings 8 and 9 on Map 6). As they moved toward their goal, about 80 yards from the mill, his men came under fire from Hunters posted in these buildings and 18-year-old Sylvanus Swete from Alexandria in Jefferson County took careful aim and fired at Johnson, hitting him with a round of "buck and ball" (a musket ball and three buckshot) on the left hip and knocking him to the ground. Sergeant John Munro assumed command, but before he could help his wounded officer, his men began to falter under a heavy crossfire from the houses and a large carriage house. Munro's shako was shot off his head but he remained cool and withdrew the remainder of his men to a nearby barn or shed. The Hunters, now behind good cover and not threatened by bayonets, pinned them down with heavy and accurate fire.[56]

By this time, Lieutenant Charles Parker of the Royal Marines, despite his wound, had joined Gowan's force with his men. Wide-eyed young Tom Bog never forgot the sight of the marine officer marching by, erect but with his useless right arm hanging at his side. Seeing the plight of his army comrades, Parker led a group of about ten marines to the rescue only to be forced back by the Hunters, who "renewed their fire with increased vigour."[57] Things were not looking good but the veteran Munro kept his head. Detailing three of his men to provide covering fire, he safely withdrew the remainder to the butternut grove in stages, where they reformed and, in turn, covered the retreat of their comrades.[58]

Throughout the land attack, Sandom's three steamers had continued their lively but useless bombardment of the mill to the great delight of the invaders, whose spirits were raised by the sight of roundshot bouncing off the structure.

Sandom's gun crews knocked about the wings of the mill and demolished its roof but, with the exception of one 18-pdr. shot that entered a window and caused some excitement for the men inside when it ricocheted a couple times off the interior walls, the building was unharmed. The gun crews fired as fast as they could – perhaps too fast because, on the *Experiment*, the 18-pdr. carronade overheated and discharged prematurely before its crew could get clear. Seaman Samuel Wade, who was ramming the round when it went off, lost his hand, and when the weapon recoiled, it sliced off three of Seaman John McDermott's fingers.[59]

The major result of the bombardment was to attract the attention of the people of Ogdensburg. Shortly after it commenced, a large crowd, estimated to be between one thousand and fifteen hundred, gathered at Mile Point, across the St. Lawrence from the mill, to watch the fun. According to editor Tyler of the local paper, almost all business in Ogdensburg was dropped that day in favour of "gossip and sight seeing."[60] Fascinated, the crowd watched the fighting on the far side of the river, waving scarves and little American flags, but their presence angered the Hunters, who felt abandoned by their countrymen – Wright remembered that, during lulls in the firing, "faint cheers reached us across the waves, and it embittered our hearts."[61] The British and Canadians were no happier with the spectators because "whenever they supposed any advantage had been obtained by the Pirates, or that our men were falling back in any quarter," they "wrent the air with their cheers, which were distinctly heard upon on our shores."[62] Worth and his men on board the *Telegraph* took a professional interest in the spectacle although one of Worth's officers wryly noted that, despite the Hunters' position being very "MILL-itary," it convinced him "of the *Quixotism*" of their cause.[63]

The noise of Sandom's guns carried some distance. At Maitland, ten miles up the river on the Canadian shore, the gunfire intrigued the curiosity of 11-year-old Richard Dumbrill. Determined to find out what was going on, young Dumbrill climbed to the top of the mill in that village, which was almost a twin of the structure on Windmill Point, and was excited to see the smoke from the battle.[64]

The artillery fire was also heard by the board of supervisors of St. Lawrence County, New York, who were in session that Tuesday at the village of Canton, eighteen miles away. Some of the supervisors were Hunter sympathizers and they tabled a motion to go to the assistance of the men on Windmill Point. Stating that "the patriots have made a noble stand" and were having "a severe engagement with the advocates and minions of British tyranny and oppression," and that these brave men would "meet with defeat, and sacrifice their lives in contending against a merciless and cruel foe," it was moved that the board would meet again "to rescue that Spartan band of patriotic friends, and preserve their lives from the hands of their enemies, the tyrants and advocates of the British crown." This rescue attempt, of course, would not take place until the board's next scheduled meeting on Monday, 27 November, thirteen days hence. The resolution, which promised all help short of actual aid (a classic politician's response to a crisis), did not pass.[65]

Things were not nearly as amusing for Colonels Fraser, Gowan and Young. They had pushed the invaders back from their outer positions without too much trouble but their enemies were now concentrated in the buildings immediately around the mill (Buildings 5 to 8 on Map 6) and all attempts to move forward were frustrated by heavy and deadly fire. As one of Young's officers later wrote, the enemy had been compelled to fly for refuge to the mill and two or three stone buildings close to it; but, on approaching these buildings, we found that they were well manned, and a destructive fire, by which several valuable lives were lost, being kept up from the upper windows of the mill, and a strong stone store which flanked it as completely as if built for that purpose; the troops were placed under partial cover, within one hundred yards, in the hope that a breach [in the mill] would be made by the armed steamers, from which an incessant fire of shot and shell had been maintained from the commencement of the operations.[66]

It was a situation where the Hunters' superior weapons gave them a decided advantage as many were armed with percussion rifles or muskets which, possessing a quicker and more dependable firing system than the smooth-bore muskets of their opponents, allowed them to lead a moving target with more certainty of hitting it. Particularly dangerous were the multi-round rifles, which provided many a sad surprise for a Briton or Canadian who thought that, if his opponent had fired and missed, he could move safely while the Hunter reloaded. The Hunters, a Canadian officer somewhat tartly noted, "had the advantage of a secure cover, a position particularly favourable, if not necessary, to the skill of American marksmen."[67]

The Hunters were also very good shots. Young later reported that "the rifle fire of the enemy was particularly true and steady" and the veracity of this statement is highlighted by the high proportion of head and shoulder wounds suffered by his men.[68] Private John Gillespie of 2nd Grenville was hit in the angle of the left eye by a ball that exited behind his ear, while Private John Morley of the same unit got a ball in his right shoulder that penetrated it and lodged in his chest. The casualties were carried or made their way to the little schoolhouse just west of the butternut grove (Building 13 on Map 6), where Doctor James W. Scott of Prescott and Surgeon Stewart Chisholm of the Royal Artillery were carrying out their grisly work. A former British army surgeon who had settled in Prescott in 1821, Scott was experienced in combat medicine, while Chisholm, who had wandered in the previous day while on his way to Kingston, had decided to stick around and help out. In between treating the wounded, he cheered on the troops. Scott was attending to a wounded American when, "in a frenzy of fear," the man "drew a long knife he carried on his person" and attempted to stab the doctor while his back was turned.[69] Fortunately, the doctor caught the movement out of the corner of his eye, the Hunter was overpowered, and Scott then resumed treating the man, giving him "the same careful attention" he bestowed on the British and Canadian wounded.[70]

The Hunters also took casualties. James Philips, the Canadian from Leeds County, died a few miles from his former residence when he was hit by a musket ball fired by a man of the 83rd Foot. An ardent Reformer who had fled Upper Canada in 1837, the 38-year-old Phillips was one of the few Canadians at the windmill and the only one to serve as an officer. Daniel Heustis wrote his epitaph: "He was brave and fearless in the fight, and his name and deeds will long live in the memory of freedom's votaries."[71] Another casualty was 24-year-old Charles Brown, the nephew of General Jacob Brown, who was hit in the head and chest and fell. Heustis went to succour Brown but was forced to fall back when the position was overrun by British and Canadian troops, one of whom made sure of Brown with his bayonet. He was then carried into a wooden barn (Building 10 on Map 6) just east of the butternut grove, where Surgeon Chisholm, who had moved forward with the troops, tried to

aid him but Brown died. Chisholm cut a button off his coat for a souvenir, another officer took his pocket book and Lieutenant Parker of the Marines ended up with the young man's sword. William Gates, who had been wounded in the arm, saw one of his friends from Salina "rising [from cover] to discharge his gun, receive a bullet in the forehead, when he fell upon his face – dead."[72] Hunter Charles West was badly wounded but tore open cartridges for his comrades until he expired. Throughout all this, von Schoultz actively encouraged his subordinates, running from man to man and "imparting to them the zeal and courage that fired his own bosom," by a pat on the shoulder and the words, "That's the sort, my good fellow," when they hit their targets.[73]

By now, it was about 10.30 A.M. and the situation was a stalemate. Rather than call off the attack, Young decided to make one final attempt. Although Gowan's men were closer to the mill, they were pinned down in the more open western approaches of Newport. Young and Fraser decided to attack the eastern edge of the hamlet, where broken ground, shrubbery and buildings provided better cover. Fraser gathered up the remnants of Macdonell's Highlanders and his Dundas and Grenville militia and, forming up on the Johnstown road, led them forward in person.[74]

This move took von Schoultz by surprise as he had concentrated most of his men against Gowan's force, which he regarded as the greater threat. The invaders at the eastern edge of the hamlet were caught off guard and many surrendered when Fraser's men made a sudden rush with the bayonet against a stone building that was the key to the defence of that side (possibly Building 4 on Map 6). Hunter Gates, firing from behind a nearby wall, had been having problems with his

musket and had hunkered down to clear the weapon. When he rose to fire, he was horrified to see his comrades "retreating toward the mill and myself left entirely alone, with large numbers of the enemy upon the other side of the wall, much nearer to the mill than myself."[75] Gates rose, fired a shot, and then dropped his weapon and ran, in full view of the oncoming Canadians who blazed away at him, hitting the top of his hat and the waistband of his pantaloons. He made it to safely and was "greeted with cordial feelings" by his fellow Hunters at his miraculous escape.[76]

Fraser's attack, initially successful, soon tailed off. When his men tried to move on the central part of the Hunters' po-

Good surgeon, good citizen: Doctor James W. Scott of Prescott
James Scott had been a surgeon's mate in the Royal Navy before transferring to the army and serving at Prescott in 1814-1815. He later joined the North West Fur Company but in 1820 established himself as a general practitioner in Prescott. During the week of 12-16 November 1838, he tended the casualties of both sides and continued to care for wounded militiamen for months after the battle. (Courtesy of Patricia Cox, Calgary)

sition, the mill and its immediately surrounding buildings, they were again pinned down by accurate fire. As Private MacIntosh summed it up: "They shot at us from the Windows" of the buildings and "We had no chance at them there."[77] It was nearly 11 A.M. and Young, finding "after a constant fire of some hours from Sandom's steamers and the musketry, that no impression could be made" on the mill or its attendant buildings, called off the attack.[78] His troops went to cover and remained in their positions until mid-afternoon, at which time Young, intending to renew the attack when "the assistance of heavy guns could be procured," withdrew to Fort Wellington, leaving strong pickets to cordon off the invaders.[79] Before pulling back, his men set fire to the wooden barn east of the butternut grove, incinerating the body of Charles Brown. Sandom also ceased fire and, leaving the *Cobourg* on patrol in the river, returned to Prescott with his other two vessels. From the time his steamers had opened fire to Young's withdrawal, the action had lasted about eight hours and the British and Canadian losses, as Young admitted in his official report, had been "severe."[80]

This was no understatement. Young reported losing 13 killed and 78 wounded out of a total force of about 650 men engaged, or just over 12 per cent. These numbers were compiled a week after the action but there is other evidence that suggests that some of the seriously wounded men later died. Of the units involved, the regulars and Macdonell's uniformed

The view from the mill down-river to the east
Taken from the upper floor of the windmill, this photograph shows the area east of the structure. In 1838 the road continued along the shore to the village of Johnstown, two miles away – today it comes to a dead end. On 13 November Colonel Richard Fraser made the third attack of the day along this road and his men took buildings (since removed) at the eastern edge of Newport but were pinned down by accurate Hunter rifle fire from the centre of the invaders' defensive position. (Photograph by René Schoemaker)

Glengarry Highlanders suffered the worst: the 83rd losing 1 killed and 4 wounded of 44 engaged; the Royal Marines lost 1 killed and 15 wounded, exactly half their number engaged; while the Highlanders lost 4 killed and 8 wounded, about a quarter of their strength.[81]

The reality was, of course, infinitely worse than the statistics. The open fields north of Newport and the buildings and enclosed gardens of the hamlet were littered with the dead and wounded. Hunter William Gates had no love for his enemy but even he found that "the groans and imprecations of the wounded and dying were heart-rending to hear."[82] His comrade, Stephen Wright, never forgot the dead of the Windmill Plains lying "with their eyes turned to heaven, with an imploring gaze – some had a mild benignant smile upon their marble faces," while others were wearing red coats "dyed a deeper color in blood," their only dirge the "beating of the waves against the rock-bound shore" of the St. Lawrence.[83] Young and his officers made every effort to get off their dead and wounded that were out of range of the invaders' rifles – Gates recorded seeing nine four-horse wagon loads of men being removed to Prescott – but the British and Canadian wounded within rifle range of the Hunter positions were left where they had fallen.[84]

It was a dispirited force of militia and regulars that marched wearily back to Prescott. The thirty Hunter prisoners taken in the action were incarcerated in a small room in Fort Wellington under the guard of Sergeant Smith of the 1st Grenville. His weapon having been damaged during the fighting, Smith was only armed with a bayonet and "was fearful the prisoners might overpower him and get away" but the Hunters were quiet. Things got worse for Smith after a drunken sergeant from Jessup's company challenged him to a wrestling match and he was forced to confine the man to the guardhouse. Jessup "appeared upon the scene promptly, and with much vigor of language" demanded his sergeant's release, but Smith refused, and when he threatened to report the matter to Lieutenant Colonel Plomer Young, Jessup quieted down and the man remained in custody overnight.[85]

Private MacIntosh and his comrades in Captain Nicholas Shaver's company of the 2nd Dundas, not having eaten for twenty-eight hours, were desperately hungry after the battle but all they got was a few pieces of hardtack. It did not get any better for the Dundas boys. Jerimiah Bouck's corpse was one of those retrieved and late that afternoon Allan Macintosh, his brother Lewis and other friends of the deceased gathered around a grave dug in the lawn of the Prescott seminary. There was no minister present but Lewis, knowing his brother's religious feelings, asked him to say a few words after they lowered a hastily procured coffin into the ground. The God-fearing young militiaman briefly recited the story of Jerimiah's life, emphasizing that no man "could say justly any evil of him" and recounted how only a few short hours before the two had knelt in the snow to pray. Pointing toward the American side of the river, where several hundred spectators were still visible on Mile Point, Allan MacIntosh continued:

> See yonder on the other side of the River, that dense crowd of people. We know not their interest. Perhaps to swim over and kill us, and take Canada. It stands us in our hands to live in readiness to meet death, either by Yankey Bullet or by any other cause, that when our Life leaves our tenement of clay, our Lord will be in eternal joy, like the Soul of the remains that lie before us.

MacIntosh thought his comrades "appeared pensive" as they stood silent, listening to the thump of earth on wood.[86]

Tactical problem: Defensive strongholds in Newport, Edwardsburgh Township, Upper Canada, 1838

This watercolour by Thomas Ainslie shows the butternut grove and the core of the Hunter defence, the three buildings near the mill, which were resolutely defended. The four-bay, two-storey carriage house with a flat roof provided good fields of fire against an approach from the west along the river road, while the two-storey roofless house to the left covered the approach from the north across the Windmill Plains. The Hunter stronghold, however, was not the mill; it was the three-storey, roofless building shown behind the carriage house. Situated obliquely to the river road (see Building 5 on Map 6), this was a combination tavern and store and an excellent all-round defensive position. Von Schoultz stationed himself here on the last day and the defenders of this structure were only blasted out of it by artillery fire. The Hunters completely blocked the doors and ground floor windows of these building to deny access to their opponents. The small white building to the left of the grove is the schoolhouse which served as an emergency dressing station during the battle. (Watercolour by Thomas Ainslie, National Archives of Canada, C-508)

CHAPTER EIGHT

"The last glimmer of hope went out"

Tuesday, 13 November, 3 P.M., to Friday, 16 November 1838, 12.00 A.M.

Let our victorious banners fly,
And give our bugles breath,
Forward! And let the battle-cry
Be Victory or Death!

But what is yonder darking cloud?
And what in bold array?
THE BRITON'S COME! lord: what a crowd!
GOOD GOD! LET'S RUN AWAY.[1]

When the fighting was over, Daniel Heustis discovered that his coat had been "pierced in six different places" by bullets and "several others were as thickly peppered as mine."[2] Nonetheless the Hunters were elated over their success. They believed they had beaten the entire 83rd Regiment of Foot, one thousand strong, "many of whom were veterans in the service of their mistress, Queen Victoria," supported by twelve hundred "provincial soldiers, aided by an unknown number of militia."[3] The invaders' casualties had been far fewer than their opponents, but were still significant. As in everything to do with figures relating to the Hunters, the evidence varies. Von Schoultz later stated that he lost 7 or 8 men killed and 14 wounded on 13 November, which, with the 32 men taken prisoner, brought his total loss for the day to 53 or 54 men but a Canadian source lists his casualties as 18 killed, 20 wounded and 26 prisoners, for a loss of 64 men. The Hunter wounded were taken to the mill and placed on pallets of straw from nearby barns and stables, but that was about all their comrades could do for them as the Hunter medical officer had lost his equipment during the landing. The wounded "endured their pains with manly fortitude, and with very little complaint" except the "occasional sigh or groan" which filled their comrades' "hearts with agony."[4] One man, Nelson Butterfield, babbled for a while about his mother and family and then became incoherent, and finally died.[5]

Although they had repulsed the attack, the Hunters were anxious as they had almost exhausted their limited supply of artillery ammunition and had eaten much of the food they had brought or found in the hamlet. Their situation, bad enough, could only get worse as the enemy was sure to return and there was no sign of the hundreds or thousands of Canadians who were supposed to flock to their side. There had also been no communication with either Johnston or Birge for nearly twenty-four hours and they had no idea what was happening on the far shore. To make things worse that Tuesday afternoon, it began to snow.[6]

Von Schoultz needed medical supplies and his men needed food. In the late afternoon he decided to risk sending one of his officers over in daylight in an attempt to get the needed items that night, and Daniel George volunteered along with four other men, including William Gates. The Hunters had noted that the British vessels occasionally interrupted their patrols to go into Prescott, leaving the river clear for brief periods, and they had also spotted a derelict boat on the river bank west of the mill. If George's party could get to it during one of the breaks in the British routine, there was a chance, given the poor visibility, that they could reach, if not the far bank, at least the safety of American waters 900 yards away.[7]

When the right moment came, the five crawled along the shore to the boat, only to find it half full of sand and water. Unfortunately, they were discovered by a militia picket about 250 yards away. The Canadians fired and started running towards the Hunters, who, with "a strong and hasty effort" born of desperation, tipped the boat to empty it, pushed out into the water and began to paddle frantically with boards they had wisely brought with them. The Canadians, frustrated, fired at them long after they were out of range.[8]

They nearly made it. In fact, subsequent inquiries showed that, although Sandom's officers denied it, George and his companions were very possibly on the American side of the international line when the *Cobourg*, which had put out from Prescott as soon as the alarm was sounded, bore down on them. The British vessel opened fire with 18-pdr. round and grape-

Iron 6-pdr. field gun

The Hunters defending the windmill had three pieces of artillery – a 3-pdr., a 4-pdr. and a 6-pdr. similar to this reproduction piece. The Hunter 6-pdr. was "borrowed" from a militia unit in Ogdensburg the day the Hunters landed. They did not have much ammunition and were reduced to using rusty nails, metal and stones as projectiles. (Photograph by René Schoemaker)

Facing page

"Heave to, or we'll fire again!" The steamer *Cobourg* takes a prize.

During the afternoon of Tuesday, 13 November, a Hunter officer, Daniel George, and four other men dared a daylight crossing of the river to request evacuation or reinforcement. They almost made it to safety but were captured by the alert crew of the *Cobourg*. (Oil sketch by Peter Rindlisbacher, courtesy of the artist)

shot which raised splashes around the Hunters' leaky craft and, as the *Cobourg* came closer, militia on her decks brought the fugitives under musket fire. Seeing it was no use, George and his companions made gestures of surrender, the *Cobourg* came alongside, a rope was thrown and the five men were hauled one by one onto the steamer. Gates was the last to be brought on board and he did not move fast enough to please a black naval rating who, having no great liking for republics or republicans, gave him a good clip upside the head with a blunt object that stretched the American senseless on the *Cobourg*'s deck.[9]

When he came to a few minutes later, Gates found himself manacled to his companions and surrounded by grinning sailors and militia. The five Hunters now discovered, as their comrades would in the days to come, that their opponents did not share their exaggerated sense of the importance of their mission to liberate the Canadas from British oppression. Far from it, the captors despised their prisoners as American marauders and cheerfully informed them that "they were to be fixed," "hung to the yardarm" or used as human targets.[10] These pleasantries over, Gates remembered, "we were stripped of every thing of value about our persons, save our clothes, and these would have been appropriated" by the militia "had they been permitted to work their desires."[11] Incredibly, Daniel George had neglected to throw away his pocket book. Inside it the *Cobourg*'s officers found the receipt for the payment George had made to the captain of the *United States* for towing the *Charlottes* from Millen's Bay to Morristown, and other documents relating to the landing, including a list of weapons ready for loading at Millen's Bay and the number and location of various Hunter units and sub-units. Some of these documents were in a code so childishly simple that the naval officers were able to crack it within minutes.[12]

News of this find spread around Prescott as did word of another document taken from the body of a dead Hunter officer, possibly the Canadian James Philips, which contained instructions for a spy and suggestions on how the people of the village should be treated:

The man must first go to Brockville and ascertain whether any regular soldiers are at Brockville; also what steamboats are there and the exact situation of all things.

Persons to be marked in Prescott are: Major Young, Dr. Jessup; John Blakey, Capt. McDonald and Brother Alpheus Jones, Dr. Scott, squire McMillan, Hooker & Henderson.

The arms in possession of the inhabitants are to be immediately taken. Arms stored in Col. Young's house and at the Barracks.

Two companies ought to be sent to Merrickville, one to Kemptville, two companies to Farmersville [now Athens].

Crane has about 50 men in his employ and is friendly.[13]

The note did not elaborate what "marked" meant but the worst connotation was placed on it since the persons so indicated were the military commander at Prescott, the collector of customs, militia officers, two local doctors who were at the moment serving in the military, and prominent merchants. The story soon made the rounds that a "list of proscribed persons in Prescott, who were to suffer death, men, women & children" had been found.[14] When word of this got out, the attitude of the Canadian militia toward their enemy, bad enough already, truly began to harden.

Nonetheless, folks in Prescott had a good laugh over the foiled escape attempt and hoped it meant their unwelcome visitors would, as Captain Hamilton Jessup (himself on the notorious list) put it, begin "to shift their quarters in rowboats to the Land of Liberty."[15]

The Hunters had witnessed the capture of George's party. Furious, they opened a long distance bombardment on the *Cobourg* with their artillery but soon gave it up. After dark, the British dead lying nearby were searched for anything useful or valuable. By this time Lieutenant Johnson of the 83rd had died and, after the invaders had scared the rooting hogs away from his corpse, it was stripped and hung by its heels from a nearby tree. One of the Poles took Johnson's shako and scarlet coatee while Hunter Lyman Lewis picked up his sword. Lewis gave it to von Schoultz, who presented the weapon to Heustis as a token of his gallantry in the action. Unfortunately, some of the Swede's men, who lacked his genteel code of conduct, mutilated Johnson's body in a most gruesome fashion with their Bowie knives. There was no justification for this act but frightened men with sharp blades often find an excuse to use them.[16]

Von Schoultz decided to send a second messenger over the river. He asked for a volunteer to cross, find one or both of the missing leaders, and arrange for either evacuation or reinforcement. A young man named Meredith responded, and, as there were no boats, took a plank from one of the buildings and carried it down to the river bank. It was bitterly cold, the wind "blew bleak and freezing," but Meredith splashed waist deep into the water and, judging the matter nicely, waited until the British vessel on patrol was on the upriver leg of its beat and then began to paddle the 1,800-yard width of the black St. Lawrence. His hopeful comrades, who had accompanied him to the water, waited until he disappeared into the darkness and then wearily returned to the windmill.[17]

It was a wretched evening. According to Stephen Wright, the

Officer, 83rd Regiment of Foot, 1830s

Recruited primarily in Ireland, the 83rd Foot, commanded by Lieutenant Colonel Henry Dundas was in garrison at Kingston when the Hunters landed at Windmill Point. Lieutenant William Johnson, commanding a detachment of the regiment that fought in the battle of 13 November, was killed in action that day. This print shows the full dress of an officer of the 83rd, not the field dress, but there is evidence that Johnson was wearing the red coatee and shako pictured here. (Print after E. Hull, photograph by René Chartrand)

wind "whistled shrilly through the arms of the old mill, blending with the groans of the stricken and dying who lay shelterless in the night's wild storm" while the Onondaga Hunters' flag flapped "like the wings of a raven above our heads."[18]

Wednesday, 14 November 1838, was a miserable day. The high winds of the night continued, bringing a mixture of snow and sleet that covered the bodies on the Windmill Plains. In the river, one of Sandom's steamers patrolled the Canadian side of the international line while the *Telegraph* did the same on its side. The sight of this American vessel, flying the

Captain, United States Infantry, full dress uniform, 1838

When the border troubles erupted in late 1837, the greater part of the American regular army was in Florida and not available for deployment in the north. In the late spring of 1838 a new unit, the Eighth Infantry, was raised specifically for service on the northern border and stationed at Sackets Harbor. Three companies of this unit were present during the Battle of the Windmill, on board steamers in the St. Lawrence, ensuring that American neutrality was preserved. This plate shows an infantry captain in the full dress blue uniform of the period and, in the background, an enlisted man in winter dress. American uniforms were only marginally less decorative than those of the British army. (From *United States Military Magazine*, 1840)

Stars and Stripes, helping their enemies to "thwart and defeat us," continued to infuriate the Hunters who believed that their own government, by "harassing the friends of Canadian liberty, altogether unworthy of republican America."[19] To Hunter C. Vaughan, the presence of the *Telegraph* was somewhat poignant because he had recognized his father, Sailing Master William Vaughan, USN, on her deck and occasionally waved his handkerchief in greeting when the steamer was in close proximity.[20]

By this time, Colonel William J. Worth had complete control in Ogdensburg. The previous evening, he had sent the *United States* and the two *Charlottes* to Sackets Harbor under guard and had ordered a third company of the Eighth Infantry from that place to Ogdensburg on the chartered steamer *Oneida*. Although Worth found it painful to watch "his countrymen, guilty as they were, selling their lives so dearly," his duty "was plain and he would not shrink from it."[21] Sometime that Wednesday morning, a deputation of citizens from Ogdensburg, anxious to end the bloodshed, asked him to intercede with his British opposite number, Plomer Young, "to allow the intruders to surrender."[22] At first, Worth was reluctant to comply with this request as he was sure that Young would respond to such a request "indignantly and in terms perhaps offensive to the U.S. government."[23] Later, he seems to have changed his mind and proposed to contact Young to see if the British officer would agree to a clandestine evacuation of the Hunters from Canada – in return Worth would arrest the invaders and bring the full measure of American law against them. The civilians enthusiastically approved this plan, which would not only prevent further bloodshed but also let both Worth and Young off the hook, and an Ogdensburg man who knew Young was dispatched across the river to speak with him.[24]

Despite the awful weather, Wednesday was a better day for Plomer Young. At about 8 A.M., the steamers *Brockville* and *Kingston* docked at Prescott with Lieutenant Colonel Henry Dundas, four companies of the 83rd Foot, and Major Forbes Macbean's demi-brigade or half battery of Royal Artillery equipped with a 6-pdr. field gun and a 12-pdr. howitzer. Dundas, who had been warned nearly seventy-two hours before that Prescott was going to be attacked, had taken his time getting there, but his tardiness may have been due to a simple lack of transport. He had not left Kingston until late Tuesday afternoon and had reached Brockville the previous evening, where he encountered Sandom on his way back to Kingston with the prisoners captured that day. The naval commander advised Dundas that heavy ordnance was needed at Prescott and, for his part, he intended to bring up three barges and a gunboat armed with 18-pdr. guns. Dundas agreed but felt that, having come this close to the scene of the action, he should at least go and have a look at the situation in person.[25]

On his orders, Young marched out at 9.30 A.M. with such militia as he could muster under the command of Colonel Richard Fraser. They drove in the enemy pickets at both sides of Newport to allow Dundas, Macbean and Captain Francis Randolph of the Royal Engineers to inspect the invaders' position. While the three officers examined Newport from various directions and the militia sniped at the Hunters, the *Cobourg* came down the river and fired at the mill with her 12-pdr. gun. Watching the solid shot bounce off the structure convinced the British officers that the artillery with them would not "make any impression" on the Hunter stronghold and "any attempt to carry it without first effecting a breach, even if successful," would prove very costly.[26] Heavy guns were needed, at least 18-pdrs., and as these were only available at Kingston, Dundas decided to return there.[27]

This was logical but what did not make sense was that he took the four companies of the 83rd Foot, who had not even disembarked from their vessels, back with him. Since Parker's

Windmill Point by moonlight, 1895
Taken by Prescott photographer R.A. Nunn at the same time of year as the battle, this remarkable view shows the river at its lowest water and demonstrates clearly how the shallows around the point made for hazardous navigation. Note the chimney (shaped like an hourglass) between the buildings, probably a ruin of one of the buildings destroyed in the 1838 battle. (Courtesy of the Grenville County Historical Society)

Marines and the late Lieutenant Johnson's detachment of the 83rd had sailed with Sandom the previous night, this left only militia at Prescott. Dundas's orders from Lieutenant Governor Sir George Arthur allowed him latitude to deal with the situation but stressed that although he was to maintain the security of Fort Henry, his paramount duty was "not to suffer the Brigands and disaffected to occupy a spot in the province, one moment longer than the most vigorous measures can prevent."[28] Removing the regulars from Prescott was hardly a vigorous measure because they would spend most of the next few days steaming on the St. Lawrence. Dundas would be criticized by his military peers for this action because, as one remarked, to withdraw "a force upwards of sixty miles from the scene of action, under the plea of obtaining guns of a heavier calibre, when these might have been sent to him without, in any way, weakening the besieging force, has in it something so incomprehensible, that I confess I have never been able to understand the tactics that induced the measure."[29] According to Major John Richardson, a Canadian officer serving in the British army, Dundas later implied that the return of the 83rd Foot to Kingston was "absolutely necessary … as an outbreak was to be expected." Richardson thought this not only absurd but a libel on the good people of Kingston because "with a *very* few exceptions, a more loyal population is not to be found in any part, not only of Her Majesty's colonies, but of the empire itself, and Col. Dundas must have been well aware of the fact."[30] Whatever his reasons, Dundas steamed away with the regulars in the afternoon.

Young took early steps to augment his command and relieve those militia who had been on duty since Sunday by calling up three companies of "volunteer reserves" from Prescott, about 160 men in total. These were older men, aged forty to sixty, meaning that almost every male in the village capable of carrying a weapon had now turned out. By Wednesday afternoon, Young's force consisted of three companies of incorporated (or longservice) militia, twelve companies of sedentary militia, five companies of volunteer sedentary militia and a cavalry troop, a total of about 1,000 officers and men.[31]

Throughout Wednesday, the militia traded shots with the Hunters. Both sides fired at an unidentified man who lurched slowly across the fields – and both sides missed. This was blacksmith Edward Landers, who, abandoned for dead the day before, had waited until dark to crawl into the loft of a nearby building for cover before lapsing into unconsciousness. He had come to and was trying to escape. When he was recognized, Landers was rescued and carried to the surgeons but it was a miracle he was still alive. A medical board later reported that he had suffered a deep knife thrust on the right side of his neck while the top and side of his skull had been fractured, his forehead "much injured" and his jaw broken by repeated heavy blows.[32] Landers lived but suffered recurrent bouts of dizziness and was never again able to practise his trade to support his wife and five children.[33]

Colonel Richard Fraser, the most experienced of the militia officers in Prescott, was in command of the cordon around Newport that morning. The Landers incident may have prompted him to take steps to bring in those British and Canadian wounded who were still lying on the snow-covered plains, and he sent a flag of truce into Newport proposing a ceasefire to permit his men to remove them. Von Schoultz accepted and the Hunters and Canadians were soon moving about the human wreckage, placing those still alive on litters extemporized from fence rails and taking them to their respective positions. During the ceasefire, von Schoultz approached Fraser, who was supervising this grim work from his horse, and tried to speak to him, perhaps to begin negotiations leading to a surrender.[34]

If so, the Swede picked the wrong man. Richard Duncan Fraser, the 53-year-old collector of customs at Brockville, had served in the Upper Canadian militia longer than Nils von Schoultz had been alive and was known for two things: his loyalty to the Crown and his volcanic temper. During the War of 1812, Fraser had raised a troop of cavalry that had rendered good service along the St. Lawrence, including participation in the 1813 battle of Crysler's Farm. He had blotted his copybook somewhat that same year when sent to arrest a known American sympathizer. Finding the man absent, Fraser and one of his officers got drunked up and set fire to his house, which was saved only by the swift action of neighbours, and this not very bright act cost Fraser heavy damages in the civil suit the man won against him.

Fraser had not improved with age. A high Tory who was prepared to go to war for his principles, Fraser hated Reformers and anyone connected with them. Some fifteen years before, he had taken the "rod of correction" to Robert Gourlay, one of Mackenzie's predecessors as a critic of the government, and caned him on the main street of Brockville and then, using his authority as a magistrate, arrested him for seditious libel. Gourlay, in turn, had Fraser charged with assault. More recently, Fraser had let it be known that, if William Mackenzie had the temerity to show his face in Brockville, he would horsewhip the little Scot down the same main street. As if all this was not bad enough, Fraser had been one of the passengers on the *Robert Peel* robbed by Bill Johnston in May 1838 and had lost his valuables, luggage and a considerable sum of money. Richard Fraser did not wish to speak to this pretend-officer with his sword and epaulettes, this foreign brigand who had invaded his country and killed his friends and neighbours, and wheeled his horse and rode away. Possibly because of this rebuff, von Schoultz had two of the British wounded carried back to the windmill.[35]

When the ceasefire was over, both sides went back to their respective positions, firing the occasional round. The terrible weather continued as snow mixed with rain fell throughout the day. Cold and getting hungry, the Hunters huddled in their positions, anxiously watching for relief or reinforcement from the American side of the river. They had received no word from Meredith, the messenger sent across the previous night – for all they knew, he had drowned in the river.

In fact, Meredith had managed to cross a mile of water on his plank, no mean feat, and had found Birge. The Hunter leader had recovered from his apparent stomach disorder but was in hiding to avoid Marshal Nathaniel Garrow, who was very keen to talk to him. Garrow was not the only party who wanted to see Birge. In Ogdensburg, so strong was "the utmost indignation" against "the *Patriot officers and leaders*," that "their lives are almost threatened by our most respectable citizens, and they may suffer yet, for sending innocent and brave men where they *dare not go themselves*!"[36] Birge could offer Meredith nothing but promises, although, to bolster a reputation that had sagged considerably, he scribbled a note to Bill Johnston which he later had published in the newspapers. In an attempt to divert responsibility from his shoulders to those of Johnston, Birge informed the pirate that

The fate of the men on the other side of the river is in your hands. Nothing is expected of the British above Prescott; and if you can rally your men and go to Jones' Mills and kindle some fires, you will save the men and save Canada. Start fires also at Gananoque, and the British will think Kingston is being attacked. Do for God's sake, rally your men and start immediately.[37]

Jones's Mills was a small settlement on the river about five miles west of Brockville but Bill Johnston, who had his own problems with the law, had made himself scarce and nothing was done.[38]

The strength of the Hunters' position had been demonstrated the previous day and von Schoultz took steps to improve it. The doors and ground floor windows of the buildings near the mill were barricaded with bricks, stones, furniture, lumber and timber, and just about anything else that could be found until they were completely blocked. To enter the buildings, the Hunters used ladders to climb up to the second-storey windows, and once inside, these were pulled up to deny access to unwanted visitors. These measures converted the structures that formed the central core of the invaders' position into miniature, self-contained fortresses. The invaders also collected nails, spikes, door handles, hinges and other metal scrap to use as canister rounds in their artillery pieces.[39]

Work like this kept the men on Windmill Point busy, leaving little time to reflect on their grim situation. They appreciated those comrades who attempted to raise their spirits. "We had some droll specimens of humanity," Heustis later recalled, who "occasionally excited a flow of mirth, which … enabled us to look with more stoic philosophy on the dark spots." One of these "fun-provoking geniuses" was 45-year-old Garrett Hicks, a labourer from Alexandria in Jefferson County and "a coarse, careless, independent sort of fellow" who had a "wonderful knowledge of the marvellous achievements of the canine race." Hicks entertained (and perhaps bored) his comrades by recounting "some big dog story" from a seemingly inexhaustible fund of such anecdotes.[40]

When darkness fell that afternoon, the snow and sleet, which had been intermittent through the day, began to fall with increased intensity and this tended to lower everyone's spirits.

What made it worse was the plight of the wounded who were kept in the mill for safety:

> We had no fires, no beds, no suitable covering for the unfortunate sufferers. They had nothing but a couch of hay, on which to pass the tedious hours. Amid all the hopeless circumstances with which we were surrounded, our greatest anxiety was for the relief and comfort of these suffering comrades. It would be impossible to describe their melancholy condition. They endured their pains with manly fortitude, and with very little complaint. An occasional sigh or groan was heard, which filled our hearts with agony.[41]

Yet, despite the dark prospects before them, Heustis boasted that his comrades were proud to have "struck a blow in the cause of freedom."

Late that same evening, Dundas and Macbean docked in Kingston. The townspeople were aware of the attack on Prescott and anxious for news. The militia had flocked in from the surrounding area, and although there was no danger of Kingston being attacked, its people were concerned about their neighbours down the river. There was little concrete information – the *Chronicle and Gazette* could only tell its readers that the "Yankee Pirates having been compelled to take refuge in the Windmill (the tower of which is of extraordinary strength)," heavy guns were required to "level it."[42]

Procuring those weapons and getting them ready was Major Forbes Macbean's responsibility and being the son of a Royal Artillery officer, Macbean was born to the business. He had been commissioned as a second lieutenant after graduation from the Royal Military Academy, the training school for British gunners and engineers, in 1804 and had served throughout the Napoleonic wars. Promotion in the artillery, which went by seniority, was slow and it had taken Macbean thirty-three years to reach his present rank. But that long period of service had made him a professional to the core and on the return voyage from Prescott he drew up a list of the tasks that had to be completed so that his men could go immediately to work.[43]

The actual weapons, iron tubes measuring 9 feet and weighing about 4,300 pounds, were available at either the Stone Frigate or Fort Henry. The problem would be getting the proper carriages for them as the equipments of Macbean's field battery were too light for this purpose. If necessary, Macbean and his men were capable of making them, because the construction of gun carriages and other vehicles was an essential part of a Royal Artillery officer's training. Seasoned wood was usually kept in store for this purpose and Macbean's battery included skilled blacksmiths, carpenters and wheelwrights in its ranks. Fortunately for him, the proper carriages were available at Kingston and, as soon as the *Brockville* and *Kingston* arrived at 10 P.M. that night, his men swung into action to procure, assemble and make ready the two guns for the return voyage.[44]

At Prescott, the weather had cleared by dawn on Thursday, 15 November. In the morning the desultory sniping started again and continued throughout the day. On the river, the *Telegraph* and HMSV *Experiment* patrolled their respective sides of the international boundary. Fowell's *Experiment* was the only British vessel on station this day as Sandom's other steamers had returned to Kingston.[45]

Lieutenant Colonel Plomer Young had no fears for the security of Prescott; he had enough militia positioned around Windmill Point to seal off the invaders and it was really a case of waiting until Dundas returned with the heavy ordnance. As a return trip to Kingston took at least twenty hours and since Macbean would also need time to get the ordnance ready, Young did not expect to see Dundas until late that night. He was therefore receptive when he received an invitation to visit Worth on board the *Telegraph* to discuss the situation.

The two officers got on well, which is not surprising as both had the same mission – ensuring that the St. Lawrence area of their respective nations remained peaceful. Worth explained his plan to evacuate and arrest the invaders but Young turned it down because of "the delicacy of the measure proposed, and the obvious charges that would be brought against" him if he consented to the escape of an enemy "who was entirely in his power."[46] During their conversation, however, either through "inadvertence or design," Young let it slip that the *Experiment* would dock early that evening for some necessary maintenance and for a few hours there would be no British vessel on the river.[47]

This was all Worth needed. At dusk, when he saw the *Experiment* going into Prescott, he brought the *Telegraph* to anchor near the Ogdensburg docks and kept her there all night. When both vessels were off the river, the *Paul Pry*, which Worth had released from impoundment, crossed the river to Windmill Point carrying a delegation consisting of the Ogdensburg postmaster, Preston King, and other prominent citizens of the village. Their purpose was to convince the Hunters to withdraw to the United States, where they might have to spend a considerable period in a federal penitentiary but that was surely a brighter prospect than what awaited them in Canada.[48]

Because of the shallow water around the point, the *Paul Pry* could not get closer than about a hundred yards offshore. As King was not a Hunter or sympathizer and had never met von Schoultz, the delegation sent a Hunter ashore first to talk to the

Swede, establish King's credentials and explain the plan. Unfortunately, this man apparently did not tell von Schoultz that his men could be taken to safety but instead urged him to hold on because 600 men would cross in the morning to assist him. Von Schoultz probably did not believe this fairy tale, but since he was not informed of any other possibilities, he only requested that the *Paul Pry* take his wounded back to the United States. The emissary agreed and returned to the steamer to make the arrangements.[49]

The Hunters carried their casualties carefully down the steep bank to the water. The emissary took one of them back to the *Paul Pry* in the boat and told the waiting delegation that the Swede had refused evacuation but had asked that his wounded to be removed to the United States. The civilians, who were nervous that the British and Canadians would discover them, assented and the captain of the *Paul Pry* tried to get nearer the shore to ease the task of transferring the men in question. In doing so, he inadvertently let off steam, making a noise heard by Canadian militia pickets up the river, and they fired warning shots that brought Fowell and the *Experiment*, repairs completed, out of Prescott. The captain of the *Paul Pry*, seeing the game was up, hastily made for American waters.[50]

Von Schoultz and his men were unsure what was happening. After things had quieted down they waited patiently for three hours under a sleet storm that soaked the wretched wounded huddling in their blankets, hoping the *Paul Pry* would return. When there was no sign of her, von Schoultz had them taken back to their uncomfortable pallets at the windmill and, as Daniel Heustis remembered, it was a bitter cup for men who had

indulged the delusive hope of being taken to the opposite shore, where they would have been warmly greeted, and where their wounds would have been properly dressed, and

every effort which friendship and sympathy could devise, would have been made to alleviate their sufferings. But, alas! they were doomed to disappointment.[51]

After three days, the invading force had been weakened by combat and a steady stream of deserters – some men actually escaped later that night in an old canoe discovered in one of the buildings near the mill. They invited Heustis to join them but, to his credit, the Hunter officer refused because he "had induced several brave young men to join in this hazardous enterprise, and I would not forsake them." Heustis, however, did not blame them for leaving as "they had fought well, and seeing no other chance of escape, and no prospect of doing any good if they remained, they decided to retreat."[52] Such was the confusion in the Hunter ranks that von Schoultz was not even sure how many men he had, so the officers made an accurate count and found 117 unwounded Hunters still under arms. Their leader gave them the news that 600 men were expected to cross in the morning but added that, if these reinforcements did not arrive, their situation was hopeless. No one really believed help was coming and, in Stephen Wright's words, "the last glimmer of hope went out."[53]

That Thursday, there was a great deal of activity at the Royal Artillery Barracks in Kingston and the naval station on Point Frederick outside the town. Sandom had docked with the *Cobourg* and *Victoria* at dawn the previous day and immediately began preparing for a return. The prisoners and British casualties from the battle were landed, including Royal Marine Private Robert Kershaw, who was in a bad way and not expected to last the day. The naval commander had decided to fit out barges with 18-pdr. guns to increase the firepower he could bring against the mill and, as the squadron log recorded, Point Frederick was a busy scene throughout Wednesday and Thursday:

14 November: Employed making preparations for fitting 2 hired Barges to carry 18 pdr guns …… artificers employed preparing Gunboats. Armourers at the forge. Wind: West. ……

15 November: Carpenters and armourers preparing two barges to receive guns on board. Hired a party of artificers from the Marine Railway. Seamen putting firewood on board steam boats. Interred the remains of the late Robert Kershaw, Private Royal Marines.[54]

Kingston was full of militia who had come flooding into the town from the surrounding areas. They were joined by Mohawk warriors from Tyendinaga (Deseronto), "all most anxious for an opportunity to try the accuracy of their aim upon the pretend Patriots."[55] Fighting Yankees was a Tyendinaga tradition begun by the grandfathers of these warriors in 1776 and continued by their fathers in 1812-1814. The Mohawks were skilled watermen and Sandom promptly signed them up to serve on the gun barges.[56]

Major Forbes Macbean's gunners were also extremely busy. There was much work to do and few men to do it because one third of his men were in Lower Canada, campaigning against Nelson's *Patriotes*. The artillery officer probably obtained working parties from the 83rd Foot to assist with the heavy lifting as it was established fact among gunners that infantrymen have weak minds but strong backs.

One party went to the ordnance store and selected the two best 18-pdr. iron tubes available, making sure their choices had been well drilled, with properly centred bores that had no

The professionals: Officers of the Royal Artillery, 1830s
After the attack of 13 November had been repulsed by the Hunters' superior firepower, the point was cordoned off until Major Forbes Macbean arrived from Kingston with a demi-brigade (half battery) of the Royal Artillery equipped with two heavy 18-pdr. guns. Adding a professional element to what otherwise would have been just a vulgar brawl, the gunners provided the heavy firepower needed for the task of eliminating the invaders. The officer on the right is in full dress; the man on the left is wearing service dress, a bulky knee-length garment called a surtout. Note the oilskin cover on his leather bell-topped shako. (From a print dated 1828 in the author's collection)

pitting or cavities from hard service, and that the vents (the small aperture at the top of the breech by which the weapon was fired) were in good shape and not eroded by previous discharges. Their choice made, the gunners manhandled one of the obstinate iron tubes with ropes and handspikes along wood slides placed on the floor to the door, where it was lashed beneath a sling wagon, a solid four-wheeled vehicle used for transporting heavy ordnance. A double team of horses drew it slowly across the Cataraqui bridge to the artillery barracks, where it was placed in the yard, while the sling wagon returned for its mate. Another working party meanwhile brought two heavy grey-painted carriages, with their attendant limbers, from the carriage store, and the battery blacksmith, carpenter and wheelwright thoroughly inspected them and made good any deficiencies.

When guns and carriages were ready, the gunners erected a gyn, a lifting device not unlike a modern engine hoist, lashed one of the tubes to its ropes, and raised it by block and tackle high enough for a carriage to be pushed underneath. The tube was then carefully lowered onto the carriage, which creaked under the strain, and the process was then repeated with the second weapon.

While the guns were being assembled, ammunition details had been busy inspecting ammunition and powder in the magazine. Having seen the target, Macbean would have wanted as much ammunition as possible and he probably ordered 300 roundshot per gun to be taken, with a due proportion of case and spherical case shot, as well as shells for the 12-pdr. howitzer. This meant that approximately six tons of weight had to be transported, and since roundshot was awkward stuff to move, given its shape, it was a slow process to load the steady stream of wagons that made their way to the wharves where their cargoes were transferred to the hold of the *Brockville*.[57]

Back at the artillery yard, the battery farrier and his assistants inspected the horses of the unit, weeding out unhealthy animals. They also checked the harness and tack, repairing or replacing strapping. When all was ready, the guns were hooked to their teams and limbers and drawn to the wharf, where the horses were unhitched, led carefully on board, and placed in hastily erected stalls on the decks. Guns and limbers followed, pushed up the gangplanks by main strength and lashed securely.

All these tasks completed, the officers and gunners of Major Forbes Macbean's No. 4 Company, 5th Battalion, Royal Regiment of Artillery, who had been working for nearly twenty-four hours without pause, may have taken a few minutes to draw breath and congratulate themselves but more likely they did not have time. Their real work lay ahead of them down the river, and late Thursday evening the gunners and four companies of the 83rd Foot embarked on the steamers *Brockville* and *Kingston* and headed for Prescott.[58]

At Windmill Point, Friday, 16 November 1838, dawned clear and cold. Anxious eyes searched for the promised reinforcements but saw only the patrol vessels cruising up and down. "The 600 men who were to come to our assistance, if they ever started," Heustis later commented wryly, "must have taken a very circuitous route, for we have never yet seen them."[59] It was four days since the invaders had landed and they were tired, hungry, running low on ammunition and depressed in spirit. By now, most had lapsed into silence and the hours "passed dreamily away."[60] Visibility up the St. Lawrence, which runs fairly straight above Prescott, was excellent, and just before noon the lookouts reported smoke from vessels coming down the river. It was the *Brockville* and *Kingston* – the British army had returned.

CHAPTER NINE

"The troops immediately commenced to bayonet:"
The end of the hunt

Friday, 16 November, 12 A.M. to midnight, Saturday, 17 November 1838

A bank was raised to hide our breast,
Not that we thought of dying,
But that we always take a rest,
Unless the game is flying.
Behind it stood our little force,
None wished it to be greater,
For every man was half a horse,
And half an alligator.

> *Oh, Kentucky,*
> > *The Hunters of Kentucky,*
> *Oh, Kentucky,*
> > *The Hunters of Kentucky.*

They did not let their patience tire,
Before they showed their faces,
We did not choose to waste our fire
So snugly kept our places,
But when so near we saw them wink,
We thought it time to stop 'em,
And it would have done you good, I think,
To see Kentuckians drop 'em.

> *Oh, Kentucky, etc.*[1]

It can be said with some degree of certainty that the officers and men of Her Britannic Majesty's 83rd Regiment of Foot forming up near a Prescott wharf shortly after noon on Friday, 16 November 1838, had never heard "The Hunters of Kentucky," the song of their enemy. The 83rd did not fight in the famous 1815 battle of New Orleans which the ballad celebrated, but these Irishmen (for the regiment was recruited largely in the Dublin area) would be quick to tell you that, if it had, the Yanks would not be singing about it now. When the fourth and final company had come down the gangplank, the order was given and the grey-coated column, just over 300 officers and men strong, under Dundas's second-in-command, Major Botet Trydell, a thirty-three-year veteran of the army, marched through Prescott. The entire village was out to greet them: men and women cheering, pretty (and other) girls waving, dogs barking, snorting hogs making way, and small boys trailing alongside, trying to keep in step. With the exception of the girls, the Irishmen ignored the commotion as they tramped along Water Street. They had seen it all before and, besides, civilians are essentially tricky people to deal with – cheer you on one moment, complain about you to the officers the next. The lads of the 83rd winked at the colleens from under their shakos,

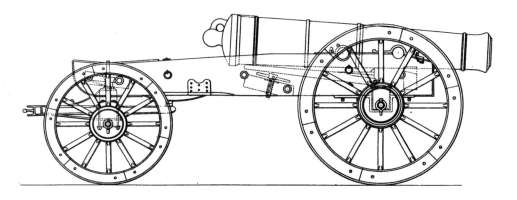

The problem was getting there: 18-pdr. gun on a travelling carriage

Because of its weight, the tube was shifted to a second set of trunnion holes to provide a more equal distribution of weight for movement. When the gun came into firing
position, the tube was shifted forward to the firing trunnion holes and unlimbered.
The 18-pdr., weighing 7,300 pounds with its carriage, was a heavy and awkward
weapon to move any distance and Macbean's men had considerable difficulty getting
them down the narrow gangplanks of the steamers. Outlined beneath the tube is the
elevating screw which lowered or raised a hinged wooden plate on which rested the
breech of the gun. (From *Aide Memoire to the Military Sciences*, 1847)

marked the location of the Pigeon Hole or one of its fellow establishments for future reference, and marched steadily west.[2]

When the wharf was clear, Macbean's gunners got to work.
The two 18-pdrs. and their limbers were manhandled down the
narrow gangplanks. Next, the horses were landed, probably
with some difficulty as Dobbin is a nervous creature at the best
of times and prefers solid ground under foot, not this hard
wood stuff with its bothersome echoes. Macbean later complained that "the narrowness of the Wharf and confined gangway of the Steamers" caused delay and that was probably an
understatement.[3] He had brought only eight horses from Kingston and, by regulation, thirty animals were required to haul
the 12-pdr. howitzer and the two heavy 18-pdrs, each of which,

with carriage and limber, weighed 7,300
pounds. The shortage of draught animals
was not a problem as Macbean quickly procured extra teams in village, but harnessing
them up to the guns took more time and it
was a considerable period before the three
weapons were moving slowly along streets
deep in mud from "excessive heavy rain."
There were willing volunteers to lend a hand,
however, and Macbean's artillery made
stately but steady progress to the firing positions he had selected two days before. Once
the guns were away, his men began the more
laborious job of unloading the ammunition.
Civilian wagons were procured to transport
it, but such was the enormity of the task that
it was to take nearly three hours from the
time the battery docked until Macbean's
gunners were ready to open fire.[4]

Dundas could not begin his attack until
Macbean was ready and Sandom had arrived from Kingston
with his squadron. While he waited, the British commander deployed his infantry, both regular and militia, on the Windmill
Plains (see Map 8). He placed three companies of the 83rd Foot
on the northern extremity of the fields, out of rifle range of the
Hunter positions. They were flanked on either side by the militia, who extended their line to the river bank on both sides of
Windmill Point, while the light company of the 83rd was directed to take post on the river road below the mill. Formed in
a two-rank line and stood at ease, the regulars leaned on their
muskets and talked quietly among themselves about how long
this matter might take (if it ever got started), and just hard it
might be to finish off the Yankees – judging by the number of

bodies on the fields in their front, it had been a toughish business three days before.[5]

It was best not to fuss about it, they told each other, because it was all in a day's work and a day's work for Her Majesty Queen Victoria earned a private soldier one shilling (less, of course, "stoppages" or deductions for food, some clothing and issue items which often amounted to as much as four shillings a week). Neither were the Irishmen of the 83rd much fussed about fighting Americans because accepted wisdom in the lower ranks of the British army held that Yankees preferred fighting from behind cover and the only reason the redcoats had lost the Revolutionary War was because they had been stabbed in the back by the wretched French. The British enlisted man was a firm believer that a bayonet with a positive attitude behind it would solve most tactical problems, but if that didn't work you had to call in those overrated and overpaid gunners (private soldiers in the artillery received 4 ¼ pence more per day than their infantry counterparts). That step had obviously been taken because, craning necks confined in stiff leather stocks, the redcoats could see Macbean's sweating gunners dragging and pushing their 18-pdrs. into position.[6]

It was a different matter for the Canadian militia, who took the situation much more personally. Standing in line that cold afternoon were men from the entire St. Lawrence "front" from Cornwall to Brockville and from the townships back of the river. In politics, some of these men were Reformers, and some may have even at one time supported William Lyon Mackenzie, but this business at the windmill was now beyond politics – they had turned out to fight a foreign invasion mounted by Americans who, ironically, had been incited by the same bad-tempered William Lyon Mackenzie. The militia would fight hard, as they had the previous Tuesday, to protect their families,

Heavy weapon: An 18-pdr. gun in position
Because of its size, the iron 18-pdr. was normally deployed in prepared positions. This 1850s print shows it emplaced behind a protective parapet of gabions, wicker baskets filled with earth. Note that the gun is placed on a platform of heavy planks, to ease the task of running it back up to its firing position. Macbean's gunners would not have had time to for such elaborate measures on 16 November. (Author's collection)

farms and homes from the Yankee pirates they could see moving about Newport in their long-tailed coats.

What bothered the waiting British and Canadians was the sight of the dead from the earlier action, "frozen white, and as naked as the day they were born," lying on the Windmill Plains.[7] This was particularly true of the militia, who were "anxious to have the bodies of their friends, the field of battle being too near the mill for them to attempt to approach it."[8] Since he had time on his hands, Dundas decided to do something about it and, just before 1 A.M., sent an officer to von Schoultz under a flag of truce with a request for a one-hour cessation of hostilities so that the dead could be removed for burial.

On Windmill Point, the Hunters had watched their doom, in the form of Dundas's regular and militia infantry and Macbean's artillery, move into position around them. A former artillery officer, von Schoultz easily identified the two heavy British guns as 18-pdrs. and he could predict exactly what Macbean would do, and about how long it would take. It was obvious to the invaders that this thing was going to end badly, very badly. There would be no help from the far shore, as the *Telegraph* and the recently chartered steamer *Oneida* cruised slowly up and down, cutting off contact with the United States.

The sight of those steamers flying the Stars and Stripes made it clear to the Hunters that Prescott was not going to be a replay of Texas in 1836. There would no rescue by their fellow countrymen nor would they get help from the very people they had come to liberate. Not a single Canadian had joined their ranks since Monday, and even the simple folk of Newport had long departed the scene. The greatcoated companies of the 83rd Foot waiting patiently in line to the north of the hamlet were not Generalissimo Antonio Lopez de Santa Anna's half-starved and poorly-armed Mexican levies; they were British regulars. The Hunters had fought some of these men on Tuesday but there were now hundreds of these steady-looking troops, each with his triangular-sectioned bayonet that they had good reason to respect, and there were also the two black 18-pdrs., squat on their carriages, surrounded by their sweating detachments. By early afternoon it was apparent to the Hunters that their stand at the windmill would resemble Texas in only one thing – like the defenders of the Alamo, they were all going to die.

The invaders were hungry, tired and above all frightened. In later years, those who survived the next few hours would boast that their comrades remained steady until the end. "We felt how hopeless was our situation," commented Wright, "but there was no whining, and no regrets, and in case we were put to the sword, we all had resolved to die like men."[9] There may have been some who would fight to the last, men who muttered curses and threats, whetted the blades of their Bowie knives on the stones of their firing positions, or notched the butts of their rifles to mark their kills. But it is unlikely that young men, boys really, such as 19-year-old Rouse Bennet from Norway in Herkimer County or 17-year-old Hiram Hall from Orleans in Jefferson County, whose lives had just begun, or older men such as 59-year-old Jeremiah Winegar, a labourer from Brownville, or 61-year-old Eli Clark, a farmer from Oswego, who had family responsibilities, felt the same way. Men like these took their fate into their own hands and hid themselves in the lofts, cellars and sheds of Newport or in the bushes along the river bank, hoping to survive the coming storm long enough to surrender or escape.[10]

Their leader was also looking for a way out. When Dundas's request for a ceasefire arrived, von Schoultz was quick to agree, and for the better part of an hour the men of both sides worked together to remove the stiff corpses from the field, Heustis remembering that it was common for "the enemy to assist us, and for us, in return, to assist them."[11] Private Allan MacIntosh was shocked by the condition of the dead, who had been stripped to their underclothes – the Hunters blamed the militia while the militia blamed the "poor of the land" – but worse was the fact that the hogs "had nearly eat some up them up."[12] The body of Lieutenant Johnson of the 83rd Foot was picked up by a working party, and when word spread that it had been badly mutilated, the "greatest indignation" swept through the British and Canadian ranks – "the 83rd vowed vengeance and the militia swore to a man they would give no quarter."[13]

There was also the matter of the two wounded Canadians brought to the mill during the previous truce. Von Schoultz saw their return as being an opportunity to open surrender negotiations and scribbled a note on the back of an old summons that he sent with the Hunters who took the two men back to their comrades. It was a polite but strangely-worded communication that not only attempted to put the onus on Dundas to end the fighting but also revealed that the Swede believed his opponents would treat him as the officer and gentlemen he believed himself to be.

To the commander of the queen's troops, at Prescott:

I send you two of your wounded, because I cannot attend to them, and give them the care they require.

In requitance, I beg you to treat my wounded with kindness.

If, on your honour, you can assure me that we are not perceived, by the people here, as liberators, it depends upon you to put a stop to further bloodshed.[14]

If von Schoultz actually thought Lieutenant Colonel the Honourable Henry Dundas was going to let him march out, drums beating and flags flying (metaphorically at least) to give up his sword in formal surrender, he was soon disabused of this illusion. The British commander, annoyed by this pompous missive from a man he regarded not as a soldier but a marauding bandit, and angered over the condition of Johnson's body, replied with a curt statement that he would only accept a surrender "at discretion" – that is to say, unconditional surrender.[15]

The Hunter officers argued the matter. Abbey and Woodruff were in favour of giving up; von Schoultz, Heustis and others wanted to fight to the end. Apparently they made no decision but some of their men took matters into their own hands and nailed a white flag to one of the tattered wings of the mill, where it was seen by Worth and his officers on the *Telegraph*, who recorded the fact. It was also seen by Dundas but he chose to ignore it.[16]

About 2 P.M., just as the working parties were completing their grim labour of removing the bodies, the lookouts on top of the mill reported steamers coming down the river. The Royal Navy had arrived.

Sandom had left Kingston at 5.30 A.M. that morning and, despite having to tow three heavy gun barges, and possibly his gunboat, he had made fairly good progress. He had now assembled at Prescott almost every vessel in his heterogeneous squadron: HMSV *Experiment*, the armed steamers *Cobourg* and *Victoria*, two gun barges each armed with an 18-pdr. gun, a third barge with an 18-pdr. carronade and a gunboat with two 18-pdr. carronades and 5.5-inch mortar. After communicating with Dundas, Sandom deployed for the forthcoming attack. He took up a position down-river from the mill with the three steamers, leaving the four smaller vessels above the invaders' position.[17]

The British naval commander was not happy to learn of the events of the previous night, particularly the movement of the *Paul Pry*, which he had believed to be impounded by the American authorities. As there was communication between Ogdensburg and Prescott, news had come over that several Hunters had escaped in the night, and this enraged Sandom, already deeply suspicious of the American authorities, who, he felt, "connive at the daring outrages" of the Hunters.[18] Having some time to spare, he crossed the river to the *Telegraph* to see Worth about the matter and to tell him that a major attack against his fellow countrymen would soon take place. It is not certain whether Worth explained to the British naval officer just why the *Paul Pry* had been on the river during the night – he probably did not, if only to protect Young's reputation. The American commander did, however, promise to use every exertion "to prevent communication from their shores, and in every manner to aid in putting an end to the species of warfare heretofore aided so much by their citizens."[19]

Pleased with this assurance, Sandom returned to his command. The squadron was ready for action. During the voyage from Kingston, his crews had made their preparations, checking the moorings or tackle which controlled the recoil of the 18-pdr. guns, replacing any weak or worn ropes, lest they break when fired, while those manning carronades of the same calibre examined the wooden slides, which provided a similar function for these weapons. The crews paid careful attention to the flintlock firing mechanisms affixed to the breech of the guns, inserting fresh flints, and replacing any worn parts. Attention was also paid to the ammunition. The cartridges were inspected and rolled gently, to break up any solidification of the powder inside, while the solid shot were "scaled" through a brass gauge of the correct diameter, and any rounds not true were put aside. Finally, the decks were sanded to provide grip in action.

After that, it was a matter of waiting until the army was ready, and since it was established wisdom in the navy that the army was always late, that might take some time. Sandom's sailors did not care as they were in a jolly mood. Service in the Lake Ontario squadron was far more pleasant than in the crowded lower decks of the main fleet, and cruising the Thousand Islands certainly beat mucking about the South Atlantic trying to intercept American slavers coming out of Africa, one of the Royal Navy's major operational tasks at this time. Accommodation on board the civilian steamers was excellent, there were friendly women and cheap drink in Kingston and, despite its awful weather, Upper Canada seemed to be a place where a man from the lower levels of British society could make his way and have a good chance of owning property. Besides, this windmill business was a break in routine, and sailors, like all servicemen, love a break in routine. The tars passed the time, swapping stories, critically inspecting the seamanship of their American counterparts on the *Oneida* and *Telegraph*, speculating whether prize money might be forthcoming and enthusiastically predicting just how and where it would be spent. These reveries were interrupted when the lookouts reported red-coated troops approaching on the river road from Johnstown. As the strangers got closer, observers identified them, by their diced bonnets and kilts, as Highland infantry.

The newcomers were the grenadier company of the 93rd (Highland) Regiment of Foot and they were in a foul temper – and had reason to be. The 93rd had landed at Montreal from Halifax on 31 October and was immediately sent on to Toronto, where it arrived on 6 November. The next day, it was ordered to turn in its tracks and move as fast as possible to Lower Canada to repel Nelson's invasion. Five days of forced marches in bad weather, alleviated by an occasional steamer passage, brought the Highlanders to Beauharnois on the south shore of the St. Lawrence by the evening of 12 November, only to find that the crisis was over. The good news was that they learned they would get a rest period and Lieutenant Andrew Agnew of the 93rd recorded that he and his fellow officers, expecting to live in clover for a few days, "set about catering."[20] They cheerfully

got a sitting room into order, collected plenty of feather beds and got fires lighted, but not *one full* bottle of wine could we find nor any viands in the larder. Late at night we got our rations of salt pork like the men served out and cooked. The only plunder we came in for in the whole town being a few casks of excellent apples and some jars of butter. However, this was good campaigning, we had capital beds and by dint of stealing some bread and sending our servants to milk the cows in some neighbouring fields we made excellent breakfasts.

Better still, Beauharnois was near Montreal, where the officers of the regiment had left their baggage and the married men their wives and children. Chances now looked good that the officers might get some warm clothing (which was needed as the weather was abysmal) while the married men might get a chance, if only brief, to resume conjugal relations.[21]

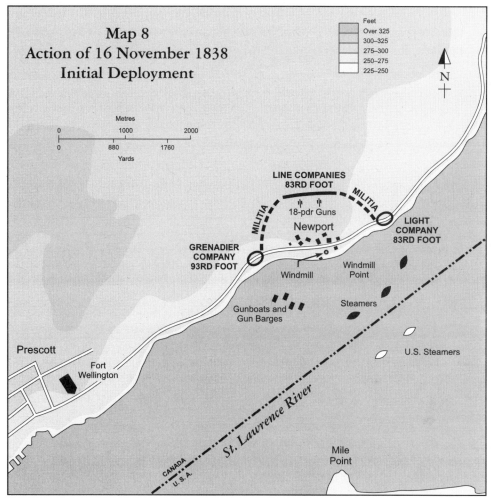

Unfortunately, this idyll came to an end on the morning of 13 November 1838 when a dispatch rider galloped in with a message for Lieutenant Colonel Robert Spark, the commanding officer of the 93rd. It informed him that his unit's services were urgently required at Prescott in Upper Canada, where a force of 500 American invaders had taken up a strong position.

Spark wasted no time in placing his Highlanders in motion. A horrified Agnew recorded that, "on as villainous a forenoon as can be conceived we were ordered instantly under arms and literally to start in *ten minutes*!!! for Prescott."[22]

That afternoon, the 93rd crossed to the north shore of the St. Lawrence where "all the carts in the country were pressed" to transport them, and at 8 P.M. set off on a tortuous journey in the slow and uncomfortable vehicles to reach Coteau du Lac the following morning. Here they boarded the steamer *Neptune* but, delayed by bad weather, did not reach Cornwall until

Thursday morning, 15 November. At this point, Spark decided to push the grenadier company under his second in command, Major John Arthur, ahead by farm cart. Agnew of that company recalled that his comrades were "two thirds frozen" when they reached Mariatown at 10 P.M. that night, where they rested until dawn before setting out to cover the remaining thirty-five miles to Prescott. After nearly eight hours in the slow, lurching vehicles, they reached Johnstown, where they disembarked and marched the remaining distance, arriving on the Windmill Plains shortly after 2 P.M. in the afternoon, having travelled nearly 750 hard miles in sixteen days.[23]

If any Irish comedians in the ranks of the 83rd thought to shout out a joke about Donald the Scotsman, not only slow-witted but slow moving, they probably thought better of it when they glimpsed the faces of the new arrivals. The Scots soldier tends to be undemonstrative, even dour, but if angered he can become ferocious to a frightening degree. And so it was with the grenadiers of the 93rd, who were big men (the average

Officers and man of the 93rd (Highland) Regiment of Foot, 1838
The grenadier company of this unit arrived just in time to take part in the final action of 16 November. They were not in a good mood as they had travelled some 750 hard miles in the previous two weeks and 35 miles that day alone. This print shows the full dress uniform of the 93rd; the company that fought in the battle were wearing their kilts but had probably substituted their forage cap – a Kilmarnock bonnet with a diced border – for the high bonnet with its ostrich feather plumes. The average height of a man in the grenadier company was 5 feet 10 inches and the grenadiers were cold, tired and angry when they arrived at Prescott, and looking for someone to take their troubles out on – the Hunters at the windmill would suit that purpose very well. (From Burgoyne, *Historical Records of the 93rd Foot*, 1883)

height in the company was 5 foot, 10 inches) and true High-landers, as they were recruited from the hill country north of Inverness. Tired, hungry, muddy, half frozen in their kilts, and not a few nursing blasted hopes of marital interludes, they were in a bloody-minded mood and looking for someone to pay for their troubles. The invaders at the windmill would suit this purpose very well as the 93rd had fought at New Or-leans in 1815 but had not had an opportunity since to discuss the matter with the Americans. As Lieutenant Agnew put it, with some understatement, the big Scots grenadiers, their kilts and legs covered in mud, were "all anxiety to get a rap" at the Yankees when they formed on the river road west of the mill.[24]

By this time, nearly 3 P.M., the Irishmen of the 83rd, who had been waiting for more than two hours, were beginning to grow impatient with those overpaid gunners who had still not opened fire. Everyone wanted to finish this thing as there were only about two hours of daylight left and a freezing wind from the west was sweeping down their ranks, causing them to blow on their hands. This cold breeze would not have been wel-come to Captain John Emslie of the 83rd as, when engaged in putting down the Kandyan Revolt in Ceylon twenty-two years before, he had been trampled by a herd of wild elephants, one of which had unfortunately stepped on his chest. Since that oc-currence, Enslie had a tendency to wheeze a bit and, in fact, he had already put in the paperwork to obtain a medical discharge from the service.[25]

It was Sandom who got the ball rolling. At 3 P.M., the naval commander moved his three gun barges and gunboat to a po-sition 450 yards up-river from the mill and ordered them to open fire. From the decks of the *Oneida* and *Telegraph*, in American waters opposite the mill, Worth and his men watched with professional interest as the "floating batteries" (their term for the gun barges) fired round after round at the Hunter citadel and the nearby buildings.[26] It was clear that the defenders were affected by their fire as the waiting British and Canadians could plainly see the "Pirates dressed in the regular Yankee garb with their long tailed surtouts & cloaks … running from one building to another in great confusion."[27] As Heustis remembered, the Hunter gunners tried to reply:

We had now fired away all our cannon-balls. In this emer-gency we contrived to load our pieces, a few times, with links of chains and scraps of old iron. The enemy were so very ac-commodating as to send us, occasionally, a ball which ex-actly fitted our six-pounder [probably a grapeshot]. We lost no time in returning all such compliments to the British, and invariably "gave them as good as they sent." Our brave boys did not wait for that ball to stop rolling, before they started in pursuit of it; and we hurled it back with more pre-cision and effect than it had been sent to us. In some in-stances we could perceive that it did good execution.[28]

These were brave words but there is no evidence that through-out the week the Hunter gunners ever hit one of their targets and after a few discharges they ceased fire.

Finally, at 3.30 P.M., Macbean was ready. Both 18-pdrs. were now positioned on rising ground about 450-500 yards directly north of the mill and the gun detachments could see the upper part of the door of the structure and the top of the stone wall erected by the Hunters to protect it. To Macbean, the politics of this business were of no concern – he had a mission and the means to accomplish it. His primary task was either to topple the mill or to "breach" it – blow an opening through its wall so

How they may have looked.

This photograph of an artillery detachment of the Kansas militia, taken twenty years after the battle, shows how the Hunter gunners may have appeared in 1838. These men are manning an iron 6-pdr. field piece, the same calibre as the invader's weapon at the mill. Note the variety of headgear – bonnet, straw and slouch hats – cotton shirts of various types, trousers and suspenders. The gun carriage appears to be home made; the Hunter gun carriages were better, being manufactured for the New York State militia. (Courtesy, Kansas State Historical Society)

that the infantry could enter. The iron 18-pdr. was not normally employed as a breaching weapon in siege work, a task usually reserved for the heavier 24-pdr. Its normal role was counter-battery fire against the enemy's guns, but 18-pdrs. were what Macbean had and they were good weapons, known for their range and accuracy. The artillery officer's secondary task was to bring down the houses occupied by the enemy, and he therefore ordered "one gun to play upon them and the other upon the Mill, intending when they were driven from the houses, to direct the fire solely on the former."[29]

Macbean's men were good. The first shot from the gun fired at the windmill, propelled by a 6-lb. charge at an elevation just over point blank, hit directly above the door of the target. Macbean personally aimed and fired the first round from the other weapon at a stone house fronting the Windmill Plains (possibly Building 6 on Map 6) and it "made a considerable breach in the building."[30] Once the two gun detachments had the correct range, they got down to work, firing at a steady rate of about one round every two minutes or so, letting the smoke clear from the previous discharge, and trying to make every shot count. The "Practice upon the houses never missed," Macbean reported, "and would have shortly brought them down; that on the Mill does not appear to have been so effective, the Shot having glanced" or bounced off.[31] Meanwhile, the 12-pdr. howitzer detachment fired explosive shell and spherical case, or shrapnel, against the houses to keep the Hunter riflemen away from the windows. Lieutenant Andrew Agnew of the 93rd remembered that "the artillery practice was beautiful" and there was "immense cheering at every shot which almost invariably told."[32]

Macbean's probable firing position

In this photograph, taken from the probable position of one of the 18-pdr. guns on high ground north of Windmill Point, the mill can be seen on the river bank. At this range, Macbean's gunners put their first round just above the door of the mill, an indication of their professionalism. (Photograph by Dianne Graves)

"Fire!"

Modern re-enactors, dressed in Royal Artillery uniforms, fire a 6-pdr. field piece during the making of a recent film about the battle. In the afternoon of Friday, 16 November, Macbean's hardworking men would have put their coats aside and worked in shirts and braces. Note the smoke produced by a minimal charge; there would have been much more around the 18-pdr. guns firing at the windmill, as each round was propelled by six pounds of powder. (Photograph by René Schoemaker)

Queen Victoria's door knocker: Iron 18-pdr. gun
Manufactured by the Walker Foundry between 1800 and 1820, about 9 feet in length and weighing nearly 4,300 pounds, this 18-pdr. gun at Fort Wellington is a similar weapon to those used against the windmill in 1838 and it may even be one of the two pieces that took part in the final bombardment. The Royal Artillery's employment of these weapons brought a quick and decisive end to the five-day occupation of Windmill Point. (Photograph by René Schoemaker)

As each gun fired, obscuring the men around it in a cloud of acrid powder smoke, and recoiling back six to eight feet, its detachment would swing into action. The bore would be swabbed, the loaders would bring the cartridge in its stiff paper casing and insert it in the muzzle, followed by the 18-pdr. shot, and both would be rammed home while the ventsman sealed the vent with a leather thumbstall to prevent any smouldering fragments in the bore flaring up and causing a premature discharge. When projectile and cartridge were seated safely, the ventsman would prick the charge with a brass wire attached by a chain of the same metal to his shirt front – for the gunners were in shirts and braces by now and did not feel the cold – by shoving it down the vent and breaking open the charge inside. This done, he would insert a tube containing mealed powder in the vent and stand back. The gun commander, always an experienced NCO, would now "lay" or aim the piece, using the screw fixed to the carriage to raise or lower a hinged wooden plank upon which rested the breach of the gun, and issue orders to the two men at the handspikes inserted into the trail of the carriage to traverse it right or left, as required. He would sight along the barrel and, when he was satisfied, give the order to "fire," and after he and the ventsman were clear of the recoil, another gunner would discharge the piece by reaching over the left wheel and touching off the tube with a portfire, a tightly-wrapped paper tube containing a combustible mixture that burned slowly and steadily. When the gun had finished rolling back, it would all begin again.

Macbean and his two subalterns, Lieutenants Henry Gardiner and George Kennedy, left their gun commanders to their work and restricted their involvement to observing the fall of shot and occasionally shifting targets. It was hard work but Macbean and his men were having a good time as to a gunner there is no greater fun than knocking down buildings. And they were proficient at it – Dundas later reported that "nearly every shot perforated" the houses around the windmill although that structure seemed impervious to damage.[33]

On and on it went, from land and water, for nearly two hours. If Sandom's rate of fire was the same as Macbean's (and it probably was), during that time Windmill Point was hit with more than 800 rounds of shell, shot and shrapnel fired from

A useful weapon: 12-pdr. field howitzer, 1838
In addition to his two 18-pdr. guns, Major Forbes Macbean also employed a 12-pdr. field howitzer against the windmill on 16 November 1838. A lighter and more mobile weapon, it could fire a variety of projectiles: solid shot, explosive shell, canister and shrapnel. Note the elevating screw connected directly to the breech. (From *Aide Memoire to the Military Sciences*, 1847)

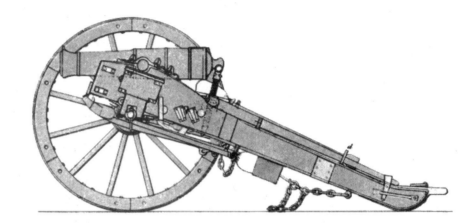

four 18-pdr. guns, eight 18-pdr. carronades, one 12-pdr. gun, two 12-pdr. carronades, one 12-pdr. field howitzer and a 5.5-inch mortar.[34]

Sheltering in the seemingly indestructible mill or in the houses near it, the Hunters were paralysed with fear. The despised British had brought up "the heaviest artillery that could be procured in Kingston, if not in the whole province" – 74-pdr. guns according to William Gates although no such calibre existed.[35] Added to the fire of these non-existent behemoths was that of "fifteen field pieces perfectly armed and ammunitioned," not to mention the weapons on Sandom's vessels. As round after round bounced off the walls of the mill, raising clouds of dust inside, or crashed through the upper floors of the houses, they huddled together, terrified.

After an hour, Dorephus Abbey could stand it no longer and went to von Schoultz to state that, in view of "our exhausted and critical situation," he should surrender. He found the Swede in a house, probably the large three-storey tavern build-

ing which the Hunter leader regarded as crucial to the defence (see Building 5 on Map 6). Von Schoultz told Abbey "to do as he thought best, himself, but by no means to encourage others to lay down their arms." According to Heustis, Abbey then returned to the mill and advised the men sheltering inside "to hold out to the last moment in the hope of receiving assistance" before running alone toward the British lines with a white flag.[36]

He was collared by Ensign Edward Smith and the men of Jessup's Volunteer Company. Colonel Richard Fraser was close by and, seeing the Hunter officer with his epaulettes, rode over and, without saying a word, gave Abbey a good whack across the back with the flat of his sword, nearly knocking him to his knees. Abbey complained that he was under a flag of truce, whereupon Fraser told him that, if that was true, he could damned well go back to the mill and take his chances with the rest of his pirate friends. The Hunter, however, refused to leave the safety of the British lines and after a few minutes Fraser relented and Abbey was led away under guard, bruised but alive.[37]

Hometown hero: Captain Hamilton Jessup (1806-1892)

This photograph shows Hamilton Jessup, the son of the Loyalist founder of Prescott, in old age. Jessup raised a volunteer company in February 1838 to defend the village. It was on duty during the night of Sunday, 11 November 1838, when the Hunters attempted to land and it fought throughout the week that followed. The Prescott Volunteers bagged the "famous Polish General Vanshulsh" on Friday night, 16 November, and they were not kind to the man – they beat him, stripped him, robbed him and, if British regulars had not intervened, would have cheerfully dispatched von Schoultz on the spot. The hometown boys had reason to be angry as nearly one third their number had been wounded in the previous five days. In later years, Hamilton Jessup served five one-year terms as the mayor of Prescott and completed another half-century of militia service. (Courtesy of the Grenville County Historical Society)

As the bombardment continued, Lieutenant Colonel Henry Dundas rode slowly up and down in front of his men. According to Private MacIntosh, the "Ginral" (to MacIntosh all officers higher in rank than his own captain were "ginrals") started at one end of the line and "as he drove his horse," kept shouting, "No quarter! No quarter!" to make sure everyone got the message.[38] Although the white flag was in plain view at the top of the mill, both British commanders, in Sandom's words, ignored it "as long as daylight lasted."[39]

The light, however, was beginning to fade and Dundas decided to move his regulars closer to the hamlet while the militia would hang back on the flanks to "prevent the escape of the brigands" along the river bank.[40] The regulars removed their knapsacks, haversacks, canteens and greatcoats, to be left under the guard of a trusted man. On order, they fixed bayonets – click-clack – and then, according to Private MacIntosh, the "Ginral" ordered "March!" and they advanced, with Dundas leading on horseback, straight at the windmill.[41] Lieutenant Agnew of the 93rd watched as the line companies of the 83rd marched south across the Windmill Plains in extended order, while on the river road his grenadiers moved in on the objective from the west just as the 83rd light company closed in from the east. As Dundas's men neared the hamlet, "a fire of musketry" was opened from a house, probably the stone tavern building defended by von Schoultz, and a private of the 83rd was killed.[42] Dundas ordered Macbean to bring forward his 12-pdr. howitzer and within minutes his gunners were firing case shot and shrapnel through the north and west windows of the tavern, cooling the ardour of the occupants, who temporarily stopped shooting.[43]

At the east end of Newport, the light company of the 83rd formed a skirmish line and advanced along the river road, section by section, one advancing while another put down covering fire, the sections then reversing roles. Their movements were admired by Worth's American regulars, one of whom watched the British light infantry "advancing from below after some skirmishing" and setting fire to "one of the houses adjacent to the mill, which soon burst forth into volumes of smoke, and afterwards into mountains of flame."[44] The Canadian militia, meanwhile, began to get excited and started to fire at random, which, in the opinion of Lieutenant Agnew of the 93rd, "was nearly as dangerous as the rebels."[45] Dundas, determined to lose "as few men as possible," ordered the regulars to lie flat on the ground for a few minutes while the artillery fired over their heads.[46]

The light was waning fast when Heustis and the officers inside the mill decided it was time to quit. They could hear the bugle calls of the 83rd light company and their lookouts at the upper windows could see the British moving toward them "with the evident intention of storming our fortress."[47] Some still wanted to fight, but most wanted to give up before it was too late, and it was agreed to send out a delegation. Four men, including Heustis, left the mill carrying a white flag but they came under immediate fire and ran back inside for cover.[48]

It was now about 5 P.M. and Macbean regretfully stopped firing as he could no longer identify targets in the dusk. The hamlet was a shambles but not one round had done any serious damage to the mill, although Macbean was sure he could "have breached it with both guns by noon of the next day," if his men had been given the chance.[49] Sandom's gun barges, manned by the proficient Mohawks, had worked themselves to within 350 yards of the point, but the naval gunners had no better luck with the invaders' stronghold than their army counterparts and Sandom, "fearing our [army] friends might by accident suffer," also ceased firing.[50]

The final act was about to begin. Fascinated, Worth and his officers watched as "more than a thousand troops, hundreds of them regulars, were now perceptible," deployed, awaiting the order to attack.[51] They had mixed feelings about what they were watching – as one remarked, their fellow countrymen had "behaved with a constancy and courage worthy of a better fate."[52] The bombardment had also attracted the usual crowd of spectators from Ogdensburg, who braved the biting wind to watch the show from Mile Point across the river. This day, however, there were few cheers.

Dundas gave the order and the regulars, followed by the militia, closed in on the Hunter position. Rather than fight a separate battle for each of the fortified houses, the 83rd and 93rd set them on fire to drive the Hunters out from cover. The redcoats kicked or poked holes in the barricades at the doors and lower windows and threw torches or flaming brands inside. When the fires had taken and the Hunters inside were forced out by flames, the soldiers drove the invaders "like rats from one [house] to the other at the point of the bayonet and as their wounded of course perished in the flames, their courage began to fail."[53] Some Hunters were still fighting. In the ranks of the 93rd, Agnew remembered that "bullets whistled pretty sharply among our bonnets." At one point Major John Arthur fell and the Highland officer ran over "to him thinking he was shot, the men nearest him supported him and he looked round with the most amusing semi comic face hardly knowing himself whether he should live or not."[54]

It was now quite dark and Sandom decided to land to coordinate activities with Dundas. As he was being rowed in toward the shore, the naval officer's boat came under fire from the tavern building that had earlier received special attention from Macbean's howitzer, and he was struck by a spent round which bounced off his chest. Sandom found Dundas near the howitzer and the two commanders discussed the situation. By this time Dundas had changed his mind and had decided to take prisoners rather than attempt to kill all the invaders on the spot. As Agnew recalled, this was not popular with the men of the 93rd:

He has been much blamed for this [decision to take prisoners], as it is impossible to hang wholesale so large a body and great dissatisfaction is naturally felt in the country that such ruthless [marauders] should in any measure escape, but having been on the spot and heard his own arguments I think he acted with discretion when it is considered that it was night, that the tired troops must have remained otherwise in the field all night and had great loss storming so strong a natural position [as the mill] against desperate and well armed men next day. I think he saved much trouble by taking prisoners.[55]

Sandom and Dundas sent Lieutenant Leary, RN, to the mill with a flag of truce to inform the Hunters that their surrender would be accepted and he returned in a few minutes with Christopher Buckley.[56]

As Buckley approached, Richard Fraser rode up out of the darkness to give the man his traditional greeting, a blow across the back with the flat of his sword. The Hunter was driven to his knees and, cowering before the somewhat embarrassed Sandom (Dundas having moved off in the interim), whom he addressed as "General," Buckley pleaded for the lives of his comrades, who were "a deluded set of poor creatures or words to that effect" who had been "led astray to commit the act which they had committed."[57] Sandom pointed out that fire was still coming from the notorious house (the tavern defended by von Schoultz) but Buckley insisted that he could only speak for the men in the mill and had no control over those in the other buildings. Sandom told him to bring out all who wished to surrender and he would guarantee their lives.[58]

At this point, Dundas ordered his men to close in on the mill. "It was a fine sight," according to Agnew, "the flames throwing a rich gleam over the bayonets and appointments of the soldiers and the darkness adding much to the effect by doubling the numbers as the troops closed nearer and nearer on the fated rascals flocking to their last hold."[59] The fascinated American regulars on their two vessels in the river watched "column after column of the British forces" move through Newport and buildings being set alight, which "urged by the wind which blew a hurricane" soon became "a mass of flame."[60] While the 83rd and 93rd deployed on the road near the mill, the militia wandered around the houses, collaring Hunters as they were flushed from their hiding places by the fires.

The big Highlanders of the 93rd, intent on settling their grievances, went to work with a will on the running figures. The "troops immediately commenced to bayonet," Lieutenant Agnew recalled, but Dundas, "riding in front with great difficulty" restrained the furious Scotsmen and placed a strong guard from the grenadier company of the 83rd on those invaders who surrendered.[61]

The Canadian militia were as bad, if not worse. "No mercy was shown," Private MacIntosh remembered, and the slightest hesitation or sign of resistance was met with extreme violence.[62] That gentle soul never forgot the "moans of the dieing, while the point of the Bayonet passed through them and struck the wall." Alexander Wright, a Canadian Hunter who had resided in Ogdensburg, refused to surrender and "was shot down and stabbed through the heart with bayonets," while John Morisette from Lower Canada (probably Jean Morisette) "was stabbed in the side with a bayonet and cut on the shoulder with a sword, but not mortally wounded."[63] Unable to get to safety, some wounded Hunters died in the flames as did one man, Leonard Root, who made the fatal mistake of crawling into a bake oven to hide.[64]

About 6 P.M. Buckley emerged from the mill with fifty to sixty terrified men, among them Heustis and Stephen Wright. They passed through two lines formed by the grenadiers of the 83rd and it was well they did because the Canadian militia crowded around, howling for blood. Wright later thanked the Irish soldiers in print for saving his comrades' lives because he believed that "the ferocious militia would have torn us in pieces, had it not been for their timely protection."[65] He was probably right but what neither Wright nor his fellow Hunters understood was that during the last five days they had created eight new widows and twenty-eight fatherless children in Dundas, Glengarry, Grenville and Leeds counties and their friends, neighbours and comrades were determined to exact retribution.[66]

They also wanted souvenirs and loot. Heustis had wisely left Johnson's sword in the mill but still he and his comrades were stripped of their "money, watches, caps, clothes, and every thing our ferocious captors could lay their hands on, leaving some half naked, while every kind of insult was offered to us."[67] The grenadiers of the 83rd patiently warded off the blows aimed at the prisoners and finally formed a cordon around them to protect them from the militia, who "resembled ravenous fiends more than decent Christian men."[68]

Frustrated, the Canadians resumed looking for the man every British and Canadian soldier wanted to talk to, the "famous Polish General Vanshulsh," as MacIntosh termed him.[69] The celebrated fugitive had defended the tavern building as long as he could, even when Macbean's gunners caused the roof to "crumble over our heads."[70] He managed to survive when the regulars set the building on fire, and in the dark and confusion scurried down to the river bank, where he hid with other fugitives in the thick cedar bushes lining the shore.

The militia combed the hamlet again, but though they flushed other prey, they did not find the Swede. Across the river, on the *Telegraph*, the American regulars could hear spaced shots, "each report the knell of a patriot" they presumed, and then "for a moment, all was still, save the roar of the conflagration."[71] The Canadians were tense and quick to fire. Captain George Drummond of the Brockville Cavalry Troop was trapped by fire on the second storey of one house and went to a window to call for help, only to be shot dead by his own men. From time to time, a wretched figure would be driven by bayonet and musket butt to join the protective fold established by the regulars. Some did not make it.[72]

Major Forbes Macbean arrived at the mill to claim, as was his right as artillery commander, the captured weaponry and military stores. He was somewhat annoyed to find that Plomer Young had already taken away one of the guns for the use of the militia, while another had gone to Sandom, "who declined giving a receipt for it or to give it up, considering it as the prize of the navy force." Sandom's sailors also got eleven kegs of musket and rifle ammunition they found in the mill and "the remainder, as well as the Small Arms, were taken away by the Volunteers 5 minutes after the Prisoners had quitted the Mill, and before I could get to the spot." If Macbean really thought the militia were going to give up those fine percussion rifles, excellent weapons for bagging deer, he did not understand the average Canadian farmer. To add insult to injury, sometime that night the locals got at his battery stores and he was forced to report the loss of six axes, six handspikes, one linstock, a wadhook, sponges, whips, currycombs and various useful and attractive bits of harness. The artillery officer was later able to examine two of the captured pieces and reported that one was an iron 4-pdr. of British manufacture, cast in the reign of King George III, while the other was a brass 3-pdr. gun was marked "SNY". The carriages of these pieces were "the work of the United States Arsenals, being complete," and many of the weapons, ammunition and provisions had the "U.S." mark. Sandom recorded that a large quantity of 18-pdr. shot was found in the windmill and prisoners told him that "several pieces of artillery of that calibre were left at Millen's Bay and other places for want of vessels and secure opportunities to convey them down to Ogdensburgh."[73]

Everyone was after souvenirs, useful or not, and even Lieutenant Governor Arthur later made a determined but unsuccessful effort to procure von Schoultz's pistols. There were enough weapons to go around because the Hunters had been well armed – Captain Hamilton Jessup was firmly convinced that each one had been issued a rifle, a brace of pistols and a Bowie knife. The wicked-looking Bowie knives, which the British and Canadians called "dirks," were the subject of much comment and soon a small pile was collected. The Onondaga Hunters' flag was taken down from the mill and examined by Jessup who, impressed with the workmanship, estimated it cost at least $125.[74]

General "Vanshulsh" was still at large nearly two hours after Buckley's surrender. As the flames died down, the militia combed the cellars of some of the buildings only to find mangled and half burnt corpses – in MacIntosh's words, "Trunks with heads and legs burnt off, Others with heads on, burnt all flesh off face and head, Their eyes sticking or protruding out of their skull horribly burnt."[75] But there was no sign of the Swede. While the regulars deployed along the road through the hamlet to seal off the river, the militia formed "beating" lines and with lanterns began to scour the bushes along the bank.[76]

Von Schoultz was finally captured at about 9 P.M. and, unfortunately for him, he was taken by Captain Hamilton D.

Jessup's Prescott Volunteers, local men who had more reason than most to despise him. Five of the seventeen men in the little unit had been wounded since the sentry on the dock had first sighted the *Charlottes* coming down the river on Monday, and the Prescott boys were not happy about it. They dragged the Polish general from under his bush, battered him to the ground with musket butts and stripped him of his hat, coat, epaulettes, sword (Jessup admired the silver-plated scabbard, "blade of fine metal" and "an eagle and other carved work on the outside"), his watch, wallet and a locket around his neck bearing the likeness of one of his many lady friends.[77] So much for the honours of war. They would cheerfully have dispatched the Swede on the spot to save the Crown the expense of a trial and a goodly length of rope but their shouts of triumph attracted the attention of a British officer, who managed to call them off long enough to get von Schoultz taken away by the regulars.[78]

Despite all efforts, some of the invaders eluded capture. Hunter Nathan Williams, hiding in the river bank, was missed by militia parties that came within thirty feet of him. With a few other fugitives, he crawled along the shore to safety but became separated from his companions when they were fired upon by sentinels. Williams made his way to the Johnstown area, where he was sheltered by a Canadian farm family for a few days until he was able to construct a small raft and cross the river. Later that night, a Polish Hunter, wearing Johnson's shako and coatee, passed through the pickets and found a skiff in which he returned to the United States. There were still many fugitives at large the following day and the militia brought in a half dozen men, including Hunter Vaughan.[79]

The battle of the windmill was over and it had been a costly affair. The final British and Canadian casualties were over 80 killed and wounded during the week of 12-16 November 1838. On the Hunter side, of the 250 who may have invaded Upper

Canada during that bloody week, perhaps as many as 50 were dead and 160 were eventually captured (including 17 wounded). The remainder had escaped back to the United States. The Hunter dead were buried in common graves hastily dug either on the battlefield or near the windmill and, according to Sergeant John Smith of Prescott, the bodies were thrown into them "naked, without any regard to order or decency."[80]

At about 10 P.M., except for those luckless souls ordered to remain on guard at Windmill Point, Dundas formed up for the return to Prescott. As the column made its way along the river road, in the centre were about one hundred beaten, robbed, half-naked and thoroughly dejected prisoners, tied separately to a long rope with a line of Irishmen from the 83rd Foot marching on either side. When the tail end of the column had disappeared into the darkness between the mill and the village, one of Worth's officers, gazing on the stone mill, its walls flickering with shadows cast by the pyres of Newport, reflected that this was all that remained of the invaders and "there it stood, gray and lonely, the melancholy monument of them, and of their folly."[81] The guns across the river had finally ceased firing.

For the victors, the march through Prescott to the wharf was one of triumph; for the vanquished, it was the beginning of a new ordeal. All the wounded invaders who could possibly do so were made to walk, and Heustis never forgot the shrieks of 23-year-old Monroe Wheelock from Watertown, badly wounded in the thigh, as he was dragged along by two of his comrades.[82]

Worse things were in store. The people of Prescott had illuminated their houses for the occasion and lanterns and candles burned in almost every window. Most of the villagers, human and animal, were assembled to greet the victorious heroes and castigate the Yankee brigands. "In the streets," recorded Heustis, "a vile set of wretches amused themselves with trying to insult and abuse us."[83] Wright remembered being "buffeted and spit upon by the Prescott mob," and the insults, which were accompanied by stones, blows and clods of mud, "made us feel doubly our desolate condition."[84] As the Hunters shuffled wearily along Water Street, von Schoultz got the loudest reception and also "the vilest treatment" of "jeers and scoffs."[85] The dejected men finally arrived at the wharf and were shoved into the hold of the *Brockville*. It was a tight squeeze as

A souvenir of von Schoultz

This finely-worked wing on display at Fort Wellington is claimed to have been worn by Nils von Schoultz at the windmill. If so, it was stripped off the Swede by the men of Jessup's Prescott Volunteer Company on Friday night, 16 November. An accompanying handwritten label (not shown) dating from the 19th century states that "it was part of the uniform of the leader of the Yankee marauders, the Pole Von Schoultz, captured at Prescott, Upper Canada, hanged at Kingston U.C. Dec 1838." It resembles wings worn by regular United States Light Dragoon officers during the War of 1812. (Courtesy Parks Canada, photograph by René Schoemaker) the space not being sufficient for us to lie or sit down, except a few at a time. Here we had the wounded in our midst, and very soon the air became exceedingly foul and unwholesome, in consequence of being breathed over so many times, unrenewed by ventilation. Faintness, headache, and other complaints, were now added to extreme exhaustion, both of mind and body. Altogether, our situation was such that death would have been a happy relief.[86]

None of their captors were particularly concerned about the matter as they despised men who, under international law, were not legitimate belligerents but pirates and in 1838 piracy received swift and merciless punishment.

When the prisoners were safely stowed, the militia not otherwise detailed were released from duty and the celebrations began, either in the many establishments on Water Street or, for the officers, in private homes. In the taverns, soldiers and civilians bellied up to the bar – the former spinning yarns, the latter buying drinks – and a great, glorious and noisy time was had by all well into the night. A roaring trade was done in souvenirs and more than one perfectly common sword was profitably passed off as General "Vanshulsh's" very own personal weapon presented to him by the King of Poland in honour of his bravery. The most marketable items were the large Bowie knives because grim stories were already going around about the condition of Johnson's body, which many had seen when it was taken back to the village in a wagon. Dundas's regulars and Sandom's sailors would have liked to join the fun but, being under tighter discipline than the militia, they were confined to their camps or vessels under guard. It was no matter because there was always a friendly Canadian who, for a small fee, would procure a little cheer for the lads, with some going to the obliging sentry who looked the other way at the right time, and

it is pretty certain that the redcoats, gunners, marines and sailors had their own good time. Thirsts slaked and trades concluded, many sought the warrior's other traditional divertissement because men who come close to death are very keen to get close to life again. None of the pretty girls evident earlier in the day were to be seen, however, as no respectable woman in Prescott would be caught dead on Water Street after dark but that didn't matter because, in a busy river port, all essential services are provided and it is possible that, throughout the previous week, reinforcements of ladies of easy virtue had poured in from the other river towns to process Prescott's expanded male population.

It must be said that this description of the celebrations in Prescott that Friday night in November 1838 is sheer speculation as not a word of such activities is contained in the official reports, personal letters or memoirs that have survived. But human nature being what is and soldiers being what they are, it is likely that this is what happened, and, of course, human nature being human nature, two other things are also certain – Private Allan MacIntosh avoided the festivities in favour of solitary prayer and nobody spared a thought for the men suffocating in the hold of the *Brockville*.[87]

The bright lights of the village were clearly visible to Colonel William Worth's men on the St. Lawrence. To one American, the sight of the people of Prescott illuminating their houses after their so-called "deliverers had been slaughtered" was proof that the "people of Canada are *not* disaffected," as the ill-fated Hunter invaders had believed. Having witnessed the events of the previous week, this man was firm in his belief that his fellow citizens had to realize that Canadians, "content as they are, *ask not*, WANT NOT, *WILL NOT HAVE*, their aid; and evince the most determined resolution to reward all patriots with buck and ball, instead of land and silver."[88]

It was nearly noon on Saturday, 17 November 1838, before Dundas and his regulars left for Kingston, a late departure probably caused by the time required for Macbean's gunners to re-embark their weapons, equipment and ammunition. For von Schoultz and his companions, "closely imprisoned in the crowded and unwholesome forecastle" of the steamer *Brockville*, the voyage up-river seemed longer than the eleven hours it actually took.[89] Some, including von Schoultz, slept, while Heustis took the opportunity to destroy two letters he had found in his pockets from Bill Johnston which would have been disastrous for him if discovered by his captors. All of the Hunters were hungry but it was not until mid-afternoon "when some half-boiled fresh beef, without a particle of salt, bread, or potato, was brought down to us."[90] According to Heustis, it was such miserable stuff that his comrades "could not eat it, notwithstanding we had been so long without food." What Heustis and the other Hunters, most of whom were essentially pampered civilians, did not realize was that they had just received standard British army rations and the regulars on the decks above them were eating the same food with relish. In time, the prisoners would learn to like what they were given.[91]

At 11 P.M., the *Brockville* docked at Scobel's wharf in Kingston. The townspeople, who had witnessed Dundas and Macbean's departure two days before, were anxious to learn the result of the expedition, and within minutes it seemed, word of the victory and the fact that the captured pirates would be marched through Kingston to Fort Henry, their place of confinement, spread through the town. "It was no sooner ascertained what the result was, and that the Prisoners were to be landed," crowed the *Chronicle and Gazette*, "than the principal street through which the triumphal cavalcade was to pass, was brilliantly illuminated" and lined by spectators numbering "some thousands."[92] Wanting to emphasize his regiment's suc-

cess before the people of Kingston, Dundas formed a proper procession. The band of the 83rd, hastily called out from the Tête de Pont Barracks, was placed at the head, followed by the light company. Next came the hundred or so prisoners, tied in couples to a large rope with von Schoultz in front, and a line company of the 83rd on either side, while the rear was brought up by the grenadier company and a wagon from which grinning soldiers displayed the captured weapons. Unfortunately, there is no evidence that Macbean's weary gunners, facing yet another heavy job getting their guns and ammunition off the steamers and back into store, were included in the festivities. When all was ready, Dundas gave the order, the band struck up "Yankee Doodle" and off they went.[93]

Kingston went wild. Excited people lined the route along Front Street, shouting loud "huzzas of thanks to the British Grenadiers that defend us," or giving a "groan of derision" when the prisoners appeared.[94] If anything, the Kingstonians were even more abusive than the people of Prescott. Many of the young prisoners "wept bitterly, and buried their heads in their bosoms"; others appeared to be indifferent, while von Schoultz marching "bare-headed in the front, maintained an erect port and unmoveable countenance; but the effort cost him so much that his face wore an unearthly appearance" and his eyes "glared and protruded as if he were on the rack."[95] The prisoners were "pelted with clubs, and spit upon with impunity" and, again, von Schoultz got the worst of it.[96] One aggressive bystander managed to get through the sentries long enough to strike the patriot leader a blow "on the hip, which caused a lameness from which he never recovered." Heustis and another Hunter were hit "by men whom we knew, and who may yet have occasion to repent." The spectators were fascinated by "the abominable weapons which the Pirates had carried about them," commented the *Gazette* reporter, particularly the Bowie knife, which "is certainly a fit instrument in the hands of such a set of cutthroats."[97]

The column made its way slowly along streets lined with Canadians cheering, jeering, spitting, or derisively shouting the words of their American neighbours' favourite patriotic tune as loudly as possible:

> Yankee Doodle went to town
> A-riding on a pony,
> He stuck a feather in his cap
> And called it macaroni.

When the procession got to the Tête de Pont barracks, the wives of the 83rd were there to greet their menfolk and add their own taunts (probably directed at the virility of the Hunters) to the chorus of verbal invective that fell on the wretched men along with stones, dirt and saliva. To the prisoners' relief, the torment began to lessen as they neared the long wooden bridge over the Cataraqui River with its seventeen arches and wry toll gate sign: "Let my care be no man's sorrow: Pay today, I'll trust tomorrow."[98] And then, finally, it was over the bridge and into the blackness beyond where Fort Henry waited.

PART III

Her Majesty's justice

The execution of Lount and Matthews, April 1838
Samuel Lount and Peter Matthews were the only two Canadian rebels executed as a result of the
1837 Rebellion. Note the white cloth pulled over the heads of the condemned and the binding of
the feet and hands. Similar scenes took place during the execution of eleven Hunters at Kingston
for their role in the Prescott invasion. (From *Mackenzie's Almanack*, 1837, author's collection)

 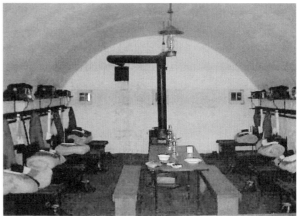

Where the invaders ended up

The front gate of Fort Henry in Kingston, the place of imprisonment of the Hunters captured at the windmill. The strongest defence work in Upper Canada, the fort had just been completed when the rebellions broke out in 1837 and played a crucial role in the defence of the province. Today, completely restored, it is one of the most popular tourist attractions in Canada. The second photo shows a typical casemate at the fort. The prisoners from the windmill were jailed in quarters such as this until they were executed, transported to a penal colony or released. The accommodation was crowded but bearable and the interiors were kept clean and ventilated. Despite frequent complaints in published Hunter accounts about their imprisonment, official delegations from the United States were unanimous that the prisoners were properly cared for and they praised Sheriff Allan Macdonell of Kingston, who supervised their confinement. This casemate has been restored as a typical barrack room of the 1860s. (Photographs by Ron Ridley, Fort Henry)

CHAPTER TEN

"Where are sinners equal to them?"
The courts martial

November 1838 to January 1839

This is the scheme that Mac built,
These are the people who worked at the scheme that Mac built,
These are the knaves held up by the people who winked at the
*   scheme that Mac built*
*   This is the Patriot all tattered and torn*
*   Who prowls like a wolf from night till morn;*
*   He has joined the plundering lawless band,*
*   And bears the name of a "stout brigand";*
*   And he raises the cry of the "Canadas free,"*
*   To seize on his neighbours' property,*
He is one of the knaves held up to the people who winked at
*   the scheme that Mac built*

These are the bandits! Lo they stand
Bound with manacles hand and hand
And surrounded by an armed band
As they gaze with a wild and vacant eye
On the gallows tree where they're doomed to die.
No trophies of war shall bestrew their bier,
Not theirs the sigh, or the friendly tear,
No friendly hand shall adorn their grave;
No! these are reserved for the loyal and brave.
But their names shall go down the course they run
Unwept – unhonoured – and unsung.[1]

The Patriot Hunters captured at Prescott, having committed acts of "armed hostility" against Upper Canada, were liable for prosecution under "An Act to protect the Inhabitants of this Province against Lawless aggression from Subjects of Foreign Countries at Peace with Her Majesty," passed in January 1838. This meant they would face a military court martial and Lieutenant Governor Sir George Arthur wasted no time in putting the machinery in motion. On 20 November, four days after the surrender at the windmill, he issued a general order directing a court martial of fifteen militia officers from the Midland District to convene at Kingston. This town was selected as the venue rather than Prescott, so as to lessen the tension in that village, and the members of the court were drawn from units that had not fought in the battle. To serve as judge advocate or prosecutor, Arthur chose Lieutenant Colonel William H. Draper from Toronto, a militia officer and the solicitor general of Upper Canada. The appointment of such a senior legal official was no accident as Arthur and his superior, Sir John Colborne, were fully aware that the proceedings would come under intense international scrutiny and they wanted them to be without blemish. The 37-year-old Draper, a determined, meticulous and conscientious man, was a good choice.[2]

The judge advocate's legal task was relatively simple. Under the legislation, Draper had to prove three things: that the accused was a British subject or a citizen of a foreign country at peace with Britain; that the accused had been at Windmill Point in the company of traitorous or rebellious British subjects; and that he had, "armed with guns and bayonets, and other warlike weapons, feloniously killed," or attempted to kill British subjects. The act, inspired by the border raids of the previous winter, was punitive in the extreme. If found guilty, the penalty was death, although the court martial could make a recommendation for mercy.[3]

The board convened at Fort Henry on 26 November but was adjourned for two days to allow Draper time to prepare. At Arthur's direction, his first responsibility was to compile a list of the prisoners "with such information or particulars … as can be extracted from each."[4] Every man was questioned by either Draper or Magistrate George Baker as to his nationality and the reasons for his presence in Upper Canada when he was captured. No duress was used and prisoners were permitted to alter the information provided, if they wished. These statements were then sworn and became the basis on which charges were laid against each man.[5]

The prisoners, trying hard to lessen their guilt, came up with some ingenious excuses for landing on Windmill Point, in fact almost any reason except for the purpose of fighting. Not a few declared that they were drunk and had innocently taken passage on the *United States*, only to find, when they sobered up, that they were in a foreign country. "A very considerable number," Draper reported,

> deny that they were connected with the party, and assert that they were mere passengers down the river on their own affairs, that they were forced out of the steam-boat into the schooners, and confined in the hold, and landed against their wills, and in despite of their resistance, at the windmill. Some go on to say that they took arms by compulsion, but would not use them, or only fired one harmless shot; others that they refused to take arms at all; some that they remained all the time concealed in cellars or out-of-the-way places, and others that they were kept confined the whole time from the landing to the surrender. It is probably too much to say that there was not an individual case of this description, but it is self-evident that, generally speaking, it is impossible that these statements can be true.[6]

Most of these claims were so preposterous that Draper had little problem in demolishing them during the proceedings.

The judge advocate found that his greatest problem was establishing the correct nationality of the prisoners. This was not surprising in a time when governments possessed little information about their citizens and formal identification papers were minimal. Following his initial interviews, Draper compiled a list of 148 men captured in the Prescott area between 12 and 17 November whom he proposed to bring to trial. He had already decided not to try some men because the evidence against them was so thin or they had agreed to serve as Crown witnesses. Appendix D contains a list of 189 men known to have fought at Prescott, 12 November–16 November 1838, and, of these, 151 were unquestionably American citizens, 25 were British subjects, and 13 were Europeans. Of the total, only 17 could be classified as possible Canadian rebels who had fled the Canadas in the wake of the rebellions of the previous year, 8 from Lower and 9 from Upper Canada. The Lower Canadians were mostly very young, very frightened, French-Canadian boys but the men from Upper Canada were somewhat older and more committed to the cause of rebellion.[7]

Clearly these seventeen Canadians were in the worst position and Draper convinced three of them, Levi Chipman from Upper Canada, and Jean-Baptiste Rousseau (sometimes Raza) and Laurent Mailhotte (called Alonzo Myatt in some accounts) from Lower Canada, to act as Crown witnesses. The 20-year-old Rousseau and 18-year-old Mailhotte were of little use because they did not know any of the American Hunters, but Chipman, a 40-year-old farmer from Leeds County, who had fled the province the previous winter, proved to be Draper's mainstay. Chipman had been an early and enthusiastic recruit to the Hunter army and it was clear from his testimony that he had been privy to the counsels of the New York leaders. One American, 25-year-old John Graves from Cosmopolitan in Jefferson County, also turned evidence for the Crown but he was too ill throughout the trials to be of much service. It says much for both the morale and loyalty of the Hunters that only four of the prisoners agreed to save their lives by testifying against their comrades.[8]

The number to be tried and the amount of evidence to be compiled and presented caused problems for Draper. "I am greatly embarrassed for proof against a large number of these rascals," he was forced to confess. "Nobody can identify them."[9] To procure additional evidence, he used Hely Chamberlain, who was inserted among the prisoners in Fort Henry. They talked freely in front of him, enabling Chamberlain to identify not only leaders such as von Schoultz, Abbey, George and Woodruff but also two men connected with the death of Lieutenant William S. Johnson of the 83rd: Sylvanus Swete of Alexandria, Jefferson County, who bragged about shooting him, and Joel Peeler from Rutland in the same county, widely regarded by the Hunters as the man who had mistreated his corpse.[10]

Draper was determined to introduce any evidence that would demonstate the character "or conduct of the prisoners." Although he found it distasteful to allude to the mutilation of Johnson's corpse, it was necessary to bring it forward to show "what atrocities some of these men were capable." It would also provide a clear contrast to "the philanthropic professions of these liberty extending Americans, and at the same time afford a just criterion to decide upon the real character of their 'sympathizing' efforts for the welfare of Canadians." Toward this end, Draper had Johnson's body examined by a military surgeon before it was released for burial.[11]

That burial took place on Tuesday, 20 November 1838. As a sign of their respect, all business and professional establishments in Kingston closed for the day while Johnson and Private Downes of the 83rd, also killed in the battle, were interred after an impressive military funeral.[12]

While Draper was making his preparations, the Hunters began their captivity in Fort Henry. When they first arrived, they were herded into one large overcrowded room, but after a few days they were transferred to five separate casemates, each containing about thirty-five to forty men. Straw mattresses were issued, one for every two men, and these were rolled up during the day to serve as couches. Each casemate was also provided with a woodstove for heating, a bucket for sanitary purposes and, as an afterthought, two bibles. Although many Hunter memoirs are bitter about conditions in the fort, official American delegations that visited them over the winter of 1837-1838 were unanimous in declaring their accommodation to be clean and comfortable. Daniel Heustis, usually the most honest and reliable of the Hunter chroniclers, regarded his comrades' situation as crowded but bearable.[13]

The prisoners were the charge of Allan Macdonell, sheriff of the Midland district. A former half-pay British officer, Macdonell had been appointed to this post the previous March and proved to be a strict but compassionate jailer. Heustis, who served as a room captain or prisoner representative for his casemate, got to know the sheriff well and described him as a "large, stout, and good-looking Scotchman" who was "not destitute of humane feelings and never insulted us, as did others, with ungentlemanly and abusive remarks, calculated to irritate and annoy us."[14] The same could not be said of the guards, who were at first militiamen who badgered the Hunters unmercifully; Stephen Wright, recovering from his wound in the new hospital (later the Kingston General Hospital), overheard them urging the doctors to cure him as quickly as possible as they could not hang a sick man. After a few weeks, the militia were replaced by regulars from the 93rd Foot whose attitude was more correct and not unsympathetic.[15]

Security was tight. In July 1838, fifteen political prisoners, American patriots and Canadian rebels, had made a dramatic escape from Fort Henry, and Macdonell was determined that there would be no repetition of this feat on his watch. Officers held snap inspections of the casemates and their inhabitants at various times of day and night, and every bedroll and article in the room was moved and examined at least once a day to ensure that there was no tunnelling.[16]

The Hunters continued to whine about the food. Gates complained about receiving boiled beef "served in a large tub, with pea soup and hard, black bread," but this was only the regular British soldier's daily fare.[17] Wright was bitter about his unvarying hospital diet of plain oatmeal with "a little allowance of milk," not realizing that this was the prescribed diet for military convalescents.[18] The prisoners' food was provided on contract by John Counter, a prominent Kingston businessman and

Judge Advocate: William Henry Draper (1801-1877)
Draper, the solicitor general of Upper Canada and an officer in the militia, acted as the judge advocate or prosecutor of the Hunters captured at the windmill. He was a conscientious and meticulous lawyer but a humane man, and agonized with Lieutenant Governor Arthur over the question of which prisoners should suffer capital punishment. This illustration dates from Draper's later life. (National Archives of Canada, C-3543)

future mayor of the town, and Counter may have cut a few corners to save on costs, but on one occasion this brought the wrath of Sheriff Macdonell down on him. The men in Heustis's cell had protested about an inedible bread issue and the sheriff, testing it himself, agreed with them. He sent for Counter and, within earshot of the delighted prisoners, tore a wide and deep strip off the merchant, a devout Methodist, by means of a diatribe "in which certain profane expressions were freely introduced, without much regard to the religious professions of the contractor."[19]

The bluff but big-hearted Macdonell proved to be a good friend to the prisoners. When New York border communities and private individuals began to send money to purchase comforts for some of the men, he collected it into a general fund from which he provided all his charges with warm clothing (many had arrived at Fort Henry nearly naked), other necessaries, and some luxuries. Under Macdonell's system, every prisoner benefited and no man went short, but it incited complaints from men whose relatives and friends sent them money for their own personal use. Several Hunters questioned the sheriff's honesty and complained he pocketed a great part of these funds, about $7,000 in their estimation, but Macdonell's correspondence with Lieutenant Governor Arthur on the subject indicates that not only were the sums involved much smaller, but he also kept careful records of what was received and what was disbursed. To get around what they regarded as ill-placed generosity on the sheriff's part, some men received private funds sewn into clothing or transmitted through the good offices of a Catholic priest, Father Patrick Dollard of Kingston, who was a daily visitor to the fort. In his capacity as a cell "captain," Heustis once complained about the matter to Macdonell. "I think you ought to allow us a little money to spend for ourselves," Heustis suggested, and the sheriff's reply was characteristic: "G_d d__n your soul, you've no right to think, there are men paid to think for you."[20]

The prisoners were, of course, the subject of intense concern on the part of their families and fellow citizens. Arthur, Draper, Dundas and Macdonell were deluged with community petitions or personal requests for mercy, particularly for the younger men. The prisoners were permitted to see family members who travelled to Kingston, and Macdonell usually provided a separate room for this purpose. Stephen Wright, who joined his fellow Hunters in the fort after he recovered from his wound, received a visit from his clergyman father but Wright did not have much to say to him. A female cousin of Daniel Heustis went to Toronto and threw herself at the knees of a somewhat disconcerted Sir George Arthur to plead for her relative, and she was not the only woman to do so.[21]

There were also a number of official American delegations that made their way to Kingston or Toronto. The first such mission, consisting of Congressman John Fine and lawyer Charles Myers from Ogdensburg, arrived in Kingston three days after the fighting had ended at Prescott, to find the hotels full of countrymen with a similar purpose. Fine and Myers were shown every courtesy and visited Fort Henry, later reporting that the food was good and sufficient and the cells "large and clean."[22] During their visit, many of the younger prisoners cried, and when they asked these boys if they needed anything, one pleaded for some candy. Moved by this experience, Fine and Myers wrote to Judge Jonas Jones of Brockville asking to him to exert his influence to obtain clemency for these lads to dry the "gushing tears" of mothers across Jefferson County.[23] The *Cornwall Observer*, learning of this correspondence, was quick to proclaim that Upper Canada "would not be thrown off its guard by any puppet shows" that Ogdensburg, "that vile nest of infamy and piracy, may choose to play" as Canadians had not forgotten the cheering "made by the thousands who lined the banks of the Tuesday of the battle," whenever the crowd "thought the pirates were making head way."[24]

Another prominent visitor was Judge Samuel Brown of Brownville in Jefferson County, who was anxious to learn of the circumstances of the death of his son Charles, killed on 13 November, and hoped to recover his body. Brown met with Dundas and Sheriff Macdonell and he also spoke with Surgeon Stuart Chisholm, who had tried to treat his son, and with the newly-promoted Captain Charles Parker of the Royal Marines, who informed him that the body had been cremated during the fighting but also made a point of restoring the young man's sword to the judge. Brown visited the men in Fort Henry, who told him they were well treated, and, on his return, reported that their cells were "airy, spacious and well-lighted, clean and comfortably warmed." He had nothing but praise for Sheriff Macdonell, who opened his accounts of the prisoners' comfort fund to Brown.[25]

There were also many written communications to the British authorities from various towns and village across northern New York pleading for mercy for local men. Typical was a petition from the citizens of Lyme in Jefferson County asking for special consideration to be given to Charles Smith of that village, a young fellow of twenty-one and basically a good boy who always cared for his aged parents but who, sadly, had been misled by wicked older men. It appears that Smith was not quite the paragon of virtue his neighbours believed him to be. A letter from a friend whose grasp of spelling was uncertain, found on Smith when he was captured, urged him not to be "like mr. Vanrensalear, but go ahead, be like M'Kenzie, do not spare a tory and if there is not rope enough to hang the tories you can by maore."[26]

Both the petition and the incriminating letter were published in the Canadian newspapers, which delighted in reproducing correspondence written to and by the prisoners, or about them. Some made for sad reading. Polly Peeler, the daughter of Joel Peeler, expressed the hope her father was "not as guilty as some are, and that we may yet see you once more this side of the grave."[27] Others verged on the comical – consider the epistle written by Lyman Lewis to a friend in Cape Vincent, which contained the astonishing statement that his fellow Hunters had now "for some cause or other, made up our mind that the good people of Canada do not wish a change in their form of government, therefore it is the height of folly to say more; so fare you well."[28] But there were also threats. The *Chronicle* published a note addressed to "the cheif Magistrate of Kingston, Upper canady," which warned that, if any of the prisoners were executed, the correspondent would invade with an army of 10,000 men "that neither fears death nor hell."[29] Arthur got a similar missive from an American who told him he would rather see the lieutenant governor's "damned head

speared then even the freedom of the Canadas and I would be your executioner."[30]

Inevitably, the man who excited the most interest was the famous Polish general. The Swede played it out to the end and his masquerade was aided by an amazing lack of sophistication on the part of North Americans, who were seemingly unable to distinguish European accents, and by articles in the press containing von Schoultz's version of his life. So strong was the popular wish that the man be the romantic figure he claimed to be, few believed it when a witness to his wedding correctly identified him as Nils Gustaf von Schoultz, a Swedish national who had deserted his family before coming to the United States. Nor did many believe the assertions of the New York Polish community that von Schoultz was not one of their countrymen and probably not a participant in the recent uprising in Poland. The Swede fooled most people who came in contact with him – among them Major John Richardson, who visited him at Fort Henry.[31]

Richardson was ushered into a casemate to find, huddled "around a stove of sheet iron, made intensely hot," a band "of shivering wretches, one half of them without coats, and either warming their fingers or cooking some article of food" which left on his mind "a sentiment of disgust." In contrast, the man he had come to see was aloof from his fellow prisoners, pacing up and down with folded arms, wearing a dark frock coat and a forage cap "lightly and comingly thrown over his brown hair, and his face, naturally pale." Richardson, like most British officers, disliked wearing uniform unless absolutely necessary and was himself clad in a Spanish fur jacket and a velvet cap with tassels hanging over his head *à la Polonaise*. Richardson thought that this somewhat outlandish costume caused von Schoultz to mistake him for a Polish "countryman," but this false assumption was dispelled when he approached the Swede and, speaking French, expressed regret that he should find a Pole as an enemy of Britain, a nation that had always supported the cause of Polish independence. These words "seemed to startle" von Schoultz (as well they should have), Richardson thought, but the Swede was a veteran *poseur* and recovered quickly, replying in French that he had been deluded but was resigned to his fate. While two young officers of the 93rd, also under the spell this man seemed to cast on everyone who came into contact with him, looked on in fascination, Richardson talked to the Hunter leader for a few minutes and then shook hands and parted. For the rest of his life, Richardson would remember that tragic figure pacing up and down a casemate in Fort Henry – but then John Richardson was a somewhat sensitive soul who had already published a number of novels and would soon leave the service to become a full-time writer.[32]

The battle of the windmill was over but American and Canadian newspapers continued to exchange fire throughout the winter of 1838-1839. Stressing that the greater part of the invaders had been misled by their superiors, a New York journalist proposed exchanging these poor misguided fellows for the true culprits – William Lyon Mackenzie, Bill Johnston and John Birge – and to "pledge the word and honor of every man in the whole line of frontier counties, in this State, that not a finger shall be lifted again in hostility to the lawful Government of the adjoining British possessions."[33] To this, the *Kingston Chronicle* responded tartly that Canadians would be glad to accept such an offer but they would have problems trusting its sincerity because the people of New York had done little to prevent their fellow citizens from invading the province "to plunder and murder us," and they "can scarcely expect that we should place much confidence in the sincerity of their profes-

sions when they promise future friendship."[34] It was now a legal matter, the *Chronicle* emphasized, and when Americans "can find public virtue enough to enforce their own laws, they will then be justified in appealing to us not to execute our own." As for the claim that many at the windmill were "seduced" to join the invasion, the *Toronto Patriot* stressed that they took part "in full knowledge of the plans of those with whom they became united" and the affair "was one of deliberate and unprovoked murder and carnage."[35] Touché.

Some American journalists appeared to have learned nothing from the recent events. The *Onondaga Standard* (which really should have known better as a number of its readers were languishing in Fort Henry) went so far as to make threats if the any of the prisoners were executed:

Shall the earth drink the blood of the victims at Kingston, and it be not found to moisten the roots of the Tree of Liberty, that they strike deeper, and its branches spread wider and farther. Had [the Canadians listened] to the dictates of policy and clemency, all might have been well. But if they go forward in the murderous work they have begun, it scarcely needs a seer to predict ... that the possession of the Canadas by a trans-Atlantic power is incompatible with the peace, safety and prosperity of the American people.[36]

To this chauvinistic volley, the *Montreal Herald* replied that, if Upper Canadians had wanted to be "free" from Britain, they would have joined Mackenzie's uprising at a time when there were no regular troops in the province – the fact that the Scotsman's followers were so few in number spoke for itself.[37] Taking direct aim at Onondaga County, the *Niagara Chronicle* noted that most of the prisoners did not profess membership in a Christian congregation and yet these same men were the "free and enlightened," who come to give civil and *religious* liberty to Canada. If so many unbaptized heathens can be collected from a county or two, as these were, how many may there be in the "Empire State." By the way, are there any Churches in Salina at all?[38]

In addition to crowing over American discomfiture, Canadian newspapers stressed that the would-be "liberators" came from a nation that maintained the institution of slavery. This was done subtly by reprinting reports of Royal Navy officers on anti-slavery patrols in the South Atlantic or, in the case of one paper, overtly by printing a rather bad piece of doggerel:

> United States, your banner wears
> Two emblems, one of fame;
> Alas! the other that it bears
> Reminds us of your shame.
>
> The white man's liberty in types
> Stands blazon'd by your stars
> But what's the meaning of the stripes?
> They mean your negro's scars.[39]

It was to be expected that, in such an exchange of paper bullets, William Lyon Mackenzie would take a prominent part. By late 1838, his *Gazette* was only printed at infrequent intervals as it was suffering from a lack of funds and subscribers, but, as ever, the Scotsman was quick into the fray. Although he disavowed any connection with the attack on Prescott he took direct aim at Colonel William Worth, whom he held responsible for the invasion. On Worth's head "does the blood rest," thundered Mackenzie, but the fractious scribbler soon switched targets to President Martin Van Buren.[40] On 21 November 1838,

under pressure to assist the Kingston prisoners, Van Buren had issued a neutrality proclamation intended to make his administration's position crystal clear on the matter of raids on the Canadas. It informed Americans that their government did not support such actions and those who "engaged in these criminal enterprizes ... whatever may be the condition to which they may be reduced," could not "expect the interference of the Government in any form, on their behalf."[41] Since this declaration struck at the heart of popular support for the patriots, Mackenzie criticized Van Buren in harsh terms as a paid tool of Britain but this was going too far for one Americans journalist, who asked why this "dirty, cowardly Scotch vagabond" was permitted "to print the grossest and most outrageous abuse of the President of the United States."[42] Another American newspaper suggested that the government trade the Canadian rebel to the British authorities for fifteen or twenty of the prisoners held at Kingston.[43]

Van Buren's proclamation was debated at public meetings in the border communities of northern New York such as Cape Vincent, Ogdensburg and Watertown during the winter of 1838. The main purpose of these meetings was to organize assistance for the prisoners at Fort Henry, but it is clear from the resolutions drafted that there had been a major shift in public opinion since the previous winter. The loss of life at Prescott had shocked many and there was much anger at the men regarded responsible, who had apparently escaped, while deluded young local boys were languishing in a British fortress. The people of the border towns admitted the guilt of these men but asked for mercy for them. Major General Winfield Scott, whom Van Buren had again sent north, was a frequent speaker at these meetings, and Scott was as blunt as ever, particularly when it came to military matters. In January 1839, he told the citizens of Ogdensburg that, if there was "sufficient cause to invade the Canadas, I would lead you on; but there is none," and "though you should effect a landing with 40,000, – 8,000 disciplined British troops would quickly annihilate or disperse the whole."[44]

Americans support for the Patriot Hunters might be declining but two events that occurred in November and December 1838 demonstrated that the clandestine organization remained a threat to Canadians. On the night of 15 November, a group of Hunters, supposedly led by one Benjamin Lett, crossed the Niagara River with the intention of apprehending or killing Captain Edgeworth Ussher, the militia officer on whose property MacNab's men had camped during the occupation of Navy Island. They forced one of Ussher's neighbours at gun point to guide them to the young officer's residence, Milford Lodge on the bank of the river, where they banged on the door. Ignoring the pleas of his wife not to answer the summons, Ussher went to the door and died instantly when a Hunter (Lett later bragged that he did the deed) shot him through a sidelight window. Having accomplished their purpose, the patriots then returned to the United States, leaving behind a province appalled by the murder of an innocent man. Arthur offered an award of £500 for information leading to the arrest and conviction of the culprits but no culprit was ever brought to justice for this crime.[45]

The second and more serious event took place on the Detroit frontier. In response to the decisions made at Cleveland the previous September, Lucius V. Bierce, the Hunter general for the northwest area, had assembled about 600 men with the intention of invading western Upper Canada as soon as he was joined by John Birge's division from northeastern New York. Birge never arrived, of course, and Beirce was further ham-pered by the ever-alert Brady, who seized most of his weapons. The Hunter commander was on the point of calling off the operation but some of his men became impatient and, hijacking a small river steamer, landed near Windsor during the early morning of 4 December. The invaders, whose battle cry was "Remember Prescott!", numbered less than 200, mostly Americans, under the command of a "General" Putnam and a "Colonel" Harvell.[46]

Moving toward the village of Windsor, the Hunters encountered resistance from a detachment of militia stationed in a civilian store used as a guardhouse. Deciding to set fire to it to flush the defenders out, they went to the nearby house of a black Canadian named Mills to get embers from his hearth fire. The Americans invited Mills to join their cause and, when he not only refused but exclaimed "three cheers for the Queen!," they killed him.[47] The guardhouse was destroyed by flames and the occupants taken prisoner, and Putnam's men continued on to Windsor, where they set fire to the steamer *Thames* in retaliation for the destruction of the *Caroline*. On their way they encountered Surgeon John Hume of the 32nd Foot, who, awakened by the alarm bells, was headed to Windsor to offer his services to the local militia. The Hunters killed Hume and mutilated his limbs with an axe before leaving the remains for the local hogs.[48]

Most of the invaders were deployed in an orchard at the edge of Windsor when they were attacked by five companies of Canadian militia. There was a brisk skirmish during which both Putnam and Harvell were killed. The latter, a 6-foot 2-inch native of Kentucky, wrapped the Hunters' flag, a tricolour with a crescent and two stars, around his body and "defended himself with a bowie knife to the very last" – or so his comrades claimed.[49] Getting the worst of the battle, the invaders then fled through the streets of Windsor toward the Detroit River "with a velocity unexampled in the annals of locomotion."[50]

It was at this point, about 6.30 A.M., that the local Canadian militia commander, Colonel John Prince, arrived on the scene. A 42-year-old native of Kent in England, a judge and an elected member of the Legislative Assembly of Upper Canada, Prince had been active in the defence of the Detroit border since the patriot troubles had begun in January. He was angry because the prisoners taken at Pelee Island in March were being treated as prisoners of war, and he was afraid that they would not suffer the full measure of the law but would simply be deported to the United States. When he learned of the deaths of Hume and Mills, he decided the culprits would not escape this time and he "resolved upon shooting at once and without a moment's hesitation every bandit that happened to be captured and brought in."[51]

The first prisoner to be executed, an unidentified American, was shot and bayoneted on Prince's personal order, while the second, a Detroit silversmith named Bennett, was apparently given a chance to run for his life. Bennett didn't make it. The execution of a third man, an American named Denison, was delayed for a few minutes while Charles Eliot, a magistrate and militia officer, argued with Prince that the man should be punished by due legal process. But Prince was adamant and Denison, wounded in one arm, was taken behind a nearby building, killed with a musket shot in the head, and thrown in the yard of the nearby Anglican church. A fourth man, 35-year-old Stephen Miller from Florence, Ohio, had been wounded in the earlier fighting and taken into the parlour of a local minister for treatment. When Prince's men reported his presence to their commander, he erupted, "Damn his eyes, have him out and shoot him!"[52] The wretched Miller was bundled into a buffalo robe, hauled into the front yard and killed by bayonets and musket fire – his disembowelled and nearly naked body lay for all to see in a Windsor street for several hours, much to the joy of the village hogs, who fell on it with gusto. The fifth and final execution, that of an unidentified man, was deliberately carried out on the river bank in full view of those on board an American vessel just to make sure the message got back to the United States.[53]

The so-called "Battle of Windsor," their last major raid on the Canadas, was yet another disaster for the patriots. Of the 164 invaders, 21 were killed, including the two leaders, and 44 captured (5 of whom were shot on Prince's orders) while the rest made good their escape, although as many as 20 may have frozen to death while trying to recross the icy river. Never again would the Hunters seriously threaten Canadians because, as Hugh Brady commented, so miserable was the fate of the invaders that American "disturbers of the Peace, are returning to their homes, and no farther attempts to violate our neutral relations, for the present are apprehended."[54]

John Prince made no attempt to hide his responsibility for the executions. On the night of the battle, he wrote in his diary:

A cold day. Awoke at 6 A.M. by an alarm gun at Sandwich. Rose & saw a fire at Windsor. Proceeded there with the Militia and found it in possession of brigands & pirates. We attacked them & killed 27 & took about 20 prisoners. I ordered the first 5 taken to be shot. We lost 4 men, & poor Dr. Hume, Asst. Staff Surgeon who was cruelly murdered by them![55]

Prince was unequivocal in his official report that several prisoners "were brought in just at the close and immediately after the engagement, all of whom I ordered to be shot upon the spot, and which was done accordingly."[56] For this remark, he was known for years afterward as "Shot Accordingly" Prince.

In Detroit, a $1,000 reward was offered for Prince alive and $800 for him dead. His actions were debated in the interna-

"Shot accordingly:"
Colonel John Prince
(1796-1870)

In December 1838, a
Hunter invasion
across the Detroit
River at Windsor was
decisively repulsed by
the local militia.
Their commander,
Colonel John Prince,
wanting to ensure that
the culprits were punished,
ordered the execution of five
American prisoners. Prince was
court martialled for this act but basically
exonerated. A price was put on his head in the United States but he
became a hero to many Canadians who shared his exasperation with
the seemingly interminable border raids. (Archives of Ontario)

the Legislative Assembly of Upper Canada when he entered to
take up his seat at the next session and feted at public dinners
held in his honour. At one of these functions, Prince not only
took credit for killing the five Hunter prisoners at Windsor but
expressed regret so many had been taken alive to "fatten in our
Jails" instead of "being (as they ought to be) swept off the face
of God's Creation, for where are sinners equal to them?"[57]

Lieutenant Colonel William Draper would have disagreed
with these sentiments because Draper believed in due legal
process. That process commenced at 10 A.M. on Wednesday, 28
November 1838, when, in accordance with Sir George Arthur's
wish that the leaders of the Prescott invasion be tried first, Daniel George and Nils von Schoultz, both handcuffed, were escorted into the officers' mess building just outside the main
gate of Fort Henry. Waiting for them, assembled around a large
table, were Draper and the fifteen members of the court martial, resplendent in their best scarlet and gold or silver lace.
Along the back wall of the room was a line of soldiers, and the
flag of the Onondaga Hunters, taken down from the windmill,
was on prominent display as were many of the Hunters' captured weapons. Also present that day was a civilian lawyer, John
A. Macdonald, who had been engaged by Daniel George's
brother-in-law to help with the Hunter officer's defence.[58]

George's relative had chosen well. John Alexander Macdonald, just twenty-three years of age, had only been called to
the bar in early 1836 but had quickly acquired a reputation as
one of the most skilful lawyers in Kingston. At the beginning of
the summer he had defended eight men accused of treason
during Mackenzie's uprising. Most people expected a guilty
verdict but Macdonald was able to win his clients an acquittal
and a Kingston newspaper had remarked that the accused were

tional press and the British parliament, and a group of his own
officers tried to have him removed from command. The irascible Prince fought a duel with one detractor, publicly horsewhipped two others, and inserted an advertisement in the local
newspaper warning his enemies that every night he set out
twelve spring-guns loaded with buckshot and two man-traps
on the grounds of his property. Lieutenant Governor Arthur,
who was not unsympathetic, arraigned Prince before a court
martial in early 1839 which, though it gave him a slap on the
wrist, basically exonerated him. Many Canadians, who shared
Prince's exasperation with the seemingly unending border depredations, heartily approved his actions and he was cheered by

defended with great skill by "Mr. J. A. Macdonald, who, though one of the youngest barristers in the Province, is rapidly rising in his profession."[59] A few weeks later, Macdonald became involved as co-counsel in another prominent case, a suit for illegal arrest brought by John Ashley against Lieutenant Colonel Henry Dundas. Ashley had been the jailer at Fort Henry on the night of 22 July when fifteen political prisoners escaped to freedom, and Dundas, certain Ashley had assisted them, imprisoned him for eight hours without a warrant. Dundas was represented by no less than Christopher A. Hagerman, attorney general of Upper Canada, local member of the Legislative Assembly and the most prominent lawyer in Kingston, but nonetheless, displaying "much ingenuity and legal knowledge," Macdonald won his plaintiff damages of £200.[60] People in Kingston were taking notice of this rising legal star and a steady stream of clients began to make their way to his law office on Quarry (now Wellington) Street.

With his career on the ascendant, it is curious that Macdonald took George's case. The citizens of Kingston, all potential future clients, hated the Hunter prisoners. Even worse, Daniel George was going to be tried by a court martial, a process in which Macdonald could only advise his client, not plead for him, as George had to conduct his own defence. Finally, George had been caught red-handed; the evidence against him, much of it contained in his own pocket book, proved his guilt beyond a doubt. It would be difficult, if not impossible, for Macdonald to get an acquittal and, given the mood of the town, even a vigorous but unsuccessful defence might arouse bad feelings against him. Despite all these negative factors, Macdonald accepted the brief.[61]

Once the members of the board had been sworn, Draper read the charges against George and asked for his plea. It was "Not Guilty." The judge advocate then called the Crown witnesses, including Levi Chipman, who identified George as an officer, and Lieutenant George Leary, RN, of the *Cobourg*, who recounted the circumstances of his capture on 13 November and elaborated on the evidence in the Hunter paymaster's notebook. George conducted his own defence and his questioning of the Crown witnesses, almost certainly directed by Macdonald, was not unskilful. George's case continued on the following day, 29 November, until noon, when the prisoner asked for time to prepare a defence statement. This request was granted and the court then took up the matter of Nils von Schoultz.[62]

The charge was read and the question put: "How say you, Nils Szoltecky Von Schoultz?" The response, "Guilty," surprised the court.[63] Draper immediately cautioned the Swede, "pointing out to him the right to be tried," the severe penalty of the law for his crime, "and the impossibility of the Court interfering in his case to modify it."[64] But von Schoultz was adamant. He had been deceived, he admitted, but it was useless to deny he was the leader of the invaders, and again said clearly, "I plead guilty." Draper then presented the considerable case he had assembled against the Swede, including his own sworn statement in which he declared that Birge and Johnston were the senior officers of the invasion and he had only assumed command to "lead the party back to the American shore."[65] Crown witness Jean-Baptiste Rousseau testified that von Schoultz was in command throughout the week, as did Levi Chipman. Captain Charles Parker described the battle of 13 November and Ensign Edward Smith of Jessup's Volunteers informed the court of the circumstances of von Schoultz's capture. Throughout all this testimony, von Schoultz remained stoically impassive, "as unmoved as a rock," and only asked a few questions.[66]

That was until Draper, following his own decision "to introduce everything which might have a tendency to throw light on the character or conduct of the prisoners," called Surgeon William Gardner of the 83rd Foot as a witness.[67] Gardner testified that he had examined the body of Lieutenant William Johnson and had discovered "several gun-shot wounds on the left hip passing through to the right" and these were the cause of death. But Gardner had also discovered "a mutilation, which I perceive to have been performed by a sharp instrument, the excision of the penis."[68]

According to those present, von Schoultz was shocked by these words. This is not surprising as the public recitation of the grim medical details shattered the persona the Swede had carefully constructed for himself as an aristocratic and freedom-loving adventurer, a knight-errant who had come from a land far away to free those suffering under the tyrant's heel. Knights-errant slay dragons and rescue fair damsels in distress, they do not desecrate corpses. There was no suggestion on the part of the court that von Schoultz had been personally involved in the mutilation but the implication was clear that, as the Hunter commander, he was being regarded as responsible for the actions of his subordinates, who, on the basis of Gardner's evidence, were clearly not the flower of chivalry.

Von Schoultz brooded on the matter and when the trial resumed on Friday, 30 November, he asked to address the court. This was granted and the Swede read a prepared statement denying he had ever shown any inhumanity to the British and Canadian dead and wounded. Far from it, he had turned over enemy wounded in his position as he "had no means of taking care of them and we had already given up all the bedding and every comfort we could for their accommodation."[69] He then came to the matter which particularly troubled him:

As regards the maltreatment of Captain Johnson's body – I tried to get the body away but the fire was such that I could

John Alexander Macdonald (1815-1891)
The family of Daniel George engaged the services of a rising young Kingston barrister, 23-year-old John A. Macdonald, to assist George during his trial. Accepting the case was a risky move on Macdonald's part as feelings in Kingston ran high against the American brigands imprisoned in nearby Fort Henry. Through George, Macdonald met Nils von Schoultz but, as the Hunter leader was determined to plead guilty, could do nothing for him except draft his will. John A. Macdonald went on to greater things, becoming the first prime minister of the new Dominion of Canada formed by Confederation in 1867. To the end of his days, however, Macdonald never forgot the haunting figure in Fort Henry whom he believed to be a noble but misled Polish freedom-fighter. (National Archives of Canada, C-10745)

not. Two men were wounded in the attempt. I put a sentinel to shoot the hogs that might approach the body and he fired to keep them off. This may show that I had no concern in mutilating his body.

"I have no witnesses to call, " he concluded. The court then rendered their verdict, which was pronounced by the president: "Nils Szoltecky von Schoultz, you shall suffer death by being hanged by the neck till dead at such time and at such place as His Excellency, the L[ieutenan]t Gov[ernor] shall be pleased to state."[70]

The Swede was removed and the trial of Dorephus Abbey commenced. It was of fairly short duration because the evidence was overwhelming and Abbey seems to have been disliked by his comrades, as the three Crown witnesses, Chipman, Mailhotte and Rousseau, were more definite about his involvement in the battle than they were with the other Hunter leaders. Abbey got no sympathy (but perhaps a few hastily-hidden smiles) from the court when they learned Colonel Richard Fraser had struck him with the flat of his sword while he was under a flag of truce. He was found guilty but the court reserved judgement until the following day.[71]

On Saturday, 1 December, the court resumed to hear Daniel George's statement in his defence. Prepared with Macdonald's assistance, it discounted the testimony of Chipman, Mailhotte and Rousseau and claimed there was no reliable evidence that George had actually been at the windmill, since he was captured on the river, and that capture was illegal because it took place on the American side of the international boundary. The court considered for a few minutes and then found George guilty, and sentenced him and Abbey to be hanged.[72]

On 3 December, a fourth Hunter officer, Martin Woodruff, appeared before the court. Draper, facing the task of trying so many men using substantially the same evidence, now began to speed up the process by bringing the prisoners before the court in batches, and four others, including William Gates, all captured with Daniel George in the boat on 13 November, appeared with Woodruff. Almost every prisoner had been taken in arms on Canadian soil and, along with British subjects, had participated in hostilities that had caused the death of British subjects, the three factors necessary to secure a conviction. For this reason, Draper was able to move the legal procedure along with celerity. Price Senter from Onondaga County remembered that the prisoners were "brought in, handcuffed between two rows of English soldiers with loaded guns" and "stood with our backs to the wall, facing judges who were seated around a large table in the centre of the room."[73] The evidence was presented, the court went into conference and, if a majority of at least two thirds of the members found the accused guilty, he was condemned. In those cases – and there were not many – where there was less than a two thirds majority convinced of the prisoner's guilt, he was acquitted.[74]

The Hunters, not comprehending how precise was the wording of the act under which they were being tried, concluded not unnaturally that their trials were perfunctory and they were being driven to the gallows with indecent haste. As Gates remarked:

Our indictment being read, we were severally asked, "Guilty? or Not Guilty?" "Not Guilty" was our response. The Queen's witness was asked if he recognized us; to which he replied, "I do not." No other questions were asked, and we were remanded back to our prison room wondering what the sentence of the court would be on such overwhelming testimony![75]

The verdict was guilty and the sentence was death.

On 5 December, eleven men, including the Swete brothers and Joel Peeler, were tried and all were found guilty. From this day until the court martial was concluded on 4 January 1839, except for a brief three-day recess, 24-26 December, at Christmas, the Hunters were tried in groups of four to fourteen. On two days, 20 and 29 December, the eight foreign prisoners "who appear to have been much put upon" or misled by the Hunter officers, appeared and translators were provided for them.[76] There were eight of these men: Philip Conrad, Henry Jantzen, Sebastian Meyers and Joseph Wagner were from the German states; Charles Horey and Peter Meyer were French; and there were two *bona fide* Poles, Ernest Berends and John Okonskie. All were found guilty.[77]

Daniel Heustis's turn came, with eleven others, on 17 December. His family had procured a lawyer for him but, given the procedure in a court martial, this man "was only permitted to remain in the room during our trial, he was not permitted to say a word."[78] The usual evidence was given by the Crown witnesses and "the members of the court busied themselves for about two minutes and a half, apparently in a very profound exchange of opinions among themselves, and then we were remanded to our prison again, without any intimation as to what the verdict was." It was guilty, and Heustis and his companions were sentenced to be hanged.[79]

Four days later, Stephen Wright appeared with eleven others, all of whom pleaded "Not Guilty." There is no record in the official transcript but Wright claims that, when he asked for an adjournment to procure witnesses, it was denied by Draper:

> I told the Judge Advocate, … that I thought it was unjust to be tried for our lives and not be allowed time to procure witnesses. He answered "that they would do no good," and I thought he was angry at my remark. I then said "the proceedings of the court-martial are more like condemning than trying the prisoners." At which he started up, and called me an insolent impertinent scoundrel, and he then proceeded to business. We were all tried and convicted, including the examination of one witness, in twenty-eight minutes, in a very summary manner. What a noble specimen of justice toward Americans in Canada.[80]

One of the few light moments came on 27 December when Garrett Hicks, that friend of the canine world, appeared before the court. It was Heustis's opinion that Hicks's uncouth appearance caused Draper to suppose that the dog lover was "three pence short of a shilling" as "the English say, when they suspect a man is a little deficient in shrewdness." If so, Hicks soon disabused the prosecutor of that notion:

> "Well, Hicks," said the Judge-Advocate, "did you fight any?"
>
> "Yes, I fit as well as I could," said Hicks, in a blunt, indifferent, care-for-nothing manner.
>
> "How many did you kill?"
>
> "Well, I don't know; I guessed I killed as many of them as they did of me."

The court enjoyed a hearty laugh at this quick reply of "Old Hicks," and "finding him not so verdant as they had imagined, let him go without further questioning." They also found Hicks guilty and sentenced him to be hanged by the neck until dead.[81] Of the 137 Hunters tried by the Kingston court martial between 26 November 1838 and 4 January, 136 of Hicks's companions were sentenced to be hanged with 20 recommended for mercy. Only four men were acquitted.[82]

CHAPTER ELEVEN

"I smile through a tear:" Punishment

December 1838 to 1844

You own I am constant, yet tell me I'm cold,
And must I my youth's early sorrows unfold?
Must I wake to remember the joys which are fled,
Now hope is extinguished and passion is dead?
I have lost in youth's morn all that life can endear,
And though I seem cheerful, I smile through a tear.

My parents, though humble, are happy and good,
We could boast of our honour, if not of our blood;
My lover – oh! how sad the tale I shall tell!
For Poland he fought, and for freedom he fell;
He was noble and brave – to my soul he was dear,
His fame claims a smile, though it shines through a tear.

In vain would I picture my agonized heart,
My parents oft soothe, yet no balm can impart –
They wept o'er the child – they could not relieve,
And the cold hand of death left me early to grieve:
They sleep in the grave – the loved and the dear,
Yet though I seem happy, I smile through a tear.[1]

Until the latter half of the 20th century, hanging was the most widely used form of capital punishment in the English-speaking world. It was, one knowledgeable commentator has written, not so much a good way to kill a man "as to advertize the fact" and since the intent was that this grim spectacle serve as a warning, most executions in Britain and its possessions were public until the late 19th century.[2] In Britain, the Crown hangman was a well known figure and usually called "Jack Ketch" after the man who held the post from 1678 to 1686. Hangmen often started out as criminals before moving to the other side of the legal fence. Jack Ketch, for example, was succeeded by John Crosland, who, having been condemned to death for horse theft along with his father and brother, was let off after he agreed to hang them, which he promptly did. Despised and feared, British executioners tended to be rather stolid types inured to insult – "I never quarrel with my customers," was the credo of James Botting, who held the post from 1817 to 1824.[3]

The sentence of the law was that the condemned person be hanged by the neck until dead (*sus per col* in the old legal terminology) but it was not the law's concern whether that death occurred almost instantly, through the fracture of the cervical vertebra, which abruptly terminates respiratory and pulmonary functions, or more slowly, by strangulation. Until the 1840s, when a board of Irish doctors calculated a table of drop distances to be used for persons of different weights and heights to try to ensure that death occurred quickly by fracture of the vertebra, hangmen followed their own judgement in the matter, and sometimes their clients died quickly, and sometimes they did not. Even after the implementation of the Irish "long drop" table, death by strangulation was not uncommon. A British parliamentary commission investigating capital punishment in the late 19th century discovered that in nine of forty hangings, the spine of the condemned had been neither broken nor dislocated. There was also the hazard that, if the hangman used too thin a rope or misjudged the drop, the condemned person might be decapitated. Such an occurrence upset everyone because it was not the punishment prescribed by law, made an awful mess that had to be cleaned up, and reduced the value of a negotiable asset, since part of a hangman's compensation often came from the sale of his client's remains to the medical profession for anatomy instruction. Hangmen usually preferred that their clients died by fracture of the vertebra because it was not only neater, it was quicker – a necessary consideration if the hangman had to process several clients at the same time.[4]

The three essentials for a good hanging are a strong and thick rope, a well-tied and properly placed knot, and a drop correctly adjusted to the weight and build of the client. The rope has to be capable of holding a ton of dead weight and experienced hangmen always stretched it beforehand to reduce the "spring" in it and thus the possibility of the noose shifting at the end of the drop. Since the knot usually slipped to the right when the trap of the gallows opened, it was best placed beside and under the left ear so it would end up under the client's chin at the end of the drop, snapping the head back and fracturing the spinal vertebra. In the words of one of the last hangmen employed in Britain,

> The knot is the secret of it. We have to put it on the left lower jaw, and if we have it on that side, when he falls it finishes under the chin and throws the chin back; but if the knot is on the right-hand side it would finish up behind his neck, and throw his neck forward, which would be strangulation. He might live on the rope a quarter of an hour then.[5]

The length of the drop is usually between eight and fourteen feet, depending on the strength and size of the client's neck muscles, and his or her height and weight. According to the same hangman quoted above, if the job is done properly, there "is not a movement on the body with a good executioner. You cannot see a movement on the body."[6]

The responsibility for carrying out the death sentences pronounced by the court martial at Kingston belonged to Sheriff Allan Macdonell, and as soon as the first "Guilty" verdict was handed down, he began construction of a new gallows in the yard behind the Kingston jail. Macdonell used local carpenters to do this job, and he had to pay them well as tradespeople thought such work degrading and would only undertake it with great reluctance. The dislike of having anything to do with executions was common in Upper Canada – the first man to suffer capital punishment in the province was hanged in 1800 by a fellow prisoner who received a pardon in payment for the service. There was no Crown executioner in the 1830s and sheriffs like Macdonell were forced to use whoever they could pay, persuade or pressure to do the business, or, failing that, to do it themselves. This was the case with the execution of the American James Morreau, hanged in July 1838 for leading the

Launching pad to eternity: Gallows in Upper Canada, 1838
Eleven of the Hunters captured at the windmill were hanged for their crimes. Six were officers or ringleaders; two were implicated in the killing and mutilation of Lieutenant Johnson of the 83rd Foot; and three had taken part in other attacks on Upper Canada. The remaining prisoners were either released or transported to a penal colony for life. Until the 1860s, executions in Canada were public and often attended by large crowds. This drawing actually shows the gallows constructed at Toronto to execute the Canadian rebels Lount and Matthews in April 1838. (National Archives of Canada, C-1242)

Short Hills raid. Sheriff Hamilton of the Niagara District failed to secure "Mr. Ketch … that sensitive functionary bolted," and was "obliged to *execute* his own duty."[7] Wishing to avoid a similar fate, Macdonell engaged two men to serve as executioners. Their names are not known but there is no evidence to substantiate the preposterous claim of one Hunter author that the sheriff asked for bids from parties wishing to contract for the work at a price "per dozen" men, gallows to be supplied "but carts, ropes, ladders, &c., to be found by the contractor."[8]

The new gallows was completed by 5 December when Macdonell received the lieutenant governor's warrant to execute Nils von Schoultz. Before signing the warrant, Arthur had requested the attorney general, Christopher Hagerman, to review the transcript of the Swede's trial and Hagerman had reported that he could find no legal grounds to mitigate the sentence passed by the court. Sheriff Macdonell was horrified, however, to see that the warrant specified that von Schoultz be hanged at 8 A.M. on 8 December 1838 "at or near Fort Henry," not at his new gallows in front of the town jail.[9] Since the instructions in a warrant of execution must be carried out exactly, he dashed off an urgent note to Arthur late in the evening of 5 December to inform him that it would be next to impossible to build a gallows near the fort in three days because local workmen would not do "disgraceful" work like this in the area of the fort which was a very "public place."[10] It is not known why the lieutenant governor directed that von Schoultz be executed on military property and it may have been a simple mistake on Arthur's part because he responded to Macdonell's note by granting him permission to hang the Swede wherever he saw fit. This confusion over the place of execution is possibly the origin of the myth (for that is what it is) that von Schoultz requested to die by a firing squad, the fate of a soldier, rather than by the rope, the fate of a criminal.[11]

Where the famous Polish general met his end: Gallows at Fort Henry

This watercolour of Fort Henry done by a British officer, Thomas Ainslie, in 1839 is unique because it shows the temporary gallows (see arrow) erected at Fort Henry for the execution of Nils von Schoultz. The lieutenant governor's execution warrant, specifying that the Swede be hanged "at or near" the fort, caused some problems for Sheriff Allan Macdonell, who had just completed a new gallows at the town jail, and he was forced to quickly erect a special "drop" for von Schoultz near the fort. The other ten Hunters executed for their role in the Prescott invasion died at the Kingston jail. To the very last, von Schoultz was always different from his fellow man and to the grave he maintained his masquerade as a Polish freedom fighter – in fact, his headstone at St. Mary's Church in Kingston describes him as a "Native of Poland." (National Archives of Canada, C-510)

On 6 December, Macdonell went to Fort Henry and read the warrant aloud to von Schoultz while standing in the door of his cell. The Swede had been expecting "the fatal news" and received it "with a pleasant smile on his countenance," according to one witness.[12] A few days before, he had sung to his cellmates a song of his own composition, quoted above, as his farewell and he now personally shook hands with each man in his casemate before accompanying Macdonell to the town jail, where he would spend his last hours. At his request, John A. Macdonald visited him to draft a will in which the Swede made bequests to his wife and mother in Sweden and several people in the United States, including his fiancee in Salina, and directed that the considerable sum of £400 be distributed to the widows and orphans of the Canadian militiamen killed at Prescott. He even tried to leave money to Macdonald, which, of course, the solicitor had to refuse. It was all very admirable and the act of a true gentleman but there is no evidence that his bequests were fulfilled because there is no evidence that he had the requisite funds.[13]

Von Schoultz also wrote a number of last letters which he entrusted to Macdonell for delivery. In them he praised the kindness of the sheriff and the officers of the 83rd Foot and stated that the prayers of him and his comrades "would be answered" if John Birge and Bill Johnston were delivered over to British authorities.[14] His last wish was that Americans not avenge his death. "Let no further blood be shed," he entreated them as "all the stories that were told about the suffering of the Canadian people, were untrue."[15] These matters taken care of, von Schoultz spent his last two nights with the Catholic priest, Father Patrick Dollard.[16]

It was about dawn on Saturday, 8 December 1838, when Sheriff Macdonell came for him. Accompanied by the faithful Father Dollard, the Swede was taken in a wagon across the Cataraqui bridge to a gallows which Macdonell had managed, by one method or another, to get built beside Fort Henry. A large crowd watched as the condemned man mounted the steps to stand on the trap while his arms and legs were bound by the hangmen. Macdonell read the charges before asking the Swede if he had anything to say. In response, von Schoultz made a short and eloquent speech which no one seems to have recorded, and then a white cloth was pulled over his head and the noose tightened around his neck. The signal was given, the lever pulled, the trap opened and death was instantaneous. The body was left hanging an hour before being taken down and transported to St. Mary's Catholic Church in Kingston for burial.[17]

Thus passed Nils Gustaf von Schoultz – failed husband, father, officer and liberator of the Canadas – whose entire life had been one continual flight from responsibility. It might be said of him, as it was said of Charles I of England, that nothing became the man so much as his own death. Perhaps the best summation of the Swede was that provided by his friend Warren Green of Salina: "I still think of him as the creature of a high-wrought fancy, rather than of sober reality; like a meteor of uncommon brilliancy, which has suddenly illumined the path of my dull existence, and as suddenly disappeared forever."[18]

Four days later, it was the turn of Dorephus Abbey and Daniel George. Attorney General Hagerman could find no legal grounds to mitigate their sentence and warrants for their execution were issued, which Macdonell read to them at the doors of their cells. According to Heustis, Abbey "received the intelligence with manly coolness, and, on leaving, shook hands with us all" but there was "a melting power in that single word 'farewell,' – when spoken for the last time, under such peculiar and distressing circumstances."[19] They were removed to the jail to spend their last days and George was attended by an Anglican clergyman although Abbey refused religious comfort. Both wrote final letters to their wives and children and, just before the sheriff came for them on the morning of 12 December, Abbey added a postscript that he had "slept soundly and quietly last night: I now feel as though I could meet the event with composure."[20]

Abbey and George were escorted into the jail yard where a large crowd had gathered to watch them pay for their crimes. On the gallows, they were bound, white caps were pulled over their heads and Macdonell then read the charges. It was a bitter, freezing morning and the correspondent for the Kingston *Spectator* noted that the two men were "much affected by cold and one placed his hands in his pockets."[21] This upset him as he

The graves of Nils von Schoultz and Martin Woodruff
Both men are buried in the cemetery of St. Mary's Catholic Church in Kingston. It was more usual for those who suffered capital punishment to be buried in unmarked graves in the grounds of the prison where they were executed. (Courtesy, Friends of Windmill Point)

did not feel it right that a man's last thoughts before he met his maker should be troubled by such banal concerns as the weather. The signal was given, the trap opened and the two Hunter officers were launched into eternity. Abbey "died without pain" but, according to the *Upper Canada Herald*, George "struggled for some time," which was a tactful way of saying that he strangled on the rope.[22] The bodies were taken down and transported to St. George's Anglican church for burial.[23]

Gates claimed that Daniel George's wife, who had come to Kingston to plead without success for her husband's life, was so overcome by his death that she fell senseless in the street at the time the execution was being carried out. It proved too much for "her overwrought heart," reason "deserted her throne," and she became a "maniac." But Gates also informs us that the new widow was "a patriot of the warmest blood, and cheerfully spent many an hour in running [casting] bullets, and in assisting the cause in whatever manner she could." Her husband and his comrades had used those bullets to kill Canadians.[24]

Martin Woodruff was next and Martin Woodruff did not have a good death. On the morning of 19 December, Sheriff Macdonell took him from his cell to the gallows in the jail yard where a crowd of 250 spectators was waiting to see his end. After the usual ceremonies, the trap opened and Woodruff dropped but, in the words of the correspondent from the *Upper Canada Herald*, through "some mismanagement of the hangman," he "was put to a great deal of unnecessary pain."[25] As the Kingston *Spectator* reported,

The knot, instead of drawing tightly under the ear, was brought to the chin. It did not slip, but left space enough to put a hand within, the chief weight of the body bearing upon the rope at the back of the neck. The body was in great agitation and seemed to suffer greatly.[26]

At this point, an experienced executioner would have quickly gone below the gallows (or more likely have sent his assistant) to grab the client's bound legs and yank down hard to snap the cervical vertebra, thus bringing the procedure to a quick and successful conclusion. Woodruff's hangmen were inexperienced and only finished their work after one climbed on the crosstree of the gallows and pulled the wretched Woodruff up by the noose "and let him fall four times in succession."[27]

A large crowd witnessed this "revolting, disgusting and disgraceful scene" and there was considerable comment on it in the pages of the Kingston newspapers.[28] The *Chronicle and Gazette*, usually a staunch defender of the Crown, printed a letter from "A Tory" criticizing the most "reprehensible manner in which Woodruff was executed."[29] The *Upper Canada Herald* blasted the *Chronicle* for this imputation on Sheriff Macdonell, who himself complained to the *Gazette* about the letter. Most Kingstonians were aware that, although the sheriff was responsible for the execution of the prisoners, he was not responsible for the actual mechanics. "Accidental failures of this nature," cautioned the *Cornwall Observer*, "should not be exaggerated, for every one knows that nothing can be farther from the intention of the Sheriff and his officers than to inflict needless pain."[30]

On the same day that Woodruff met his end, Macdonell received warrants for Joel Peeler and Sylvanus Swete. At his trial, Swete had been one of the few prisoners to plead guilty but it did not save him because Draper established to the satisfaction of the court that Swete had shot Johnson of the 83rd while Peeler was known to have mutilated the body. Sentence was carried out on 22 December, and it was a better day for Macdonell's hangmen as both Hunters died quickly.[31]

The executions of Peeler and Swete shocked Daniel Heustis, who had himself just been found guilty and sentenced to death.

Not understanding the depth of feeling about the mutilation of Johnson's corpse, he regarded them as "inoffensive" and, if such men were to die, it appeared that "an indiscriminate slaughter of all the prisoners had been decreed" because none of the other Hunters were less guilty.[32] As an officer, Heustis was worried because it was common knowledge that the leaders were marked for death and he had no way of ascertaining just how "comprehensive the tory definition of the word 'leaders' might be." He had been careful to get rid of all the trappings of his rank, swords, epaulettes, etc., before surrendering at Prescott and it says much about the loyalty of his comrades and the usefulness of those Hunters who turned evidence for the Crown, that no one appears to have identified his position to the British and Canadian authorities. "The reflections incident to such a situation," he recalled, "as may easily be imagined, were not of the most agreeable character."[33]

Heustis would have been less concerned if he knew how much Sir George Arthur agonized over the matter of the death penalty. Arthur knew it was impossible to carry out the full sentence of the court martial against all the prisoners and, on the advice of the three chief justices of Upper Canada, he and William Draper decided to classify the prisoners in terms of their age, social position, intelligence and "ferocity of character or particular atrocities," and only execute "eye for eye."[34] Arthur planned to "limit Capital executions to Fifteen! that is one for every life lost in the Prescott affair" but his problem came when choosing who was to die.[35] "Never was anything more difficult than to make the selection," he confessed to Draper. There was also another consideration. As Judge Adiel Sherwood advised him, although "the acknowledged desire of Capital Punishment is to hold out an example of terror and by that means to prevent, as far as possible" any sympathy for the offenders, too many executions might incite just such a feeling among the

Canadian public.[36] A profoundly religious man whose leisure time was often spent reading the Scriptures, Arthur's reluctance to levy the death penalty is somewhat curious in view of the fact that, during his seventeen-year tenure as governor of the penal colony at Van Diemen's land, he had signed death warrants for hundreds of men and women. It would seem that hanging British felons troubled the lieutenant governor far less than hanging American citizens.[37]

Arthur tried to share the responsibility with his Executive Council, who turned out to have fewer qualms about executing Yankees. In the last week of December, the Council examined the trial transcripts of twenty-four prisoners and recommended that six – Duncan Anderson, Christopher Buckley, Leonard Delino, Sylvester Lawton, Andrew Leeper and Russell Phelps – be executed. Duncan Anderson from Jefferson County, New York, was a man of mature age who had not only fought at Prescott but had also participated in Van Rensselaer's abortive attack on Kingston in February 1838. Evidence contained in Daniel George's notebook showed that Christopher Buckley from Salina had been a Hunter officer, sufficient cause to warrant his death. Leonard Delino from Watertown, twenty-five years of age, had belonged to a company known to be one of the better Hunter units, and witnesses had stated that he had fought well at the windmill. Sylvester Lawton from Lyme in Jefferson County had been an early recruit to the Hunter organization and, although he was only twenty-three years of age, testimony at his trial proved that he had held officer's rank. Andrew Leeper, also from Lyme, had been a frequent traveller in Upper Canada before the invasion and the council regarded him as a likely spy. At age forty-two, Leeper could not plead the ignorance of youth and evidence showed that he had fought hard at Prescott. Russell Phelps, aged forty and another native of Lyme, had not only been with Van Rensselaer on Hickory

Island but had been arrested in Kingston a few months later for trying to induce British soldiers to desert. Although Phelps had been acquitted of this charge, the councillors felt it carried weight and a public example should be made of him.[38]

Arthur received these recommendations at a Council meeting held on 26 December. The lieutenant governor argued against the execution of Delino because of his youth, while, as for Leeper, there was no real proof that he had acted as a spy. He asked the Executive Council to reconsider the matter and reminded it that forty-four men captured at Windsor would shortly go on trial and inevitably some of them would have to suffer the supreme penalty, and Arthur wanted to keep the number of executions as low as possible. The Council duly reconsidered but refused to change their recommendation and the lieutenant governor therefore signed the six warrants and sent them to Sheriff Macdonell – but he continued to have doubts and almost immediately cancelled the warrants for Delino and Leeper. Fortunately for them, Macdonell received word of this change before he carried out the sentences. By this time, the sheriff was becoming tired of hanging men, even convicted pirates, and confessed to Arthur's secretary that the reprieves were "very welcome."[39]

With good reason, William Gates never forgot the morning in early January 1839 when he was called to the door of his cell at Fort Henry, along with Anderson, Buckley, Lawton and Phelps, by Macdonell's deputy sheriff. Horror struck, he listened as the man read the four prisoners their execution warrants and told them to get their things together as they were being transferred to the town jail. This done, the deputy handed Gates a letter that had arrived for him and walked away.[40]

Duncan Anderson, Christopher Buckley, Sylvester Lawton and Russell Phelps were hanged at Kingston jail on 4 January. The weather had recently been very cold and the St. Lawrence was frozen, with the result, as the correspondent for the *Upper Canada Herald* reported, that many Americans were "present at the Execution, the travelling being good from the United States."[41] The four men were attended to the last moment by the clergy of their respective faiths and they died well, the only sour note in the proceeding being that Anderson was so weak from illness that he had to be supported while walking to the gallows.[42]

By this time, many Upper Canadians were growing weary of executions. This was certainly the case in Kingston, Draper reported to Arthur, where the townspeople believed that "capital punishment has gone far enough" although he noted that this belief was not popular down-river at Brockville and Prescott, where the locals would gladly have watched every man who landed at Prescott swing for it.[43] The Kingston newspapers were quick to expound on the sentiment that, since the Hunter leaders had paid with their lives for their crimes, their followers should receive less severe punishment. The *Chronicle and Gazette* suggested that the prisoners at Fort Henry should be exchanged for the true culprits in the affair, men like Birge, Johnston and Mackenzie, while the *Upper Canada Herald* proposed that they should be kept as hostages to the good behaviour of their fellow citizens – a number would be executed any time there was a future border incursion. By the first week of January 1839, however, the *Herald* was proclaiming that the course of justice having been served, it was now time for a course of mercy.[44]

This sentiment was not shared by the British ambassador in Washington, Henry S. Fox, who had been carefully measuring American reaction to the executions. It was his belief that

This severe and just chaztizement has I believe produced its complete effect. The example was absolutely necessary; in

order to make the Americans understand, that to wage a privateering war against Her Majesty's peaceful subjects, – to carry fire and sword into Canada, – is something more than a mere idle frolic, or fair land-speculating enterprize.

Fox did not "blame the President, or any American, for desiring to save the lives of his fellow citizens: but I think that man must be blind," who thought that Britain would be "able by gentle means, to repress the detestable crusade against Canada that has been waged by the American pirates." Fox wanted the executions to continue and it was his great regret that "the real movers of the invasion of Canada," the wealthy citizens of the border towns, who had "a deep and permanent land-speculating interest," in encouraging the Hunter attacks, would never be brought to justice.[45]

The reluctant Arthur was caught between a growing public sentiment against more executions on one side and the intransigence of his own Executive Council and officials like Fox on the other. There was also the problem of the St. Lawrence river towns which, as he confessed to Lord Glenelg, the colonial secretary, wanted "an example of terror," in Judge Sherwood's words that would, once and for all, put an end to the border raids.[46] Reluctantly, he signed warrants for the execution of six of the forty-four Hunters captured at Windsor but only one more man from the Prescott invasion went to the gallows.

This was a prisoner who had stated, when captured, that he was Lyman Leach, twenty-eight years old, from Westchester County, New York. Draper and Arthur learned from spies and an anonymous letter that he was actually Lyman Lewis from Onondaga County and that he had been a member of Bill Johnston's gang when it robbed and burned the steamer *Sir Robert Peel*. For this, Arthur signed his execution warrant. Heustis thought Lewis "one of the most daring and fearless men I ever saw" and "so perfectly reckless of danger that nothing could intimidate him."[47] The condemned man maintained that reputation to the very end. When Sheriff Macdonell came for him at Kingston jail on the morning of 11 February 1839, Lewis had not yet finished his breakfast and "insisted on being allowed to enjoy his last meal," keeping the sheriff "waiting till he had cooly and deliberately concluded his repast."[48]

Lewis brought the number of executions for the invasions at Prescott and Windsor to seventeen and in Arthur's opinion that was enough. His problem was what to do with the remaining prisoners. As he explained to Colborne and Glenelg, the colonial secretary, there were too many to be incarcerated in the small penitentiary at Kingston; they could not be used as convict labour on chain gangs in the Canadas; and, since most were Americans, simple banishment to the United States was no punishment. He decided that he would grant a pardon to some of the remaining prisoners, particularly those under the age of twenty-one, and send the remainder to a penal colony, although he did not intend to inform them of this change in their sentences until it was absolutely necessary. For the time being the prisoners could labour under the belief that they would pay for their crimes on the gallows.[49]

William Draper, who had come to know quite a bit about the prisoners in Fort Henry, had already classified them "with reference to their degree of Criminality."[50] Draper based his grading on the length of time they had served as Hunters, their knowledge of the object of the Prescott invasion, their own statements, their previous residence and their age. Of the 127 men on his list, dated 1 January 1839, 17 were of the first or "Most Criminal" class, 44 of the second or "Less Criminal Class" and 66 of the "Least Criminal" class. Many of those in the first category, including Daniel Heustis, had the letter "H" marked beside their name, which meant that Draper regarded them as men who might be chosen to pay the supreme penalty, should there be more executions.[51]

Between January and May 1839, 85 prisoners were released from custody. Four men had served as Crown witnesses, 8 were not tried because of their wounds and were subsequently pardoned, 1 man was pardoned on account of age and sickness, 3 men were pardoned on the specific recommendation of the Executive Council, 4 were discharged for lack of evidence and 4 men were acquitted. There is no doubt that some Hunters were released because of their connections. Among them was 60-year-old Eli Clark from Oswego, a former state militia officer who should have known better than to have become involved in the landing, but who just happened to be the brother of a U.S. senator. Hunter Vaughan's father was an American naval officer but being twenty-one he qualified as a youth, as did 19-year-old John Brewster from Henderson Harbor in Jefferson County, whose parents were personal friends of William Draper. One man, David Defield, a Canadian who had joined the Hunters in Salina, was freed because his mother had saved the life of a British officer during the War of 1812. Six of the youngest prisoners were freed after Judge Jonas Jones, acting on the request of Congressman Fine from Ogdensburg, exerted himself on their behalf. They were followed by 55 other young men who were released in two groups in April and sent over to Sackets Harbor, among them Justus Merriam, Price Senter and Nelson Truax.[52]

Sheriff Allan Macdonell accompanied the second group to the Harbor and, on meeting Sheriff Abner Baker of Jefferson County, there to receive them, he was his usual bluff self.

"Here I have 22 pirates," Macdonell said to the American lawman. "If you want them, write me a receipt for them. Otherwise I shall take them back."

"I do not care whether or not they are pirates," was Baker's quick response. "I accept them."[53]

In May 1839, there were still sixty men, most of them Americans, languishing in Fort Henry under sentence of death. According to Gates, they had no idea what their fate would be, although they suspected they would not be hanged. Sheriff Macdonell told them that, although death "was the sentence of the court, he could assure us upon the word of the lieutenant governor, that no more executions would take place – that the last man had been hung – for he, the governor, felt assured that the officers or ring-leaders were now disposed of, and the remainder should be treated with clemency, and probably ere long be liberated."[54] This was not the complete truth and most of the prisoners suspected that they were going to be transported but it did somewhat lift their spirits.

Sir George Arthur himself visited Fort Henry in the early summer of 1839 and addressed the men, telling them "among other things not so complimentary," that, if they "had been fighting in the right cause," they "would have been an honor to your country."[55] Right or wrong, the Americans were determined to celebrate the Fourth of July as well as circumstances would permit. Heustis proudly recollected that

Out of several pocket handkerchiefs a flag was manufactured, as nearly resembling the "star-spangled banner" as we could conveniently make it. This emblem of freedom and national independence we hoisted in our room, taking good care that the officers did not get a peep at it. We procured some lemons and sugar, which enabled us to pass round a refreshing bowl of lemonade.[56]

This done, the Hunters "let off our toasts, in which the heroes of '76 were duly remembered."

The Hunters remained at Fort Henry throughout the summer, but on 17 September they were told to start packing their belongings as they were being taken to Quebec "to receive free pardons from the governor general in person." Most did not believe this fantasy and were sure "some other disposition was to be made of us; but what that was to be, was beyond our conjecture."[57] But they were undaunted and, as they prepared to leave the casemates where they had been incarcerated for nearly ten months, they burst into song, each man singing "what pleased him best." "Hail Columbia," "The Star Spangled Banner," "Hunters of Kentucky" and "Yankee Doodle" resounded through the fort, "calling quite a crowd about the doors and windows."[58]

After a five-day trip by boat and steamer down the St. Lawrence, the Hunters arrived at Quebec and were immediately hustled on board a naval stores ship, HMS *Buffalo*, at anchor below Cape Diamond. On 22 September 1839, the *Buffalo* weighed anchor and was towed by a steamer into the Gulf of St. Lawrence – her destination the British penal colony of Van Diemen's Land.[59]

The apparent leniency shown by Arthur to the prisoners was not popular along the Canadian side of the St. Lawrence River, particularly at Prescott, whose residents had personal experience of the Hunters and their handiwork. That people in Kingston were growing weary of executions did not concern folks in Prescott – if Kingston had been attacked, its citizens would have been just as keen to see the invaders severely punished – and, besides, everyone down-river knew that the people Kingston often got ideas considerably above their station. This desire at Prescott to see the men captured at the windmill suffer the extreme penalty was fuelled by daily reminders of the events of November 1838.

There was, for example, the burned-out wreckage of Newport with its gutted and roofless houses. The property owners

Newport and the mill after the battle, 1839
For many years after the battle the gutted ruins of the hamlet of Newport served to remind the people of Prescott of those bloody five days in November 1838. Newport was never rebuilt and today there is only one house in the area that can be dated to the time of the battle. (Woodcut, Courtesy Friends of Windmill Point)

in the hamlet applied for compensation from the Crown, fifteen individuals submitting claims totalling over £6,450 for the loss of buildings and property. They received £2,250. Newport, however, was never rebuilt in its entirety and some of the ruins remained as late as the 1890s, and today there is only one house near the windmill that can be reliably dated to the time of the battle. As for the mill itself, the McQueen brothers, who owned this unprofitable structure, had visions of generous financial compensation when the military retained it over the winter of 1838 as a defence work. In April 1839 they asked for £1,754 for the building and improvements they had made to it, but the army had by this time abandoned the mill and, after two years of haggling, the McQueens accepted the Crown's offer of £285 compensation, four months after they had sold the structure for £225.[60]

A second and more compelling reminder of the invasion was the human sufferers of the battle, most of whom lived in Leeds, Grenville and Dundas counties. Many of the wounded remained in Prescott for weeks after the fighting had ended, recovering in private homes or boarding houses, and they were attended by the magnificent Dr. James Scott, who did not charge for his professional services. Alpheus Jones, the collector of customs at Prescott, acted as the treasurer for the donations that poured into the village from private individuals and organizations across North America, and his account books show that he used these funds to assist the families of the men wounded or killed in the battle, paying for food, firewood, clothing, board for the wounded, rent if required, and many other costs for families who had lost their male providers.[61]

Eventually, the Crown provided compensation for the sufferers. The widows of the militiamen killed in the battle received an annual pension of £20, regardless of the number of their dependant children, not much more than the annual pay of a private in the British army, and soldiers' families received free rations and quarters. It was paid twice yearly in instalments of £10 and the recipient had to travel to Toronto to collect it or, more likely, she utilized an agent in that city, who charged for the service. Pensions in smaller amounts were paid to men disabled by their wounds, such as Sergeant Landers, who was never again fit to practise his trade as a blacksmith; Lieutenant John Parlow, who could not farm with a shattered wrist; or Private John Gillespie, who took a musket ball in the head and was subject to "fits of giddiness" whenever he leaned over.[62]

Fortunately, this assistance was fleshed out by an additional £1,146 raised in Upper Canada and the Maritimes which was dispersed to those who had suffered from the battle. The payments made ranged from £72 paid to Margaret Linnen, the widow of Private Adam Linnen of the Grenville Cavalry, who had eight children, down to £12 paid to Harris Russell, the gentleman volunteer from Brockville who had ridden through the night to get to the battle but had broken his leg when thrown from his horse. John Parlow received £60, Edward Landers received £54 and John Gillespie £36 to relieve the financial distress caused their families by the action.[63]

This private and public aid was amplified by the efforts of friends and neighbours who helped out how and where they could, but some cases were truly heartbreaking. Hunter Gates might think that Mrs. Daniel George, who became deranged after her husband was hanged at Kingston, was a tragic figure, but consider the situation of Margaret Linnen. The £72 she received from the public subscription was a great help, but nearly two years after the battle she had still not learned if she would get a pension, and the fatherless Linnen family was reduced to such distressing circumstances that the widow Linnen informed the authorities that, if a pension was not soon forthcoming, she intended to "bind out," or indenture, her eight children as servants so they could at least get enough to eat. Happily, after the efforts of several senior militia officers, Margaret Linnen was put on the pension roll for the annual £20.[64]

Given these reminders, it is not surprising that feelings remained high along the Canadian side of the St. Lawrence and there were a number of incidents in the months that followed the battle. In April 1839, militia at Prescott opened fire on the *United States*, a vessel they had no reason to love, as it passed the village. In August, the aggressive Lieutenant William Fowell, RN, commanding the armed steamer *Montreal*, ordered his men to open fire with muskets on the American *St. Lawrence* after her captain refused his command to show her colours.[65]

The worst of these episodes took place at Brockville on 17 May 1839. Residents noticed that an American schooner, *G.S. Weeks*, which had docked to discharge some merchandise, had a 6-pdr. iron field gun on her deck. This weapon was actually destined for Ogdensburg to replace a similar piece "borrowed" from the state militia by Bill Johnston during the landing at Windmill Point and never returned. Suspecting it was intended for the use of the Hunters somewhere on the river, a crowd of Canadians attempted to board the vessel and seize the gun. The crew resisted until the local collector of customs "took possession of the vessel under some alleged irregularities of her papers."[66] As the collector at Brockville was Richard D. Fraser, this was not surprising, and the gun was dragged in triumph through the streets of Brockville and even fired a few times. The captain of the *Weeks*, however, had managed to get a message to the American side of the river and, late in the afternoon of the following day, Colonel William J. Worth arrived in the steamer *Oneida* with a hundred men from his Eighth Infantry and politely requested the return of the purloined gun. Fraser agreed to release it but neither he nor his officials, nor the small detachment of British regulars at Brockville, were able to get it away from the "excited and furious mob, many of whom were armed."[67] Matters were looking particularly grim when two steamers arrived from Kingston with a company of the 83rd Foot, sent for by the magistrates. The regulars arrested the ringleaders of the mob, returned the gun to its owners and averted what might have been a nasty international incident. Although Sir George Arthur later complained to the American government about Worth's somewhat high-handed action, there was not that much good to be said about the Canadian side of this affair, for it seems Brockville came perilously close to being as lawless as Ogdensburg had been the previous November.[68]

HMS *Buffalo* was carrying 141 prisoners when she left Quebec City. There were 78 Hunters (60 taken at Prescott and 18 at Windsor), 58 *Patriotes* captured after Robert Nelson's abortive November 1838 invasion of Lower Canada, four common criminals, and an American, suspected of being a spy, who had been arrested on Canadian soil. The prisoners were incarcerated in the lower deck, a hold below water level about 75 feet long and 35 feet wide with about 5 feet of headroom. They were allowed on the upper deck daily in groups of twelve for fresh air and exercise. During their first days at sea, conditions in the hold were terrible as a ferocious storm raged, but after that, although life on the *Buffalo* was hard, it was bearable.[69]

Some of the prisoners hoped that the ship's destination was Britain, but when the *Buffalo* cleared the Gulf of St. Lawrence and sailed south through the Atlantic, they knew they were bound for Australia. At this point, a plot was hatched to seize the ship and take it into an American port, but, according to Gates, this plan was betrayed to the captain by one of their own comrades and additional security measures were taken. As the vessel ploughed steadily south, 40-year-old Asa Priest of Auburn, New York, died and was buried at sea, leaving a wife and six children to mourn him. Two months after leaving Quebec City, the *Buffalo* made a brief stop in Rio de Janiero before sailing east round the Cape of Good Hope in a storm so bad that the prisoners had to take shifts at the pumps to keep the vessel afloat. Finally, after four months and twelve days at sea, on 10 February 1840, the *Buffalo* dropped anchor at Hobart Town, capital of the British penal colony the prisoners soon came to call "Van *Demon's* Land."[70]

Van Diemen's Land (modern Tasmania) was the main penal colony in Australia. The British system of transporting criminals to a distant place of incarceration had begun in 1787 when the first convict fleet had arrived in Botany Bay on the Australian mainland, and it was to continue until 1853, during which time more than 100,000 men, women and children suffered this punishment. From 1830 onward, as the settlements on the mainland had progressed to the point where they were attractive to free settlers, most of these unfortunates went to Van Diemen's Land, and when the *Buffalo* arrived, the island had a population of 67,000, split almost equally between convict and free inhabitants.[71]

Officials of the prison service immediately boarded the vessel and interviewed each man to record his vital information. It quickly became apparent that the service knew little about the new arrivals, most of whom were political, not criminal, prisoners and, since there was no information about the duration of their transportation, they were recorded as being sentenced "for life." These preliminaries finished, the Hunters went ashore and, as Gates later wrote, their first impressions of their new home were not good:

> We had hardly our feet on the soil when almost the first objects that greeted our vision were gibbets, and men toiling in the most abject misery, looking more degraded even than so many beasts. Such sights, and the supposition that such might be our fate, served to sink the iron still deeper into our souls.[72]

The *Buffalo* prisoners were inspected by Lieutenant Governor Sir John Franklin, who would later come to a bad but famous end as an explorer of the Canadian arctic. Lacking any instructions from his superiors, Franklin did not really know what to do with the Hunters but did give them a lengthy and almost incoherent two-hour harangue, the substance of which seemed to be

> that we were bad men – very bad men – were sent there for a very bad crime – rebellion – one of the worst crimes that

Convict life in Van Diemen's Land

These two scenes from a patriot memoir show life in the penal colony of Van Diemen's Land during the first part of the prisoners' sentence. The transported Hunters suffered only two years of labour such as this before receiving a ticket of leave which allowed them to seek paid employment anywhere in the colony. The normal sentence was six years of hard labour. (Author's collection)

could be – worse than murder – didn't know what to do with us – guess should put us on the roads awhile – work good for us – should send home for orders – send home to know what to do with us – at present put us on probation – if we behaved well on probation, get rewarded for it.[73]

Probation was not as good as it sounded. The correctional system in Van Diemen's Land (ironically developed by Sir George Arthur) consisted of two stages. When a convict first arrived, he or she was placed on "probation," which was a sentence of hard labour for a set period, usually six years, under heavy guard. Good behaviour during probation might bring the award of a "ticket of leave," which permitted the convict to seek paid employment anywhere on the island. Ticket of leave convicts were still subject to restrictions; they had to obey a curfew and had to report regularly to prison officials. With firther good behaviour, however, they might receive a pardon for their crime and, if they could raise the money for the long sea voyage, return home – not surprisingly, most never did.[74]

For the next two years, the Prescott and Windsor Hunter prisoners laboured building roads near Hobart Town. It was hard and brutal work performed in a hot climate under a draconian discipline that could result in flogging or solitary confinement for any infraction of the many rules. At least four men died during this period but most of the Hunters survived, if barely. Sundays were nominally a day of rest but, to their disgust, the Hunters found they were forced to attend two lengthy Church of England services because the prison service officials were concerned about the spiritual education of their charges. Since the head of that church was Queen Victoria, this did not sit well with men who had fought against her soldiers and sailors. In addition, the Hunters were not a very religious group of men: most did not belong to an established Christian faith and those that did were usually Baptists, Methodists or members of smaller sects. Nonetheless, every Sunday, they were "marched with soldier-like precision" to the Anglican church, where they were "forced to submit to it all, and compelled to endure the purgatory of two and three long doleful hours – rising, kneeling, and sitting according to the most precise formula, all the while holding our faces as grave as an owl."[75]

Thanks to the efforts of a remarkable woman, the prisoners' probation ended after just two years of hard labour. Maria Wait was the wife of Benjamin Wait, a Canadian who had been captured in the Short Hills raid of June 1838 and condemned to death on the gallows. He was saved from the noose by Maria, who personally interceded with Lord Durham and Sir George Arthur and won a commutation of his sentence to transportation for life. Determined to get her husband back, Maria trav-

elled across the Canadas and to England winning the support of a number of influential persons, including Durham, and her efforts were successful. In 1842, Benjamin Wait received a pardon and at the same time all the political prisoners in Van Diemen's Land were given tickets of leave. It was Heustis's belief that Maria Wait's "devoted and heroic services" should "be handed down to other generations as a bright example of conjugal fidelity and active philanthropy, worthy of an immortality of honour."[76]

The Prescott Hunters now entered into the second phase of their life as convicts. As ticket of leave men, they were free to go, under some restrictions, anywhere on the island, and they spread out to seek paid labour where they could find it: Heustis worked as a farm hand; John Berry became a shepherd in a remote area; Gates found employment as a shearer on a sheep

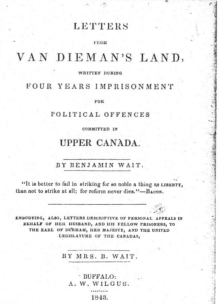

LETTERS
FROM
VAN DIEMAN'S LAND,
WRITTEN DURING
FOUR YEARS IMPRISONMENT
FOR
POLITICAL OFFENCES
COMMITTED IN
UPPER CANADA.

BY BENJAMIN WAIT.

"It is better to fail in striking for so noble a thing as LIBERTY, than not to strike at all; for reform never dies." —BACON.

EMBODYING, ALSO, LETTERS DESCRIPTIVE OF PERSONAL APPEALS IN BEHALF OF HER HUSBAND, AND HIS FELLOW PRISONERS, TO THE EARL OF DURHAM, HER MAJESTY, AND THE UNITED LEGISLATURE OF THE CANADAS,

BY MRS. B. WAIT.

BUFFALO:
A. W. WILGUS.
1843.

Transported for life

A patriot condemned to transportation for life to the penal colony of Van Diemen's Land glumly contemplates his fate. Note the shaven head. Sixty Hunters captured at Prescott were transported in 1840, and several later published accounts of their experiences. They suffered two years of hard labour before receiving a ticket of leave permitting them to take paid employment anywhere on the island. All were pardoned in 1844 and most managed to get back by 1847 although one man did not return until 1860. Some found life in Australia to their liking and became settlers. (From Benjamin Wait, *Letters from Van Dieman's Land*, 1843) farm; others worked in any capacity they could find, including two who became convict overseers. Life was still hard but it was improving, although, as the somewhat prim Stephen Wright recorded, there were dangers in the penal colony that snared a number of his comrades. Social life in Van Diemen's Land tended to be "gross and sensual," in fact so sensual that, in Wright's opinion, there was "an article which, if imported there, would command the highest price" and that was "*female virtue*" because "licentiousness, libertinism, drunkenness, and debauchery" were "the order and fashion of the day."[77] To ward off such obvious evil, Wright and some of his comrades formed a temperance society but, sadly, he recorded that some of his comrades slid down the slippery slope to end up dissipated, married or otherwise connected to local women, and became content to live out the rest of their days under the Union Jack.

Many of the Hunters, among them Gates, Heustis and Wright, served in posses organized to track down and kill or capture the numerous "bush rangers," escaped convicts who preyed on the non-criminal settlers. Heustis spent seventy-three days on the trail of one gang, which was rather a new experience for a man who had fought hard to overturn established authority. None of the Hunters showed any reluctance to join these posses in the Crown's work, because there was the added incentive that the lieutenant governor sometimes offered a pardon and a free passage home to ticket of leave men who apprehended one of the more notorious bush rangers. Aaron Dresser and Stephen Wright served in a posse that caught two infamous bush rangers, Jeffs and Conway, after a twelve-day hunt. For their efforts they got a pardon and passage and in July 1843 embarked for their homes.[78]

A year later, the remainder of the Prescott Hunters gained their freedom. The American government had been working hard on their behalf and in 1844, when an amnesty was granted to most Canadians who had taken part in the rebellions, it was extended to American citizens captured in the border raids. The Hunters were now free but they had to find their own way back to North America. Twenty-seven Prescott and Windsor men, including Heustis, were fortunate to be taken on board the American whaler *Steiglitz*, whose captain needed replacements for a mutinous crew. The Hunter officer long remembered that "joy beamed in every face" when his comrades boarded the vessel as "liberty's bright banner, the glorious stars and stripes, flaunted in triumph over my head."[79] William Gates, who by now had moved to the mainland to work on a sheep station, had saved enough money to pay another whaler captain $200 for a passage to the United States. Garrett Hicks, a dog's best friend, worked his passage home on a merchant vessel as did many others. Some decided to settle in Australia and never returned, and some simply disappeared. The evidence is fragmentary but it appears that of the 60 men captured at the windmill who were transported to Van Diemen's Land in 1840, 32 returned to their homes, 6 died either in the penal colony or on passage, 4 married in Australia, and there is no record of the fate of the remaining men.[80]

By the time the Hunters returned to North America, the patriot movement had all but disbanded. The severe punishment accorded to those captured at Prescott and Windsor, waning support for their cause in the United States, and more rigorous enforcement of the neutrality laws by U.S. authorities, combined with the increasing size of the garrison of British North America – by February 1839 there were 33,000 regulars and longservice militia under arms in the Canadas – hastened the dissolution of the secret organization. John Birge, Bill Johnston, William Lyon Mackenzie, Robert Nelson, Rensselaer

Van Rensselaer were all arrested, tried and spent time in jail. The Hunters continued to make occasional forays across the border for eighteen months after the battle of the windmill but these were single criminal acts, not military invasions. In the summer of 1839, there were several instances of arson along the Niagara frontier involving the property of prominent militia and law officers and the Anglican church at Chippawa. In July, six Hunters were captured in Cobourg after crossing Lake Ontario from Oswego on a mission to rob and murder prominent citizens. They were tried and received prison terms in the new penitentiary at Kingston. In April 1840, the Hunters blew up the monument on Queenston Heights marking the grave of Major General Sir Isaac Brock, regarded as the saviour of Upper Canada during the War of 1812. The following June, the infamous Benjamin Lett was apprehended trying to plant an incendiary device on board the Canadian steamer *Great Britain* when it was anchored at an American port. The final Hunter attempt to unsettle Upper Canada, a plot in September 1840 to destroy vulnerable locks on the Welland Canal, was foiled when it came to the attention of the military authorities.[81]

By this time the Patriot Hunters had become little more than an elaborate extortion scheme by which a knowledgeable few bilked money from many gullible members. Although there were still some hard cases in the lodges of the border states that believed they would eventually set the Canadas free, the Patriot Hunters were a spent force. The movement disappeared after President John Tyler ordered it to disband in September 1841.[82]

Perhaps the best assessment of the undeclared war that these Americans had waged against the Canadas between December 1837 and June 1840 was provided by the *New York Times*, which called it a war

instigated by men destitute of influence, and deficient in common honesty, for their own purposes.

It is a war in which the instigators eschew the dangers into which they incite others to rush headlong.

It is a war to force liberty on a people who like it so little, that they repel the advances of their liberators with the bayonet and hiss upon them when led captive through their streets.

It is a war in which success would be infamy, and where defeat is the certain prelude of ignominious death.

It is a war engaged in for a people, who when we were struggling for liberty, harassed and impeded us in the effort, as far as in them lay.

And it is a war which, if continued, in the face of the recent unsympathizing rejection of our companionship by the Canadians themselves, can only be regarded as directed to the object of piracy and plunder.

It was, the *Times* concluded, "an enterprise at once hopeless, useless and dishonorable."[83]

In the end, the political problems that had led to the rebellions and creation of the American patriot movement were solved – in a typically Canadian fashion – through peaceful means. In his report, submitted in February 1839, Lord Durham recommended that Upper and Lower Canada be joined and the executive of this new entity be drawn from an elected legislative assembly. This was done, although some of his other recommendations were shelved. In 1847 Britain granted full responsible government to the new united province of Canada and successively to the Maritime colonies of New Brunswick, Nova Scotia and Prince Edward Island. Canadians thus achieved control of their government and their future without violence and after 1867 the independent colonies of British North America confederated into the modern Dominion of Canada.

The fates of men
and a windmill

The rebels now remain at home,
We wish that they would come;
We would cut them up both day and night,
Under the command of Colonel Young.
If ever they dare return again,
They will see what we can do;
We will show them British play, my boys,
As we did at Waterloo.

    So you British boys be steady,
    And maintain your glorious name;
    May we always find bold Fraser,
    To lead us o'er the plain.

Under Captain Jessup we will fight,
Let him go wherever he will.
With powder and ball, they will surely fall,
As they did at the Windmill.
I marched this town right up and down,
With a musket on my shoulder;
That the rebels they might plainly see
Great Hector was no bolder.

    So you British boys be steady, etc.

If I was like Great Vergil bright,
I would employ my quill
And I would write both day and night,
Concerning the Windmill.
Lest to intrude, I will conclude,
And finish off my song:
We will pay a visit to Ogdensburg,
And that before too long.[1]

In the spring of 1839, the windmill was abandoned as a defended post although nearby Fort Wellington was reconstructed and garrisoned by regular troops for the next four decades. The border tensions gradually died away but for years afterward both Britain and the United States maintained garrisons on their respective sides of the international line. They were needed as a second round of troubles took place in 1866-1870 when an Irish liberation movement, the Fenian Brotherhood, launched a series of attacks from American soil against the Canadas. The Fenians were repulsed, but not without considerable trouble on the part of the American, British and Canadian governments. In 1871, the Treaty of Washington ushered in a period of good relations between the three nations and resulted in the removal of British troops from North America, except for garrisons at the naval bases of Halifax and Esquimault.

The windmill remained derelict for many years. In 1860, the American historian Benson Lossing visited the site of the battle and noted the many indentations in its walls made by Macbean and Sandom's gunners during the battle. In 1873 the mill got a new lease on life when it was taken over by the Canadian government and converted into a lighthouse. It became a well known landmark to the passenger steamboats that passed up and down the St. Lawrence and occasionally, until the late 19th century at least, organized tours were conducted for those interested in the battle. The hamlet of Newport was never rebuilt and some of its ruined buildings were still extant at the turn of the century, by which time Windmill Point had become a favourite daytime spot for summer outings and picnics organized by school, church and scout groups and often resounded with the laughter of delighted children who refought the 1838 battle many times on the actual ground. The tykes were usually gone by evening when the point, a convenient carriage drive from Prescott, served as the local trysting place for generation after generation of young couples who liked to watch the moonlight dapple the surface of the St. Lawrence while intently discussing the importance of studying history. By this time, however, most of those involved in the battle and the events surrounding it had gone to their reward.

Unhappy reminder: Windmill Point in Edwardsburgh Township, Canada West, in 1853

The ruins of Newport as they appeared fifteen years after the battle. The hamlet was never completely rebuilt and the mill functioned intermittently until 1873 when it was converted into a lighthouse. (From Franklin Hough, *History of St. Lawrence County*, 1853)

Of the Americans, President Martin Van Buren, who tried to prevent a war with Britain breaking out over the activities of the Patriot Hunters, lost the election of 1840 to William Henry Harrison. Van Buren was blamed for the depressed state of the economy and deserted by many voters in the northern border states, including his own New York, who disliked his rigid neutrality stance.[2]

Major General Winfield Scott soldiered on for another forty-three years after the battle of the windmill and won a notable victory during a risky campaign against Mexico in the war of 1846-1848. Scott failed at a bid for the presidency and was commanding general of the army when the Civil War broke out in 1861. He died at his home near West Point in 1866.[3]

Brigadier General Hugh Brady, the American commander on the Detroit frontier, was still on active service at the age of eighty-three in 1851 when he died as the result of an accident.[4]

Colonel William Jenkins Worth, whose prompt actions restored order in Ogdensburg and doomed the Hunters at the windmill, distinguished himself as a field commander during the Mexican War. Worth was a major general when he died from cholera in 1849 and he lies today under a memorial erected at the corner of Broadway and Fifth Avenue in his native New York City. Fort Worth, Texas, is named after him.[5]

The Patriot Hunter "generals" are not as well remembered. John Ward Birge and Rensselaer van Rensselaer served prison terms for violating the neutrality laws and then disappeared from view. Lucius V. Beirce, senior officer of the Ohio and Michigan Hunters, left the organization and returned to his Akron law practice and wrote local history in his spare time. Edward Theller from Detroit was also charged with neutrality violations but was acquitted. He settled in Rochester and wrote a book about the patriot movement before moving to California, where he died in 1859. Donald McLeod, the Canadian rebel from Brockville who had fought alongside Theller on the Detroit frontier, was pardoned in 1846 and returned to Upper Canada, where he became a clerk in the government patent office. McLeod published a book about the origins and course of the 1837 rebellion and died in Toronto in 1879.[6]

For a while, there was talk in Onondaga County about raising a memorial to Christopher Buckley, Nils von Schoultz and Martin Woodruff but nothing ever came of it except that a street in Syracuse was named after Buckley.[7]

The law caught up with Bill Johnston on 17 November 1838 when a detachment of Worth's regulars apprehended him on the bank of the St. Lawrence. He was arraigned before a jury in Auburn by Marshal Nathaniel Garrow on a charge of violating the neutrality law but was discharged for lack of evidence.

Garrow promptly re-arrested Johnston on earlier charges only to lose him when he escaped from jail. He was tracked down by Sailing Master William Vaughan and one of Garrow's deputies, who brought him back to Albany and charged him with having been a leader of the invasion at Prescott, a charge he vehemently denied. Such was Johnston's popularity that an Albany theatre owner staged a play, "Bill Johnston, the Hero of the Lakes," with proceeds going to the miscreant's legal fund. Johnston was found guilty and sentenced to a year in prison, and beautiful Kate, the pirate's daughter, went with her father to care for him during his stay behind bars. Bill escaped six months later and stayed at large, with help from the people of New York, until he was formally pardoned by President Harrison. He was then appointed as the lighthouse keeper on Rock Island, not far from where he had burned the *Sir Robert Peel*, but after a few years gave this up to run a popular tavern at French Creek (Clayton) on the St. Lawrence, where, still tended by dutiful Kate, the old reprobate died in 1870. So famous were the father and daughter combination that they were the subjects of at least two novels, *Empress of the Isles or the Lake Bravo* and *The Prisoner of the Border*, described as having "little merit as works of literature and none at all as history."[8] Kate married and lived in Clayton, where she died at the age of fifty-nine.[9]

In the spring of 1839, Ann von Schoultz, living with her two daughters, three-year-old Anne and four-year-old Mary, in Karlskrona, Sweden, began to hear rumours that her husband had died in North America. She had heard nothing from him since a letter written from Baltimore in June 1837 in which he told her that he soon expected to come into $75,000 for certain technical processes he had developed and that, within a month, he would send her a remittance to pay their many debts. In July 1839, Ann received a letter from a friend in New York confirming her husband's death and later she was informed by von

Newport in the later 19th century

This watercolour by an unknown artist, done after 1873, shows four small houses on Windmill Point but none near the mill, which by this time was a lighthouse. Note the gutted and ruined structure – between it and the small white building on the far left was the butternut grove. The small white building was the little school which functioned as an emergency dressing station during the battle of 13 November. (Courtesy, Friends of Windmill Point)

Schoultz's friend, Warren Green of Salina, that she would receive one quarter of the balance of the money in the Swede's estate after certain bequests were made, as would his mother. There is no evidence that this money was ever paid. Ann von Schoultz never remarried and died in 1862 at the young age of forty-nine.[10]

One by one, those Hunters who survived their transportation to Van Diemen's Land straggled home to the United States or, in the case of some, to Canada, where they attempted to pick up the threads of their lives. Stephen Wright was one of the first to arrive. Just before he left Australia, a British official asked him if he would ever again interfere with British rule in Canada and Wright replied: "Not until the Canadians are worthier of liberty than they are at the present." He arrived home in Denmark, Lewis County, New York, in February 1844 and later published a memoir of his experiences at the windmill and in prison.[11]

Daniel Heustis got back to Watertown in 1846, after a long journey by way of Hawaii and Chile that took more than a year.

His family, overjoyed to see him, "fired a cannon and called out a band of music." A short time later, Heustis visited the scene of the fighting at Prescott and, as he wrote, "the recollections of the past were still fresh in my mind, and I will leave the reader to imagine the feelings with which I trod again that field of deadly strife." Two years later he published a *Narrative of the Adventures and Sufferings of Captain Daniel D. Heustis,* which is notable for its honesty, accuracy and humour and is by far the best of the Hunter accounts of the Prescott invasion.[12]

Sometimes the homecomings were not happy. Henry Shew of Jefferson County returned in 1846 to discover that his wife, having despaired of his life, had married another man. In 1848, William Gates arrived in his home town of Cape Vincent, Jefferson County, only to discover to his horror that his mother and father had emigrated to Upper Canada and were living near Port Stanley. He visited them but, unable to stomach the thought of living under the British flag, convinced them to move to Lockport, New York. In 1850, Gates published *Recollections of Life In Van Dieman's Land,* which he hoped "would meet with encouragement sufficient to give him help to assist in maintaining his aged parents."[13]

The last of the Hunters to return was John Berry, a former resident of Leeds County, who had fled to Oswego early in 1838 before joining the Prescott expedition. Berry was working as a shepherd in such a remote area of Van Diemen's Land that he did not learn of his 1844 pardon until 1857. He got a passage on an American whaler but it took him nearly three years to make New York, from which he made his way to Cape Vincent and then boarded a steamer for Brockville. On board was William H. Draper, his former prosecutor, who recognized Berry, "shook hands with him and generously helped him onward." Twenty-two years after he had left Upper Canada, John Berry came home.[14]

The steamer *United States* was taken off the St. Lawrence route because Canadians would not travel on her and spent the rest of her days in service on Lake Ontario. The ship was broken up at Oswego in 1843.[15]

The flag of the Onondaga Hunters captured at the windmill was sent to the Tower of London, where it was briefly displayed before apparently being destroyed in a fire in 1841.[16]

Of the British military and naval officers involved in the battle, Sir John Colborne, the commander in chief in North America, returned to Britain in October 1839. Elevated to the House of Lords, he was governor of the Ionian Isles in 1843-1849 and commander of the forces in Ireland from 1855 to 1859. Loved and respected as a man and a soldier, Colborne died at Torquay in 1863.[17]

Lieutenant Governor Sir George Arthur left Upper Canada in 1841 and later served as governor of Bombay from 1842 to 1846. By seniority, he had reached the rank of lieutenant general in the army at the time of his death in 1854. Remembered with respect in Canada, Arthur is despised in Australia, where he is regarded as a bloody tyrant.[18]

Lieutenant Colonel the Honourable Henry Dundas received both a knighthood and a promotion to colonel for his role in the battle of the windmill. He returned to Britain in 1841 and was briefly an aide de camp to Queen Victoria before seeing considerable active service in India. In 1851, Dundas succeeded his father as Viscount Melville and he had reached the rank of lieutenant general when he died unmarried at the family castle near Edinburgh in 1876.[19]

The recognition given to Dundas for his role in the battle was resented by Captain Williams Sandom of the Royal Navy and Major Forbes Macbean of the Royal Artillery, who felt that their commands should have received greater credit for their efforts. Macbean complained that both Lieutenant Colonels Henry Dundas and Plomer Young had "received distinction and promotion" while his gunners, "who performed the principal service on that occasion, have been entirely overlooked!"[20] For his part, Sandom stated that Macbean's guns were never closer than 1,000 yards to the mill, which was not true, and it was the guns of his squadron that had brought the issue to a sucessful close. Nothing seems to have come of these complaints, but then such is life in the service.[21]

Williams Sandom continued as the naval commander on the Great Lakes until 1843 when he was succeeded by Lieutenant William Fowell. He returned to England, where he married in 1844, and had reached the rank of rear admiral by seniority when he died at Lowestoft in 1858.[22]

At the suggestion of the Duke of Wellington, Plomer Young, the British commander at Prescott, was given the permanent rank of lieutenant colonel for his actions. He served in various staff positions in North America until 1855 when he returned to Britain and, by seniority, had reached the rank of major general when he died at his home in Trowbridge in 1863.[23]

Major Forbes Macbean, whose gunners had added a professional element to what otherwise would have been a vulgar brawl, was promoted lieutenant colonel in 1841. Nothing is known about his later life.[24]

Lieutenant William Fowell, RN, who fought a naval action in the middle of the St. Lawrence against a vessel commanded by a drunken phrenologist, was promoted commander in 1839 and succeeded Sandom in 1843. He retired from the service as a captain in 1853 and died in 1868.[25]

Lieutenant William Johnson's fellow officers erected a plaque to their fallen comrade in St. George's Anglican Church in Kingston which recorded that he was "killed while gallantly leading an attack … against a band of American marauders who were strongly posted at Windmill point, near Prescott."[26] Unfortunately this plaque was destroyed when a fire gutted the church.

For his bayonet work at the windmill, Lance Corporal Hunn of the Royal Marines was given an accelerated promotion to sergeant. A year or two after the battle, he died of yellow fever while on anti-slavery patrol off the coast of Africa.[27]

The Royal Navy, of course, is still the Royal Navy, and the Royal Regiment of Artillery and Royal Marines continue to serve. The 83rd Regiment of Foot is today The Royal Irish Regiment, while the 93rd (Highland) Regiment of Foot, which went on to greater fame when it formed the "thin red line" at the battle of Balaclava, is now The Argyll and Sutherland Highlanders (Princess Louise's) regiment.

As for the Canadians, William Lyon Mackenzie was tried at Rochester in June 1839 for violation of American neutrality law. He conducted his own defence and made an impassioned six hour speech to the jury describing the royalist oppression in the north country that had forced him to take extreme measures. The judge allowed as to how all that might be true but the fact being that Mackenzie had broken the law, he directed the jury to consider their verdict solely on legal grounds. For their part, the jury only kept the little Scotsman waiting ninety minutes before finding him guilty. Mackenzie was fined $10 and sentenced to eighteen months in prison but was granted early release after a year because of his health. Mackenzie and his family lived for a while in Rochester, where he published a newspaper, the *Volunteer*, but moved to New York in 1842. Here he worked at various publishing ventures, launched several newspapers which usually folded for lack of funds and wrote a number a books. He became disillusioned with America and Americans and was quick to accept when the Crown offered him an amnesty in 1849.[28]

Mackenzie travelled to Montreal to test the waters, but while visiting the Legislative Library in that city unfortunately ran into his worst nightmare – Colonel John Prince. According to an eyewitness, the choleric Prince, on seeing the former rebel leader, stepped up to him "without a word" and

> laid his iron paw upon his throat and dragged him out of the Library, through the door, down the stairs, across the lobby, down another stair, across the hall, through the outer door, and pitched him into the slush in the open street, with one kind word of warning to his unresisting victim, to keep out of his way in future lest he should break his neck.[29]

As always, Prince was unrepentant and that night confided to his diary: "I turned McKenzie, the Traitor, out of The Library. *Much Excitement created thereby.*"[30]

Things got better for Mackenzie after that. He settled in Toronto and in 1851 won election to the Legislative Assembly, where he served for seven years and was active in promoting the cause of reform. But he was never an easy man to deal with and gradually became personally and politically isolated. Mackenzie was ever short of money and when a group of his admirers (and he still had a few) privately raised funds to reward him for his services to Canada by purchasing him a home for his later years, he disputed with them over how the money was to be spent. He died, in debt, in August 1861 at the age of sixty-seven, respected but not particularly liked. William Lyon Mackenzie remains as much a problem in death as he was in life and historians have found him a difficult figure to assess, but whatever his role in achieving responsible government in Canada,

he must bear a great deal of the blame for encouraging the creation of an organization that brought needless death and suffering to his fellow countrymen.[31]

Mackenzie's counterpart in Lower Canada, Louis-Joseph Papineau, sailed to France in 1839 but returned to Canada five years later to accept an amnesty from the Crown. Papineau returned to politics in 1848 and spent six years in the Legislative Assembly, where he advocated the annexation of Canada to the United States. He died at his manor at Montebello in 1871.[32]

Two other prominent rebel leaders, Charles Duncombe and Robert Nelson, stayed in the United States. Duncombe moved to California, where he died in 1867. Nelson also went to California and amassed a fortune while practising medicine during the gold rush years. He later moved to New York, where he wrote an authoritative text on cholera before dying in 1873.[33]

For his part, Colonel John "Shot Accordingly" Prince had a lengthy career in provincial politics, although towards the end of it he became an advocate of independence from Britain. Prince's marriage ended on an unhappy note and he spent his last years as a judge in Sault Ste. Marie. Prince remained a tough man to the end – at the age of seventy, following an accident, he amputated his own thumb. John Prince died in 1870.[34]

Sheriff Allan Macdonell, the bluff but good-hearted men who guarded the prisoners and, if required, executed them, was appointed inspector of the Provincial Penitentiary at Kingston in 1840. From 1838 to 1841, he was also the commanding officer of the 8th Provisional Battalion of longservice militia. In 1842, Macdonell resigned the shrievalty of the Midland District and his post as inspector of the penitentiary.[35]

William H. Draper, the man who prosecuted the prisoners, entered politics and was a leading light in creating what would become the Conservative Party of Canada. He later left politics for the judiciary and was a chief justice when he died in Toronto in 1877.[36]

One of Draper's protegés in the Conservative Party was John Alexander Macdonald, the young Kingston lawyer who had tried to assist Daniel George and Nils von Schoultz at their trials. Macdonald was elected to the Legislative Assembly for Kingston in 1844, beginning a political career that would span nearly half a century. He was a proponent of the union of the separate British North American colonies in North America and, following confederation in 1867, became the first prime minister of the newly-created Dominion of Canada. He was defeated in 1873 but returned to office five years later and was still prime minister when he died in 1891, by which time the new nation stretched from the Atlantic to the Pacific. To the end of his long and productive life, Macdonald never forgot the romantic but haunted figure of the "Polish" adventurer, Nils von Schoultz, whom he had met as a young man.[37]

Colonel Richard Duncan Fraser, the bad-tempered militia officer who liked to beat pirates with the flat of his sword, did not get any more mellow with age. In 1840, he had a falling out with Ogle Gowan, his former comrade in the battle of 13 November, whom he accused of being a coward and a fool in front of witnesses. Gowan immediately challenged him to a duel but Fraser refused to fight on the grounds that Gowan "was beneath the station of a gentlemen and not a worthy opponent." Nonetheless, a time and place was set for a meeting but, according to one account, Fraser's wife informed the local magistrates, who bound both men over to keep the peace. Not long after, certain irregularities came to light in Fraser's accounting of the customs duties he had collected at Brockville on behalf of the goverment – in fact, it turned out that he owed the Crown a considerable sum of money. Fraser pleaded that the

missing funds had been stolen by Bill Johnston when he had robbed Fraser on the *Sir Robert Peel* in June 1838 but this excuse was not accepted and in 1843 he lost his position as collector at Brockville. Richard Fraser, perhaps Canada's most cantankerous defender, spent his last years on his farm, "Fraserfield," on the banks of the St. Lawrence and died in 1857 at the age of seventy-one.[38]

Lieutenant Colonel Ogle Gowan, who received an embarrassing wound at the battle of the windmill, was elected to serve for Grenville County in 1844 and had a long and tempestuous political career. He joined the nascent Conservative Party created by William Henry Draper and for some time was associated with Draper and John A. Macdonald, but Gowan was never completely accepted by his fellow Tories as they did not regard him as a gentleman. After suffering an election defeat, he moved to Toronto in 1851, where he was active in municipal politics and the Orange Lodge. Gowan spent his last years writing a multi-volume history of the Orange order in Ireland and Canada. He died in 1876.[39]

Major John Richardson left the army in 1838 but, unable to make a living as an author in Canada, moved to New York, where he apparently starved to death in 1852. It is not an uncommon fate for writers.[40]

Captain Hamilton D. Jessup, the Prescott doctor whose militia company had defended their own homes during the battle, pursued an active career in provincial and local politics, being elected to the Legislative Assembly and serving ten times as the mayor of Prescott. Jessup never lost his interest in things military and was a lieutenant colonel when he resigned from the militia in 1883, after forty-five years of service. Hamilton Jessup died at Prescott in 1892 and was universally mourned.[41]

Sergeant John Smith, who arrested one of Jessup's men for drunkenness, returned to his farm near Prescott, where he and

Friends again: International Peace Centennial, July 1938
As the 100th anniversary of the battle approached, the town of Prescott decided to hold an International Peace Centennial to mark the event and promote tourism. The high point of the week was a commemoration ceremony at the windmill, where, among other politicians, Prime Minister Mackenzie King spoke of the heroes who had helped bring about responsible government in Canada, including the famous Polish general, Nils von Schoultz. Here, a local hotel is decorated with American, Canadian and Polish flags in celebration. (National Archives of Canada, C-27018)

Wooden nickel
Celebrating "A Century of Peace at the Crossroads of the Continent," this wooden nickel was manufactured as a souvenir by the organizers of the St. Lawrence International Peace Centennial. Although it was certainly not their intention, this gimmick ironically implies that international peace is worth about as much as a wooden nickel. (Courtesy of the Friends of Windmill Point)

his wife raised a large family. Smith continued to serve in the militia and was known to be still alive in the early 1870s.[42]

The Canadian militia from the St. Lawrence area who defended their country in 1838 are today represented on the order of battle of the Canadian Forces by three fine units: The Prince of Wales's Own Regiment in Kingston, The Brockville Rifles in that town, and The Stormont, Dundas and Glengarry Highlanders at Cornwall. Some of the soldiers serving in these units are descendants of the men who fought at the battle of the windmill, and unless their regiments are axed by a computer in National Defence Headquarters in Ottawa, they will be ready, if needed again, to serve their country.

And, finally, we come to Private Allan MacIntosh, that gentle and religious man who buried a good friend on the grounds of the Prescott seminary on the Tuesday of the battle. Allan became a circuit preacher for the Methodist Church and for many years travelled across North America dispensing not only The Word but also cuttings from the unique apple tree on his father's farm at Dundela. As a result, the MacIntosh family never achieved their ambition to make money from this delicious fruit, which has since become one of the most popular eating apples in the world – every year an estimated eight

million bushels are harvested in Canada. After a long and happy life of service to his fellow man, Allan MacIntosh died in 1899 at the age of eighty and was buried in the family plot at Dundela.[43]

The Ogdensburg–Prescott International Bridge
Completed in 1960, this bridge links Canada and the United States and is a symbol of the enduring friendship between the two nations. It was not always so – there was tension along the border for nearly forty years after the border troubles of 1837-1840, and in 1866-1870 the Fenian movement based on American territory mounted a further series of invasions. The Treaty of Washington signed in 1871 ushered in an era of better relations between the two neighbours that continues to this day. (Photograph by René Schoemaker)

In the century that followed, almost everyone forgot about the battle of the windmill. In the United States, few outside the northern states were even aware that an undeclared border war took place in 1837-1840, and if Americans today recall events from that time, they are more likely to think of Bowie, Crockett and Texas than the somewhat less than glorious last stand of the Patriot Hunters at the "Alamo of the North." In Britain, the Canadian rebellions and the attendant border troubles were only one of many colonial campaigns waged by the Royal Navy and the British army during the 19th century, and since they lacked the colour and intensity of the Indian Mutiny, the Zulu War or the Nile Expedition, they are generally overlooked. At best they get only a passing mention in regimental histories – that of the Royal Marines contains two short paragraphs about Lance Corporal Hunn on 13 November in a small print appendix listing miscellaneous battles and deeds. In Canada, the patriot raids and the invasion at Prescott have become tangled up in the public mind with the rebellions of 1837 and, as a result, there are many Canadians who still believe that the invaders at Prescott were Canadian "rebels" and "reformers," not what they really were – a rather inept group of American terrorists.[44]

Prescott, however, has always remembered that long and terrible week in its history. Memories, anecdotes and stories about the battle are still told in the river port and, up to the 1960s at least, Prescott schoolchildren were taught the militia song of the battle ("On Tuesday morning we marched out, in command of Colonel Fraser, with swords and bay'nets of polished steel, as keen as any razor"). By 1938, the centennial of the battle, the couples who parked out on Windmill Point on warm summer evenings to discuss history and watch the moon rise over the river were cuddling in horseless carriages. Local interest was perhaps at its highest this year and, as described in the prologue, Prime Minister Mackenzie King attended the memorial ceremony at the Point on 1 July and praised the efforts of his grandfather, William Lyon Mackenzie, and that Polish hero, Nils von Schoultz, who had fought to serve a "larger freedom" even if he had tried to kill Grandfather King of Macbean's brigade, Royal Artillery. (If only the Swede had been there to hear it.) Later that night, as he was being driven back to Ottawa along the river highway, King's car passed near the windmill and the prime minister was entranced by the way its flashing beacon cut through the heavy fog on the river.[45]

That beacon continued to flash as the decades passed although the myths still lay thick about the battle of the windmill. In 1970, a Prescott historian published an account of the engagement which described Nils von Schoultz as a Polish aristocrat from Cracow whose family had suffered in the uprising of 1830-1831 and who "equated the position of the 'oppressed Canadians' with that of his own countrymen in Poland."[46] Ironically, another book the following year written by a descendant of von Schoultz finally unmasked him as a Swede and provided the correct details of his life, although it cast him as a romantic and well-meaning figure.[47]

Also in 1970, a memorial was unveiled at Sandy Bay in Tasmania, the spot where the prisoners landed from HMS *Buffalo*, to mark the 130th anniversary of the event. It bears a plaque dedicated to 92 English-speaking and 58 French-speaking "exiles" from the 1837 rebellions in the Canadas and the "sacrifices" they made and states baldly that "measures taken as a re-

Memorial to an unhappy event: The Prescott windmill today
One hundred and sixty-three years after the battle, the windmill is now a National Historic Site. Operated by a non-profit group, the Friends of Windmill Point, it is open in the summer months and visitors who climb to the top of the structure can obtain splendid views of the St. Lawrence and surrounding area. (Photograph by René Schoemaker)

sult" of these uprisings "represented significant steps in the evolution of responsible government and parliamentary democracy" in Canada. Few realize that 60 of the English-speaking prisoners commemorated were convicted criminals transported (not exiled) for attacking Prescott in 1838 and that 51 of these men were Americans. The fact that these martyrs to the cause of responsible government killed or wounded more than 80 British and Canadian soldiers, sailors and civilians in those five awful days in November has somehow got lost along the way, but then you should never believe what you read on historical plaques.[48]

The windmill continued to function as a lighthouse until it was taken out of service in 1978. Today, the structure and its grounds constitute the Battle of the Windmill National Historic Site. Operated by the Friends of Windmill Point, a nonprofit organization, it is open to the public during the summer months and the interested visitor who climbs the interior staircase to the top level will be rewarded with splendid views of the St. Lawrence, Prescott and Ogdensburg, and the International Bridge completed down-river in 1960.

That long steel span linking Canada and the United States is a symbol of the special relationship that has formed between the two nations since the unhappy days of 1838. It is a relationship based on mutual respect and its enduring quality was perhaps best summed up in a phrase from the Scriptures quoted by President John Fitzgerald Kennedy when visiting Canada in 1961: "What therefore God hath joined together, let not man put asunder."

The End

APPENDIX A

British and Canadian military and naval organization, weapons and tactics, North America, 1838

GENERAL COMMAND STRUCTURE AND STRENGTH

In November 1838, the military command in British North America was vested in Lieutenant General Sir John Colborne, with the title of Commander of the Forces. Colborne's headquarters was at Quebec City but he spent much time at Montreal as he usually exercised direct command of Lower Canada, allowing Sir George Arthur the subordinate role in Upper Canada. All military units, regular and militia, reported to these officers. The naval squadron on the Great Lakes was under the operational control of Colborne or Arthur although its commanding officer also had regular contact with the commander of the North American and West Indies station at Halifax and the Admiralty in London.

By the end of 1838, Colborne commanded 12,000 regulars, 21,000 longservice militia or provincial units and 235,000 sedentary militia in the two provinces of Upper and Lower Canada.

LAND FORCES

British Regular Army

Infantry

In 1838, the infantry of the British army comprised 7 battalions of guards, 4 battalions of rifles, and 124 battalions of the line. Each line battalion was divided into a service or active component and a depot component which trained men for the active component. The service component, usually led by the battalion commander, a lieutenant colonel, consisted of six companies, each with 86 privates at full strength. The depot component, usually commanded by a junior major, consisted of four companies, each with 56 privates at full strength. Of the six active companies, one was a grenadier company, theoretically composed of the biggest and most experienced soldiers in the battalion, and one was a light company, theoretically composed of the most agile and intelligent men in the unit. The grenadier company functioned as the assault element of the battalion while the light company provided it with a skirmishing capability.

The British private soldier enlisted for a term of seven years and could re-enlist for two further periods of the same duration, after which he might, on good behaviour, receive a small pension. His pay was 1 shilling a day for the first seven years and an additional one pence per day for each successive seven-year term. "Stoppages," or deductions were made from his pay for rations, and some clothing and other issue items. The rule was, however, that the private soldier, despite all deductions owed, received at least one penny per day.

In 1838, the British soldier was dressed for effect, not comfort. Soldiers of the line infantry wore a heavy, leather bell-topped shako, a tight red wool coatee (a jacket with short tails), white pants in the summer and grey pants in the winter. All private soldiers had to wear stocks – leather collars that forced them to keep their heads upright. Buff leather shoulder belts, crossed on the chest, carried the soldier's bayonet scabbard and cartridge box.

The infantryman was armed with a .75 calibre India Pattern smoothbore flintlock musket weighing 9 lb. 11 oz. which fired a .71 calibre soft lead ball weighing just over one ounce. First manufactured in the 1790s, the Indian Pattern had been the common arm of the British infantry during the Napoleonic Wars and so many were produced that it soldiered on well into the 1840s. Its maximum range was about 200 yards, its maximum effective range was 150 yards, and the preferred range was 75-100 yards. It was a difficult weapon to load and fire but, under optimum conditions, a trained infantryman could get off between 3 and 4 rounds per minute although, in combat, the rate of fire dropped considerably. The infantryman's second weapon was his 17-inch long bayonet, with a triangular cross-section.

The India Pattern musket was an abysmally inaccurate weapon and in battle the emphasis was put on volume, not accuracy of fire – in effect, the battalion or company was the weapon, not the individual soldier. The favoured formation in the British army, for fire and manoeuvre, was the two-rank line, a formation that required considerable training to be used successfully. In a well-commanded infantry battalion, drill was therefore unceasing, usually between three and four hours a day. For individual and platoon level instruction, the 1834 *Manual and Platoon Exercises* was the established drill book; for company and battalion level training, use was made of the 1833 *Field Exercise and Evolutions of the Army*.

These manuals had not changed radically since those in use during the Napoleonic period. However, by the 1830s, some stress was being put on individual marksmanship and skirmishing tactics. By 1838, most British battalions could manoeuvre and fight, either in line, or in extended skirmish order as light infantry.

Artillery

In 1838, the artillery arm of the British army consisted of 72 Royal Artillery companies, 6 Royal Horse Artillery troops and 1 Royal Horse Artillery Rocket troop. The RHA were true mobile field artillery, the RA companies served either as garrison or field artillery, as required, and British gunners were trained to man a wide variety of ordnance, from small 3-pdr. up to 68-pdr. guns.

If an RA company was organized for field service, it usually formed a brigade (battery) which was equipped with six pieces of ordnance. Light field brigades had four or five 6-pdr. guns and one or two 12-pdr. howitzers; field brigades had four or five 9-pdr. guns and one or two 24-pdr. howitzers. The guns fired case shot (canister), spherical case shot (shrapnel) and round shot; the howitzers fired shell, spherical case and case shot. By the 1830s, it was calculated that the maximum effective range for roundshot was about 1200 yards; for shell, about 1000 yards; and for case shot about half that range although, in action, shorter ranges were more desirable. The rate of fire for field pieces was deliberately kept low, usually between 2-3 rounds per minute.

The Royal Artillery was, in all senses, an elite arm. All artillery officers were graduates of the Royal Military Academy at Woolwich, the training school for British gunners and engineers. Unlike the infantry and cavalry where the purchase system permitted a wealthy officer to gain promotion faster than his peers, artillery officers were promoted by seniority and promotion was very slow. Forbes Macbean, the RA commander at the battle of the windmill graduated from the Royal Military Academy and was commissioned as a second lieutenant in 1804. It took him ten years, in a time of constant warfare, to reach the rank of captain and a further twenty-three years to reach the rank of major. A similar case applied with the enlisted men of the artillery arm.

They were trained longer and paid better than their infantry counterparts. Artillery recruiting sergeants looked for intelligent and big men because quick-witted men learned the technical aspects of the artillery trade faster and men with physical strength were needed to handle the heavy equipment of the period.

Upper Canadian Military Units

The Canadian militia units that fought at Prescott in November 1838 were composed of either sedentary or longservice militia units.

The Sedentary Militia

By law, every male in Upper Canada between the ages of sixteen and sixty was liable for militia service, with some exceptions on religious grounds. This *levée en masse* constituted the sedentary militia which was organized by counties, populous counties having two or more regiments, each with two battalions, while less settled counties might provide only a single battalion. Under the militia act of 1829, each county regiment was to consist of two battalions, the 1st Battalion to include men no older than forty and the 2nd Battalion to consist of those over that age. In 1840, the sedentary militia of Upper Canada totalled 117,000 men organized into 248 battalions.

Prior to the outbreak of the 1837 Rebellion, the sedentary militia was indifferently armed and poorly trained. Uniforms were not provided but each man was supposed to possess a "good and sufficient musket, fusil, rifle or gun" with a certain proportion of ammunition but few bothered to obey this regulation. Once a year, on 4 June, the annual muster day, each militiaman had to turn out with his company "to be reviewed and exercised." The result was often ludicrous, but it was never intended to use the sedentary militia for operational purposes; the organization was basically a mobilization scheme. Companies were called out as needed, usually from the younger and more active men of the 1st Battalions. Fortunately, there was in the province a cadre of men who had previous military service, either with the British army or with the militia during the War of 1812, who could provide competent leadership for active companies.

In terms of training and tactics, the Upper Canadian militia followed established British army doctrine and the more fortunate units were trained by regular army instructors.

Longservice Militia

When the border troubles started in December 1837, it quickly became obvious that there was a need for more permanent militia units who would receive a higher level of training. Over the next year, various units of incorporated, provisional and volunteer militia infantry, artillery and cavalry were raised – the differences in name having to do more with their terms of service than their military qualities – totalling just under 20,000 men. These units varied in quality. The best were colonial regulars, being armed, uniformed and equipped by the Crown, and usually trained by British army instructors while other were home defence companies but all were generally superior to the sedentary militia.

Among the major longstanding units were six regiments of incorporated militia, each 500 strong, authorized in December 1837, four raised in the Toronto area, and two on the Niagara frontier. These regiments were disbanded in June 1838 when the border tensions subsided but the rise of the Hunters caused a new wave of longservice units to be created. In the autumn of 1838, four battalions of incorporated militia were raised to serve for eighteen months and twelve provisional battalions for six months service. In addition, nearly 9000 men served in independent companies created at "revolt stations," threatened or sensitive points along the border.

In terms of training and tactics, the longservice militia followed the British model. Throughout 1838, there were shortages of uniforms and weapons for these units but these problems gradually eased as materiel became available in 1839.

The Canadian militia that fought at Prescott in November 1838 included elements of the sedentary, longservice and volunteer militia. Appendix B below is the order of battle for these units.

NAVAL AND MARINE FORCES

In April 1838, Captain Williams Sandom, RA, was sent to Kingston to revive the naval station on the Great Lakes which had been closed down in 1836. Gradually, over the next few months, detachments of sailors and marines were successively transferred from the North America and West Indies squadron, stationed at Halifax until Sandom was in command of 267 officers and men, including a small Royal Marine detachment of one officer and 41 marines.

Sandom commissioned the shore station at Point Frederick near Kingston as HMS *Niagara* and quickly extemporized a squadron from purchased and chartered vessels. He commissioned HMS *Bullfrog,* a schooner, as a depot ship and bought the steamer *Experiment,* which was brought into service as Her Majesty's Steam Vessel *Experiment.* He also constructed or purchased gunboats and gun barges and chartered civilian steamers, which he armed. Details of the vessels in his squadron will be found in Appendix B.

The Royal Marines were armed and equipped as their land-service comrades.

Sandom came under the command of Sir John Colborne or Sir George Arthur for operational matters but in administrative matters he reported to Vice Admiral Sir Charles Paget, the naval commander in chief of North America at Halifax, and to the Admiralty or naval headquarters in London.

Sources

Public Record Office, Kew, Surrey: Admiralty 1, Captains' Letters, 1838; War Office 17, General Monthly Returns, Canada; National Archives of Canada: Colonial Office 42; Record Group 8 I, British Military and Naval Records; *Army List*, 1838 and 1839; Charles R. Sanderson, ed., *The Arthur Papers*, 3 vols., Toronto, 1957; *Field Exercise and Evolutions of the Army*, Horse Guards, London, 1833; *List of Officers of the Royal Regiment of Artillery …*, Greenwich, c. 1840; *Manual and Platoon Exercises*, Horse Guards, London, 1834; Howard Blackmore, *British Military Firearms. 1650-1850*, London, 1961; J. Mackay Hitsman, *Safeguarding Canada, 1763-1831*. Toronto, 1968; B.P. Hughes, *British Smooth-Bore Artillery*, London, 1969; M.E.S. Laws, *Battery Records of the Royal Artillery, 1716-1859*, Woolwich, 1952; Frederick Myatt, *The British Infantry 1660-1945*, Poole, 1983; George Stanley, *Canada's Soldiers. The Military History of an Unmilitary People.* Toronto, 1974; Hew Strachan, *From Waterloo to Balaclava. Tactics, Technology, and the British Army, 1815-1854.*

Order of battle, British and Canadian forces at Prescott, 12–17 November 1838

* indicates that unit was in action on 13 November 1838

N.B. Strength figures include all ranks unless otherwise noted

Command

Lieutenant Colonel Plomer Young, a regular officer, was in command on 12 and 13 November. On 14 November, Lieutenant Colonel Henry Dundas of the 83rd Foot took over command for the day but departed in the late afternoon and Young resumed command, retaining it until noon on 16 November when Dundas returned.

When he was present on 13 and 16-17 November, Captain Williams Sandom, RN, exercised naval command. In his absence, naval command was vested in the senior RN officer on station at Prescott.

BRITISH REGULAR FORCES

ARMY

83rd Regiment of Foot (300)
Officer Commanding: Major Botet Trydell
  Grenadier company
  Light Company
  Two Line Companies

Detachment, 83rd Regiment of Foot (44)*
Officer Commanding: Lieutenant William S. Johnson

93rd (Highland) Regiment of Foot (est. 75-80)
Officer Commanding: Major John Arthur
  Grenadier company

No. 4 Company, 5th Battalion, Royal Regiment of Artillery (est. 90)
Commanding Officer: Major Forbes Macbean
  1 x 6-pdr. gun, 1 x 12-pdr. howitzer present on 14 November
  2 x 18-pdr. guns, 1 x 12-pdr. howitzer present on 16 November

ROYAL NAVY

Commander: Captain Williams Sandom, RN

Detachment, Royal Marines (30)*
Officer Commanding: Lieutenant Charles Parker

HMSV *Experiment*, Lieutenant William Fowell, RN
  Displacement: 100 tons
  Engine: Single engine, 30 horsepower
  Armament: 1 x 18 pdr. carronade, 2 x 3-pdr. brass guns

Cobourg (chartered steamer), Commander Gibson, RN
> Displacement: 440 tons
> Engine: Double engine, 120 horsepower
> Armament: 4 x 18-pdr. carronades

Queen Victoria (chartered steamer), Lieutenant Harper, RN
> Displacement: 220 tons
> Engine: Single engine, 60 horsepower
> Armament: 1 x 12-pdr. gun, 2 x 12-pdr. carronades

Gun Boat No. 1
> 2 x 18-pdr. carronades
> 1 x 5.5 in mortar

Gun Boat No. 2 (Barge)
> 1 x 18-pdr. gun

Gun Boat No. 3 (Barge)
> 1 x 18-pdr. gun

Gun Boat No. 4 (Barge)
> 1 x 18-pdr. carronade

UPPER CANADA MILITIA

Incorporated Militia (148)
Lancaster Glengarry Highlanders (84)*
Commanding Officer: Captain George Macdonell

9th Provisional Battalion (64)
Commanding Officer: Lieutenant Colonel Ogle Gowan (8 staff)*
> Captain William Stewart's Company (53)*

Volunteer ("Revolt") Companies (86)
Brockville Independent Company (69)*
Officer Commanding: Captain Robert Edmondson

Prescott Volunteer (Independent) Company (17)*
Officer Commanding: Captain Hamilton D. Jessup

Sedentary Militia (643)
1st Dundas Regiment (53)
Commanding Officer: Colonel John Crysler
> Captain John P. Crysler's Company (53)*

2nd Dundas Regiment (108)
Commanding Officer: Colonel George Merkeley
> Captain John Dorrin's Company (54)*
> Captain Nicholas Shaver's Company (54)*

1st Grenville Regiment (437)
Commanding Officer: Colonel Hugh Munro
> Captain John Adams's Company (78)*
> Captain Dunham Jones's Company (120)*
> Captain Thomas McCargar's Company (53)*
> Captain Simon B. Fraser's Company (40)
> Captain John Lawrence's Company (64)*
> Captain Philip Dulmage's Company (82)*

1st Grenville Cavalry Troop (45)
Officer Commanding: Captain William Kay

2nd Grenville Regiment
Commanding Officer: Colonel Richard D. Fraser

Emergency Volunteers (256)
Grenville Loyal Sedentary Volunteer Company (28)*
> Officer Commanding: Captain Edwin Pridham

Captain Archibald Campbell's Augmentation of Grenville Volunteers (65)*

First Company of Prescott Reserves (19)
Officer Commanding: Captain John Kearnes

Second Company of Prescott Reserves (75)
Officer Commanding: Captain Chauncey Johnson

Third Company of Prescott Reserves (69)
Officer Commanding: Lieutenant Lang Robertson

Because various regular and militia units were coming and going from the area of Prescott throughout the period 11 November–17 November 1838 no attempt has been made to provide a total for the British and Canadian soldiers who saw service during those six days. A calculation of the units and numbers that actually saw combat on 13 November and 16 November will be found in Chapters 7 and 9, respectively, above.

It should be noted that the militia records for this period are very confused. Men are recorded as holding various ranks and belonging to different units according to the different records consulted. The most complete study of the units and Canadian militiamen is Arthur Robinson, *The Grenville Militia Regiments and Other Local Militia Regiments. November 1838*, which is based on pay and pension records. Those interested in the subject of the militia at the battle of the windmill, should consult this work.

Sources

Archival
Archives of Ontario, Toronto: MS 521, Hamilton Jessup, "Battle of the Windmill"; *National Archives of Canada*, Ottawa: CO 42: vol. 409, pt 2: Young to Halkett, 14 Nov 1838; Fowell to Sandom, 14 Nov 1838; Dundas to Arthur, 18 Nov 1838; Sandom to Arthur, 18 Nov 1838; vol. 451, Fowell to Sandom, 12 Nov 1838; Sandom to Arthur, 14 Nov 1838; MG 19 A39, 365, Young to Halkett, 20 Nov 1838; MG 27 I E30, Gowan, "Memoir": RG 5 B40 & B41, evidence of Fowell, Leary, Parker and Sandom; RG 8 I, vol. 750, 65, Macbean to Cubitt, 27 Nov 1838. *Public Record Office, Kew, Surrey, UK*: Admiralty 1, vol. 2563, Statement of British Steam Vessels on Lake Ontario; vol. 2564, A List of Vessels and Boats Employed on Canadian Waters, 1 Oct 1839; vol. 2565, Sandom to Admiralty, 14 May 1839; War Office 17, vol. 1542, Distributionn of the Troops in Canada, 1 Nov 1838. *Friends of Windmill Point, Prescott*: Memoir of Private Allan MacIntosh; Sergeant John Smith, "Recollections."

Published
Kingston Chronicle and Gazette, 17 Nov, 27 Nov 1838; Thaddeaus Leavitt, *A History of Leeds and Grenville*, 1879, 49-51, summary by a British officer; Prescott *Sentinel*, 24 Nov 1838; Arthur Robinson, *The Grenville Militia Regiments and Other Local Militia Regiments. November 1838*, author, Victoria, BC, 2000; *Upper Canada Herald*, 4 Dec 1838, Naval force at Prescott.

The Upper Canada militia at the battle of the windmill, 1838

by Arthur J. Robinson

The first Militia Act for Upper Canada was passed in 1793 and provided for the appointment of county lieutenants, who in turn had authority to appoint officers of militia in their respective counties. All males sixteen to fifty years old were enrolled. The act allowed the militia to be called out once a year "to be reviewed and exercised." The captains were authorized to (and did) call out their companies not less than twice a year to inspect arms and to be instructed.

New militia acts were created periodically. In 1808 the upper age limit was raised to sixty years. The Militia Act of 1812 extended the 1803 act. There followed numerous amendments. In 1829 the militia was reorganized (General Order No. 87). Each regiment was to consist of two battalions, the first to include men not exceeding forty years of age and the second was a reserve battalion of men from that age to the upper limit established by law. A new act in 1838 proved to be insufficient and was superseded by a new act in 1839. It provided for all males eighteen to sixty to be enrolled.

The militia in a county was formed into a regiment of five to ten companies, each company to be composed of not more than fifty privates and no less than twenty. However, there were variances in the maximum, as in 1812 when Brock's Militia Act increased the maximum number of rank and file in a company to 100. This provision was rescinded in 1813 and the maximum number was once again made. In counties with smaller populations, a battalion of five to eight companies was formed. Where there were not enough men to form a regiment or a battalion, independent companies were formed. There was a provision for troops of cavalry.

By November 1838, the infantry companies were organized with a captain, a lieutenant, three sergeants and between thirty-four and 115 privates. Some companies had additional officers and non-commissioned officers such as ensigns and corporals. A typical troop of cavalry consisted of a captain, a lieutenant, a cornet, a sergeant major, six sergeants and about thirty-five privates.

Each militiaman was to provide his own "good and suficient musket, fusil, rifle or gun" with at least six pounds of powder and ball. Uniforms were not provided. As a result, while the men may have had the military spirit, formations often did not have a military bearing.

For their service during the conflict captains received a military allowance of 13 shillings (s.) and 10 pence (d.) per day, lieutenants received 7s. 9d. per day, sergeants 2s. 2d. per day, corporals 1s. 7d., and privates 1s. 2d. In addition many of the men received a billeting allowance of 4d. per day. Because the militia did not have any uniforms, an allowance was given them in lieu of clothing. The amount of the allowance was based on their days of service.

The Militia Units at Prescott, 1838

Among the local militia units that participated in the battle in various ways were six companies from the First Grenville Militia Regiment (companies commanded by Captain John Adams, Captain Dunham Jones, Captain Thomas McCargar, Captain Simon B. Fraser and Captain John Lawrence and a troop of cavalry commanded by Captain William Kay) and part of the Second Grenville Militia Regiment (Captain Edwin Pridham's Grenville Loyal Sedentary Volunteer Company, Captain Joseph Adams's Company, Captain Archibald Campbell's Company of Augmentation of Grenville (Gentlemen) Volunteers and a detachment of Captain Lang's Company). There were four militia units in Prescott – the Prescott Independent Company or the Prescott Volunteer Company (as it was sometimes called) commanded by Captain Hamilton Jessup, and three companies of Prescott Reserves, commanded by Lt. Col. George Hamilton.

Other militia units that participated included the Brockville Independent Company (commanded by Captain Robert Edmondson), three companies of the Royal Dundas Militia (Captain John Crysler's Company, Captain John Dorin's Company and Captain Nicholas Shaver's Company), The Lancaster Glengarry Highlanders (Captain George Macdonell's Company and parts of nine companies of the 4th Regiment commanded by Colonel Angus McDonell) and the Queens Royal Borderers (the Ninth Provisional Battalion commanded by Lieutenant Colonel Ogle Gowan).

The paylists of these militia units that were called out during the emergency that occurred in the middle of November 1838, show the military allowance received by the officers, non-commissioned officers, and other ranks in their company for service during this emergency. The company commanders submitted these paylists, including the billeting allowance that was received. The company clerk recorded the name, rank, date of service and amount of military allowance received. Each person was then re-quired to sign the paylist beside his name to indicate that he had received his allowance. When the individual was unable to write, he made an "X" for his name.

It appears that the paylists for most of the militia units did not contain the names of those killed or seriously wounded, although some of the ones listed in other accounts as wounded appear on the paylists. They may not have been badly wounded and were able to return to duty quickly. The Dundas and Lancaster Glengarry companies did list those killed and some of the wounded.

The nominal rolls of the militia units were derived from the paylists submitted for the time period of the emergency. The name and rank of the individual is given as well as the date of service and whether or not the individual received a billeting allowance. In extracting the names from the paylists, every effort was made to ensure that the correct name appears on the lists. However, as the lists were handwritten, some error is inevitable. In a number of cases the handwriting is open to interpretation, e.g. the name could be "Mcaluse" or "Mcalue". Generally the clerk wrote down what he thought he heard the name to be. In some cases, his version of a name differs from the actual signature; e.g. the clerk wrote Robertson and the individual signed Robinson. In some cases the individual's name is spelled differently on different paylists. Where there is more than one version of the surname for an individual, the alternate version(s) are given in brackets.

The following nominal rolls or paylists of the various militia units that participated in the emergency are drawn from my work *The Grenville Militia Regiments and Other Local Militia Regiments*. Additional information on these militia units, including the billeting allowance and the clothing allowance, is contained in this book, which may be obtained from the Grenville County Historical Society in Prescott, Ontario.

PAYLISTS OF THE MILITIA UNITS FOR THE PERIOD 1 TO 31 NOVEMBER 1838

Abbreviations

Adj.	Adjutant
APM	Acting Paymaster
BA	Billeting Allowance
Blr.	Buglar
Capt.	Captain
Cnt.	Cornet
Col.	Colonel
Cpl.	Corporal
CSgt.	Colour Sergeant
Ens.	Ensign
Dmr.	Drummer
KIA	Killed in Action
Lt.	Lieutenant
LtCol	Lieutenant Colonel
Pte.	Private
PMS	Paymaster Sergeant
Q.M.	Quartermaster
QMS	Quartermaster Sergeant
Sgt.	Sergeant
SMaj.	Sergeant Major
Surg.	Surgeon
Tpr.	Trumpeter
WIA	Wounded in Action

Rank	Name	Date of Service

Brockville Independent Company

Capt.	Edmondson, Robert	1-30
Lt.	Schofeld, Jn- L.	1-30
Ens.	Fraser, Thomas W.	1-30
CSgt.	Freeman, James	15-30
CSgt.	Murphy, John D.	1-15
Sgt.	Freeman, James	1-15
Sgt.	Haley, James	20-30
Sgt.	Hall, Thomas	20-30
Sgt.	Neeves, Mathew	1-30
Cpl.	Haley, James	1-20
Cpl.	Hall, Thomas	1-20
Cpl.	Honer (Homer), Francis	20-30
Cpl.	Reilly, Adam	20-30

Cpl.	Stuart, William	20-30
Cpl.	Willson (Wilson), Thomas	20-30
Dmr.	Ross, Wm.	1-30
Pte.	Algate, Ward	17-30
Pte.	Alvert, George	5-30
Pte.	Anderson, Alexander	8-30
Pte.	Barry, Michael	1-30
Pte.	Blackmer, Alvin	9-30
Pte.	Boman (Bowman), Wm.	1-30
Pte.	Bono, William John	26-30
Pte.	Brinston (Bunniston), Henry	1-30
Pte.	Brown, William	1-30
Pte.	Carter, Thomas	22-30
Pte.	Causeor, John	1-4
Pte.	Chappeles (Chappell), Edward	1-30
Pte.	Churchill, William	13-30
Pte.	Crawford, James	1-4
Pte.	Davis, John	1-30
Pte.	Day, James	1-30
Pte.	Devine, Peter	12-30 WIA
Pte.	Dobson (Dodson), Joseph	2-30
Pte.	Donally (Donnelly), Patrick	1-30
Pte.	Dunnegham, John	5-30
Pte.	Dyer, Ormond	8-30
Pte.	Dyer, Samuel	1-30
Pte.	Eris (Iris), George	1-30
Pte.	Everts, George	27-30
Pte.	Farrell, Charles	30-30
Pte.	Folay, John	1-30
Pte.	Fraser, Alex	6-30
Pte.	Gray, William	10-30
Pte.	Gray, William Jr.	10-30
Pte.	Haley, Patrick	20-30
Pte.	Harbison, John	2-30
Pte.	Harley, Timothy	14-30
Pte.	Harris, Robert	1-30
Pte.	Harrison (Hamisfam), John G.	1-30
Pte.	Hewitt, Robert	26-30
Pte.	Honer (Honner), Francis	1-20
Pte.	Howard, Thomas	1-30
Pte.	Jelly, Andrew	1-30
Pte.	Joynt, Thomas	1-30

Pte.	Laidlaw, Andrew	1-30
Pte.	Lancaster, John	1-30
Pte.	Laney, Wm.	1-30
Pte.	Lewis, John	21-30
Pte.	Lipton, George G.	1-27
Pte.	Looby, Michael	12-30
Pte.	Loude (Loose), Isaac	6-30
Pte.	Lyttle, William	3-30
Pte.	Mahonny (Mahoney), Alan	1-30
Pte.	Mans, Phillip	5-30
Pte.	McDole, Matthew	3-30
Pte.	McGill, Henry	1-30
Pte.	McKay, John	2-30
Pte.	McLean, Hector	9-30
Pte.	McRae, Daniel	20-30
Pte.	Miller, William	17-30
Pte.	Moon, Charles	1-30
Pte.	Mooney, John	12-30
Pte.	Morris (Norris), William	1-30
Pte.	Murphy, Nicholas	1-30 WIA
Pte.	Payne, William	7-30
Pte.	Pye, Richard	18-30
Pte.	Randal (Randell), John	5-30
Pte.	Rely (Reilly), Adam	1-20
Pte.	Rely (Reilly), Robert	1-30
Pte.	Rely (Reilly), William	1-30
Pte.	Reynolds, Thomas	5-30
Pte.	Robinson, Wm.	1-30
Pte.	Stoddard, Alonson	1-30
Pte.	Stuart, Dann	1-30
Pte.	Stuart, William	1-30
Pte.	Thornhill, Henry	2-30
Pte.	Togaberry (Togabury), Henry	1-30
Pte.	Vahay, William	1-30
Pte.	Watson, Robert	1-30
Pte.	Weddows, Adam	1-30
Pte.	Weddows, William	1-30
Pte.	Willson, (Wilson), Robert	1-30
Pte.	Wilson, Thomas	1-20

Royal Dundas Militia

Some of the men and officers served at Prescott and others elsewhere.

Capt. John Pliney Crysler's Company

Capt.	Crysler, John Pliney	5-30
Lt.	Rose, Isaac N.	5-30
Ens.	Loucks, John W.	5-30
Sgt.	LaPoint, John	5-30
Sgt.	Schwardfegor, William	5-30
Sgt.	Shaver, John	5-30
Cpl.	Pierce, Roland	5-30
Cpl.	McCeachen, Archibald	5-30
Cpl.	Stala, Simon	5-30
Dmr.	Heagle, Peter	5-30
Tpr.	Nash, Edward	19-30
Pte.	Armstrong, John	5-30
Pte.	Baker, John	5-30
Pte.	Barclay, George A.	5-30
Pte.	Barclay, Mathew	5-30
Pte.	Bedsted, Alexander	5-30
Pte.	Bedsted, James	5-30
Pte.	Bedsted, John	5-30
Pte.	Bilows, Michael	5-30
Pte.	Biustius (Binstine), John	5-30
Pte.	Calquhoun, John	5-30
Pte.	Christy, William	5-30
Pte.	Church, John	5-30
Pte.	Dillabough, Daniel	5-30
Pte.	Dillabough, Jacob	5-30
Pte.	Dillabough, Lewis	5-30
Pte.	Dix, Henry	5-30
Pte.	Dixson, George	5-30
Pte.	Dunlap, William	5-30
Pte.	Duval, Charles	5-30
Pte.	Fetterley, Peter	5-30
Pte.	Fetterley, Gordon	5-30
Pte.	Fowler, George	5-30
Pte.	Fox, Edward	5-30
Pte.	Froats, John	5-30
Pte.	Froats, Richard	5-30
Pte.	Frymire, Nicolas	5-30
Pte.	Gale, Henry	5-30
Pte.	Hawn, William	5-30
Pte.	McMartin, Malcolm	5-30
Pte.	Merkley, John	5-30
Pte.	Munro, William	5-30

Pte.	Phillips, James	5-30
Pte.	Reddick, George	5-30
Pte.	Reddick, William	5-30
Pte.	Redmond, George	5-30
Pte.	Reid, Michael	5-30
Pte.	Schwerdfiger, Adam	5-30
Pte.	Second, William	5-30
Pte.	Stata, Cephreues	5-30
Pte.	Ulman, William	5-30
Pte.	Watson, Henry	5-30
Pte.	Weegar, Amos	5-30
Pte.	Weegar, William	5-30

The following was listed as being wounded during the battle, but for some reason was not listed on the paylists of the 1st Dundas Companies:

Pte.	Errington, William	WIA

Captain John Dorin's Company of 2nd Royal Dundas Militia

Capt.	Dorin, John	1-30
Lt.	Parlow, John	1-30 WIA
Ens.	Carman, George	1-30
Sgt.	McDonnel, Alexander	1-30
Sgt.	McIntosh, David	1-30
Sgt.	Van Allen, Henry	1-30
Cpl.	Casselman, Warner	1-30
Cpl.	Gore, John	1-30
Cpl.	Night, Charles	1-30
Dmr.	Casselman, Christian	1-30
Pte.	Barkley, John	1-30
Pte.	Billingsby, William	1-30
Pte.	Bouch, Jerimiah	1-13 KIA
Pte.	Bouch, John	1-30
Pte.	Bouch, John C.	1-30
Pte.	Brown, David	1-30
Pte.	Bush, William	1-30
Pte.	Caiss, Charles	1-30
Pte.	Carrington, William	1-30
Pte.	Casselman, Simon	1-30
Pte.	Cook, George	1-30
Pte.	Coons, Samuel	1-30
Pte.	Crowder, Charles	1-30
Pte.	Devilin, James	1-30 WIA
Pte.	Dillabough, David	1-30
Pte.	Dillabough, James	1-30
Pte.	Droppo, Francis	1-30

Pte.	Droppo, John	1-30
Pte.	Hamilton, John	1-30
Pte.	Hare, Henry	1-30
Pte.	Hentner, John	1-30
Pte.	Keeler, Daniel	1-30
Pte.	King, James	1-30
Pte.	Lapain, Solomon	1-30
Pte.	Lavis, Samuel	1-30
Pte.	Lowery (Lasory), Robert	1-30
Pte.	Madden, John	1-30
Pte.	McClument (McCliment), John	1-30
Pte.	McIntosh, Charles	1-30
Pte.	McIntosh, John	1-30
Pte.	Mcloughling, Michael	1-30
Pte.	McMahon, Andrew	1-30
Pte.	Merkley, Michael	1-30
Pte.	Mumbey, William	1-30
Pte.	Myers, William	1-30 WIA
Pte.	Robertson, David	1-30
Pte.	Seipeo, Jacob	1-30
Pte.	Sellers, William	1-30
Pte.	Shaver, Simon	1-30
Pte.	Shenack, Edward	1-30
Pte.	Smith, James	1-30
Pte.	Turner, William	1-30
Pte.	Wyley, William	1-30
Pte.	Younge, John	1-30

Captain Nicholas Shaver's Company of 2nd Royal Dundas Militia

Capt.	Shaver, Nicholas	1-30
Lt.	Struder, John	1-30
Ens.	Coons, David	1-30
Sgt.	Rose, Reuben	1-30
Sgt.	Service, John	1-30
Sgt.	Wallison, Anthony	1-30
Cpl.	Ault, Philip	1-30
Cpl.	Boden (Bouden), William	1-30
Pte.	Barkley, Evert	1-30
Pte.	Barkley, Michael	1-30
Pte.	Barkley, Thomas	1-30
Pte.	Bouch, David	1-30
Pte.	Bourgon, David	1-30
Pte.	Bell, James	1-30
Pte.	Car (Case), John	1-30
Pte.	Carlin, Thomas	1-30
Pte.	Carlin, James	1-30

Pte.	Clearwater, George	1-30
Pte.	Connor, Edward	1-30
Pte.	Connor, Nicholas	1-30
Pte.	Coons, Ruben	1-30
Pte.	Crowder, Anthony	1-30
Pte.	Crowley, Timothy	1-30
Pte.	Fader, George	1-30
Pte.	Fader, Phillip	1-30
Pte.	Fader, Wilson	1-30
Pte.	Fitzsimmons, James	1-30
Pte.	Foster, Edward	1-30
Pte.	Hanford (Harford), James	1-30
Pte.	Heck, George	1-30
Pte.	Johnson, James	1-30
Pte.	Johnson, John	1-30
Pte.	Kelly, Samuel	1-30
Pte.	Kelso, (Keeler), George	1-30
Pte.	Landers, William	1-30
Pte.	Leman, James	1-30
Pte.	Leman, William	1-30
Pte.	Loosasse, Emos	1-30
Pte.	Lornson, Samuel	1-30
Pte.	Lossan, Charles	1-30
Pte.	Marchant, William	1-30
Pte.	McGovern, John	1-30
Pte.	McIntosh, Allan	1-30
Pte.	Norton, William	1-30
Pte.	Redman, Nicholas	1-30
Pte.	Ringland, George	1-30
Pte.	Service, Peter	1-30
Pte.	Shaver, William	1-30
Pte.	Soles, George	1-30
Pte.	Stormburg, William	1-30
Pte.	Thomson, David	1-30
Pte.	Wacka, John	1-30
Pte.	Woodna, John	1-30

The following were listed as being killed or wounded during the battle, but for some reason were not listed on the paylists of the 2nd Dundas Companies:

Pte.	Boulton, Richard	WIA
Pte.	Conovers, James	WIA
Pte.	Fye, Francis	WIA
Pte.	McMartin, J.	KIA

Richard Boulton died of his wounds.

First Grenville Militia Regiment

Captain John Adams' Company

Capt.	Adams, John	12-17
Lt.	Beach, William	12-17
Sgt.	Hunter, Samuel	12-17
Sgt.	Shaver, Elija J.	12-17
Sgt.	Shaver, Nicholas J.	12-17
Cpl.	Grant, Peter	12-17
Pte.	Ager (Egan)(Uger), James	12-18
Pte.	Aiken, James	12-18
Pte.	Allen, Christopher	12-18
Pte.	Boyd, Andrew	12-18
Pte.	Brown, William	12-18
Pte.	Buckles, James	12-18
Pte.	Cameron, Allen	12-18
Pte.	Carson, Andrew	12-18
Pte.	Christie, Archibald	12-18
Pte.	Christy, Alexander	12-18
Pte.	Christy, Henry	12-18
Pte.	Christy, James	12-18
Pte.	Coleman, Robert	12-18
Pte.	Cummins, John	12-18
Pte.	Cummins, Peter	12-18
Pte.	Cummins, William	12-18
Pte.	Dunlop, Samuel	12-18
Pte.	Evans, John	12-18
Pte.	Gamble, John	12-18
Pte.	Gardiner, John	12-17
Pte.	Gilmore (Gilmour), Thomas	12-18
Pte.	Grant, Alexander	12-18
Pte.	Grant, Daniel	12-18
Pte.	Grant, John	12-18
Pte.	Grant, Lewis	12-18
Pte.	Gray, Samuel	12-18
Pte.	Hall, Peter	12-18
Pte.	Hunter, Nelson	12-18
Pte.	Johnston, David	12-18
Pte.	Johnston, Isaac	12-18
Pte.	Johnston, John Jun.	12-18
Pte.	Johnston, John Sen.	12-17
Pte.	Johnston, Joseph	12-18
Pte.	Johnston, Simon	12-18
Pte.	Johnston, Thomas	12-18
Pte.	Lamerick, James	12-18
Pte.	Law, Samuel	12-18

Pte.	Lawson, William	12-18
Pte.	Leddy (Laddy) (Ledda), John	12-18
Pte.	Leddy, William	12-18
Pte.	Mcaluse (Mcluce), Patrick	12-18
Pte.	McCahil, Barnaby	12-18
Pte.	McCahil, John	12-18
Pte.	McCarger, George	12-18
Pte.	McDowell (McDowl), John	12-18
Pte.	McDowell (McDowl), William	12-18
Pte.	Miller, George	12-18
Pte.	Moren, Edward	12-18
Pte.	Northway, William	12-18
Pte.	Prosser, Charles	12-18
Pte.	Quackenbush, David	12-18
Pte.	Quackenbush, Eliazer	12-18
Pte.	Quackenbush, Elijas	12-18
Pte.	Rath, William	12-18
Pte.	Saghaw (Siaghaw), David	12-18
Pte.	Sharp, William	12-18
Pte.	Shaver, Gordon	12-18
Pte.	Shaver, Lewis	12-18
Pte.	Smith, William	12-18
Pte.	Snider, John H.	12-18
Pte.	Stone, James	12-18
Pte.	Thomkim, Benjamin	12-18
Pte.	Thompson, William	12-18
Pte.	Todd, John	12-18
Pte.	Todd, Nathanial	12-18
Pte.	Todd, Patrick	12-18
Pte.	Todd, Samuel	12-18
Pte.	Tweed, James	12-18
Pte.	Whaley, David	12-18
Pte.	Whaley, Thomas	12-18
Pte.	Wilson, Samuel	12-18
Pte.	Wood, Mathew	12-17
Pte.	Workman, William	12-18

Captain Dunham Jones' Company

Capt.	Jones, Dunham	8-19
Lt.	Fraser, John	8-19
Ens.	Campbell, Robert	8-19
Sgt.	Henry, James	12-19
Sgt.	Johnston, John	8-19
Sgt.	Robinson, William	8-19
Pte.	Alkinton (Alkinson), Wm.	12-17
Pte.	Allen, Thos.	12-17
Pte.	Allen, George	12-17
Pte.	Armstrong, James	12-17
Pte.	Ball, John G.	12-16
Pte.	Bancroft, Sam'l.	12-19
Pte.	Baynham, Thos.	8-17
Pte.	Bell, Alexander	12-19
Pte.	Bell, James	8-19
Pte.	Bell, Robert	12-19
Pte.	Borden (Bourden), Alex'r.	8-19
Pte.	Brasher, Samuel	12-17
Pte.	Brown, Albert	8-19
Pte.	Brown, Elisha	12-16
Pte.	Brown, James	9-11
Pte.	Brown, Wm.	12-18
Pte.	Burgayne (Burgoin), Thos. F.	12-17
Pte.	Carter, George	8-19
Pte.	Cassy (Casey), Thos.	12-19
Pte.	Caughlan, Patrick	12-19
Pte.	Christy, John	12-19
Pte.	Colligan, Patrick	12-19
Pte.	Connell, Richard	8-11
Pte.	Countryman, Wm.	12-19
Pte.	Curby (Kirby), Thos.	12-19
Pte.	Davison, Thos.	12-17
Pte.	Disset, Thomas	8-19
Pte.	Dixon, Charles	12-17
Pte.	Dowsley, John	12-17
Pte.	Duclow, James	9-11
Pte.	Duncan (Dunigen), Edward	12-17
Pte.	Emberson, John	12-16
Pte.	Farley, John	10-19
Pte.	Fell, Erastus	12-16
Pte.	Fell, Ichabod	12-18
Pte.	Fell, James	12-19
Pte.	Fell, John	12-19
Pte.	Fisher, Samuel	9-11
Pte.	Flagg, Alfred	9-11
Pte.	Fraser, Wm.	12-17
Pte.	Fulcher, Edward	12-17
Pte.	Gardener, Samuel	8-19
Pte.	Gillard, James	12-17
Pte.	Glasgow, John	12-17
Pte.	Glasgow, Robert	12-17
Pte.	Goldsmith, Wm.	12-16
Pte.	Goodin, Richard	12-15
Pte.	Gore, James	9-11
Pte.	Gould, James	9-19
Pte.	Hall, James	12-17
Pte.	Henry, Wm.	12-16
Pte.	Hines (Hanse), James	12-17
Pte.	Hutchcroft (Huchcroft), Robert	10-19
Pte.	Johnston, James	12-19
Pte.	Kelsey (Kelsay), Hugh	12-17
Pte.	Knapp, Abraham	12-17
Pte.	Knapp, John	8-19
Pte.	Knapp, Silas	12-16
Pte.	Knapp, Van Rumpelleur	8-19
Pte.	Knowles, Robert	12-19
Pte.	Lane, Benjamin	12-19
Pte.	Lane, John	12-15
Pte.	Lane, Wm.	8-19
Pte.	Laughead, Joseph	12-19
Pte.	Magee, John	12-17
Pte.	Manion, Michael	12-19
Pte.	Martin, William	8-19
Pte.	Maxwell, James	12-17
Pte.	McAuley, Daniel	12-19
Pte.	McCarthy, Dan'l.	12-17
Pte.	McCarthy (McCarty), Sandy	12-17
Pte.	McFarlane (McFarlin), Michael	12-17
Pte.	McGee, Wm.	12-17
Pte.	McLeod, Alex'r.	12-15
Pte.	McMurray, John	12-15
Pte.	McMurray (Murray), Thos.	12-14
Pte.	Millar, Joseph	12-17
Pte.	Mills, Samuel	9-11
Pte.	Moore, James	12-17
Pte.	Morrison, James	8-19
Pte.	Newberry, Silas	9-19
Pte.	Nugent, John	12-16
Pte.	O'Neil, John	9-11
Pte.	Peoples, Arch'd.	9-11
Pte.	Perrin, Andrew	12-15
Pte.	Perrin, Emanuel	8-19
Pte.	Perrin, Marcus	12-19
Pte.	Perry, John	12-16
Pte.	Perry, Robert	12-16
Pte.	Pitman, Thomas	8-19
Pte.	Pitman, Thos. Senr.	12-19
Pte.	Plumb, Isaac (Jr.)	8-19
Pte.	Polite, David	12-19
Pte.	Poor, Wm.	8-19
Pte.	Portray (Portra), Francis	8-19
Pte.	Raney, Neil	9-11
Pte.	Raycroft, Joseph	12-18
Pte.	Robinson, George	12-19
Pte.	Robinson, Thos.	12-17
Pte.	Rolston, Rob't.	12-14
Pte.	Scott, Geo.	12-17
Pte.	Sherwood, Joseph	9-19
Pte.	Sherwood, Wm.	12-17
Pte.	Smith, Alex'r.	12-15
Pte.	Smith, Hamilton	12-16
Pte.	Smith, John	12-19
Pte.	Smith, Wm.	12-17
Pte.	Stevenson, Wm.	9-11
Pte.	Swart, John	12-17
Pte.	Walker, John	12-19
Pte.	Walsh, Michael	12-19
Pte.	Whitmore, Solomon D.	12-19
Pte.	Wolf, John	9-11
Pte.	Youker, John	12-19

Captain Thomas McCargar's Company

Capt.	McCargar, Thomas	12-30
Sgt.	Beach, Abraham	12-30
Sgt.	Christie, Duncan	12-30
Sgt.	Holmes, Andrew	12-30
Cpl.	Beach, Benjamin	12-30
Cpl.	Boggart, Giles W.	12-30
Pte.	Allen, Christie	12-30
Pte.	Anderson, John	12-30
Pte.	Blackburn, William	12-30
Pte.	Bleakey, Francis	12-30
Pte.	Boyce, David Junr.	12-30
Pte.	Boyce, David Senr.	12-30
Pte.	Brandon, John	12-30
Pte.	Buchanan, William	12-30
Pte.	Buchannan, William Jr.	12-30
Pte.	Burk, Henry	12-30
Pte.	Burns, James	12-30
Pte.	Christie, Thomas	12-30
Pte.	Christie, William	12-30

Pte.	Coleman, Samuel	12-30
Pte.	Conley, John	12-30
Pte.	Connor, Denis	12-30
Pte.	Craig, William	12-30
Pte.	Crambe, Samuel W.	12-30
Pte.	Cummins, John	12-30
Pte.	Dool, Hugh	12-30
Pte.	Dool, John	12-30
Pte.	Fitzgerald, Thomas	12-30
Pte.	Graham, Thomas	12-30
Pte.	Herman (Herran), Michael	12-30
Pte.	Kumminwray, Deluer	12-30
Pte.	Long, Joseph	12-30
Pte.	MacKey, Thomas	12-30
Pte.	Main, John	12-30
Pte.	Martin, Hugh	12-30
Pte.	McCrannel, Patrick	12-30
Pte.	McGovern, James	12-30
Pte.	McGovern, Patrick	12-30
Pte.	McGovern, Richard	12-30
Pte.	Murphy, Thomas	12-30
Pte.	O'Neil, Peter	12-30
Pte.	Rany, William	12-30
Pte.	Rutherford, Alexander	12-30
Pte.	Smith, Barney	12-30
Pte.	Sopha, Jarel	12-30
Pte.	Sopha, Stephen	12-30
Pte.	Stewart, Samuel	12-30
Pte.	Stewart, Jacob	12-30
Pte.	Storey, Robert	12-30
Pte.	Swords, John	12-30
Pte.	Uere, Walter	12-30
Pte.	Van Buren, James	12-30
Pte.	Wood, Ezra	12-30

Captain Simon B. Fraser's Company

Capt.	Fraser, Simon B.	13-19
Lt.	Peters, Stephen	13-19
Ens.	Forrester, John S.	13-19
Sgt.	Gore, James	13-19
Sgt.	Hunter, Allan	13-19
Sgt.	Newman, William	13-19
Pte.	Armstrong, Thomas	13-19
Pte.	Bennett, John	13-19
Pte.	Connell, Thomas	13-19
Pte.	Doyle, Lawrence	13-19
Pte.	Ducklow, Charles	13-19

Pte.	Ducklow, James	13-19
Pte.	Freland (Ferland), Francis	13-19
Pte.	Fisher, Samuel	13-19
Pte.	Gamble, James	13-19
Pte.	Hodge, James	13-19
Pte.	Hodge, Joseph	13-19
Pte.	King, Jacob	13-19
Pte.	King, Stephen	13-19
Pte.	Lammon, Robert	13-19
Pte.	Lavier, John	13-19
Pte.	McDonald (McDonnell), John	13-19
Pte.	Mcgammon, John	13-19
Pte.	Mcgammon, Peter	13-19
Pte.	McGangagan, John	13-19
Pte.	McKever, Hugh	13-19
Pte.	Mills, Daniel	13-19
Pte.	Newman, Abraham	13-19
Pte.	Newman, Joseph	13-19
Pte.	Raney, Neal	13-19
Pte.	Smell, William	13-19
Pte.	Stephenson, William	13-19
Pte.	Stirtan, Geo.	13-19
Pte.	Stitt, James	13-19
Pte.	Strahan, Wm.	13-19
Pte.	Watson, James	13-19
Pte.	Wells, Samuel	13-19
Pte.	Whitney, John	13-19
Pte.	Wilson, James	13-19
Pte.	Wilson, Joseph	13-19
Pte.	Wilson (Willson), Thomas	13-19
Pte.	Wolf, John	13-19

Captain John Lawrence's Company

Capt.	Lawrence, John	12-17
Lt.	Beach, Melon (Malcolm)	12-17
Ens.	Dulmage, Samuel	12-17
Sgt.	Gibson, James	12-17
Sgt.	Jackson, John	12-17
Sgt.	Keeler, James	12-17
Cpl.	McFadden, Joseph	12-17
Pte.	Adam, Louis (Levis)	12-17
Pte.	Augley, Joseph	12-17
Pte.	Bank, Stephen	12-17
Pte.	Barr, Rob't.	12-17
Pte.	Bennett, Andrew	12-17

Pte.	Bennett, John	12-17
Pte.	Bennett, Rick	12-17
Pte.	Bennett, William	12-17
Pte.	Brown, Sylvester	12-17
Pte.	Campbell, Hector	12-17
Pte.	Christie, Andrew	12-17
Pte.	Christie, Duncan	12-17
Pte.	Cooke, John	12-17
Pte.	Cousins, Wm.	12-17
Pte.	Dempsey, Edward	12-17
Pte.	Ellcock, Joseph	12-17
Pte.	Ellcock, Richard	12-17
Pte.	Ellcock, William	12-17
Pte.	Gibson, Geo.	12-17
Pte.	Gibson, Wm.	12-17
Pte.	Graham, Arbny	12-17
Pte.	Grue, Baptiste	12-17
Pte.	Hirset, John	12-17
Pte.	Hobbs, Patrick	12-17
Pte.	Hodge, James	12-17
Pte.	Hurley, James	12-17
Pte.	Irvine, Thomas	12-17
Pte.	Kearns, Alexander	12-17
Pte.	Kearns, Thomas	12-17
Pte.	Keeler, Daniel	12-17
Pte.	Keeler, Enlamin	12-17
Pte.	Kyle, Arthur	12-17
Pte.	Laidly, Andrew	12-17
Pte.	Lawrence, John Sr.	12-17
Pte.	McDonald, John	12-17
Pte.	McFadden, Benjamin	12-17
Pte.	McGandry, David	12-17
Pte.	McLary, Patrick	12-17
Pte.	McNeil, John	12-17
Pte.	Mitchell, Andrew	12-17
Pte.	Murphy, Patt	12-17
Pte.	Nickales, James	12-17
Pte.	Payne, William	12-17
Pte.	Pew, Geo.	12-17
Pte.	Pew, John	12-17
Pte.	Richardson, Robert	12-17
Pte.	Robinson, Abraham	12-17
Pte.	Robinson, George	12-17
Pte.	Robinson, Jacob	12-17
Pte.	Scott, Frank	12-17
Pte.	Sellick, Geo.	12-17
Pte.	Sellick, James	12-17
Pte.	Tate, Henry	12-17

Pte.	Tate, Joseph	12-17
Pte.	Tate, Samuel	12-17
Pte.	Tate, Thomas	12-17
Pte.	Wilson, Abraham	12-17

1st Troop of Cavalry of the 1st Grenville Militia under the command of Captain William Kay

Capt.	Kay, William	12-17
Lt.	McKnoyle, John	12-17
Cnt.	Blakey, James	12-17
SMaj	Gray, John	12-17
Sgt.	Adams, Abel H.	12-17
Sgt.	Burrows, Earl	12-17
Sgt.	Harding, John	12-17
Sgt.	McFadden, John	12-17
Sgt.	McFadden, William	12-17
Sgt.	Thrasher, Zedock	12-17
Pte.	Adams, Beldon	13-17
Pte.	Adams, Edmond B.	13-16
Pte.	Adams, George	13-14
Pte.	Adams, Thomas	13-17
Pte.	Bass, William	13-14
Pte.	Belwell, Joseph	13-16
Pte.	Bickam, Robert	13-14
Pte.	Dodge, Ashby	13-17
Pte.	Dodge, William J.	13-14
Pte.	Forrester, William	13-13
Pte.	Froom, David	13-14
Pte.	Froom, John	12-17
Pte.	Girnash (Gisnash), John	12-16
Pte.	Grue, John	12-15
Pte.	Hopper, Samuel	12-16
Pte.	Kennedy, William	12-17
Pte.	Larabee, Henry	13-17
Pte.	Mains, John	13-17
Pte.	Marlatt (Molatt), Abram	13-17
Pte.	Marlatt (Molatt), William	13-17
Pte.	McFadden, James	12-16
Pte.	Miller, George	12-17
Pte.	Miller, John	12-15
Pte.	Montgomery, Samuel	13-15
Pte.	Robinson, Isaac	12-17
Pte.	Rose, William	12-14
Pte.	Selleck, Joseph	13-13
Pte.	Smaills (Smells), Andrew	13-15

Pte.   Snyder, Andrew   13-15
Pte.   Spencer, William   13-15
Pte.   Spencer, Edwin   13-15
Pte.   Stitt, John   14-15
Pte.   Stitt, Richard   13-17
Pte.   Thrasher, Hamilton   12-14
Pte.   Whitney, Emery   13-16

The following were listed as being killed or wounded during the battle, but for some reason were not listed on the paylists of the First Grenville Regiment Companies:

Pte.   Allis, William   WIA
Pte.   Drummond, George   KIA
Pte.   Landers, Edward   WIA
Pte.   Linnen, Adam   KIA
Pte.   Polite, David   WIA
Pte.   Porta, Francis   WIA

Second Grenville Militia Regiment

Grenville Loyal Sedentary Volunteer Company under the Command of Captain E. Pridham

Capt. Pridham, Edwin   12-16
Ens.   Horner, Ralph   12-16
Sgt.   Engleson, Samuel   12-17
Cpl.   Gallaghar, Andrew   12-16
Pte.   Burns, John   12-16
Pte.   Cacy, Joseph   12-17
Pte.   Cameron, John 1st   12-16
Pte.   Cameron, John 2nd   12-17
Pte.   Connor, Abner   12-16
Pte.   Cook, Carrol   12-17
Pte.   Evatts, David   12-17
Pte.   Fairburn, Arch.   12-15
Pte.   Garland, Thomas   12-17
Pte.   Hall, William   12-17
Pte.   Hastings, Patrick   12-16
Pte.   Kelly, James   12-16
Pte.   Kelly, Patrick   12-16
Pte.   Livingston, Hugh   12-17
Pte.   McLean, Charles   12-16
Pte.   McVicar, Archibald   12-17
Pte.   Murray, Alexander   12-16
Pte.   O'Brien, Daniel   12-15

Pte.   Ogilvy, Samuel   12-16
Pte.   Richie, Richard   12-16
Pte.   Steel, Samuel   12-16
Pte.   Timbas, Joseph   12-17
Pte.   Tompkins, Robert   12-15
Pte.   Williamson, James   12-15

A Detachment of Captain Lang's Company Stationed at Carillon for Nov 12th to 17th, 1838

Capt. Lang, John   12-17
Sgt.   Hockins, John   12-16
Sgt.   Lowe, Ralph   12-16
Cpl.   Lowe, James   12-17
Pte.   Anderson, James   12-17
Pte.   Anderson, Joseph   12-17
Pte.   Berry, Joseph   12-17
Pte.   Bird, John   12-15
Pte.   Brooks, George   12-17
Pte.   Cameron, Laughlin   12-17
Pte.   Clarke, John Junr.   12-17
Pte.   Downing, James   12-15
Pte.   Driscol, Michael   12-17
Pte.   Grunday, William   12-16
Pte.   Hunt, Edwin   12-15
Pte.   Longburn, James   12-16
Pte.   Longburn, James Jr.   12-15
Pte.   McCallagan, William   12-17
Pte.   McEwans, James   12-17
Pte.   McGuire, William   12-15
Pte.   McPhee, Murdock   12-16
Pte.   Murray, Thomas   12-17
Pte.   Murray, William   12-17
Pte.   Owens, William   12-17
Pte.   Pringle, James   12-15
Pte.   Reeves, Christifer   12-15
Pte.   Smith, George   12-15
Pte.   Stewart, Andrew   12-15
Pte.   Stockdale, Benj'n.   12-16
Pte.   Wilson, James   12-17

Captain Joseph Adams's Company

Capt. Adams, Joseph   12-18
Sgt.   Cameron, John   12-18
Sgt.   McCarty, Alexander   12-18
Sgt.   McNeill, James   12-18
Pte.   Adams, Elisha   12-18
Pte.   Adams, Reuben   12-18

Pte.   Anderson, Levi   12-18
Pte.   Anderson, Peter   12-18
Pte.   Armstrong, Robert   12-18
Pte.   Becket, Michael
         (Micheal)   12-18
Pte.   Bigham, Robert   12-18
Pte.   Bigham, William   12-18
Pte.   Boulton (Bolton), John 12-18
Pte.   Boulton (Bolton),
         William   12-18
Pte.   Brown, William   12-18
Pte.   Burnside, John   12-18
Pte.   Bush, William   12-18
Pte.   Bush, Jerimiah   12-18
Pte.   Cameron, William   12-18
Pte.   Cleland (Clealen),
         Thomas   12-18
Pte.   Freeland, Richard   12-18
Pte.   Gamble, James   12-18
Pte.   Graham, Andrew   12-18
Pte.   Grames, John   12-18
te.   Hamilton, John   12-18
Pte.   Humes, John   12-18
Pte.   Long, Hugh   12-18
Pte.   Main (Mane), Thomas   12-18
Pte.   Marlatt (Malat), Marcus 12-18
Pte.   McLaughlin, Hugh   12-18
Pte.   Morrison, John   12-18
Pte.   Pinkerton, William   12-18
Pte.   Pitt, William   12-18
Pte.   Prossor, Edward   12-18
Pte.   Robertson, Alexander   12-18
Pte.   Robertson, Thomas   12-18
Pte.   Spotswood, Joseph   12-18
Pte.   Turner, Richard   12-18
Pte.   Webb, Silas   12-18

The following were listed as being killed or wounded during the battle, but for some reason were not listed on the paylists of the Second Grenville Regiment Companies:

Lt.   Dulmage, John   KIA
Pte.   Fox, Adam   WIA
Pte.   Gillespie, J. (John)   WIA
Pte.   Morey, John   WIA
Pte.   Perrine, J.   WIA

J. Perrine died of his wounds.

Captain Archibald Campbell's Company of Augmentation of Grenville Volunteers

Capt. Campbell, Arch'd   12-16
Lt.   Cameron, Donald   16
Ens.   Campbell, Colin   16
Sgt.   Crawford, John   12-16
Sgt.   McNeil, Hugh   16
Sgt.   Woodward, Thos.   12-16
Cpl.   Ferrara, Manuel   16
Pte.   Bates (Beats), George   12-16
Pte.   Bates, Robert   16
Pte.   Bates, Wm.   12-16
Pte.   Beathun (Bethune)
         (Beaton), Don   12-16
Pte.   Beathun (Bethune)
         (Beaton), Malcalm   12-16
Pte.   Blackburn, William   16
Pte.   Brown, Mark   16
Pte.   Brown, Vernor   12-16
Pte.   Brown, Wm.   12-16
Pte.   Buttler, Patrick   12-16
Pte.   Cameron, Archibald   12-16
Pte.   Campbell, Colin   12-16
Pte.   Campbell, Dugald   16
Pte.   Campbell, Ewin   12-16
Pte.   Campbell, John   12-16
Pte.   Campbell, Kenneth   16
Pte.   Campbell, Robert   12-16
Pte.   Campbell, William   16
Pte.   Connell, Owen   12-16
Pte.   Connelly, Edward   12-16
Pte.   Coteau, Louis   16
Pte.   Cousins, Andrew   12-16
Pte.   Cousins, William   16
Pte.   Craig, Joseph   12-16
Pte.   Dewar, Martin   12-16
Pte.   Fallon, John   12-16
Pte.   Fox, William   12-16
Pte.   Hanlon, Michael   12-16
Pte.   House, John   16
Pte.   House, Nath'l   16
Pte.   House, Sameul   16
Pte.   Hutton, Byron   16
Pte.   Johnson, Charles   16
Pte.   Johnston, Patrick   12-16
Pte.   Kelly, James   12-16

Pte.	Kelly, Jonathon	16
Pte.	Mahanson (Malcalmson), Alex	12-16
Pte.	Mathews, Peters	12-16
Pte.	McArthur, James	12-16
Pte.	McCallan, Duncan	16
Pte.	McCallum, Arch'd	16
Pte.	McCallum, Donald	16
Pte.	McDonald, Roderick	16
Pte.	McLean, Duncan	16
Pte.	McLeod, Alexander	12-16
Pte.	McLeod, Duncan	16
Pte.	McLeod, Jas.	12-16
Pte.	McLevay (McElway), James	12-16
Pte.	McLothasme, Donald	12-16
Pte.	McNeil, Anthony	16
Pte.	McNeil, David	16
Pte.	McRea, Murdock	16
Pte.	McTague, John	12-16
Pte.	McTague, Michael	16
Pte.	McTague, Patrick	16
Pte.	McTague, Tony	16
Pte.	Milner, John	16
Pte.	Moore, John	16
Pte.	Moore, Oliver	12-16
Pte.	Pierce, Joseph	16
Pte.	Pierce, Wm.	12-16
Pte.	Prossel, Thomas	16
Pte.	Quinn, Patrick	16
Pte.	Simeuton, Adam	16
Pte.	Vallesley, George	16
Pte.	Williamson, Hugh	12-16
Pte.	Young, James	16

The following were listed as being wounded during the battle, but for some reason were not listed on the paylists of the Grenville Volunteer Company:

Pte.	Russell, Harris	WIA
Pte.	Wilson, J.	WIA

Lancaster Glengarry Highlanders

Capt. George Macdonell Company (Stationed at Prescott)

Capt.	Macdonell, George	1-30
Lt.	Stewart, John	1-30
Ens.	Macdonell, Angus	1-30
CSgt.	Fraser, John S.	1-30
Sgt.	Coulter, Thos. S	1-30
Sgt.	Gauthier, Hyacinth	1-30
Sgt.	McIntosh, Arch'd	1-30
Cpl.	Edwards, John	1-30
Cpl.	Hynes, Edward	1-30
Cpl.	Reardon, Eugen	1-30
Cpl.	Ross, Donald	1-30
Blr.	Sizland, James (John) Sr.	1-30
Blr.	Woods (Wood), Joseph	1-30
Pte.	Adams, James	1-30
Pte.	Bunton (Burton), John	1-13 KIA
Pte.	Black, William	1-30
Pte.	Brennan, Michael	1-30
Pte.	Butler, Harvey	1-30
Pte.	Cahill, William	1-30
Pte.	Cameron, Dougal	1-13 KIA
Pte.	Chinuton, Wm.	1-30
Pte.	Collins, Path	1-30
Pte.	Connor, Edward	1-30
Pte.	Cooper, William	1-3 WIA
Pte.	Easter, Jacob	1-30
Pte.	Elvin, George,	1-30
Pte.	Emery, John	1-30
Pte.	Fitzgerald, Morris	1-30
Pte.	Fitzgerald, Pat	2-30
Pte.	Fitzgerald, Pat	2-30
Pte.	Fitzpatrick, Edward	1-30
Pte.	Forrester, Wm.	1-30
Pte.	Fraser, Donald	28-30
Pte.	Fuller, John	1-30 WIA
Pte.	Garmie (Germe), Joseph	1-30
Pte.	Gill, David	1-30
Pte.	Gore, William	1-13 KIA
Pte.	Harris, Thos.	1-30
Pte.	Harrison, Joseph	1-30
Pte.	Hughes, Henry	1-30
Pte.	Lee, James	1-30
Pte.	Lydford, Thos.	1-13 KIA
Pte.	Manning, Jerimiah	6-30
Pte.	McCormack, Nick	1-30
Pte.	McCutcheon, Hugh	1-30
Pte.	McDonell, Alex G.	1-30
Pte.	McDonell, Dougal	1-30
Pte.	McDonell, Edward	1-30
Pte.	McDonell, John	1-30

Pte.	McDonell, Isaac	14-30
Pte.	McDuncan, Donald	13-30
Pte.	McGlore, Pat	1-30
Pte.	McGovern, Pat	1-30 WIA
Pte.	McPherson, Jos.	1-30
Pte.	McPherson, Thos.	1-30
Pte.	McWalter, Wm.	1-30
Pte.	Munro, Wm.	1-30
Pte.	Nahnie, Joseph	1-30
Pte.	O'Conner, Dan	1-30
Pte.	O'Mara, Pat	1-30
Pte.	Perrin, Henry	1-30
Pte.	Pierce, Peter	1-30
Pte.	Rea, Peter	5-30
Pte.	Richardson, David	1-30
Pte.	Robinson, Charles	1-30
Pte.	Rumble, Thos.	1-30
Pte.	Russell, Peter	1-30
Pte.	Sheely, Francis	1-30
Pte.	Shup, Robert	1-30
Pte.	Sigyn, David	30-30
Pte.	Sizland, Jas. Jun.	1-30
Pte.	Sizland, Wm.	5-30 WIA
Pte.	Spicer, Robert	1-30
Pte.	Straton, Cyrenus	23-30
Pte.	Sutherland, Wm.	1-30
Pte.	Tilley, George	1-30
Pte.	Topper, Wm.	5-30
Pte.	Westcomb, Jas.	28-30
Pte.	Westcomb, Wm.	28-30
Pte.	White, James	1-30 KIA
Pte.	Williamson, Thos.	1-30
APM.	MacDonnell, George	1-30

The following were listed as being wounded during the battle, but for some reason were not listed on the paylists of the Lancaster Glengarry Regiment Companies:

Pte.	Black, John	WIA
Pte.	Corfe (Cross), George	WIA

Muster Roll and paylist of parts of nine companies of the 4th Regiment Glengarry Militia commanded by Col. Angus McDonell and served at Beauharnois and Windmill Point in Month of November 1838.

Col.	McDonell, Angus	7-30
LCol.	McDonell, Alex	7-30
Capt.	Kennedy, John	7-30
Capt.	McDonald (McDonell), Niel	7-30
Capt.	McDonald, Allan	7-30
Capt.	McDonell, Angus	7-30
Capt.	McDougald, Angus	7-30
Capt.	McDougald, Lauchin	7-30
Capt.	McKenzie, John	7-30
Capt.	McKinnon, Alex	7-30
Lt.	Campbell, Alexander	7-30
Lt.	Chisholm, Colin	7-30
Lt.	McDonald, Angus	7-30
Lt.	McDonald, Arch'd	7-30
Lt.	McDonald, John	7-30
Lt.	McDonald, Donald	7-30
Lt.	McDonell, Angus	7-30
Lt.	McLennan, Kenneth	7-30
Lt.	Stewart, Alexander	7-30
Ens.	Kennedy, Donald	7-30
Ens.	Kennedy, Duncan	7-30
Ens.	McCulloch, James	7-30
Ens.	McDonald, Angus	7-30
Ens.	McDonell, Allan	7-30
Ens.	McGillis, Angus	7-30
Ens.	McMaster, Donald	7-30
Ens.	McMillan, Miles	7-30
Ens.	Urquhart, James	7-30
SMaj.	Sproul, John	7-30
Sgt.	Cameron, Angus	6-30
Sgt.	Campbell, John	6-30
Sgt.	Campbell, Malcom	6-30
Sgt.	Chisholm, Donald	6-30
Sgt.	Grant, Angus	6-30
Sgt.	Kennedy, Alexander	6-30
Sgt.	McCay, James	6-30
Sgt.	McCrae, John	6-30
Sgt.	McDonald, Angus	6-30
Sgt.	McDonald, Arch'd.	6-30
Sgt.	McDonald, Charles	6-30
Sgt.	McDonald, Duncan	6-30

Sgt.	McDonald, Duncan	6-30
Sgt.	McDonald, John	6-30
Sgt.	McDonell, Alexander	7-30
Sgt.	McGillis, Angus	6-30
Sgt.	McIntyre, Duncan	6-30
Sgt.	McKenzie, James	6-30
Sgt.	McKinnon, Alexander	6-30
Sgt.	McKinnon, Duncan	6-30
Sgt.	McMillan, Angus	6-30
Sgt.	McMillan, Arch'd.	6-30
Sgt.	McMillan, Ewen	6-30
Sgt.	McPhee, Arch'd.	6-30
Sgt.	Sproul, Will	6-30
Cpl.	Campbell, Duncan	8-30
Cpl.	Campbell, John	9-30
Cpl.	McDonald, Angus	7-30
Cpl.	McDonald, Donald	9-30
Pte.	Campbell, John	9-30
Pte.	Forbes, Christopher	9-30
Pte.	Forbes, David	7-30
Pte.	Fraser, Alexander	11-30
Pte.	Fraser, Colin	11-30
Pte.	McCrae, Duncan	9-30
Pte.	McDonald, Alexander	9-30
Pte.	McDonald, Angus	9-30
Pte.	McDonald, Angus	9-30
Pte.	McDonald, Donald	9-30
Pte.	McDonald, Duncan	14-30
Pte.	McDonald, Finlay	7-30
Pte.	McDonald, Hugh	9-30
Pte.	McDonald, James	9-30
Pte.	McDonald, John	9-30
Pte.	McDonald, John	7-30
Pte.	McDonald, John	14-30
Pte.	McDonald, John	9-30
Pte.	McDonald, John	9-30
Pte.	McDonald, Ronald	9-30
Pte.	McDougald, Angus	11-30
Pte.	McDougald, Angus	11-30
Pte.	McPherson, Alexander	9-30
Pte.	McPherson, Duncan	9-30
Pte.	Urquhart, Olias	7-30

Prescott Volunteer (Independent) Company (Captain Jessup)

Capt.	Jessup, Hamilton D.	2-30
Lt.	Smith, Edward	13-30
Sgt.	Thompson, John	6-30

Sgt.	Weeks (Weekes), John D.	6-30
Cpl.	Territt, Thomas	9-30
Cpl.	Turner, Thomas	10-30
Pte.	Adding, Benjamin	8-30
Pte.	Anderson, Hugh	9-30
Pte.	Brown, James	6-30
Pte.	Call, Rufus	26-30
Pte.	Dodridge, Thos.	30-30
Pte.	Duclow, James	29-30
Pte.	Edwards, Joseph	28-30
Pte.	Finamore (Finnamore), Wilbert (Willard)	9-30
Pte.	Fingham, Michael	6-30
Pte.	Fraser, Thomas	26-30
Pte.	Gallagher, John	20-30
Pte.	Gatran (Place), Martin	23-30
Pte.	Jackson, Alexander B.	10-30
Pte.	Lucas (Lasson) (Lennon), George	24-30
Pte.	Lucas, John	9-30
Pte.	Ludlow, Thomas	26-30
Pte.	McEllen, James	26-30
Pte.	McKnight, Robert	29-30
Pte.	Montgomery, Wm.	10-30
Pte.	Murdock, Robert	6-30
Pte.	Newman, James	19-30
Pte.	O'Brien, Cornelus	26-30
Pte.	O'Sulivan, Denis	10-30
Pte.	Plantz, Jacob	28-30
Pte.	Poor, Wm.	26-30
Pte.	Rattery, James	27-30
Pte.	Rayland (Bingham), Joseph	19-30
Pte.	Steel, John G.	10-30
Pte.	Thompson, Wm.	28-30
Pte.	Willson, Thos.	23-30

The following were listed as being wounded during the battle, but for some reason were not listed on the paylists of the Prescott Volunteer Company:

Sgt.	Fraser	WIA
Pte.	Fraser, William	WIA
Pte.	Slavin, Francis	WIA

First Company of the Prescott Reserves

Capt.	Kearnes, John	14, 21, 28
Lt.	Kellog, Elijah	14, 21, 28
Ens.	Parker, Wm.	14, 21, 28
Sgt.	Davis, Casias	21, 28
Sgt.	Kearney, Patrick	14, 21, 28
Pte.	Anderson, James	21, 28
Pte.	Bates, Thos.	21, 28
Pte.	Baxter, Samuel	21, 28
Pte.	Belfas, Francis	21
Pte.	Benson, John	21, 28
Pte.	Blaney, Sproull	21, 28
Pte.	Bradley, Henry Jr.	21, 28
Pte.	Bradley (Bradly), Henry Sr.	21, 28
Pte.	Brownrick, Henry	21, 28
Pte.	Burton, John	21, 28
Pte.	Call, Patrick	21, 28
Pte.	Cameron, John	14
Pte.	Campbell, Esken	21, 28
Pte.	Charles, Edward	14
Pte.	Cole, Robert	21, 28
Pte.	Cutt (Couts), George	21, 28
Pte.	Downing, Philip	21, 28
Pte.	Erratt (Errett), Isaac	14, 21, 28
Pte.	Frith, James	21, 28
Pte.	Garrett, Joseph	14
Pte.	Gates, Charles	21, 28
Pte.	Gordon, John	21, 28
Pte.	Henderson, David	21, 28
Pte.	Holmes, Henry	14, 21
Pte.	Holmes, John	14, 21, 28
Pte.	Holmes, William Jr.	21, 28
Pte.	Holmes, William Sr.	21
Pte.	Hughes, Hum'y	14, 21, 28
Pte.	Hughes, Humphry	21, 28
Pte.	Hughes, James	14, 21
Pte.	Hughes, James Jr.	21, 28
Pte.	Hughes, James Sr.	21, 28
Pte.	Hughes, John	14, 21, 28
Pte.	Hughes, John	21, 28
Pte	Hunter, William	21, 28
Pte.	Johnston, William	21, 28
Pte.	Kelley, Bartholmy	21
Pte.	Little, James	14, 21, 28
Pte.	Little, Thos.	14, 21, 28
Pte.	Longral, Joseph	14, 21, 28

Pte.	McAuley (McAulley), Charles	21, 28
Pte.	McAuley, Francis	28
Pte.	McAuley (McAulley), James	21, 28
Pte.	McCalligen, James	14, 21, 28
Pte.	McCrank, James	21, 28
Pte.	McCuscer, James	14, 21, 28
Pte.	McDonald, Thomas	21
Pte.	McElroy, Alex'r	21
Pte.	McGregor, Duncan	21
Pte.	McIntyre, William	21, 28
Pte.	McKiney (McKinley), Hugh	21, 28
Pte.	McLean, David	21, 28
Pte.	McLean, Hugh	21, 28
Pte.	McQuinse, John	21
Pte.	Melvin, Patrick	21
Pte.	Metcalf, Henry	21, 28
Pte.	Moffett, James	21
Pte.	Muorarty (Murarty), Eugene	28
Pte.	Powell, James	28
Pte.	Powell, Joseph	21, 28
Pte.	Presley, George	21, 28
Pte.	Proudfoot, James	21
Pte.	Rennick, James	21, 28
Pte.	Rhatigon, Thos.	21, 28
Pte.	Ryan, John	21, 28
Pte.	Ryan, Michael	28
Pte.	Scott, Robert	21, 28
Pte.	Sergeant, John	14, 21, 28
Pte.	Shea, Thomas	21, 28
Pte.	Sheahan, Moses	21, 28
Pte.	Sheilds, Alex'r.	21, 28
Pte.	Skelly, Donald (Soulby, Daniel)	21, 28
Pte.	Smith, John	21
Pte.	Walton, George	21, 28
Pte.	Wilkinson, Samual	21, 28
Pte.	Wilks, John	21, 28

Second Company of the Prescott Reserves

Lt.Col.	Hamilton, George	14
Capt.	Johnson, Chauncey	14, 21, 28
Lt.	Cozens, William J.	14, 21, 28
Ens.	Sturdy (Sturey), Thomas	14, 21, 28

Sgt.	Sylvester (Silvester), John	14, 21, 28
Sgt.	Cross, James	14, 21, 28
Pte.	Allan, Henry	14, 21, 28
Pte.	Allan, Richard	14, 21
Pte.	Bailey, James	14, 21
Pte.	Bangs, Alonzo	14, 21, 28
Pte.	Barton, Augustus	14, 21
Pte.	Barton, William	14, 21, 28
Pte.	Bencroft, Asa	14, 21, 28
Pte.	Burke (Birk), Thomas	14, 21, 28
Pte.	Blany, John	21
Pte.	Broad, John	14, 21, 28
Pte.	Brown, George	21, 28
Pte	Burton, John	14
Pte.	Butler, Andrew	14
Pte.	Cass, Alfred	14, 21, 28
Pte.	Cass, James	14, 21, 28
Pte.	Cass, Josiah	14
Pte.	Cento (Centeu), Anson	14, 21, 28
Pte.	Cento (Centeu), Lewis	14, 21, 28
Pte.	Cento, Luther (Centeu)	14, 21, 28
Pte.	Cento (Centeu), Philetus	14, 21, 28
Pte.	Chamberlain, John	14, 21, 28
Pte.	Cole, Robbert	21, 28
Pte.	Conroy, Michael	14, 21, 28
Pte.	Countrey, Robbert	14, 21, 28
Pte.	Cross, George	14, 21, 28
Pte.	Cross, John	21, 28
Pte.	Davidson, John	21
Pte.	Davidson, Peter	21
Pte.	Doake, Samuel	14
Pte.	Doyle, William	14, 21, 28
Pte.	Dubois, Charles	14, 21, 28
Pte.	Dumming, Gregory	14, 21, 28
Pte.	Dumming, Levi	14, 21, 28
Pte.	Emma, Joseph	14, 21, 28
Pte.	Gale, John	14, 21, 28
Pte.	Granter, William	14, 21, 28
Pte.	Hagarty, William	14, 21, 28
Pte.	Hall, William	14, 21, 28
Pte.	Hanney, John	21
Pte.	Hanston, Jerimiah	14, 21, 28

Pte.	Harstrus, Joaiah	14, 21, 28
Pte.	Helm, Andrew	14, 21
Pte.	Helm, James	14, 21, 28
Pte.	Higginson, William	14, 21, 28
Pte.	Horan, James	21, 28
Pte.	House, Joseph	14, 21, 28
Pte.	House, William	14, 21, 28
Pte.	Ireland, Joseph	14, 21, 28
Pte.	Jackson, Richard	14, 21, 28
Pte.	Johnson. Alexis	14, 21, 28
Pte.	Johnson, Chauncy Jr.	21, 28
Pte.	Jouey (Loue), Havie	21, 28
Pte.	Kellogg, Coloney	14, 21, 28
Pte.	Kellogg, Elijah Jun.	21
Pte.	Kellogg, Thomas	14, 21, 28
Pte.	King, William	21
Pte.	La Clair, Pierre	21, 28
Pte.	Landriman, Caung.	21, 28
Pte.	Leavitt, John	14, 21, 28
Pte.	Le Daust, Hyciath	21, 28
Pte.	Le Duke, Erangelish	14, 21
Pte.	Lolhelat (Leviolet), Clare	14, 21
Pte.	Leviolet, Joseph	21, 28
Pte.	Locke, Robert	14, 21
Pte.	Longlorieu, Autrine	21, 28
Pte.	Lytle, John	14, 21, 28
Pte.	Marston, C.R.	14, 21, 28
Pte.	Mathews, John	14, 21, 28
Pte.	McIntyre, Guy	14, 21, 28
Pte.	McKay, Archibald	14, 21, 28
Pte.	McMahon, George	14, 21, 28
Pte.	McMaster, Angus	14, 21, 28
Pte.	McMaster, Earin	21
Pte.	Moran, Richard	14, 21, 28
Pte.	O'Brien, Peter	14, 21, 28
Pte.	O'Losin, Nathaniel	21
Pte.	Pullet, Charles	21
Pte.	Reed, William	14, 21, 28
Pte.	Reed, William	14, 21
Pte.	Robbinson, William	14, 21
Pte.	Ryan, Michael	14, 21, 28
Pte.	Sharp, Patrick	14, 21, 28
Pte.	Shaw, Archibald	14, 21, 28
Pte.	Shaw, John	14, 21, 28
Pte.	Sylvester, William	14, 21, 28
Pte.	Taylor, Patrick	14, 21, 28
Pte.	Thomson, Donald	14, 21, 28

Pte.	Tweed, Alexander	14, 21
Pte.	Valley, Godfrey	14, 21, 28
Pte.	Vilnaue, Michael	21, 28
Pte.	Wallace, William	21, 28
Pte.	Whitcomb, James	21, 28
Pte.	Wilcox, William	21, 28

Third Company of the Prescott Reserves

Lt.Col.	Hamilton, George	14
Lt.	Robertson, Lang	14, 21, 28
Ens.	Stewart, Neil	14, 21, 28
Sgt.	McCann, Thomas	14, 21, 28
Sgt.	McPhee, Daniel	14, 21, 28
Pte.	Barton, Thos.	14, 21, 28
Pte.	Blaynay, George	14, 21, 28
Pte.	Boyd, John	14, 21, 28
Pte.	Brown, John	14, 21, 28
Pte.	Cameron, Murdock	14, 21, 28
Pte.	Campbell, John	14, 21, 28
Pte.	Cook, Hiram L.	14, 21, 28
Pte.	Davidson, David	14, 21, 28
Pte.	Davidson, William	14, 21, 28
Pte.	Fitzpatrick, Johnson	14, 21, 28
Pte.	Fraser, Alex	14, 21, 28
Pte.	Fraser, Alex'r	14, 21, 28
Pte.	Fraser, Alex'r. W.	14, 21, 28
Pte.	Fraser, John	14, 21, 28
Pte.	Fraser, Malcom	14, 21, 28
Pte.	Gibson, James	14, 21, 28
Pte.	Hammell, Joseph	14, 21, 28
Pte.	Harkins, Roger	14, 21, 28
Pte.	Higginson, John	14, 21, 28
Pte.	Hunter, John	14, 21, 28
Pte.	Lock, William	14, 21, 28
Pte.	Long, Elisha B.	14, 21, 28
Pte.	Made, George	14, 21, 28
Pte.	McArthur, Robert	14, 21, 28
Pte.	McCann, James	14, 21, 28
Pte.	McCann, Samuel	14, 21, 28
Pte.	McCaskell, Alex'r.	14, 21, 28
Pte.	McCaskell, John	14, 21, 28
Pte.	McCaskell, John	14, 21, 28
Pte.	McCaskell, Donald	14, 21, 28
Pte.	McCrimnu (McCrumma), Duncam	14, 21, 28
Pte.	McCrimon, Farg.	14, 21, 28
Pte.	McInnis, Donald	14, 21, 28
Pte.	McIntosh, Finlay	14, 21, 28

Pte.	McKeiger (McKinger), James S.	14, 21, 28
Pte.	McKellican, Benjamin	14, 21, 28
Pte.	McLeod, Angus	14, 21, 28
Pte.	McLeod, Norman	14, 21, 28
Pte.	McNally, Henry	14, 21, 28
Pte.	McNee, John	14, 21, 28
Pte.	McNulty, Hugh	14, 21, 28
Pte.	McRae, Alex'r.	14, 21, 28
Pte.	McRae, Arch'd.	14, 28
Pte.	McRae, Donald	14, 21, 28
Pte.	McRae, Donald	14, 21, 28
Pte.	McRae, Finlay	14, 21, 28
Pte.	McRae, John	14, 21, 28
Pte.	McRae, Norm'n.	14, 21, 28
Pte.	McRae, Malcolm	14, 21, 28
Pte.	McRae, Patrick	14, 21, 28
Pte.	McThistlewait, Robert	14, 21, 28
Pte.	Reid, Robert	14, 21, 28
Pte.	Renick, Lady	14, 21, 28
Pte.	Robinson, Murdock	14, 21, 28
Pte.	Sample, John	14, 21, 28
Pte.	Sharp, John	14, 21, 28
Pte.	Sherman, Jonathan	14, 21, 28
Pte.	Shields, Andrew	14, 21, 28
Pte.	Summerland, John	14, 21, 28
Pte.	Van Kleek, Peter	14, 21, 28
Pte.	Vogan, George	14, 21, 28
Pte.	Vogan, Samuel	14, 21, 28
Pte.	Walker, Henry	14, 21, 28
Pte.	Watson, Robert	14, 21, 28
Pte.	Waite (Wait), Simeon	14, 21, 28

Ninth Provisional Battalion, Queens Royal Borderers

First Company of the Ninth Provisional Battalion

LtCol.	Gowan, Ogle Robert	7-30 WIA
Maj.	Grant, Alexander	10-30
Adj.	Mathewson, Alexander	10-30
PMtr.	Hebbell, Ephraim James	10-30
Surg.	Buchanan, Charles William	10-30
Q.M.	Mair, David	10-30
SMaj.	Boyd, Alexander	10-30

QMS.	Anderson, Adam	10-30
PMS	Upton, George Graham	10-30
Capt.	Stewart, William	10-30
Lt.	Hopkins, Nicholas	10-30
Ens.	Reynolds, Thomas	10-30
Sgt.	Burland, Thomas	10-30
Sgt.	Graham, William	10-30
Sgt.	Kelly, William	10-30
Cpl.	Bradley, John Ross	10-30
Cpl.	Godkins, William	10-30
Cpl.	Running, William	10-30
Dmr.	Beauford, William	10-30
Dmr.	McGowan, Robert	10-30
Fifer	Hayes, Henry	10-30
Pte.	Brown, Hugh	10-30 WIA
Pte.	Campbell, James	10-30
Pte.	Channing, Edward	10-30
Pte.	Criichton (Creghton), John	22-30
Pte.	Courtney, Patrick	12-30
Pte.	Crawford, James	10-30
Pte.	Cusac, George	15-30
Pte.	Cusac, William	10-30
Pte.	Diamond (Dimond), Patrick	15-30
Pte.	Dobson, William	10-30
Pte.	Dooles (Doolas), William	12-30
Pte.	Draper, Richard	10-30
Pte.	Duffy, James	10-30
Pte.	Durand, James	19-30
Pte.	Ebbe, Walter	10-30
Pte.	Elliot, Thomas	10-30
Pte.	Ferguson, Daniel	15-30
Pte.	Fortier, George	15-30
Pte.	Galt, Alexander	10-30
Pte.	Godkin, Abel	10-30
Pte.	Godkin, John	10-30
Pte.	Godkin, Thomas, Jr.	10-30
Pte.	Godkin, Thomas, Sr.	10-30
Pte.	Hardy, Alexander R.	15-30

Pte.	Harrol, John	10-30 WIA
Pte.	Harvey, Henry	10-30
Pte.	Johnston, Richard G.	10-30
Pte.	Kellings, William	10-30
Pte.	Kenney, John	15-30
Pte.	Kerr (Carr), Jonathan	10-30
Pte.	Lang, Alexander	15-30
Pte.	Low, Edward	15-30
Pte.	Mason, George	10-30
Pte.	McIntyre, Hugh	10-30
Pte.	McKee, Adam	10-30
Pte.	Meaby, William	10-30
Pte.	Mee, James	10-30
Pte.	Moore, James	10-30
Pte.	Mulrainy, James	10-30
Pte.	O'Hara, Peter	10-30
Pte.	Oliver, Nathaniel	10-30
Pte.	Pratt, James	10-30
Pte.	Reynolds, James	10-30
Pte.	Rogers, John	10-30
Pte.	Shicely, Edward	23-30
Pte.	Sinclair, George	10-30
Pte.	Spencer, John	10-30
Pte.	Stewart, John	10-30
Pte.	Stewart, Nathaniel	10-30
Pte.	Taylor, Joseph	10-30
Pte.	Tommy, John	10-30
Pte.	Turner, Samuel	10-30
Pte.	Weir, George	15-30
Pte.	Williamson, John	13-30
Pte.	Wilson, James	10-30
Pte.	Woods, John	22-30

The following were listed as being wounded during the battle, but for some reason were not listed on the paylists of the Ninth Provisional Battalion:

Pte.	Brownlee, Alexander	WIA
Pte.	Glistor, Christopher	WIA

Sources

Archival

The records of the Upper Canadian Militia in Record Group 9 in the National Archives of Canada are the primary source for the information on men serving in the militia units. The lists of the men serving in the various militia units has been primarily drawn from the paylists and nominal rolls created in 1838-39 and found in RG 9, WO 13, vols 3675, 3677, 3681, 3682, 3683, 3701, 3702, and 3705. Canadian Militia and Volunteers 1838-39.

Published

J. Smyth Carter, *The Story of Dundas, being a history of the County of Dundas from 1784 to 1904*, St. Lawrence News Publishing House, Iroquois. 1905; Goldie A. Connell, *Augusta Royal Township Number Seven*, St. Lawrence Printing Company Limited, Prescott, 1985; James Croil, *Dundas or a Sketch of Canadian History, and More Particularly of the County of Dundas*, B. Dawson & Son, Montreal, 1861; *Chronicle and Gazette* (Kingston), 26 October 1839; Elizabeth Hancock, "Distribution of Loyalist Relief Following the Battle of the Windmill near Prescott, Ontario, 1839," *Canadian Genealogist*. Vol. 3, No. 1, 1981. pp. 46-47; John Grahm Harkness, *Stormont, Dundas and Glengarry. A History 1784-1945*. 1949; Thaddeus W.H. Leavitt, *History of Leeds and Grenville, Ontario, from 1749 to 1879, with... Biological Sketches of Some of its Prominent Men and Pioneers*, Recorder Press, Brockville, 1879; J.A. Morris, *Prescott 1810 - 1967*. The Prescott Journal. Prescott, 1967; Arthur J. Robinson, *The Grenville Militia Regiments and Other Local Militia Regiments - November, 1838*, Victoria, BC, 2000; K.F. Scott, *The Battle of the Windmill*, St. Lawrence Printing Co. Ltd. Prescott, 1969.

APPENDIX D

The Patriot Hunters who fought at Prescott, November 1838

The following list provides information about 189 men who are known to have served with the Patriot Hunters at Windmill Point near Prescott, 12-17 November 1838. Based on a number of sources, it allows some analysis to be made of their nationality, place of residence, age, occupation and fate.

Nationality

The breakdown is as follows:

Americans		
Nationality confirmed:	142	
Nationality probable:	8	
Naturalized American:	1	
Total:	151	151
British subjects		
From the British Isles:	6	
From the Canadas:	17	
Possible Canadians:	2	
Total:	25	25
European		
From France:	3	
From Germany:	5	
From Holland:	1	
From Poland:	3	
From Sweden:	1	
Total:	13	13

It is clear that the majority of the invaders were Americans. Of the 189 men on the list, 142 can be positively identified as American citizens, 8 were probable American citizens and one a Canadian who had been so long in the United States that he has to be regarded as an American citizen. This latter man was William Johnston, the pirate of the St. Lawrence who left Canada in 1812, served in the American armed forces during the War of 1812, was married to a woman from Jefferson County and had resided in French Creek (Clayton, NY) for more than 20 years at the time of the battle.

The 25 British subjects can be broken down as 17 men from the Canadas, 2 possibly from the Canadas, and 6 from the British Isles. Of this latter group, most had been in the United States for a number of years and must be regarded as economic immigrants, not professional rebels.

The 17 certain Canadians, who form the most interesting single group, can be further sub-divided into economic immigrants (1); young men from Lower Canada (8); and patriots or rebels from Upper Canada (8). The economic immigrant was Justus Merriam from Haldimand Township in Northumberland County who had moved to Jefferson County, NY, sometime before the 1837 Rebellion to look for work. He was caught up in the Patriot Hunters, fought at the windmill and was captured, found guilty but was pardoned and released.

· The 8 men from Lower Canada (the Aubré brothers, Blondeau, Gagnon, Leforte, Mailhotte, Morrisette, Rousseau or Raza) were, with an average age of only 19 (nearly eight years below that of the other men on the list), thus very young men who were probably unemployed and had drifted into the United States looking for work only to get caught up in the border wars. Of this group, Benjamin Aubré was killed in action, Mailhotte and Rousseau (sometimes Raza) turned evidence for the Crown, Oliver Aubré and Gagnon were found guilty but pardoned and only Leforte and Morisette were severely punished by being transported.

This leaves the third group of 8 Upper Canadians, the only men who can truly be considered as hardcore rebels (or, if you will, Reformers). Of these, David Defield was from the Niagara area and, given his age, probably drifted into the United States looking for work. Samuel Laraby was living in Rossie, St. Lawrence County just prior to the invasion but there is some evidence that he was a former native of Prescott. Ezra Brockaway and James Cummings were natives of Prescott, the former escaped and the latter, who was mentally unstable, was acquitted and released. The remaining four Upper Canadians were natives of the St. Lawrence area and all had a record as having been involved in the political turmoil that predated the 1837 Rebellion: James Philips, and Levi and Truman Chipman from Bastard Township, Leeds County; and John Berry from Brockville. All four had fled to the United States immediately after the failed uprising. If we discount Cummings, who was clearly mentally unfit, only 6 men for certain and possibly a seventh (Laraby) can be classified as diehard Canadian rebels.

The fact that only 7 men of the 189 Hunters known to have landed in Prescott in November 1838 can be termed hardcore Canadian rebels is the most compelling evidence that this attack was predominantly an American operation.

There are 13 Europeans on the list: 3 Frenchmen; 5 Germans; 3 Poles; 1 Swede and 1 Dutchman. Another Pole is known to have fought at the windmill but his name is unknown — he escaped using Lieutenant William Johnson's uniform. Some of these Europeans had been in the United States for as little as five months, others for a number of years. As a group, they resemble the 8 Lower Canadians, being caught up in a process that they did not fully understand.

Residence

The last known places of residence for the men on the list are as follows:

United States		
New York State		
	Jefferson County	88
	Onondaga County	37
	St. Lawrence County	20
	Oswego County	17
	Cayuga County	4
	Lewis County	4
	Monroe County	2
	Franklin County	1
	Herkimer County	1
	Montgomery County	1
	New York City	1
	Oneida County	1
	Westchester County	1
Europe		3
The Canadas		
Lower Canada		2
Upper Canada		1

Again, the predominance of American residences is noteworthy particularly the border counties of Jefferson and St. Lawrence which account for over two-thirds of the men. Onondaga County, with 37 men, and Oswego County, with 17, were the two other hotbeds of Hunter sentiment. Between them, these four counties account for about 85% of the known places of residence.

Age and Occupation

Ages are known for 178 men and the average (calculated only on the most generally accepted age of each man) was 26.8 years. Essentially, the Hunters were young men.

In terms of their occupations, information is available for 132 men. The largest single group were unskilled manual labourers, followed by skilled tradesmen; those engaged in commercial activites; farmers; professionals and government officials.

The occupational breakdown is as follows:

Labourer		65
Skilled tradesman		44
Apprentice	1	
Carpenter	8	
Blacksmith	7	
Cooper	4	
Maso:	3	
Shoemaker or cobble:	3	
Wagon maker	3	
Hatter	2	
Salt factory worker	2	
Cabinet maker	1	
Chair maker	1	
Cook	1	
Joiner	1	
Machinist	1	
Printer	1	
Saddler	1	
Tailor	1	
Tinsmith	1	
Weaver	1	
Wheelwright	1	
Commercial activities		12
Dealer (not specified)	2	
Storekeeper	2	
Tavernkeeper	2	
Clothier	1	
Factory owner	1	
Pedlar	1	
Salt manufacturer	1	
Farmer:		8
Professional		2
Chemist	1	
Teacher	1	
Government official		1

As a matter of interest, only 6 men admitted to having served in the regular or militia forces of the United States or other nations. However, this could well be due to the fact that those Hunters captured were reluctant to admit to British authorities during questioning that they had military experience as it might have weighed against them at their courts martial.

Fates

Of the 189 men, 15 were killed during the battle but this is by no means all the fatal casualties suffered by the Hunters during the action as other men, for whom there is no surviving records, died in the battle. As stated in the main text, Hunter casualties during the period, 12-17 November, may have been as high as 50. Nineteen men were wounded, of whom 3 later died of their wounds, while 8 men who were known to have fought escaped, either during or immediately after the action.

The evidence on the number of men captured is extremely variable as even the official British and Canadian records provide different figures. Based on information from the sources listed below, 136 men are known to have been taken prisoner by Crown forces of whom 5 died in captivity. Of this number, between 134 and 138 (records vary) were tried by courtmartial while 16 men (many of them wounded in the fighting) were released without trial.

Of those tried, their fates were as follows:

Condemned but later pardoned and released	86
Transported	60
Executed	11
Acquitted on the evidence	3
Acquitted on grounds of insanity	1

Of the 60 men transported to Van Diemen's Land (modern Tasmania), their fates were as follows:

Known to have returned to North America	32
Fate unknown	18
Died on passage or in Van Diemen's Land	6
Married in Van Diemen's land and settled there	4

THE HUNTERS WHO FOUGHT AT THE WINDMILL, 1838

In the following list, the most common variation of the last name of the Hunter is in capital letters. Variations on names are listed in lower case following "aka" (also known as). The most common age listed for each man in the records is listed followed by alternate ages in brackets. Residences listed are the last known residence of the man prior to the invasion.

Key to abbreviations used in the list

*	On the Crown List, see National Archives of Canada, Colonial Office 42, vol. 456, Alphabetical List of Persons taken near Windmill Point
aka	also known as
Co	County
DOW	Died of Wounds
GSD	Found guilty, sentenced to death
JC	Jefferson County
KIA	Killed in action
LC	Lower Canada
OnC	Onondaga County
OsC	Oswego County
Pd	Pardoned
R/M	Recommended for mercy
RWT	Released without trial
SLC	St. Lawrence County
VDL	Van Diemen's Land
T/VDL	Sentence commuted to transportation to Van Diemen's Land
UC	Upper Canada
Wd	Wounded

Name	Age	Last Known Residence(s)	Occupation	Nationality	Additional Information	Fate
*ABBEY, Dorephus aka Dorethus, Doropheus, Doropheas, Dorotheus, Dorotheas	48 (47)	Pamelia, JC, NY	Printer	American	Second in command under von Schoultz. Former militia officer	GSD. Hanged 12 Dec 1838
ALGER, Philip	23 (32)	Salina, OnC, NY	Labourer	American		Wd. RWT.
*ALLEN, Charles	24	Scriba, OsC, NY	Labourer	American		GSD. RWT.
*ALLEN, David	37 (24)	Volney, OsC, NY	Labourer	American		GSD. T/VDL. Returned 1844
*ANDERSON, Duncan aka Launcen	48	Lyme, JC, NY	Labourer	American		GSD. Present at Hickory Island Feb 1838. Hanged 4 Jan 1839
AUBRÉ aka Aubry, Obrey, Benjamin	18	Montreal, LC, lately of Madrid, SLC, NY		Canadian		KIA
AUBRÉ aka Aubry, Obrey, Oliver	21 (20)	Montreal, LC, lately of Madrid, SLC, NY		Canadian		Wd. RWT.
*AUSTIN, Samuel	17 (21)	Madrid, SLC, NY	Labourer	American	Captured 13 Nov 1838	GSD. Pd.
*BAKER, Thomas	47	Hannibal, Cayuga Co, NY	Labourer	American	Resided for a time in UC	GSD. T/VDL
*BARLOW aka Barton, Hiram W.	19	Morristown, SLC, NY	Labourer	American		GSD. Pd
*BENNET, Rouse	17 (19)	Norway, Herkimer Co, NY	Carpenter	American		GSD. Pd.
*BERENDS aka Berentz, Barance, Berius, Ernest	40 (41, 44)	Formerly of Cracow, Poland, lately of Salina, OnC, NY		European (Polish)	Former officer in Polish Army. Captured 13 Nov 1838	GSD. R/M. Pd.
*BERRY, John	40 (42)	Oswego, OsC, NY	Farmer	Canadian	Native of Elizabethtown, UC. Left province in Dec 1837, suspected of treason	GSD. T/VDL. Returned 1860.
*BLODGETT aka Blodgit, Blodget, Orland, aka Orlin, Orland	23 (19)	Philadelphia, JC, NY	Carpenter	American		GSD. T/VDL
*BLONDEAU aka Blondon, Bloudeau, George	19 (21)	Native of LC, lately of Ogdensburg, SLC, NY	Labourer	Canadian		GSD. Pd.
*BRADLEY, John	30 (28)	Native of Co Antrim, Ireland, lately of Sackets Harbor, JC, NY	Hatter	British (Ireland)		GSD. T/VDL.
*BREWSTER, John	19 (16)	Henderson, JC, NY	Wheelwright	American	On guard at the windmill	GSD. R/M. Pd.
BROCKAWAY aka Brockway, Ezra		Prescott, UC	Storekeeper	Canadian		Escaped.
BROMLEY aka Brownley, John	38	Depeauville, JC, NY		American		Wd. DOW in hospital
BROWN, Charles E.	24	Brownville, JC, NY		American	Son of Judge Samuel Brown and nephew of General Jacob Brown	KIA, 13 Nov 1838
BROWN, Charles S.	20	Hastings, OsC., NY	Labourer	American		GSD. Pd.
*BROWN, George T.	22 (23)	Evans Mills, JC, NY	Blacksmith	American	Captured on 13 Nov 1838	GSD. T/VDL. Returned 1846
*BUCKLEY aka Bulkley, Christopher	30 (25)	Salina, OnC, NY	Salt manufacturer	American	Hunter senior officer and recruiter	GSD. Hanged 4 Jan 1839

Name	Age	Last Known Residence(s)	Occupation	Nationality	Additional Information	Fate
*BUGBEE aka Bugby, Bugbie, Chauncey or Chauncy	22	Lyme, JC, NY	Farmer	American		GSD. T/VDL. Returned 1846
BUTTERFIELD, Nelson aka George	22	Philadelphia, JC, NY		American		KIA 13 Nov 1838
*CERVANTES aka Carpenter, Cervanter, Cerventes, Cerventer, Paschall or Paschal	20	Leroy, JC, NY	Labourer	American		GSD. Pd.
CHIPMAN, Levi	45	Bastard Township, Leeds Co, UC, lately of Westchester Co, NY	Farmer	Canadian	Fled Canada after rebellion of 1837. Turned Crown Evidence	RWT.
CHIPMAN aka Shipman, Truman	44	Bastard Township, Leeds Co, UC, lately of Morristown, SLC, NY	Farmer	Canadian	Fled province in Dec 1837. Captured 13 Nov 1838	GSD. Pd.
*CLARK, Culver S. aka Calvin S.	19 (18)	Fort Covington, Franklin Co, NY	Labourer	American		GSD. Pd.
*CLARK, Eli	61 (60)	Oswego, OsC, NY	Labourer	American	Related to US Congressman. Officer in NY Militia artillery NAC RG5 A1 Vol 214 Draper to Arthur, 1 Jan. 1839	GSD. T/VDL. Pd. on account of age and infirmities
COFFIN, Nathan	27	Liverpool, OnC., NY		American		KIA.
COLQUHOUN aka Calhoun, Hugh	35 (25, 23)	Formerly of Ireland, lately of Salina, OnC., NY	Labourer	British (Irish)		GSD. T/VDL.
*COLLINS, Robert G.	21 (32, 34)	Ogdensburg, SLC, NY	Shoemaker	American		GSD. T/VDL.
COLTON aka Coultman, Hiram	21 (19)	Philadelphia, JC, NY		American		Wd. RWT.
*CONRAD aka Coonrod, Conrod, Condrat, Philip	21 (22)	Native of Germany, lately of Salina, OnC, NY	Labourer	European (German)		GSD. R/M. Pd.
*CRONKER aka Cranker, Craoker, Peter	19 (23)	Orleans, JC, NY	Labourer	American		GSD. Pd.
*CRONKHITE aka Cronkheit, John	29 (30)	Alexandria, OsC, NY	Blacksmith	American		GSD. T/VDL. Returned 1845
*CROSSMAN, Charles F.	19	Watertown, JC, NY	Wagon maker	American		GSD. Pd.
*CUMMINGS aka Cummins, James	40 (38)	Augusta township, Grenville Co, UC, lately of Orleans, JC, NY	Yeoman (farmer)	Canadian	Captured 13 Nov 1838. Subject to fits and temporary derangement	Acquitted and released on account of insanity
*CURTIS, Lysander	33 (35)	Ogdensburg, SLC, NY	Shoemaker	American		Wd. Csd. T/VDL. Died in VDL
*DARBY, Luther	48	Watertown, JC, NY		American		GSD. T/VDL. Returned 1845
*DEFIELD aka Duffield, Dufield, Deffield, David	28 (22)	A native of the Niagara District, UC, lately of Salina, OnC, NY	Labourer	Canadian	Pardoned because of his mother's record during the War of 1812	GSD. T/VDL. Pd.
*DELINO aka Delano, Deline, Leonard	26 (24)	Watertown, JC, NY	Blacksmith	American	Also a farm owner	Wd. GSD. T/VDL. Returned 1845
*DENIO, William	21 (18)	Leroy, JC, NY	Labourer	American		GSD. Pd.

Name	Age	Last Known Residence(s)	Occupation	Nationality	Additional Information	Fate
*DODGE, Joseph	28 (30)	Salina, OnC, NY	Labourer	American		GSD. R/M. Pd.
DRAKE, Rensselaer	23	Salina, OnC, NY		American		KIA
*DRESSER aka Deeper, Aaron Jr	24 (22)	Alexandria, JC, NY		American	Officer in the Hunters. Captured 13 Nov 1838	GSD. T/VDL. Returned 1843
*DRUMMOND aka Drumma, Joseph	22 (21)	Salina, OsC, NY	Labourer	American		GSD. Pd.
DUNTEN aka Dunton, Robert		Probably Watertown, JC, NY		Probably American	Presumed landed	Missing noted in *Watertown Jeffersonian*, 16 Nov 1838
*DUTCHER aka Deutscher, Moses A.	23	Brownville, JC, NY	Carpenter	American		GSD. T/VDL.
*ELMORE, John	19 (18)	Leroy, JC,NY	Tinsmith	American		GSD. Pd.
EMPY, Adam	40	Rossie, SLC, NY		American		KIA
ESTES, ——		French Creek, JC, NY	Believed to have commercial interests	American	A mysterious figure and a senior leader and recruiter in the Hunters. Known to have landed in Canada on the night of 12 Nov 1838	Escaped
EVANS, Selah or Shelah	35	Leroy, JC, NY		American		Wd. RWT.
*FELLOWES aka Fellows, Elon, aka Elom, Ebon	23	Dexter, Montgomery Co, NY	Cooper	American		GSD. T/VDL. Returned 1845
*FINNEY aka Phinney, Lorenzo F.	21	Watertown, JC, NY	Machinist	American		Wd. RWT.
FOSTER, Edmund	22	Alexandria, JC, NY		American		KIA
*FRAER aka Friar, Frear, Michael	23	Clay, OnC, NY	Cooper	American		GSD. T/VDL.
FULTON, Benjamin		Unknown		Unknown, probably American		Escaped
*GAGNON aka Gagnion, Gaynion, Ganyo, François aka Francis	18	Native of LC, lately of Ogdensburg, SLC, NY	Labourer	Canadian		GSD. R/M. Pd.
*GARRISON aka Garison, Emanuel J.	26	Brownville, JC, NY	Blacksmith	American		GSD. T/VDL. Returned 1846
*GATES, William	24 (23)	Cape Vincent, JC, NY	Labourer	American	Captured 13 Nov 1838	GSD. T/VDL. Returned 1845
*GEORGE, Daniel	28	Lyme, JC, NY	Teacher	American	Captured 13 Nov 1838. Paymaster of the Hunters	GSD. Hanged 12 Dec 1838
*GILMAN aka Gillman, John	38	Brownville, Oneida Co, NY	Labourer	American		GSD. T/VDL. Returned 1845
*GOODRICH, Cornelius	18 (16)	Salina, OnC, NY	Labourer	American	Captured 13 Nov 1838	GSD. Pd.
*GOODRICH aka Gooderich, George S. aka Gideon	43	Salina, OnC, NY	Labourer	American	Father of Cornelius	GSD. T/VDL.
*GOULD, David aka Price	24 (21)	Alexandria, JC, NY	Labourer	American		GSD. R/M. Pd.
GRAVES, John	25	Cosmopolitan, JC, NY		American	Testified for the Crown	RWT.
*GRIGGS, Jerry E.	21 (22)	Salina, OnC, NY	Labourer	American		GSD. T/VDL. Returned 1845

Name	Age	Last Known Residence(s)	Occupation	Nationality	Additional Information	Fate
*GRIGGS, Nelson T.	28	Salina, OnC, NY	Labourer	American	Captured 13 Nov 1838	GSD. T/VDL. Returned 1845
*HALL, Hiram	17 (15, 16)	Orleans, JC, NY		American		GSD. Pd.
HATHAWAY, William		Unknown		Probably American		Escaped
HAYNES, Moses	20	Salina, OnC, NY		American		KIA
HERALD aka Herod, Jacob aka Jacques	27	Native of Lorraine, France.		European (French)	Arrived in America 5 months earlier	Wd. RWT.
*HEUSTIS aka Hustace, Daniel D.	32	Watertown, JC, NY	Storekeeper, Grocer	American	A captain in the Hunters	GSD. T/VDL. Returned 1845
*HICKS, Garret	27 (45)	Alexandria, JC, NY	Farmer	American		GSD. T/VDL. Returned 1846
*HOLMES, Edmund aka Edward	24 (29)	Salina, OnC, NY	Labourer	American		GSD. Pd.
*HOREY aka Hovey, Horiz, Horiez, Hover, Hariz, Charles	22	Native of Paris, France, lately of Lyme, JC, NY	Labourer	European (French)		GSD. R/M. Pd.
*HOWTH aka House, Houth, Huff, David	26 (24)	Alexandria, JC, NY	Labourer	European (Dutch)		GSD. T/VDL. Returned 1845
*INGLIS aka Inglish, Ingles, James	28 (30)	Native of Paisley, Scotland, lately of Adams, JC, NY	Weaver	British (Scot)		GSD. T/VDL.
JACKSON, O.	18	Unknown		American		Probably RWT.
*JANTZEN aka Jantzer, Jentzen, Jautzen, Jancken, Johnson, Henry aka Heinrich	29	Native of Germany, lately of New York City		European (German)		GSD. R/M. Pd.
JOHNSTON, William (Bill)	55	French Creek, JC, NY	Tavern keeper and smuggler	Canadian but had lived in the United States for 26 years	Born in LC. Arrested 1812 Kingston for treason. Escaped. Served as river pilot for U.S. Army 1813-14. At Navy Island Dec 1837. Burned *Sir Robert Peel*, May 1838. Commodore in Patriot Navy. Known to have landed at windmill	Arrested in Nov 1838 and later imprisoned
*JONES, John M.	35 (37)	Philadelphia, JC, NY	Hatter	American	Captured 13 Nov 1838	GSD. Commuted. Pd.
*KIMBALL aka Kimbalt, Kemble, George H.	20 (18, 19)	Brownville, JC, NY		American	Brother of John R. Kimball	Wd. GSD. Pd.
KIMBALL aka Kimbalt, Kemble, John R.		Dexter, JC, NY	Factory owner in Dexter	American	Officer. Prominent in recruiting in Jefferson County	Escaped 12 Nov 1838
*KINNEY aka Kenney, Hiram	20	Palermo, OnC, NY	Labourer	American		GSD. R/M. Pd.
LAMEAR, Paul		Ogdensburg, SLC, NY		American		KIA
LARABY, Samuel	35	Rossie, SLC, NY		Canadian?	Possibly Canadian from Prescott area	KIA
*LAWTON aka Lanton, Oliver	22 (23)	Auburn, Cayuga Co, NY	Wagon maker	American		GSD. Pd.
*LAWTON aka Lanton, Sylvester A.	28 (23)	Lyme, JC, NY	Farmer	American	Hunter officer and hanged for it	GSD. Hanged 4 Jan 1839
*LEE, Joseph	21	Palermo, OsC, NY	Joiner	American		GSD. Pd.

Name	Age	Last Known Residence(s)	Occupation	Nationality	Additional Information	Fate
*LEEPER, Andrew	44 (42)	Lyme, JC, NY	Labourer	American	Suspected spy who travelled in UC prior to the battle. Death sentence commuted by Arthur	GSD. Ordered hung but reprieved. T/VDL. Died in VDL
*LEFORTE aka Lefore, Lefort, Lefoen, Fefore, Lafore, Joseph	29 (19, 21, 31)	Native of Montreal, LC, lately of Cape Vincent, JC, NY	Stonemason	Canadian	Captured 13 Nov 1838	GSD. T/VDL. Returned
*LEWIS aka Leach, Lyman L. aka Leman	28 (40)	Salina, OnC, NY	Dealer	American	Believed to have aided the destruction of the *Sir Robert Peel*	GSD. Hanged 11 Feb 1839
*LISCUM aka Liscomb, Liskum, Daniel	22 (40)	Lyme, JC, NY		American		GSD. T/VDL. Returned 1846
LIVINGSTON, Samuel	40	Lisbon, SLC, NY		American	Captured 13 Nov 1838	RWT.
*LOOP, Hiram	25 (26)	Scriba, OsC, NY	Labourer	American	Captured 13 Nov 1838	GSD. T/VDL.
*MARTIN, Foster	34 (32)	Antwerp, JC, NY	Labourer	American	Captured 13 Nov 1838. Proved to have assisted working the artillery at the windmill	GSD. T/VDL. Died in VDL.
*MARTIN, Jehiel aka Tehiel, Jemal	32 (31)	Oswego, OsC, NY	Mason	American		GSD. T/VDL. Returned 1846
*MATHERS aka Matthews, Calvin	25 (24)	Lysander, OnC., NY	Labourer	American		GSD. T/VDL.
*MATHERS aka Matthews, Chauncey	25 (24)	Liverpool, OnC, NY		American	Captured 13 Nov 1838	GSD. T/VDL.
MAILHOTTE aka Milhiot, Mayatt, Myatt, Mailhotte, Maillotte, Milhieu, Mignoteth, Laurent, aka Lenson, Lonson, Alonzo, Laurente	18	Native of LC		Canadian	Turned Crown Evidence	RWT.
*MERRIAM aka Miriam, Meriam, Justus	18 (17)	Formerly of Haldimand township, Northumberland Co, UC, lately of Brownville, JC, NY	Shoemaker	Canadian	Had emigrated to the US to look for employment. Captured on 13 Nov 1838	R/M. RWT.
*MEYER aka Myer, Moyer, Mier, Peter	20 (21)	Native of France, lately of Salina, OnC, NY	Salt maker	European (French)		R/M. RWT.
*MEYERS aka Mayers, Meyer, Myer, Sebastian	21 (20)	Native of Bavaria, Germany, lately of Rochester, Monroe Co, NY	Cook	European (German)	Said he was hired as a cook	GSD. R/M. Pd.
*MILLER, Phares aka Pheris	18	Watertown, JC, NY	Wagon maker	American	Drummer in Watertown Hunter Lodge	GSD. Pd.
MILLOW aka Meslo, Mealo, Milow, Frederick	21	Hannover, Germany		European (German)	Servant of Nils von Schoultz	DOW
*MOORE aka More, Andrew	26	Adams, JC, NY	Labourer	American		Wd. GSD. T/VDL.
*MORRISETTE aka Morriseau, Morisset, Marriset, Jean, aka John	20 (22, 26)	Native of LC, lately of Lewis Co, NY	Labourer	Canadian		Wd. GSD. T/VDL. Returned 1844
MYER, Oster	30	Native of Poland		European (Polish)		KIA
*NORRIS, Joseph	35 (26)	Rossie, SLC, NY	Carpenter	American		Acquitted
*OKONSKIE aka O'Koinski, Okoinski, O'Koyinski, O'Koyinsky, Jean aka Ivan	31 (32)	Native of Cracow, Poland, lately of Salina, OnC, NY		European (Polish)	Captured on 13 Nov 1838	Wd. GSD. RM. Pd.

Name	Age	Last Known Residence(s)	Occupation	Nationality	Additional Information	Fate
*O'NEILL aka O'Neil, William	42 (38)	Alexandria, JC, NY	Labourer	American	Captured 13 Nov 1838	Acquitted
*OWEN, Alson	27 (24)	Palermo, OsC, NY,	Labourer	American	On guard at the windmill. An epileptic	GSD. T/VDL. Died in VDL
PADDOCK, Jacob	18 (17)	Salina, OnC, NY	Labourer	American		GSD. T/VDL.
*PECK aka Peek, Lawton S., aka Lanton	20	Brownville, JC, NY	Labourer	American		GSD. R/M. Pd.
*PEELER, Joel	41 (50)	Rutland, JC, NY	Farmer	American	Implicated in mutilation of Johnson's body	GSD. Hanged 22 Dec 1838
*PENNY, Ethel, aka Ithol	19 (18)	Lyme, JC, NY	Labourer	American		GSD. Pd.
*PHELPS, Russell aka Russel	38 (50)	Lyme, JC, NY	Tailor	American	Implicated in destruction of *Sir Robert Peel*	GSD. Hanged 4 Jan 1839
PHILIPS, James, aka Phillips	38	Formerly of Bastard township, Leeds Co, UC, lately of Ogdensburg, SLC, NY	Tavern keeper	Canadian	Officer in the Hunters. Fled UC in Dec 1837	KIA 13 Nov 1838
*PIERCE, James	22 (19)	Orleans, JC, NY	Labourer	American		GSD. T/VDL. Returned 1846
*POLLY aka Polley, Ira	22 (23)	Lyme, JC, NY	Carpenter	American		GSD. T/VDL. Returned 1845
POWERS, Gaius aka Gayus, Geaus, D.S.	24	Brownville, JC, NY		American	Captured 13 Nov 1838	RWT.
*PRIEST, Asa	45 (40, 43, 42)	Auburn, Cayuga Co, NY	Probably a farmer	American		Wd. GSD. T/VDL. Died on passage 19 Oct 1839
*PUTMAN aka Putnam, Jacob	24 (19)	Palermo, OsC, NY	Labourer	American		GSD. R/M. Pd.
*PUTNAM aka Putman, Levi	21	Lyme, JC, NY	Labourer	American		GSD. Pd.
*RAWSON aka Ransom, Rosin, Timothy P.	24 (21)	Alexandria, JC, NY	Blacksmith	American	Captured 13 Nov 1838	GSD. Pd.
*REILLY aka Riley, Rielley, O'Reilley, Lawrence	46 (43)	Lyme, JC, NY	Labourer	American		GSD. Pd.
ROUSSEAU aka Razeau, Ruza, Raza, Jean Baptiste	20	Native of Montreal, LC		Canadian	Turned Crown evidence	RWT.
*REYNOLDS, Solomon	33	Salina, OnC, NY	Labourer	American		GSD. T/VDL.
*REYNOLDS, William	19 (33)	Orleans, JC, NY	Labourer	American		GSD. T/VDL.
*RICHARDSON aka Richards, Andrew	28 (38)	Rossie, SLC, NY	Carpenter	American	Captured 13 Nov 1838. Brother-in-law in Brockville	GSD. R/M. Pd.
*RICHARDSON, Asa H.	24 (23)	Formerly of UC, lately of Oswego, OsC, NY	Labourer	Not established possibly Canadian		GSD. T/VDL.
ROGERS, Charles		Philadelphia, JC, NY		Probably American		Captured. RWT?
ROGERS, Edgar	18	Watertown, JC, NY		Probably American		Captured. RM?
ROGERS, Orson	19 (23)	Philadelphia, JC, NY		Probably American		Wd. RWT.
ROOT, Lysander	27	Sackets Harbor, JC, NY		American		KIA
SAVOY, ——	44	Lewisburg, Lewis Co, NY		American		KIA
*SENTER aka Seuter, Price	18	Salina OnC, NY	Chairmaker	American	Cook to the Hunters	GSD. R/M. Pd.

Name	Age	Last Known Residence(s)	Occupation	Nationality	Additional Information	Fate
*SHARP, Hiram	25 (24)	Salina, OnC, NY	Labourer	American		GSD. T/VDL. Returned 1846
*SHEW aka Shaw, Henry	28 (23)	Philadelphia, JC, NY	Pedlar	American		GSD. T/VDL.
*SMITH aka Smyth, Andrew	21	Orleans, JC, NY		American		GSD. Pd.
*SMITH, Charles	21	Lyme or Cape Vincent, JC, NY		American	Emigrated with family from UK in 1834. Captured 13 Nov 1838	GSD. Pd.
*SMITH, Orrin W. aka Orin, Owen, Orren	32 (26, 36)	Orleans, JC, NY	Farmer	American		GSD. T/VDL. Returned 1845
*SNOW, James L.	20 (21)	Hastings, OsC, NY	Labourer	American		Wd. GSD. Pd.
*STEBBINS, William	18	Brownville, JC, NY		American		GSD. Pd.
*STEWART, Joseph	25	Syracuse, OsC, NY	Clothier	American		GSD. T/VDL.
*STOCKTON aka Stackton, Thomas	40 (26, 40)	Fell's Mills, JC, NY	Blacksmith	American	Captured 13 Nov 1838	GSD. T/VDL. Died in VDL
*SWANBERG aka Swansberg, Swansburgh, John G.	28 (27)	Alexandria, JC, NY	Labourer	American		GSD. T/VDL. Returned 1845
SWETE aka Sweet Dennis (William D.),	19 (20)	Alexandria, JC, NY	Cooper	American	A committed Hunter to the last. Brother of Sylvanus Swete	GSD. T/VDL.
*SWETE aka Sweet, Sylvanus	21 (18)	Alexandria, JC, NY	Cooper	American	Implicated as man who killed Johnson of 83rd Foot	GSD. Hanged 22 Dec 1838
THOMAS, Giles	27 (34)	Salina, OnC, NY		American		Wd. RWT.
*THOMAS, John	26	Madrid, JC, NY		American	Had lived in Canada. Officer in the Hunters	GSD. T/VDL. Returned 1845
THOMPSON, John	24	Morristown, SLC, NY		American		Captured.
*THOMPSON, John	27 (44, 49)	Native of Hexham, Northumberland, England, lately of Madrid, SLC, NY	Carpenter	British (English)	Captured 13 Nov 1838. Formerly a private with 68th Foot. Reported to have deserted 7-8 years earlier in Canada at Fort George	GSD. R/M. Pd.
*THOMPSON, Joseph	26 (22)	Lyme, JC, NY	Labourer	American		GSD. T/VDL. Returned 1845
*TIBBETTS aka Tibbetts, Tibbet, Tibbitt, Samuel	25 (19)	Salina, OnC, NY	Labourer	American		GSD. Pd?
*TOWNSEND, Abner	19 (17)	Philadelphia, JC, NY	Labourer	American		GSD. Pd.
TRACY, ——		Unknown		Probably American		Escaped
*TRUAX aka Trucax, Nelson	20 (21)	Antwerp, JC, NY	Saddler	American	Captured 13 Nov 1838	GSD. Pd.
*TUCKER, Oliver	22 (17, 18)	Rutland, JC, NY	Labourer	American		GSD. Pd.
*VAN AMBER aka Venambler, Van Ambler, George	23 (17)	Alexandria, JC, NY		American		GSD. Pd.
*VAN SLYKE aka Vanslike, Van Slyk, Van Slick, Martin	23 (21)	Watertown, JC, NY	Labourer	American	Captured 13 Nov 1838	Acquitted

Name	Age	Last Known Residence(s)	Occupation	Nationality	Additional Information	Fate
*VANWERMER aka Van Wermer, Van Wormer, Van Warner, Charles	21	Ellisburg, Lewis Co, NY	Mason	American		GSD. Pd.
*VAUGHAN, Hunter C.	21 (19)	Sackets Harbor, JC, NY	Gentleman	American	Son of William Vaughan, US naval officer. Captured 17 Nov 1838. Reason to believe he held a commission in the Hunters	GSD. Pardoned after intercession of his father.
VENALSTINE aka Van Alstine, Tenike, aka Hendrik, Heinrich	30	Salina, OnC, NY		American		KIA
*VON SCHOULTZ, Nils Gustaf Szoltereky, aka Sczoltevki, Szolteveky, Szolteocky, Sultuskie	43 (31)	Salina, OnC, NY former Swedish	Chemist, artillery officer	European (Swedish)	In command of the Hunters	GSD. Hanged 8 Dec 1838
*WAGNER, Joseph	24 (22)	Native of Germany, lately of Salina, OnC, NY	Salt maker	European (German)		GSD. R/M. Pd.
*WASHBURN aka Washbourne, Wasburn, Samuel aka Saul	23 (25)	Oswego, OsC, NY		American		GSD. T/VDL.
*WEBSTER, Simeon H.	21 (20)	Salina, OnC, NY	Labourer	American		GSD. Pd.
WEST, Charles aka Lorenzo	26	Salina, OnC, NY		American		KIA, 13 Nov 1838
*WHEELOCK, James Monroe	23 (22)	Watertown, JC, NY	Machinist	American		DOW
*WHITE, Patrick	25 (22)	Native of Rathkeale, Co Limerick, Ireland, lately of Rochester, Monroe Co, NY	Labourer	British (Irish)	Emigrated to Canada 6 years earlier. Acted as a sentry on 13 Nov 1838	GSD. T/VDL.
*WHITING aka Whitney, Nathan	45 (43, 48)	Liverpool, OnC, NY	Labourer	American	Returned 1845	GSD. T/VDL.
*WHITNEY, Reilly aka Riley	28 (27)	Leroy, JC, NY	Labourer	American		GSD. T/VDL. Returned 1846
*WILEY, Sampson A.	20	Watertown, JC, NY	Apprentice	American	Drummer in Watertown Hunter Lodge	GSD. Pd.
WILKEY aka Wilkie, Henry E. aka Hosea	20 (19)	Orleans, JC, NY	Labourer	American	Captured 13 Nov 1838	GSD. Pd.
WILLIAMS, Nathan		Possibly Oswego, OsC, NY		American		Escaped 16 Nov 1838
*WILSON, Charles	23 (18)	Lyme, JC, NY	Labourer	British (probably English)	Emigrant to the US from Britain	GSD. Pd.
WILSON, Edward A.	27 (23)	Ogdensburg, SLC, NY	Cabinet maker	American		GSD. T/VDL.
*WINEGAR, Jeremiah	59	Brownville, JC, NY	Labourer	American		GSD. R/M. Pd.
*WOODBURY, Bemis aka Bemas, Beman	22 (24, 25)	Auburn, Cayuga Co, NY		American		GSD. T/VDL. Returned 1845
*WOODRUFF, Charles	21 (19)	Salina, OnC, NY	Labourer	American		GSD. Pd.
WOODRUFF, Jonah		Unknown		Unknown but probably American	Possible brother of Charles Woodruff	Escaped.
*WOODRUFF, Martin	34 (40)	Salina, OnC, NY	Sheriff	American	Former sheriff of Onondaga County. Officer in the Hunters	GSD. Hanged 19 Dec 1838

Name	Age	Last Known Residence(s)	Occupation	Nationality	Additional Information	Fate
*WOOLCOTT aka Woolcot, Wolcot, William	20	Clay, OnC, NY	Blacksmith	American		Wd. GSD. Pd.
WRIGHT, Alexander	21	Formerly of UC, lately of Ogdensburg, SLC, NY		Canadian		KIA 16 Nov 1838
*WRIGHT aka White, Stephen S.	25	Denmark, Lewis Co, NY	Carpenter	American		Wd. GSD. T/VDL. Returned 1843

Sources

Archival

Archives of Ontario, Toronto, AO Pamph 1897, No. 88, Price Senter, "The Patriot War;" Friends of Windmill Point, Prescott, Memoir of Justus Merriam; National Archives of Canada, Ottawa: CO 42: vol 450, Griffin to Arthur, 20 Nov 1838; vol. 452, 373, Deposition of Hely Chamberlain, 22 Dec 1838; vol. 456: Minutes of Executive Council, 26 Dec, 31 Dec 1838, 1 Jan 1839; Arthur to Glenelg, 1 Jan 1839; Draper to Arthur, 4 Feb 1839; Report of Executive Council, 24 Dec, 26 Dec 1838; Alphabetical List of Person taken near Windmill Point; Minutes of Executive Council, 2 Feb 1839; Arthur to Glenelg, 5 Feb 1839; MG 24, B98, vol. 1, Vaughan to Jones, 3 Dec 1838; RG 5 A1: vol. 211: Draper to Arthur, 5 Dec, 9 Dec 11 Dec 1838; Macdonell to Arthur, 14 Dec 1838; Classification of the Prisoners ... with reference to their degree of criminality, 29 Dec 1838; RG 5, B40, B41, State Trials, Records of the Courts Martial of the Prisoners; vol. 212, Anonymous Note to Arthur, 22 Dec 1838; vol 214, Draper to Arthur, 27 Dec 1838; Macdonell to Arthur, 3 Jan 1839; Queen's University Archives, Kingston, Memoir of Nelson Truax.

Published Primary and Secondary Sources

Charles Anderson, *Blue Bloods and Rednecks* (Burnstown, 1995); *Brockville Recorder*, Nov 1838-Jan 1839; *Cornwall Observer*, Nov-Dec 1838; Jack Cahill, *Forgotten Patriots: Canadian Rebels on Australia's Convict Shores* (Toronto, 1999); Edwin C. Guillet, *The Lives and Times of the Patriots* (Toronto, 1938, 1964); William Gates, *Recollections of Life in Van Dieman's Land ...* (Lockport, NY, 1850); Franklin B. Hough, *A History of Jefferson County in the State of New York* (Albany, 1854) and *A History of St. Lawrence and Franklin Counties* (Albany, 1853); Daniel Heustis, *Narrative of the Adventures and Sufferings of Captain Daniel D. Heustis ...* (Boston, 1848); Oscar Kinchen, *The Rise and Fall of the Patriot Hunters* (New York, 1956); *Kingston Chronicle and Gazette*, Nov 1838–Feb 1839; *Kingston Spectator*, Nov 1838-Jan 1839; David Lee, *The Battle of the Windmill*, Ottawa, 1974; Donald McLeod, *A Brief Review of the Settlement of Upper Canada ...* (Cleveland, 1841); *Montreal Gazette*, Dec 1838-Jan 1839; Ella Pipping, *Soldier of Fortune* (Toronto, 1971); Charles Saunders, ed., *The Arthur Papers ...* (3 vols., Toronto, 1957), Vol. II; Stuart Scott, "The Patriot Game: New Yorkers and the Canadian Rebellions of 1837-1838," *New York History*, July 1987, 281-295; Charles P. Stacey, ed., "An American Account of the Prescott Raid of 1838," *Canadian Defence Quarterly*, 9 (1932), 393-398; George F. Stanley, "William Johnston: Pirate or Patriot," *Historic Kingston*, 6 (1957), 13-28; "The Battle of the Windmill, *Historic Kingston*, 3 (1953), 41-55; E.A. Theller, *Canada in 1837-1838* (2 vols., New York, 1841), II; *Upper Canada Herald*, Kingston, Nov 1838-Feb 1839; Benjamin Wait, *Letters from Van Diemen's Land* (Buffalo, 1843); Stephen Wright, *Narrative and Recollections of Van Diemen's Land ...* (New York, 1844).

British and Canadian fatal casualties resulting from the battle of the windmill, 1838

The official casualty reports for the fighting that took place at the windmill between 12 November and 16 November 1838 included only the names of the officers who were killed in action or later died of their wounds. A recent search of all available archival sources has revealed the names of a total of seventeen Britons and Canadians who died as a result of the Patriot Hunter invasion of Prescott in November 1838 and it is believed that there may be one or two names missing from this list. Where this information is known, the marital status of the casualty and number of dependant children have been added.

It should also be remembered that a civilian, Mrs. Belden Taylor of Newport, was killed as a result of the action of 13 November and her daughter, Eliza, was badly wounded.

Nationality	Unit	Family Status
British		
Lieutenant William S. Johnson	83rd Regiment of Foot	
Private Downes	83rd Regiment of Foot	
Private Robert Kershaw	Royal Marines	
Canadian		
Captain George Drummond	1st Cavalry Troop, Grenville Militia	Married, three children
Lieutenant John Dulmage	2nd Regiment of Grenville Militia	Married, four children
Private Jerimiah Bouck	2nd Regiment of Dundas Militia	Single
Private Richard Boulton	Dundas militia	Married, six children
Private John Bunton	Lancaster Glengarry Highlanders	Single
Private Dugald Cameron	Lancaster Glengarry Highlanders	Single
Private William Gore	Lancaster Glengarry Highlanders	Married, two children
Private Adam Linnen	1st Cavalry Troop, Grenville Militia	Married, eight children
Private Thomas Lydford	Lancaster Glengarry Highlanders	Married
Private J. McMartin	2nd Regiment of Dundas Militia	Single

Nationality	Unit	Family Status
Private J. Perrine	1st Regiment of Grenville Militia	Married, two children
Private John Raney	1st Regiment of Grenville Militia	
Private John White	Lancaster Glengarry Highlanders	Married, three children
Private Joseph Kendrick*	1st Regiment of Grenville Militia	Married, ten children

* Private Kendrick's death resulted from illness contracted due to his exertions during the battle of 13 November, not from military action. His widow, however, was granted a pension because his death resulted from active service.

Sources

National Archives of Canada: Record Group 9 I B4, Upper Canada, Pension List, vols. 4 to 7; Public Record Officer, Kew, Surrey, UK, Admiralty 51, vol. 3641, Log HMS *Niagara*, 15 Nov 1838; *Kingston Chronicle and Gazette*, various issues Nov and Dec 1838; 26 Oct 1839: Arthur Robinson, *The Grenville Militia Regiments*.

APPENDIX F

The songs of the battle

"The Battle of the Windmill" or "The Prescott Volunteers"
This song was composed and sung in the Prescott area shortly after the battle of the windmill. In 1904, a researcher for the Ontario Archives recorded some verses from Lieutenant Colonel Thomas Bog who had been a 12-year-old witness to the 1838 action. More verses were recorded during the centennial of the battle in 1938 from the Dawson brothers of Prescott who had heard their fathers' friends singing it. A slightly different version was contributed that same year by Judson Polite of Domville near Prescott.

The song was sung to the music of "The Girl I've Left Behind Me," a catchy, lively tune that, from the late 18th century onward, became one of the most popular British army "loth-to-departs," played when a regiment left its station for the last time. The British historian Lewis Winstock believed that, from the most common words to this song, it dates from the Seven Years War (1756-1763) but there is some evidence that the tune itself may predate that period.

As explained below (p. 247, note 1 in Chapter 7), the words of "The Battle of the Windmill," as recorded from Bog, the Dawsons and Polite, were in four-line verses but should probably be in 8-line verses to accord with the form of "The Girl I've Left Behind Me." There is a strong possibility that, as originally sung in the 19th century, the battle song had a 4-line chorus.

The version reproduced here is substantially the same as recorded from Bog and the Dawsons but arranged in 8-line verses.

On Tuesday morning we marched out,
In command of Colonel Fraser[1],
With swords and bay'nets of polished steel,
As keen as any razor.
Unto the Windmill Plains we went,
We gave them three loud cheers,
To let them know, that day, below,
We're the Prescott Volunteers[2].

Oh, we're the boys that feared no noise,
When the cannons loud did roar;
We cut the rebels left and right,
When they landed on our shore.
Brave Macdonell[3] nobly led,
His men into the field;
They did not flinch, no not an inch,
'Til the rebels had to yield.

He swung his sword right round his head,
Saying "Glengarrys, follow me,"
"We'll gain the day, without delay,
And that you'll plainly see!"
The rebels now remain at home,
We wish that they would come,
We'd cut them up, both day and night,
By command of Colonel Young[4].

If e'er they dare return again,
They'll see what we can do;
We'll show them British play, my boys,
As we did at Waterloo.
Under Captain Jessup[5] we will fight,
Let him go where he will;
With powder and ball, they'll surely fall,
As they did at the Windmill.

If I were like great Virgil bright,
I would employ my quill,
I would write, both day and night,
Concerning the Windmill.
Lest to intrude, I will conclude,
And finish off my song,
We'll pay a visit to Ogdensburg,
And that before too long.

"The Hunters of Kentucky"

Composed by American songsmith Samuel Woodworth (who also wrote "The Old Oaken Bucket"), "The Hunters of Kentucky" was set to a traditional tune called "Ally Croker." The same tune was used for a popular song of the early 19th century called variously "The Unfortunate Miss Bailey," "Miss Bailey's Ghost" or "The Captain from Halifax" which has been credited to George Colman the elder (1732-1794) and his son of the same name (1762-1836).

"The Hunters of Kentucky," which celebrates the exploits of the Kentucky riflemen at the battle of New Orleans in 1815, was adopted by Andrew Jackson's adherents as his campaign song in 1829 and was very popular throughout the United States during the 1830s. In 1838, the Patriot Hunters took it as their marching song.

Ye gentlemen and ladies fair
Who grace this famous city[6],
Just listen, if you've time to spare,
While I rehearse a ditty;
And for the opportunity,

Conceive yourselves quite lucky,
For 'tis not often here you see,
A hunter from Kentucky.

 Oh, Kentucky,
  The Hunters of Kentucky,
 Oh, Kentucky,
  The Hunters of Kentucky

We are a hardy free-born race,
No man to fear a stranger,
Whate'er the game we join in chase,
Despising toil and danger.
And if a daring foe annoys,
Whate'er his strength or forces,
We'll show them that Kentucky boys,
Are alligator-horses.,

 Oh, Kentucky, etc.

I s'pose you've read it in the prints,
How Pakenham[7] attempted
To make Old Hickory Jackson[8] wince,
But soon his scheme repented;
For we with rifles ready cock'd,
Thought such occasion lucky,
And soon around the general flock'd
The Hunters of Kentucky.

 Oh, Kentucky, etc.

You've hear, I s'pose, how New Orleans
Is famed for wealth and beauty,
There's girls of every hue, it seems,
From snowy white to sooty.
So Pakenham, he made his brags,
If, he in fight was lucky,
He'd have their girls and cotton bags,
In spite of old Kentucky.[9]

 Oh, Kentucky, etc.

Now Jackson he was wide awake,
And wasn't scared at trifles,
For well he knew what aim we take
With our Kentucky rifles.
So he led us up to a Cypress swamp,
The ground was low and mucky,
There stood John Bull in martial pomp,
And here was old Kentucky

    Oh, Kentucky, etc.

A bank was raised to hide our breast,
Not that we thought of dying,
But that we always take a rest,
Unless the game is flying.
Behind it stood our little force,
None wished it to be greater,
For every man was half a horse,
And half an alligator.

    Oh, Kentucky, etc.

They did not let their patience tire,
Before they showed their faces,
We did not choose to waste our fire
So snugly kept our places,
But when so near we saw them wink,
We thought it time to stop 'em,
And it would have done you good, I think,
To see Kentuckians drop 'em.[10]

    Oh, Kentucky, etc.

They found, at last, 'twas vain to fight,
Where lead was all their booty[11],
And so they wisely took to flight,
And left us all the beauty.
And now if danger e'er annoys,
Remember what our trade is,
Just send for us Kentucky boys,
And we'll protect ye, ladies.

    Oh, Kentucky, etc.

Sources

On "The Battle of the Windmill," see Friends of Windmill Point Collection, Memories of Colonel Bog (c. 1904); Ernest Green, "The Song of the Battle of the Windmill," *Ontario Historical Society, Papers and Records*, vol 34 (1942), 43-45; *History of the Founding and Growth of the St. Lawrence District* (Prescott, 1838; Lewis Winstock, *Songs and Music of the Redcoats. 1642-1902.* (London, 1979).

On "The Hunters of Kentucky," see *The Burl Ives Song Book* (New York, 1963) and Denes Agay, *Best Loved Songs of the American People* (New York, 1975)

Notes

1. Colonel Richard Duncan Fraser of Brockville, who commanded one of the two columns that attacked the windmill on 13 November 1838.
2. Captain Hamilton D. Jessup's volunteer company raised in Prescott.
3. Captain George Macdonell, who commanded the Lancaster Glengarry Highlanders, a longservice militia company, during the attack of 13 November 1813.
4. Lieutenant Colonel Plomer Young, the British commandant at Prescott and the officer who led the attack of 13 November.
5. Captain Hamilton D. Jessup, who led the Prescott Volunteer Company during the battle.
6. In this case, New Orleans, as the words are addressed to the inhabitants of that place.
7. Major General Sir Edward Pakenham, brother-in-law of the Duke of Wellington and commander of the British army that attacked New Orleans in late 1814.
8. Major General Andrew Jackson, victor at New Orleans and later President of the United States.
9. This verse is a reference to the popular myth in the United States that the password of the British army that attacked New Orleans was "Booty and Beauty."
10. In actual fact, despite the boasting of the Kentucky riflemen, the majority of British casualties during the battle of 8 January 1815 were caused by American artillery fire.
11. A direct reference to the "Booty and Beauty" myth.

End notes

Abbreviations

Owing to their great number, highly abbreviated forms of the published and unpublished sources for *Guns Across the River* have been used in the notes. The full citation for published sources will be found in the bibliography which follows.

Adm	Admiralty
AO	Archives of Ontario, Toronto
Arthur	Charles Saunders, ed., *The Arthur Papers …* Toronto: University of Toronto, 1957, 3 vols
BR	*Brockville Recorder*
CHR	*Canadian Historical Review*
CMH	*Canadian Military History*
CO	Colonial Office
CO	*Cornwall Observer*
DAB	*Dictionary of American Biography*
DCB	*Dictionary of Canadian Biography*
DNB	*Dictionary of National Biography*
FWP	Friends of Windmill Point Collection, Prescott
GCHS	Grenville County Historical Society
JSAHR	*Journal of the Society for Army Historical Research*
KCG	*Kingston Chronicle and Gazette*
KS	*Kingston Spectator*
MG	Manuscript Group
MG	*Montreal Gazette*
NAC	National Archives of Canada, Ottawa
NYHS	New York Historical Society, New York
OH	*Ontario History*
PRO	Public Record Office, Kew, Surrey,
QUA	Queen's University Archives, Kingston
RG	Record Group
UCH	*Upper Canada Gazette*, Toronto
UCH	*Upper Canada Herald*, Kingston
WO	War Office

Prologue

1. FWP, Programme, Prescott International Peace Centennial, July 1938.
2. *Ottawa Citizen*, 2 July 1938.
3. *Ottawa Citizen*, 2 July 1938.
4. NAC, MG 26J, Mackenzie King Diary, 1 July 1938.

5. NAC, MG 26J, Mackenzie King Diary, 1 July 1938.
6. NAC, MG 26J, Mackenzie King Diary, 1 July 1938.

Chapter 1: "A brave stroke of liberty!" The Canadian rebellions of 1837

1. "New Words to an Old Song; or John Gilpin Travestied," published in the Toronto *Patriot*, 7 February 1838. The "Mac" referred to in the words is, of course, William Lyon Mackenzie.
2. Unless otherwise noted, my account of the background and course of the Upper Canada Rebellion of 1837 is based on Craig, *Upper Canada*, 188-251, Guillet, *Lives and Times*, 1-14; Kilbourn, *Firebrand*; and Read and Stagg, *Upper Canada Rebellion*.
3. *Colonial Advocate*, quoted in Tait, *One Dominion*, 163.
4. On Mackenzie's life before 1837, see *DCB*, William L. Mackenzie; and Kilbourn, *Firebrand*.
5. *Constitution*, 4 July 1836, quoted in Kilbourn, *Firebrand*, 144.
6. Senior, *Redcoats*, 3-20.
7. *Constitution*, 5 July, 1837, quoted in Craig, *Upper Canada*, 244.
8. Lizars, *Humours of 1837*, 93-94.
9. Kilbourn, *Firebrand*, 154.
10. On the course of the rebellion in Lower Canada, see Senior, *Redcoats*, 43-146.
11. *DCB*, Charles Duncombe.
12. Read and Stagg, *Upper Canada Rebellion*, lii.
13. Guillet, *Lives and Times*, 248.
14. On population figures, see Durham, *Report*.
15. Preston, *Residence*, II, 175.
16. Guillet, *Lives and Times*, 59.

Chapter 2: "Sturdy fear-nothing boys:" The rise of the Patriot movement

1. "The Battle of Black Rock, 12 January 1838," a song commemorating the march of the Buffalo City Guards from that city to near Navy Island. When they arrived at Navy Island, they turned around and marched back. From *Historical Sketch D Co. Buffalo City Guard*, 31-35.
2. Ketchum, *History of Buffalo*, I, 157.
3. Corey, *Crisis*, 29-30. On Chapin, see Graves, "Willcocks," 63; Ketchum, *History of Buffalo*, I, 155-158; Roach, "Journal," 144.

4. Welch, *Recollections*, 276.
5. McLeod, *Brief Review*, 195; also Corey, *Crisis*, 30-31, 45.
6. Craig, *Upper Canada*, 241-243; Current, Freidell and Williams, *History*, 411-416; Cruikshank, "Navy Island," 15; Facey-Crowthers, *New Brunswick Militia*, 52-72.
7. Kinchen, *Hunters*, 15.
8. Corey, *Crisis*, 17-18; Long, *Duel*, 22-51. An excellent study of the philosophy of the "Go Ahead" men that can be read with both profit and pleasure is Davis, *Three Roads to the Alamo*.
9. *DAB*, Andrew Jackson; Prucha, *Sword*, 129-134, 307-311; Rimini, *Andrew Jackson*, I; Current, Friedel and Williams, *History*, 510-511.
10. Travis to the People of Texas, 24 Feb 1836, quoted in Davis, *Three Roads*, 541.
11. *Columbian Centinel*, 11 May 1836, quoted in Long, *Alamo*, 271. There is some evidence that Crockett survived the battle to be taken prisoner but was executed on the orders of Santa Anna. For contrasting views on this subject, see Long, *Duel*, 259, and Davis, *Three Roads*, 737-738.
12. On Travis, see Davis, *Three Roads*.
13. *National Review*, Jan 1832, quoted in Corey, *Crisis*, 16.
14. Editorial in *Lexington Intelligencer* quoted in Corey, *Crisis*, 17.
15. *New York Observer*, 16 Dec 1837.
16. McLeod, *Brief Review*, 195.
17. McLeod, *Brief Review*, 196.
18. A "stand of arms" is a period term that includes a musket, bayonet with scabbard and belt, and cartridge box and belt.
19. McLeod, *Brief Review*, 197-198; Cruikshank, "Navy Island," 15-16; Lindsey, *Mackenzie*, 411-412.
20. Gates, *Recollections*, 7.
21. Dickinson in Hinchen, *Hunters*, 14.
22. Heustis, *Narrative*, 56.
23. Rensselaer van Rensselaer, quoted in Cruikshank, "Navy Island," 15-16.
24. Kinchen, *Hunters*, 14-17.
25. *Buffalo Commercial Advertiser*, quoted in Corey, *Crisis*, 35.
26. *Buffalo Commercial Advertiser*, 27 Dec 1837; McLeod, *Brief Review*, 197-198, Cruikshank, "Navy Island," 18-19.
27. Report of Captain Biscoe in Cruikshank, "Navy Island," 65-66.

28. Guillet, *Lives and Times*, 256-257.
29. Cruikshank, "Navy Island," 17-19, 32; Guillet, *Lives and Times*, 74-76; Kilbourn, *Firebrand*, 198, 201; Corey, *Crisis*, 34.
30. Quoted in Cruikshank, "Navy Island," 29.
31. *Buffalo Journal*, 26 Dec 1837; also Corey, *Crisis*, 35; Cruikshank, "Navy Island," 20-25.
32. Corey, *Crisis*, 35; Guillet, *Lives and Times*, 83; Kilbourn, *Firebrand*, 200-201; Lindsey, *Mackenzie*, 412-413, 418-419.
33. *Rochester Democrat* letter dated 20 Dec 1837, quoted in Cruikshank, "Navy Island," 26.
34. Cruikshank, "Navy Island," 33; Fryer, *Volunteers*, 57.
35. Head to Colborne, Dec 1837, quoted in Cruikshank, "Navy Island," 35.
36. Cruikshank, "Navy Island," 41-42; Guillet, *Lives and Times*, 78.
37. Cruikshank, "Navy Island," 39-46.
38. Heustis, *Narrative*, 28; also Cruikshank, "Navy Island," 48-50.
39. Gates, *Recollections*, 8.
40. Guillet, *Lives and Times*, 79-81, 260-261.
41. Garrow to Van Buren, 28 Dec 1837, quoted in Prucha, *Sword*, 37.
42. Corey, *Crisis*, 44-45; Cruikshank, "Navy Island," 38, 55.
43. Corey, *Crisis*, 57; Prucha, *Sword*, 313; *American State Papers: Military Affairs*, vol. 6, 1022, Strength of the Army, 1837.
44. Stacey, "Scott", 411, Scott to Secretary of War, 12 Jan 1839.
45. Prucha, *Sword*, 314, Secretary of War to Scott, 5 Jan 1838.
46. Scott, *Auto-Biography*, I, 312.
47. Johnson, *Scott*, 131, Scott to Worth, 11 Jan 1838.
48. Cruickshank, "Navy Island," 43, 78; Wallace, *Worth*, 38-39.
49. Corey, *Crisis*, 65; Cruikshank, "Navy Island," 55, 77-78; Guillet, *Lives and Times*, 84-85.
50. Corey, *Crisis*, 45; McLeod, *Brief Review*, 218; Stanley, "William Johnston," 17; Heustis, *Narrative*, 29-30.
51. Heustis, *Narrative*, 29.
52. Heustis, *Narrative*, 29-30; McLeod, *Brief Review*, 218.
53. Kinchen, *Hunters*, 25; Guillet, *Lives and Times*, 88.
54. Corey, *Crisis*, 32-33; Guillet, *Lives and Times*, 88-89; Prucha, "Brady," 64, Brady to Jones, 29 June 1838.
55. Guillet, *Lives and Times*, 90.
56. Guillet, *Lives and Times*, 90-93.
57. McLeod, *Brief Review*, 208-211, 214-215; Guillet, *Lives and Times*, 93-94.
58. McLeod, *Brief Review*, 215.
59. McLeod, *Brief Review*, 214-216; Guillet, *Lives and Times*, 95-98.
60. Martyn, "Pelee Island," 154-156.
61. Martyn, "Pelee Island," 156-162; Morgan, *Sketches*, 353.
62. Hough, *St. Lawrence*, 657.

63. Cruikshank, "Navy Island," 69-70; Heustis, *Narrative*, 30-32; Hough, *St. Lawrence*, 657; Lindsey, *Mackenzie*, 424.
64. Heustis, *Narrative*, 30-31.
65. Preston, *Residence*, II, 140.
66. *UCH*, 27 Feb 1838; also Bonnycastle, *Upper Canada*, II, 73-74; Fryer, *Volunteers*, 70-71.
67. Cruikshank, "Navy Island," 80.
68. Heustis, *Narrative*, 32; also Hough, *Jefferson County*, 520-521.
69. Gibson to Graham, 23 Feb 1838, in Summers, "Patriots," 31; also Lindsey, *Mackenzie*, 439. In fairness, Van Rensselaer is later said to have recanted and apologized to Mackenzie, see Lindsey, *Mackenzie*, 430.
70. Lindsey, *Mackenzie*, 433; *DCB*, Mackenzie; Kilbourn, *Firebrand*, 208-209.
71. Senior, *Redcoats*, 152-153.
72. Senior, *Redcoats*, 152-154.
73. PRO: Adm 1, vol. 2563, Sandom to Paget, 21 Apr 1838; WO 17, vol. 1542, Distribution of the Troops, 1 Nov 1838; Fryer, 93-94; Hitsman, *Safeguarding Canada*, 134-136.
74. "An Act to protect the Inhabitants of this Province against Lawless Aggression from Subjects of Foreign Countries at Peace with Her Majesty." *Statutes*, 1 Vic., cap. III.
75. *DCB*, George Arthur; Read and Stagg, *Upper Canada Rebellion*, lxxxii-c.
76. *KCG*, July 1838, quoted in Corey, *Crisis*, 91.
77. Creighton, *Young Politician*, 50-51.

Chapter 3: "Do you snuff and chew?" The coming of the Hunters

1. "The Hunters of Kentucky" was written by Samuel Woodworth and set to the tune of "The Unfortunate Miss Bailey," an old folk song. It became Andrew Jackson's campaign song in 1828 and was popular throughout his presidency and after. It was adopted by the Patriot Hunters as their marching song.
2. Colborne to Head, 24 Mar 1838, quoted in Senior, *Redcoats*, 154.
3. Brady to Scott, 14 Mar 1838, in Prucha, "Brady," 63.
4. Worth to Secretary of War, 3 Mar 1838, quoted in Stacey, "Scott," 408.
5. Johnson, *Scott*, 132.
6. Corey, *Crisis*, 44-57.
7. Senior, *Redcoats*, 141-163.
8. Levi Woodbury, collector of customs at Oswego, to Secretary of the Treasury, 14 Sep 1838, in Kinchen, *Hunters*, 37. For the creation and spread of the Patriot Hunters, see Kinchen, 31-34, 37-38.
9. Hough, *Jefferson County*, 528-529.
10. Corey, *Crisis*, 75-76; Kinchen, *Hunters*, 39-42, 133.
11. Kinchen, *Hunters*, 55-56.

12. Kinchen, *Hunters*, 57, also 54-55.
13. Kinchen, *Hunters*, 56-58.
14. Bishop, "Patriot War," 416-418.
15. Bishop, "Patriot War," 418.
16. Daniel Rorabaugh, *The Alcoholic Republic: An American Tradition* (New York, 1979), 233, quoted in McKee, *Gentlemanly Profession*, 452.
17. NAC, CO 42, vol. 451, 445, Deposition of Anthony Flood, 21 Nov 1838.
18. Kinchen, *Hunters*, 41-44; Corey, *Crisis*, 75-77.
19. Kinchen, *Hunters*, 58-59.
20. Hough, *St. Lawrence*, 657-658.
21. Hough, *Jefferson County*, 521-523; Stanley, "William Johnston," 22-23.
22. Arthur quoted in Stanley, "William Johnston," 23; also Guillet, *Lives and Times*, 158-159; Hough, *St. Lawrence*, 657-659.
23. Ormsby, *Crisis*, 78, Grey to father, 39, 17 Jul 1838.
24. Ormsby, *Crisis*, 53, Grey to father, 25 June 1838.
25. Van Buren to Congress, 20 Jun 1838, in Guillet, *Lives and Times*, 185.
26. Corey, *Crisis*, 45, Secretary of War to Macomb, 12 Jun 1838.
27. Hough, *Jefferson County*, 524; Wallace, *Worth*, 41-42; Stanley, "William Johnston," 24.
28. Scott, *Battle of the Windmill*, 12.
29. Stanley, "William Johnston," 23-24.
30. NAC, CO 42, vol. 285, Young to Hall, 30 May 1838.
31. Guillet, *Lives and Times*, 158-160; Stacey, "American Account," 395.
32. Prucha, "Brady," 63, Brady to Jones, 8 June 1838.
33. Corey, *Crisis*, 74-75; Guillet, *Lives and Times*, 104-113; Lindsey, *Mackenzie*, 448-449; NAC, MG 27, E I30, Gowan, "Memoir." It should be noted that, after Papineau and Mackenzie fell out with the *Patriotes* and the patriots, respectively, they tried unsuccessfully to start their own competing movements, see Corey, *Crisis*, 77 and Lindsey, *Mackenzie*, 434-435.
34. Kinchen, *Hunters*, 38-39; Lindsey, *Mackenzie*, 440-441.
35. Kinchen, *Hunters*, 38-39, 64-65.
36. Kinchen, *Hunters*, 38-40, 45. Preston, *Residence*, II, 159, states that the Hunters had 7.5 million dollars but this is almost certainly too large an amount.
37. NAC, MG 24, B 97, Regulations and Pay of The North Western Army, on Patriot Service in Upper Canada.
38. *DCB*, John Lambton, Lord Durham.
39. Hitsman, *Safeguarding Canada*, 135-136; Fryer, *Volunteers*, 93-101.
40. NAC, CO 42, vol. 285, Colborne to Somerset, 5 June 1838.
41. Burns, *Fort Wellington*, 94-95; Fryer, 97-101; NAC, MG 27 I E30, Gowan, "Memoir"; Lee, *Battle of the Windmill*, 114, 117.

Chapter 4: "Brothers from a land of liberty:" The New York Hunters and their plans

1. Cazenovia NY Public Library, Jabez Abel Scrapbook, 36; Heustis, *Narrative*, 42-43; Kinchen, *Hunters*, 69-70; McLeod, *Brief Review*, 254-255; Guillet, *Lives and Times*, 132-133. On background of Hunter leaders, see CO 42, vol. 456, Alphabetical List of Persons Taken Near Windmill Point.
2. Heustis, *Narrative*, 43.
3. Kinchen, *Hunters*, 70.
4. Hough, *Jefferson County*, 357-359.
5. Heustis, *Narrative*, 41; NAC, CO 42, vol. 456, Alphabetical List of Persons taken near Windmill Point; Guillet, *Lives and Times*, 132-133.
6. Heustis, *Narrative*, 41; Hough, *Jefferson County*, 359; NAC, CO 42, vol. 451, 445, Deposition of Anthony Flood, 21 Nov 1838; vol. 456, Alphabetical List of Persons Taken Near Windmill Point.
7. On Stone and the officers, see NAC, CO 42, vol. 456, Alphabetical List of Persons Taken near Windmill Point; Pipping, *Soldier of Fortune*, 136-137.
8. Guillet, *Lives and Times*, 283, letter of Warren Green, 28 Dec 1838.
9. Guillet, *Lives and Times*, 283, letter of Warren Green, 28 Dec 1838.
10. Guillet, *Lives and Times*, 283, letter of Warren Green, 28 Dec 1838.
11. For von Schoultz and his debts, see *DCB*, von Schoultz entry. On the Foreign Legion, see Porch, *French Foreign Legion*, 13-19. There is a recent study of the Polish rebellion of 1830-1831 that argues that von Schoultz was actually a mercenary in the uprising, see Witold St. Michalowski, *Najemnicy Wolnosci*, 46. This makes good sense because his technical background as an artillery officer would have made von Schoultz a useful adjunct to the insurgent forces.
12. Pipping, *Soldier of Fortune*, 52-114, 128-132.
13. *KCG*, 19 Jan 1838.
14. NAC, CO 42, vol. 451, 445, Deposition of Anthony Flood, 21 Nov 1838.
15. Heustis, *Narrative*, 43.
16. Bonnycastle quoted in Guillet, *Lives and Times*, 179. Information on Prescott Hunters from NAC, CO 42, vol. 456, Alphabetical List of Persons Taken Near Windmill Point; Heustis, *Narrative*, 62-66; and sources listed in Appendix D.
17. QUA, Memoir of Nelson Truax.
18. Gates, *Recollections*, 12.
19. On compensation to be offered to the Hunters who attacked Prescott, see Corey, *Crisis*, 28-29, 70-71; Guillet, *Lives and Times*, 133; NAC, RG 5 B 40, Trial of Daniel George, George's Notebook. Various Hunters captured at the windmill gave evidence as to the financial induce-

ments they had been offered, see NAC CO 42, vol. 456, Alphabetical List of Prisoners taken near Windmill Point.
20. NAC, CO 42, vol. 450, 350, evidence of Elon Fellowes.
21. Corey, *Crisis*, 105; also Guillet, *Lives and Times*, 134. The New York Hunters amassed an impressive inventory of weapons and provisions for the attack on Prescott. They had at least 8 pieces of artillery (although only 3 were actually landed in Canada) ranging in calibre from 3-pdr. to possibly 18-pdr. guns. Longarms included surplus American military muskets, probably 1795 and 1814 pattern Springfield or contractor manufactured weapons, some being percussion conversions. There were also a number of the latest multi-round longarms, including Cochran, Colt, Knox and Wurfflinger types which were either provided free to marksmen or sold at nominal cost. Many of the Hunters had flintlock or percussion pistols while edged weapons included boarding pikes, cutlasses or dirks (probably Bowie knives as the British confused them). Ammunition and provisions included powder, lead, musket rounds, "buck and ball" rounds (1 ball and 3 buckshot in a single cartridge), flour, apples and hardtack. Much of the provisions and ammunition were packed in containers marked "US" and "SNY," or "State of New York," indicating that they came from government sources.
    On Hunter weapons, see: NAC: CO 42, vol. 409, pt 2, 360, Dundas to Arthur, 18 Nov 1838; 362, Sandom to Arthur, 18 Nov 1838; vol. 432, 373, Deposition of Hely Chamberlain, 22 Dec 1838; vol 451, 445, Deposition of Anthony Flood, 21 Nov 1838; vol. 456, Draper to Arthur, 4 Feb 1839; RG 5 B40 and B41, evidence of Leary, Parker, Sandom, Smith, and many others: RG 8 I, vol. 750, 65, Macbean to Cubitt, 27 Nov 1838; PRO, Adm 1, vol. 2563, Sandom to Admiralty, 19 Nov 1838; AO, MS 521, Jessup, "Battle"; Leavitt, *Leeds and Grenville*, summary by a British officer, 48-51; Heustis, *Narrative*; Gates, *Recollections*; Wright, *Narrative*; *KCG*, 17 Nov, 27 Nov 1838; and Guillet, *Lives and Times*, 133-134, 138.
22. Heustis, *Narrative*, 42-43.
23. Heustis, *Narrative*, 42-43.
24. NAC, CO 42, vol. 451, 445, Deposition of Anthony Flood, 21 Nov 1838.
25. *KCG*, 24 Nov 1838.
26. Wright, *Narrative*, 5.
27. Descriptions of the Hunters' flag flown at the battle of the windmill vary. Heustis (*Narrative*, 44), states that it "had an eagle and two stars, wrought on a ground of blue, and was a very neat and beautiful specimen of woman's handiwork." Wright, (*Narrative*, 5) records that "it bore upon its face the device of an eagle and twin stars upon a ground of blue" In contrast, Lt. Leary, RN, gave evidence at the court martial (NAC, RG 5, B41)

that the flag was "white, with a blue border, an eagle in the middle and the word 'liberated' over the eagle and 'Onondaga Hunters' also on the flag." The Prescott *Sentinel* (quoted in *BR*, 22 Nov 1838) states that the flag had an eagle with a single star above and the words "Liberated by the Onondaga Hunters." The flag was of fine quality, Hamilton Jessup estimated that it must have cost $125 to make (see AO, MS 521, Jessup, "Battle").
    Since Leary also testified that there was some confusion over the flag on 13 Nov because the British and Canadians, seeing its white field, thought it was a flag of surrender, it is probable that the flag was predominantly white. Gates and Wright may mean that the eagle and stars were on backgrounds of blue, not that the flag was blue.
    Putting all this together, it seems likely that the flag of the Hunters had a white field and a blue border; contained a republican eagle with outspread wings with one or two stars above it, both probably on backgrounds of blue; and a scroll or scrolls beneath with the words "Canada Liberated" or "Liberated " and "Onondaga Hunters", or "Liberated by the Onondaga Hunters." This is the flag described in the main text.
    After the battle, the captured flag was sent to the Tower of London where it was briefly displayed before apparently being burned in a fire in the early 1840s.
28. Pipping, *Soldier of Fortune*, 139.
29. *Arthur*, I, 368, Arthur to Cox, 14 Nov 1838.
30. NAC, MG 27 I E30, Gowan, "Memoir"; Lee, *Battle of the Windmill*, 116.
31. Senior, *Redcoats*, 164-195.
32. *KCG*, 3 Nov, 1838; PRO, WO 17, vol. 1542, Distribution of the Troops, 1 Nov 1838.
33. CO 42, vol. 451, 445, Deposition of Anthony Flood, 21 Nov 1838.
34. Heustis, *Narrative*, 43.
35. NYHS, Worth to Eustis, 13 Nov 1838; Heustis, *Narrative*, 43.
36. NAC, CO 42, vol. 451, 445, Deposition of Anthony Flood, 21 Nov 1838.
37. NAC, CO 42, vol 452, 373, Deposition of Hely Chamberlain, 22 Dec 1838.
38. *Oswego Commercial Advertiser*, 13 Nov 1838, quoted in *BR*, 6 Dec 1838.
39. Hough, *St. Lawrence*, 660.
40. *BR*, 6 Dec 1838, letter of Hiram Denio, 13 Nov 1838. This letter was unsigned but it could only have been the work of Hiram Denio given its contents.
41. *BR*, 6 Dec 1838, letter of Hiram Denio, 13 Nov 1838; Hough, *Jefferson County*, 352-353; Hough, *St. Lawrence*, 660; MMGL, James Van Cleve memoir.
42. *BR*, 6 Dec 1838, letter of Hiram Denio, 13 Nov 1838; Hough, *St. Lawrence*, 660; MMGL, James Van Cleve

memoir; NAC, CO 42, vol. 451, 445, Deposition of Anthony Flood, 21 Nov 1838; Stacey, "American Account," 395.

43. Heustis, *Narrative*, 43.

Chapter 5: "Repel the midnight assassins"

1. "The Coming Struggle," by "Miletius" appeared in the *Toronto Patriot* in November 1838.

2. NAC, CO 42, vol. 451, 445, Deposition of Anthony Flood, 21 Nov 1838.

3. NAC, CO 42, vol 451, 445, Deposition of Anthony Flood, 21 Nov 1838.

4. *DNB*, entry for Henry Dundas; NAC, CO 42, vol 451, 445, Deposition of Anthony Flood, 21 Nov 1838.

5. *DCB*, entry for Williams Sandom; PRO, Adm 1, vol. 2563, Sandom to Paget, 21 Apr 1838.

6. NAC, CO 42, vol 451, 445, Deposition of Anthony Flood, 21 Nov 1838.

7. NAC, CO 42, vol 432, 373, Deposition of Hely Chamberlain, 22 Dec 1838; PRO, Adm 51, vol. 3641, Log of HMS Niagara, 3 Nov 1838.

8. PRO, Adm 1, vol. 2564, Sandom to Admiralty, 26 Feb 1839; NAC, CO 42, vol. 451, 445, Deposition of Anthony Flood, 21 Nov 1838.

9. NAC, CO 42, vol 451, 445, Deposition of Anthony Flood, 21 Nov 1838.

10. *BR*, 6 Dec 1838, letter of Hiram Denio, 13 Nov 1838.

11. *KCG*, 15 Dec 1838; Hough, *St. Lawrence*, 660; *BR*, 6 Dec 1838, letter of Hiram Denio, 13 Nov 1838.

12. Hough, *St. Lawrence*, 660.

13. Hough, *St. Lawrence*, 660; MMGL, Memoir of James Van Cleve.

14. *BR*, 6 Dec 1838, letter of Hiram Denio, 13 Nov 1838.

15. Hough, *St. Lawrence*, 660; also *BR*, 6 Dec 1838, letter of Hiram Denio, 13 Nov 1838; Wright, *Narrative*, 1.

16. *BR*, 6 Dec 1838, letter of Hiram Denio, 13 Nov 1838; Hough, *St. Lawrence*, 661.

17. *BR*, 6 Dec 1838, letter of Hiram Denio, 13 Nov 1838; Hough, *St. Lawrence*, 661.

18. Heustis, *Narrative*, 43.

19. Heustis, *Narrative*, 43; Hough, *St. Lawrence, 660*.

20. Heustis, *Narrative*, 43-44.

21. Heustis, *Narrative*, 44.

22. *BR*, 27 Dec 1838, testimony of Martin Van Slyke.

23. *UCH*, 4 Dec 1838, Naval force at Prescott. This letter is probably the work of Lieutenant Fowell, RN.

24. Morris, *Prescott*, 21.

25. *DCB*, Plomer Young; Senior, *Redcoats and Patriotes*, 154; Anderson, *Bluebloods and Rednecks*, 171-182; Lee, "Battle of the Windmill," 112-115.

26. AO, MS 521, Jessup, "Battle"; NAC, MG 27 I E30, Gowan, "Memoir"; Anderson, Lee, *Battle of the Windmill*, 114; *BR*, 12 Jul 1838; Fryer, *Volunteers*, 78-83, 94, 1-2-103;

Robinson, *Grenville Militia*, 3-20; Senior, *Redcoats*, 154-155.

27. NAC, RG 8 I, vol. 606, 148, Young to Halkett, 29 Apr 1838.

28. NAC, MG 27, I E30, Gowan, "Memoir."

29. *MG*, 17 Nov 1838, letter of Alpheus Jones, 13 Nov 1838.

30. Leavitt, *Leeds and Grenville*, 48, summary by a British officer. Given the amount of specific detail he provides about the attack on Prescott, the author of this account was probably Plomer Young.

31. *MG*, 17 Nov 1838, letter of Alpheus Jones, 13 Nov 1838.

32. *MG*, 17 Nov 1838, letter of Alpheus Jones, 13 Nov 1838.

33. Leavitt, *Leeds and Grenville*, 48, summary by a British officer.

34. Heustis, *Narrative*, 44-45.

35. AO, MS 521, Jessup, "Battle."

36. *MG*, 17 Nov 1838, letter of Alpheus Jones, 13 Nov 1838; AO, MS 521, Jessup, "Battle"; Leavitt, *Leeds and Grenville*, 48, summary by a British officer.

37. Leavitt, *Leeds and Grenville*, 48, summary by a British officer.

38. *UCH*, 4 Dec 1838, Naval force at Prescott; NAC, CO 42, vol. 451, 555, Fowell to Sandom, 12 Nov 1838.

Chapter 6: "A dose of John Bull's powders"

1. "No Surrender," poem in the *KCG*, 17 November 1838.

2. Heustis, *Narrative*, 44; *UCH*, 4 Dec 1838, Naval force at Prescott.

3. Kinchen, *Hunters*, 71.

4. Heustis, *Narrative*, 44

5. Heustis, *Narrative*, 45; Hough, *St. Lawrence*, 662.

6. Wright, *Narrative*, 6; Heustis, *Narrative*, 45; Hough, *St. Lawrence*, 662.

7. Leavitt, *Leeds and Grenville*, 49, summary by a British officer.

8. Leavitt, *Leeds and Grenville*, 49, summary by a British officer; *UCH*, 4 Dec 1838, Naval force at Prescott.

9. Hough, *St. Lawrence*, 662-663; AO, MS 521, Jessup, "Battle."

10. Hough, *St. Lawrence*, 662.

11. Hough, *St. Lawrence*, 662.

12. Hough, *St. Lawrence*, 532; Ogdensburg *Times and Advertiser*, 12 Nov 1838.

13. *BR*, 6 Dec 1838, letter of Hiram Denio, 13 Nov 1838; also Hough, *St. Lawrence*, 662; *MG*, 17 Nov 1838, letter of Alpheus Jones, 13 Nov 1838; QUA, Hiram Denio to wife, 14 Nov 1838.

14. Hough, *St. Lawrence*, 662; and Heustis, *Narrative*, 45.

15. *Prescott Sentinel*, 17 Nov 1838, quoted in *UCH*, 27 Nov 1838.

16. *UCH*, 4 Dec 1838, Naval force at Prescott; NAC, CO 42, vol. 451, 555, Fowell to Sandom, 12 Nov 1838; PRO, Adm 1, vol. 2563, Statement of British steam vessels on Lake Ontario.

It should be noted that HMSV *Experiment* was flying the White Ensign because the senior naval officer

on the North American and West Indies Station was Vice Admiral of the White Sir Charles Paget. If Paget had been a vice admiral of the blue, the *Experiment* would have been flying a Blue Ensign. The White Ensign did not become the battle standard of all Royal Navy warships until 1864.

17. *UCH*, 4 Dec 1838, Naval force at Prescott; NAC, CO 42, vol. 451, 555, Fowell to Sandom, 12 Nov 1838; *BR*, 6 Dec 1838, letter of Hiram Denio, 13 Nov 1838.

18. *UCH*, 4 Dec 1838, Naval force at Prescott; NAC CO 42, vol. 451, 555, Fowell to Sandom, 12 Nov 1838.

19. Hough, *St. Lawrence*, 663; Hough, *Jefferson*, 353; *BR*, 6 Dec 1838, letter of Hiram Denio, 13 Nov 1838.

20. QUA, Hiram Denio to wife, 14 Nov 1838.

21. MMGL, Van Cleve memoir; FWP, Recollections of Colonel Thomas Bog; AO, MS 521, Jessup, "Battle"; Hough, *St. Lawrence*, 663; *UCH*, 4 Dec 1838, Naval force at Prescott; NAC, CO 42, vol. 451, 555, Fowell to Sandom, 12 Nov 1838.

22. *Ogdensburg Times & Advertizer*, 12 Nov 1838.

23. *BR*, 6 Dec 1838, letter of Hiram Denio, 13 Nov 1838; also Hough, *St. Lawrence*, 663; MMGL, Memoir of Van Cleve.

24. *BR*, 6 Dec 1838, letter of Hiram Denio, 13 Nov 1838.

25. Leavitt, *Leeds and Grenville*, 49, summary by a British officer; AO, MS 521, Jessup, "Battle"; *MG*, 17 Nov 1838, letter of Alpheus Jones, 13 Nov 1838; NAC, MG 27 I E30, Gowan, "Memoir"; Scott, *Battle of the Windmill*, 19.

26. Wallace, *Worth*, 44.

27. NAC, CO 42, vol. 451; 394, Sandom to Arthur, 14 Nov 1838; 445, Deposition of Anthony Flood, 21 Nov 1838; PRO, Adm 51, vol. 3641, Log, HMS *Niagara*, 11-12 Nov 1838.

28. On *Brockville*, see NAC, vol. 432, 373, Deposition of Hely Chamberlain, 22 Dec 1838.

29. Stacey, "American Account," 395; NYHS, Worth Papers, Worth to Eustis, 13 Nov 1838; NAC, CO 42, vol. 451, 394, Sandom to Arthur, 14 Nov 1838; PRO, Adm 51, vol. 3641, Log of HMS *Niagara*, 3 Nov 1838.

30. Stacey, "American Account," 395.

31. Stacey, "American Account," 395-396; NAC, CO 42, vol. 451, 394, Sandom to Arthur, 14 Nov 1838; PRO, Adm 51, vol. 3641, Log of HMS *Niagara*, 11-12 Nov 1838; NYHS, Worth Papers, Worth to Eustis, 13 Nov 1838.

32. NAC, CO 42, vol. 451, 394, Sandom to Arthur, 14 Nov 1838; PRO, Adm 51, vol. 3641, Log of HMS *Niagara*, 11-12 Nov 1838.

33. Heustis, *Narrative*, 44-45; Burns, *Fort Wellington* (1995), 33-42.

34. On construction of the windmill, see Burns, *Fort Wellington* (1995), 33-35; and Lee, *Battle of the Windmill*, 124.

35. Heustis, *Narrative*, 45; NAC, RG 5, B41, evidence of Leary, Sandom, and John Thomas.

There is considerable confusion over the calibres of the three artillery pieces landed and used by the Hunters at the windmill. Most sources agree that there were three guns but, on the subject of calibres, they radically diverge. Gates, (*Recollections*, 15) stated that the invaders had two brass 7-pdr. guns and one 12-pdr. gun, which he implies was iron. Wright (*Narrative*, 7) identifies one of the pieces as a 6-pdr. gun as does Heustis (*Narrative*, 55). No guns of 7-pdr. calibre ever existed in American or British artillery inventories so Gates may be referring to 6-pdrs. A more informed witness, Captain Williams Sandom, stated that all three guns were 6-pdrs. (PRO, Adm 1, vol. 2563, Sandom to Admiralty, 19 Nov 1838) and also reported (NAC, CO 42, 362, Sandom to Arthur, 18 Nov 1838) that two "pieces are newly cast, and bear the stamp and number of a part" of a recent large casting of American ordnance. For his part, Jessup (AO, MS 251, Jessup, "Battle") states that one gun was a 9-pdr. Finally, Lieutenant Colonel William Draper, who had an opportunity to examine much of the evidence of the battle stated (NAC, CO 42, vol. 456, Draper to Arthur, 4 Feb 1839) concluded that the Hunters had two 6-pdr. guns and one 3-pdr. gun. Thus we have three weapons ranging in calibre from 6 to 12-pdr.

The most expert witness to examine the Hunter artillery was Major Forbes Macbean. He reported the following (RG 8 I, vol. 750, 65, Macbean to Cubitt, 27 Nov 1838) of the Hunter artillery all of which were mounted on carriages made by "United States Arsenals, being complete, and made with Cheeks."

1. Iron gun, British origin, cast in the reign of George III (1760-1820), length (from muzzle face to rear of base ring), 5 feet, 6 inches, with a bore diameter of 3 1/4 inches.
2. Brass 4-pdr. gun, from US arsenal, length of 3 feet, 8 1/2 inches, bore diameter of 3 inches, marked "IMP" and "SNY."
3. Brass gun obtained or given to the Canadian militia.

With reference to Gun 1, the information on weight, dimensions, casting date and bore diametre identifies this weapon as probably being an obsolescent type which was used both in British land and naval service in the mid to late 18th century. The 4-pdr. calibre (3.21 inch bore diameter) was very rare in British service but some were apparently cast in limited numbers. A 4-pdr. gun could fire 3-pdr. shot but would not be able to fire 6-pdr. shot. For information on this weapon and an illustration, see McConnell, *British Smooth-Bore Artillery*, 92-93.

By its bore diameter, Gun 2 was not a 4-pdr. but a 3-pdr (3.01 inch diameter). The mistake is probably due to the fact that Macbean did not personally examine this weapon because Sandom's triumphant sailors had hauled it away as a trophy. Its markings, "IMP" and "SNY" identify this as an American piece and translate as "John Mason, Pittsburgh" and "State of New York." Mason was a gun founder at Pittsburgh in the War of 1812 who purchased the well known Columbia Foundry in Georgetown in 1816, and became one of the largest manufacturers of ordnance in the United States in the 1820s. Prior to about 1830, "J" was inscribed as "I" in formal markings, following the Roman style, hence "IM" rather than "JM." On Mason, see Graves, "American Ordnance" and Peterson, *Roundshot and Rammers*.

Macbean provides no details of Gun 3. A later witness, Benson Lossing, who visited Fort Wellington in 1860 reported (Lossing, *Fieldbook*, 584) seeing a brass gun marked "SNY 1834, taken from the rebels in 1837 [sic]" but gives no further details. As it is known that Bill Johnston "borrowed" a brass 6-pdr. from the Ogdensburg state militia artillery unit in that village on 12 Nov (Hough, *St. Lawrence*, 662), is possible that this was the same 6-pdr. weapon but no further identification can be made based on available information.

Putting all this together, it would appear that the Hunter artillery probably comprised three weapons: a brass 6-pdr. gun cast for the state of New York in 1834; an iron British 4-pdr. gun cast in the mid to late 18th century; and an American brass 3-pdr. gun cast a few years before the battle. The fact that Draper stated that there were two 6-pdrs. is probably attributable to the fact that the 4-pdr. and 6-pdr. calibres could easily be confused as there was only about a half inch difference in their bore diameters and the iron 4-pdr. used at the windmill was larger and heavier than the most modern 6-pdrs. in service in 1838.

36. FWP, Memoir of Justus Merriam. Accurate information on Hunter numbers is difficult to find – Gates, *Recollections*, 19, states that there were 250 men in Newport on the evening of 12 Nov 1838, Heustis, *Narrative*, 45, states that there were less than 200. On the stores in the *Charlotte of Oswego*, see Theller, *Canada in 1837-1838*, II, 282.
37. Gates, *Recollections*, 32.
38. Heustis, *Narrative*, 46; NAC, RG 5 A1, B40, B41, evidence of Bass, Graves and Mosher; *BR* 20 Dec 1838.
39. NAC, RG A1, B40, evidence of Bass.
40. NAC, RG 5A1, B40, evidence of Bass and Mosher; B41, evidence of John Graves; Robinson, *Grenville Militia Regiments*.
41. Scott, *Battle of the Windmill*, 18; *KCG*, 1 Dec 1838, statement of von Schoultz. Theller, *Canada in 1837-1838*, II, 287-288 offers an alternate explanation – Canadians did not join the Hunters because they were terrified by the number of militia surrounding the windmill.

42. Morris, *Prescott*, 156; Leavitt, *Leeds and Grenville*, 49-50, summary by a British officer; AO, MS 521, Jessup, "Battle"; Scott, *Battle of the Windmill*, 19.
43. NAC, MG 27, I E30, Gowan, "Memoir"; Robinson, *The Grenville Militia Regiments*; Leavitt, *Leeds and Grenville*, 49-50, summary by a British officer.
44. Robinson, *The Grenville Militia Regiments*; Neale, "John Crysler," 53-54. On the battle of Crysler's Farm, 1813, see the author's book, *Field of Glory: The Battle of Crysler's Farm* (Toronto, 1999).
45. FWP, MacIntosh, Memoir; and information from Mr. Pember MacIntosh, Ottawa.
46. FWP, MacIntosh, Memoir.
47. On Hunter numbers, see Heustis, *Narrative*, 45 and Gates, *Recollections*, 19; *BR*, 20 Dec 1838; QUA, Denio to wife, 14 Nov 1838. On Abbey, see *CO*, 20 Dec 1838.
48. Heustis, *Narrative*, 46.
49. Gates, *Recollections*, 22; Heustis, *Narrative*, 46; and Wright, *Narrative*, 6.
50. Gates, *Recollections*, 29.
51. Wright, *Narrative*, 6.
52. *KCG*, 19 Dec 1838; also *KCG*, 1 Dec 1838, statement of von Schoultz; Wright, *Narrative*, 6.
53. Heustis, *Narrative*, 46.

Chapter 7: "The rifle fire of the enemy was particularly true and steady"

1. This song, known as "The Battle of the Windmill," or "The Prescott Volunteers," was written by a Prescott militiaman who fought in the battle of 13 Nov 1838. It was sung to the tune of "The Girl I Left Behind Me," the most famous of all the "loth-to-depart" tunes of the British army. There are a number of versions extant; the one reproduced in the text here was published in *Ontario Historical Society, Papers and Records*, Vol 34 (1942), 43-45 . Note the reference to Richard Fraser and George Macdonell and the use of the term "rebels" for the Hunters.

I have, however, placed the words in eight-line verses which accord with the verse form in "The Girl I Left Behind Me." We know from another version of this song contributed by Judson Polite of Domville to the *History of the Founding and Growth of the St. Lawrence District*, a pamphlet published for the centennial of the battle in 1938, that the song had a chorus. The four-line verse used as a chorus here was chosen because it did not fit smoothly anywhere in the text of the song when formed into eight-line verses.

Polite's version of the first three verses of the song are as follow. Polite probably did not have all the words correct (note the repetition of "bold" four times in the first verse).

Come on all you lads, both stout and bold,
That loves your native land;
Rejoice unto the victory,
Bold Fraser gave command.
Bold Fraser gave the old command
And that you soon shall see,
We fought like any lions bold,
To set the Windmill free.

    So you British boys be steady,
    And maintain your glorious name;
    May we always find bold Fraser,
    To lead us o'er the plain.

When to the Windmill plains we went,
We gave them three loud cheers;
To let the know that day be long[ed]
With the Prescott Volunteers.
Captain Macdonell so nobly led,
His men into the fight;
They did not flinch, no not an inch,
Till the rebels had to yield.

    So you British boys be steady, etc.

He swung his sword right round his head,
Saying "Glengarry, follow me,
We shall gain the day without delay
As that you soon shall see."
As we are the boys that fear no noise,
Where the cannons loud did roar,
We would cut the rebel right and left,
As they landed on our shore.

    So you British boys be steady, etc.

2. NYHS, Worth Papers, Worth to Eustis, 13 Nov 1838.
3. Stacey, "American Account," 394-395; also NYHS, Worth Papers, Worth to Eustis, 13 Nov 1838; and Hough, *St. Lawrence*, 662-663.
4. NAC, CO 42, vol. 451, 394, Sandom to Arthur, 14 Nov 1838.
5. NAC, CO 42, vol. 451, 394, Sandom to Arthur, 14 Nov 1838; Leavitt, *Leeds and Grenville*, 48-49; PRO, Adm 1, vol. 3641, Log, HMS *Niagara*, 13 Nov 1838.
6. NAC: CO 42, vol. 409, pt 2, 361, Young to Halkett, 14 Nov 1838; vol. 451, 394, Sandom to Arthur, 14 Nov 1838; MG 27 I E30, Gowan, "Memoir"; Adm 51, vol. 3641, Log, HMS *Niagara*, 13 Nov 1838; units and strengths from Robinson, *Grenville Militia Regiments*; Leavitt, *Leeds and Grenville*, 49-50, summary by a British officer.
7. *KCG*, 26 Nov 1838, letter from an officer.
8. Morris, *Prescott*, 156.
9. FWP, Smith, "Recollections."
10. On militia units, see Robinson, *The Grenville Militia Regiments* and Appendix B; NAC, RG 9 I B4, Upper Canada Militia Pensions: 464, Petition of Harris Russell; 998, Petition of Christopher Leeson, 4 Aug 1841.
11. FWP, Smith, "Recollections."
12. Carr, *Kemptville*, 9.
13. Carr, *Kemptville*, 10.
14. FWP, MacIntosh, Memoir.
15. FWP, MacIntosh, Memoir; NAC, MG 27, I E30, Gowan, "Memoir"; NAC, CO 42, vol. 409, pt 2, 361, Young to Halkett, 14 Nov 1838; Leavitt, *Leeds and Grenville*, 48-49, summary by a British officer.
16. Wright, *Narrative*, 1.
17. Gates, *Recollections*, 17-18.
18. Gates, *Recollections*, 19.
19. On Hunter numbers on 13 Nov 1838 see: Gates, *Recollections*, 19; Heustis, *Narrative*, 45; and Wright, *Narrative*, 6.
20. The difference between physical and moral courage has been succinctly defined by Major Sedley F.C. Sweeny of the Royal Canadian Engineers, who had good reason to know: "Physical courage is the ability to think clearly under abnormal circumstances, and moral courage is the ability to act decently under the same circumstances." S.F.C. Sweeny to his son, 22 Nov 1939, quoted in William Reid, "The Governor-General's Gold Medal," in Marion Harding, ed., *The Victorian Soldier: Studies in the History of the British Army, 1816-1914* (London, 1993), 220.
21. NAC, CO 42, vol. 451, 394, Sandom to Arthur, 14 Nov 1838.
22. For details of the armament of Sandom's squadron, see PRO, Adm 1, vol. 2564, A List of Vessels and Boats Employed on the Canadian Waters, 31 oct 1838.
23. On this subject, see Sandom's correspondence with the Admiralty and the commander, North America and West Indies station, Apr to July 1838, in PRO, Adm 1, vols. 2563 and 2564.
24. QUA, Hiram Denio to wife, 14 Nov 1838.
25. AO, MS 521, Jessup, "Battle."
26. NYHS, Worth Papers, Worth to Eustis, 13 Nov 1838; on Europeans, see NAC, RG 5, B41, evidence of Chipman. On Hunter artillery, see Wright, *Narrative*, 7.
27. Gates, *Recollections*, 21.
28. Heustis, *Narrative*, 47; QUA, memoir of Nelson Truax. On red uniforms attracting fire, see NAC, MG 27 I E30, Gowan, "Memoir."
29. *UCH*, 27 November 1838.
30. Graves, *Merry Hearts*, 242.
31. Birge was wearing a uniform of his own design (see Kinchen, *Hunters*, 71) but most of the Hunter officers were apparently wearing civilian clothes with the martial addition of epaulettes or wings (see illustration on page 157) and were also armed with swords as opposed to longarms. On the Hunter's flag, see NAC RG 5 A1, B 41, Trial of Solomon Reynolds, Captain Parker's evidence and Note 27 in Chapter 4 above.
32. On the Hunter deployment, see Gates, *Recollections*, 23-24; Heustis, *Narrative*, 47-48 and Wright, *Narrative*, 7.
33. Heustis, *Narrative*, 47; NAC, RG 5, B41, evidence of Bass. See also Wright, *Narrative*, 7; NAC Rg 5, B41, evidence of Bass and Mosher; *UCH*, 22 Jan 1839.
34. Leavitt, *Leeds and Grenville*, 49, summary by a British officer; NAC: MG 27 I E30, Gowan, "Memoir"; RG 5 A1, B 41, evidence of Captain Parker, 26 Nov 1838; MG 27, I E30, Gowan, "Memoir"; C) 42, vol. 409, pt 2, 361, Sandom to Arthur, 14 Nov 1838; Gates, *Recollections*, 24; Wright, *Narrative*, 7.
35. *Ogdensburg Times and Advertizer*, 13 Nov 1838.
36. Gates, *Recollections*, 24.
37. FWP, MacIntosh Memoir.
38. NAC, MG 19, A 39, 365, Young to Foster, 20 Nov 1838; FWP, Smith, "Recollections"; FWP. MacIntosh, Memoir.
39. Gates, *Recollections*, 24.
40. NAC, MG 27, I E 30, Gowan, "Memoir"; Leavitt, *Leeds and Grenville*, 50-51; *KCG*, 26 Nov 1838, letter by a British officer.
41. NAC, MG 27, I E 30, Gowan, "Memoir."
42. The sources for the technique of bayonet fighting come from McClellan, *Manual of Bayonet Exercise*, and the author's own training on the FN C1 rifle as conducted in the 1960s under the guide of Canadian Army Military Training Manual 7-51, *Rifle and Bayonet*. The NCO instructor's injunctions, "Don't be shy, lad, stick it in the soft part, lad, stick it in his guts!" still ring in the author's ears.
43. Field, *Britain's Sea Soldiers*, II, 334.
44. Morris, *Prescott*, 59.
45. Morris, *Prescott*, 59.
46. Preston, *Residence*, II, 167.
47. Gates, *Recollections*, 23; Wright, *Narrative*, 7.
48. NAC, MG 27 I E30, Gowan, "Memoir."
49. NAC, MG 27, I E30, Gowan, "Memoir."
50. NAC, RG 9 I B4, Upper Canada Militia Pension, 998, Petition of Christopher Leeson, 4 Aug 1841; *KCG*, 26 Nov 1838. On Gowan, see *DCB*, Ogle Gowan.
51. QUA, memoir of Nelson Truax; NAC, MG 27, I E30, Gowan, "Memoir."
52. NAC, MG 27, E I 30, Gowan, "Memoir."
53. NAC, MG 19, A39, 365, Young to Foster, 20 Nov 1838; MG 27, I E30, Gowan, "Memoir." Gowan states that he was wounded by one of his own men, others think he was wounded by a Hunter, see Akenson, *Orangeman*, 203, and McLeod, *Brief Review*, 258.
54. QUA, Memoir of Nelson Truax.
55. PRO, WO 25, vol. 495, Statement of Service of W.S. Johnson of the 83rd Reg. of Foot; Anderson, *Anglican Churches*, 35.

56. NAC, CO 42, vol. 452, 373, Deposition of Hely Chamberlain, 22 Dec 1838; RG 5 A1, B40, evidence of Surgeon Gardiner: *KCG*, 26 Nov 1838. On the Hunter use of "buck and ball," a favoured American projectile, see *KCG*, 24 Nov 1838.
57. *KCG*, 26 Nov 1838.
58. FWP, Memoir of Tom Bog; *KCG*, 26 Nov 1838.
59. Burns, *Fort Wellington* (1995), 43; Gates, *Recollections*, 30; PRO, Adm 51, vol. 3641, Log, HMS *Niagara*, 13 Nov 1838.
60. *Ogdensburg Times and Advertizer*, 13 Nov 1838.
61. Wright, *Narrative*, 7.
62. AO, MS 521, Jessup, "Battle."
63. Stacey, "American Account," 395.
64. FWP, "Richard Dumbrill," clipping from a Strathroy, Ontario, newspaper, c. 1890s.
65. Hough, *St. Lawrence*, 668-669.
66. Leavitt, *Leeds and Grenville*, 50-51, summary by a British officer; *KCG*, 26 Nov 1838.
67. NAC, CO 42, vol. 456, Draper to Arthur, 4 Feb 1839.
68. NAC, CO 42, vol. 409, pt 2, Young to Halkett, 14 Nov 1838.
69. FWP, Smith, "Recollections."
70. FWP, Smith, "Recollections". Also, *KCG*, 9 Jan 1839; NAC, RG 9 I B4, 612, Certificate of R.D. Fraser for John Gillespie; 727, Certificate of R.D. Fraser for John Morley; MG 27 I E30, Gowan, "Memoir." On Chisholm, see Kane, *List*; NAC, RG 5 A1, vol. 212, Young to Cubitt, 12 Dec 1838. Information on Scott supplied by Paul Fortier of Prescott.
71. Heustis, *Narrative*, 49.
72. Gates, *Recollections*, 25.
73. Wright, *Narrative*, 7-8; also Gates, *Recollections*, 26; *KCG*, 9 Jan 1839; Anderson, *Bluebloods*, 140-142, 152-154.

74. NAC, CO 42: vol. 409, pt 2, Young to Halkett, 14 Nov 1838; NAC, MG 27 I E30, Gowan, "Memoir"; vol. 451, 394, Sandom to Arthur, 14 Nov 1838; Leavitt, *Leeds and Grenville*, 50-51, summary by a British officer.
75. Gates, *Recollections*, 26.
76. Gates, *Recollections*, 26; also NAC, MG 27 I E30, Gowan, "Memoir"; and Leavitt, *Leeds and Grenville*, 51.
77. FWP, MacIntosh Memoir.
78. NAC, C) 42, vol. 409, pt 2, 361, Young to Halkett, 14 Nov 1838.
79. NAC, C) 42, vol. 409, pt 2, Young to Halkett, 14 Nov 1838.
80. NAC, CO 42, vol. 409, pt 2, Young to Halkett, 14 Nov 1838; also *Ogdensburg Times & Advertizer*, 13 Nov 1838; *BR*, 15 Nov 1838; Hough, *St. Lawrence*, 665; Wright, *Narrative*, 9; NAC, MG 27, I E30, Gowan, "Memoir"; *KCG*, 26 Nov 1838.
81. NAC, MG 19 A39, 365, Young to Foster, 20 Nov 1838;

Robinson, *The Grenville Militia Regiments.*
82. Gates, *Recollections*, 26.
83. Wright, *Narrative*, 9.
84. Gates, *Recollections*, 27.
85. FWP, Smith, "Recollections." On prisoners taken, see NAC, CO 42, vol. 451, 394, Sandom to Arthur, 14 Nov 1838; RG 5, B40, evidence of Arthur.
86. FWP, MacIntosh, Memoir.

Chapter 8: "The last glimmer of hope went out"
1. "Yankee Song of Triumph" from the *Toronto Patriot*, 2 Mar 1838.
2. Heustis, *Narrative*, 50.
3. Gates, *Recollections*, 27.
4. Heustis, *Narrative*, 51.
5. Heustis, *Narrative*, 49-50. On Hunter casualties, see Gates, *Recollections*, 9; Heustis, *Narrative*, 51; *KCG*, 12 Dec 1838, statement of von Schoultz; *KCG*, 26 Dec 1838, von Schoultz to Parker, 1 Dec 1838.
6. On weather, see Wright, *Narrative*, 9; on supplies, see Heustis, *Narrative*, 50, 52.
7. Gates, *Recollections*, 32; Heustis, *Narrative*, 50.
8. Gates, *Recollections*, 32.
9. Gates, *Recollections*, 33-34; PRO, Adm 51, vol. 3641, Log, HMS *Niagara*, 13 Nov 1838.
10. Gates, *Recollections*, 34.
11. Gates, *Recollections*, 34.
12. Gates, *Recollections*, 34-35; NAC, CO 42, vol. 451, 394, Sandom to Arthur, 14 Nov 1838; PRO, Adm 51, vol. 3641, Log, HMS *Niagara*, 13 Nov 1838; *Montreal Gazette*, 8 Dec 1838; *KCG*, 15 Dec 1838.
13. Morris, *Precott*, 57.
14. AO, MS 521, Jessup, "Battle."
15. AO, MS 521, Jessup, "Battle."
16. On Hunter artillery firing at the *Cobourg*, see Gates, *Recollections*, 35. On the mutilation of Johnson's body, see Heustis, *Narrative*, 49; NAC, RG 5 A1, B40, evidence of Surgeon William Gardiner; *UCH*, 20 Nov 1838; *KCG*, 1 Dec 1838, statement of von Schoultz. Although it seems sensational, a number of sources confirm the story of the Polish Hunter who escaped from Windmill Point wearing Johnson's shako and uniform, see Wright, *Narrative*, 9; Stacey, "American Account," 397; *New Yorker*, 24 Nov 1838, letter of Doty, 16 Nov 1838.
17. On weather, see Heustis, *Narrative*, 51; on Meredith, see Scott, *Battle of the Windmill*, 28; AO Pamph 1897 No. 88, "The Patriot's War," Price Senter.
18. Wright, *Narrative*, 9.
19. Heustis, *Narrative*, 55.
20. Heustis, *Narrative*, 52, 56; NYHS, Worth Papers, Worth to Eustis, 13 Nov 1838; Stacey, "American Account," 396.
21. *Ogdensburg Times & Advertizer*, 29 November 1838.
22. NYHS, Worth Papers, Worth to Eustis, 13 Nov 1838.

23. NYHS, Worth Papers, Worth to Eustis, 13 Nov 1838.
24. Hough, *St. Lawrence*, 666-667.
25. NAC, RG 8 I, vol. 750, 65, Macbean to Cubitt, NAC, CO 42, vol 409, pt 2, 362, Dundas to Arthur, 15 Nov 1838; vol. 451, 394, Sandom to Arthur, 14 Nov 1838; NAC, MG 11.
26. NAC, CO 42, vol. 409, pt 2, Dundas to Arthur, 15 Nov 1838.
27. NAC, CO 42, vol 409, pt 2, 359, Dundas to Arthur, 15 Nov 1838; RG 8 I, vol. 750, 65, Macbean to Cubitt, 27 Nov 1838. On Randolph, see Lee, *Battle of the Windmill*, 117.
28. *Arthur*, I, 367, Fraser to Dundas, 14 Nov 1838.
29. Richardson, *Eight Years*, 65.
30. Richardson, *Eight Years*, 66.
31. On militia units and strengths, see Robinson, *The Grenville Militia Regiment.*
32. NAC, RG 9 I B4, 352, Description of Wounds of Edward Landers.
33. Morris, *Prescott*, 58-59; NAC, RG 9 I B4, vol. 6, 347, Petition of Edward Landers.
34. Heustis, *Narrative*, 55; *KCG*, 1 Dec 1838, statement of von Schoultz; Scott, *Battle of the Windmill*, 29; Wright, *Narrative*, 10; Theller, *Canada in 1837-1838*, II, 282, Leavitt, *Leeds and Grenville*, 47.
35. *DCB*, Richard D. Fraser; *KCG*, 1 Dec 1838, statement of von Schoultz; NAC, RG 5 A1, vol. 26, Campbell to Halton, 27 Feb 1816; RG 8 I, vol. 700, 67, Memorial of Richard Fraser, 17 Jan 1815; Guillet, *Lives and Times*, 157; Anderson, *Bluebloods*, 96.
36. *New Yorker*, 24 Nov 1838, letter by D.M. Doty.
37. Scott, *Battle of the Windmill*, 29.
38. AO Pamph 1897, No. 88, "The Patriot War," Price Senter.
39. McLean, "Windmill Revisited," 68; Heustis, *Narrative*, 55.
40. Heustis, *Narrative*, 78.
41. Heustis, *Narrative*, 51.
42. *KCG*, 14 Nov 1838.
43. On Macbean's career, see Kane, *List*, 30.
44. On the size and weight of the 18-pdrs., see Hughes, *British-Smooth Bore Artillery*, 30.
45. PRO, Adm 51, vol. 3641, Log, HMS *Niagara*, 14-15 Nov 1838; *KCG*, 14 Nov 1838.
46. Hough, *St. Lawrence*, 666.
47. Hough, *St. Lawrence*, 666.
48. Stacey, "American Account," 396; Hough, *St. Lawrence*, 666-667; Heustis, *Narrative*, 53.
49. Hough, *St. Lawrence*, 666-667; Heustis, *Narrative*, 53; *KCG*, 1 Dec 1838, statement of von Schoultz.
50. Hough, *St. Lawrence*, 667; Heustis, *Narrative*, 53; *KCG*, 1 Dec 1838, statement of von Schoultz.
51. Heustis, *Narrative*, 53.
52. Heustis, *Narrative*, 54.

53. Wright, *Narrative*, 10; also Heustis, *Narrative*, 54.
54. PRO, Adm 51, vol. 3641, Log, HMS *Niagara*, 14-15 Nov 1838.
55. *KCG*, 14 Nov 1838.
56. PRO, Adm 51, vol. 3641, Log, HMS *Niagara*, 15 Nov 1838.
57. My estimate of Macbean's ammunition scale is based on his reports, see NAC RG 8 I, vol. 750, 65 Macbean to Cubitt, 27 Nov 1838; vol. 1229, Return of Ammunition, Small Stores, etc., 22 Nov 1838. Macbean recorded firing 118 roundshot from his two 18-pdr. guns in ninety minutes on 16 November, or about 39 rounds per gun per hour. He was confident that he could have knocked down the mill by noon the next day and he would not have made that statement unless he had the ammunition to do so. If he had opened fire at first light or about 7 AM on 17 November, he would have had five hours of firing until noon and would have therefore expended a further 200 rounds per 18-pdr. gun. As Macbean was a competent officer, he would have wanted some ammunition spare, so it is reasonable to assume that he ordered 300 rounds to be taken to Prescott for each 18-pdr. gun.
58. On Macbean's company, see Laws, *Battery Records*, 212.
59. Heustis, *Narrative*, 53.
60. Wright, *Narrative*, 10.

Chapter 9: "The troops immediately commenced to bayonet:" The end of the hunt

1. "Hunters of Kentucky," the marching song of the Patriot Hunters.
2. On Major Botet Trydell, see NAC, RG 8 I, vol. 1001, 140, Jackson to Young, 30 July 1842. The strength of the four companies of the 83rd is taken as an average from the six companies of the unit at Kingston on 25 Oct 1838, see PRO, WO 17, vol. 1542, Distribution of the Troops in Canada, 1 Nov 1838.
3. NAC, RG 8 I, vol 750, 65, Macbean to Cubitt, 27 Nov 1838.
4. NAC, RG 8 I, vol. 750, 65, Macbean to Cubitt, 27 Nov 1838. On the regulation number of horses for the three pieces, see Hughes, *Smooth-Bore Artillery*, 105.
5. NAC, CO 42, vol. 409, pt 2, Dundas to Arthur, 18 Nov 1838; *KCG*, 17 Nov 1838; McLean, "Battle;" 68-69.
6. On British army pay in 1838, see Chartrand, *Canadian Military Heritage*, II, 125; and Kane, *List*.
7. FWP, MacIntosh, Memoir.
8. McLean, "Battle of Windmill," 69.
9. Wright, *Narrative*, 10.
10. For details and sources for information on the Hunters who fought at the windmill, see Appendix D.
11. Heustis, *Narrative*, 54.
12. FWP, MacIntosh, Memoir.

13. McLean, "Battle of the Windmill," 68.
14. *MG*, 1 Dec 1838.
15. NAC, CO 42, vol. 409, pt 2, 360, Dundas to Arthur, 18 Nov 1838.
16. Stacey, "American Account," 397; NAC, CO 42, vol. 409, pt 2, 360, Dundas to Arthur, 18 Nov 1838; 362, Sandom to Arthur, 18 Nov 1838.
17. NAC, CO 42, vol. 409, pt 2, Sandom to Arthur, 18 Nov 1838; PRO: Adm 1, vol., 2563, Statement of British Steam Vessels on Lake Ontario; vol. 2564, A List of Vessels and Boats Employed on Canadian Waters, 1 Oct 1838; vol. 2565, Sandom to Admiralty, 14 May 1839; Adm 51, vol. 3641, Log, HMS *Niagara*, 16 Nov 1838.
18. NAC, CO 42, vol. 451, 394, Sandom to Arthur, 14 Nov 1838.
19. NAC, CO 42, vol 409, pt 2, Sandom to Arthur, 18 Nov 1838.
20. McLean, "Battle of the Windmill," 67.
21. McLean, "Battle of the Windmill," 67; Burgoyne, *Historical Records*, 70-77.
22. McLean, "Battle of the Windmill," 67.
23. Account of journey from Beauharnois to Prescott from McLean, "Battle of the Windmill," 67-68; Burgoyne, *Historical Records*, 78-79.
24. McLean, "Battle of the Windmill," 68. On height of grenadier company, see Burgoyne, *Historical Records*, 74. On uniforms of the 93rd in November 1838, see Cavendish, *An Reisimeid Chataich*, 328, 333, 335. Burgoyne, *Historical Records*, 78, notes that the 93rd had suffered during their voyages and marches because they were wearing kilts in a Canadian November.
25. On Emslie, see NAC, RG 8 I, vol. 1000, 147, Hardy to Emslie, 18 Sep 1822; 153, Memorial of Captain John Emslie.
26. Stacey, "American Account," 397.
27. AO, MS 521, Jessup, "Battle."
28. Heustis, *Narrative*, 55.
29. NAC, RG 8 I, vol. 750, 65, Macbean to Cubitt, 27 Nov 1838. On role of 18-pdr. gun, see Hughes, *Smooth-Bore Artillery*, 93.
30. McLean, "Battle of the Windmill," 69.
31. NAC, RG 8 I, vol. 750, 65, Macbean to Cubitt, 27 Nov 1838.
32. McLean, "Battle of the Windmill," 69; also NAC, RG 8 I, vol. 750, 65, Macbean to Cubitt, 27 Nov 1838; NAC, CO 42, vol. 409, pt 2, 360, Dundas to Arthur, 18 Nov 1838.
33. NAC, CO 42, vol. 409, pt 2, Dundas to Arthur, 18 Nov 1838. On Macbean's subordinates, see Kane, *List*.
34. Calculation based on Macbean's expenditure of ammunition as contained in his report to Cubitt, see NAC, RG 8 I, vol. 750, 65, Macbean to Cubitt, 27 Nov 1838, and the naval armament known to have been mounted on Sandom's squadron, see PRO, Adm 1, vol. 2564, A

List of Vessels … employed on the Canadian Waters, 31 Oct 1838; vol. 2565, Sandom to Paget, 14 May 1839.
35. Gates, *Narrative*, 9.
36. Heustis, *Narrative*, 56.
37. Heustis, *Narrative*, 56; RG 5 A1, B40, evidence of Ensign Smith.
38. FWP, MacIntosh, Memoir.
39. NAC, CO 42, vol. 409, pt 2, 362, Sandom to Arthur, 18 Nov 1838.
40. NAC, CO 42, vol. 409, pt 2, Dundas to Arthur, 18 Nov 1838.
41. FWP, MacIntosh, Memoir.
42. NAC, CO 42, vol. 409, pt 2, 360, Dundas to Arthur, 18 Nov 1838.
43. NAC, CO 42, vol. 409, pt 2, 360, Dundas to Arthur, 18 Nov 1838; 362, Sandom to Arthur, 18 Nov 1838; McLean, "Battle of the Windmill," 69.
44. Stacey, "American Account," 397.
45. McLean, "Battle of the Windmill," 69.
46. McLean, "Battle of the Windmill," 69; NAC, CO 42, vol. 409, pt 2, 360, Dundas to Arthur, 18 Nov 1838; 362, Sandom to Arthur, 18 Nov 1838; *KCG*, 17 Nov 1838.
47. Heustis, *Narrative*, 56.
48. Heustis, *Narrative*, 56; Wright, *Narrative*, 11.
49. NAC, RG 8 I, vol. 750, 65, Macbean to Cubitt, 27 Nov 1838.
50. NAC, CO 42, vol. 409, pt 2, 362, Sandom to Arthur, 18 Nov 1838.
51. Stacey, "American Account," 397.
52. Stacey, "American Account," 397.
53. Mclean, "Battle of the Windmill," 69.
54. McLean, "Battle of the Windmill," 71.
55. Mclean, "Battle of the Windmill," 69-70.
56. On the decision to accept a surrender, see NAC: C0 42, vol. 409, pt 2, 360, Dundas to Arthur, 18 Nov 1838; 362, Sandom to Arthur, 18 Nov 1838; RG 5, B41, evidence of Jones, Leary, Noble and Sandom; Heustis, *Narrative*, 57
57. NAC, RG, B41, evidence of Sandom.
58. NAC: CO 42, vol. 456, Draper to Arthur, 4 Feb 1839; MG 11, vol. 409, pt 2, 362, Sandom to Arthur, 18 Nov 1838; *KCG*, 17 Nov 1838; Heustis, *Narrative*, 57.
59. McLean, "Battle of the Windmill," 70.
60. Stacey, "American Account," 398.
61. McLean, "Battle of the Windmill," 69.
62. FWP, MacIntosh, Memoir.
63. Heustis, *Narrative*, 57.
64. On Root, see Heustis, *Narrative*, 57.
65. Wright, *Narrative*, 11.
66. Number of Widows and orphans extrapolated from *KCG*, 26 Oct 1839, Statement of sums paid … for the relief of the loyalist who suffered by the invasion of the brigands, etc, at the Windmill near Prescott, U.C.

67. Heustis, *Narrative*, 57.
68. Wright, *Narrative*, 11.
69. FWP, MacIntosh, Memoir.
70. Von Schoultz to Parker, quoted in Heustis, *Narrative*, 57-58.
71. Stacey, "American Account," 397.
72. On Drummond's fate, see *KCG*, 17 Nov 1838.
73. NAC, RG 8 I, vol. 750, 65, Macbean to Cubitt, 27 Nov 1838. On Macbean's loss of equipment and tools at Prescott, see NAC, RG 8 I, vol. 1229, Return of Ammunition, Small Stores, etc. 22 Nov 1838.
74. On Arthur, see NAC RG 5 A1, Macdonell to McCauley, 17 Dec 1838. On "dirks," see AO, MS 521, Jessup, "Battle."
75. FWP, MacIntosh, Memoir.
76. NAC, RG 51, B40 and B41, evidence of Smith; *KCG*, 17 Nov 1838; Guillet, *Lives and Times*, 279, Williams to Dickens, 21 Dec 1838.
77. AO, MS 521, Jessup, "Battle."
78. NAC, RG5, B40, evidence of Smith.
79. Williams to Dickinson, 21 Dec 1838, *Toronto Mirror*, 8 Feb 1839, contained in Guillet, *Lives and Times*, 279; Stacey, "American Account," 397; NAC, RG 5 A1, vol. 214, List of Prisoners taken by the 93rd and examined by the A. Jones, Magistrate.
80. FWP, Smith, "Recollections." On British casualties, see NAC, CO 42, vol. 456, Draper to Arthur, 4 Feb 1839; MG19 A39, vol. 1, Young to Halkett, 20 Nov 1838; and Lee, *Battle of the Windmill*, 151. On Hunter casualties, see Draper Report, Wright, *Narrative*, 9; *KCG*, 17 Nov and 26 Dec 1838; *Prescott Sentinel*, 24 Nov 1838; *BR*, 20 Dec 1838. Lieutenant Agnew of the 93rd noted that the Hunters apparently threw some of their dead in the St. Lawrence. An eyewitness who walked over the ground the day after the surrender counted 50 dead Hunters from the actions of 13 and 16 November, see *UCH*, 20 Nov 1838. Lee (*Battle of the Windmill*, 133) states that a local source holds that 9 men were buried in one grave about 150 yards west of the mill and 80 yards from the river, under the location of the present railway tracks. A letter published in the Prescott *Sentinel*, 31 Dec 1937, states that the Americans were buried in several trenches on the battlefield. A very careful historian, Lee (*Battle of the Windmill*, 152) estimates that a minimum of 20 Hunters were killed during the battle.
    The official records also contain conflicting evidence on the number of men captured at the windmill. The generally accepted figure is 159 men, see Lee, *Battle of the Windmill*, 156, but the author's research has revealed that there may been as many as ten more men apprehended in the days immediately following the battle.
81. Stacey, "American Account," 397.
82. Heustis, *Narrative*, 59.

83. Heustis, *Narrative*, 60.
84. Wright, *Narrative*, 11-12.
85. Heustis, *Narrative*, 60.
86. Heustis, *Narrative*, 60.
87. There was no shortage of drink in Prescott during the the week of the battle, a merchant was offering 150,000 gallons of whisky for sale in the village, see *Prescott Sentinel*, 24 Nov 1838.
88. Stacey, "American Account," 397.
89. Heustis, *Narrative*, 61.
90. Heustis, *Narrative*, 61.
91. On the voyage to Kingston, see Heustis, *Narrative*, 61 and Wright, *Narrative*, 12.
92. *KCG*, 17 Nov 1838.
93. *KCH*, 17 Nov 1838; *UCH*, 20 Nov 1838; Heustis, *Narrative*, 61; Wright, *Narrative*, 11. Wright, 11, states that a band played "Yankee Doodle" when the Hunters were paraded through Prescott. His memory may have been playing tricks but, if there was a band during the procession through Prescott, it was probably a civilian organization as it was unlikely that Dundas, with a shortage of shipping space, would have brought the regimental band from Kingston to the windmill.
94. *KCG*, 17 Nov 1838.
95. *UCH*, 20 Nov 1838.
96. Heustis, *Narrative*, 61.
97. *KCG*, 17 Nov 1838.
98. Britton Smith, *Kingston! Oh Kingston!*, 293.

Chapter 10: "Where are sinners equal to them?"
The courts martial

1. "The Scheme that Mac Built," a poem published in a Kingston newspaper in November 1838, see Stanley, "Battle of the Windmill," 55-56. "Mac" of course was William Lyon Mackenzie.
2. *DCB*, William H. Draper entry; *BR*, 29 Nov 1838, Militia General Order, 20 Nov 1838; Lee, *Battle of the Windmill*, 137-138.
3. Lee, *Battle of the Windmill*, 137-140.
4. *Arthur*, II, 382, Arthur to Draper, 20 Nov 1838.
5. Lee, *Battle of the Windmill*, 139-140; *MG*, 8 Dec 1838.
6. NAC, CO 42, vol. 456, Draper to Arthur, 4 Feb 1839.
7. For information on the prisoners and the sources from which it was compiled, see Appendix D.
8. Lee, *Battle of the Windmill*, 138-139.
9. NAC, RG 5 A1, vol. 211, Draper to Arthur, 11 Dec 1838.
10. NAC, CO 42, 452, 373, Deposition of Hely Chamberlain, 22 Dec 1838.
11. NAC, RG 5 A1, vol. 211, Draper to Arthur, 9 Dec 1838.
12. *MG*, 4 Dec 1838.
13. Gates, *Recollections*, 36, 39-40; Heustis, *Narrative*, 62, 67-68; Wright, *Narrative*, 12.
14. Heustis, *Narrative*, 79.

15. Wright, *Narrative*, 12; Gates, *Recollections*, 40-41. I am indebted to William Patterson of Kingston for information on the location of the hospital.
16. Wait, *Letters*, 91; Gates, *Recollections*, 40-41.
17. Gates, *Recollections*, 39.
18. Wright, *Narrative*, 12; *Instructions ... Concerning the Regulations of the Sick and the Hospitals*.
19. Heustis, *Narrative*, 68. For information on Counter, see Margaret Angus, "John Counter."
20. Heustis, *Narrative*, 79. On Sheriff Macdonell and the collection and distribution of money for the prisoners, see NAC, RG 5 A1, vol. 211, Macdonell to Arthur, 14 Dec 1838; vol. 212, Macdonell to McCaulay, 17 Dec 1838.
21. Gates, *Recollections*, 51-52; Heustis, *Narrative*, 76; Wright, *Narrative*, 14.
22. Hough, *St. Lawrence*, 670.
23. *CO*, 28 Dec 1838, Jones to Fine, 17 Dec 1838.
24. *CO*, 28 Dec 1838; also Hough, *St. Lawrence*, 670.
25. *Jefferson County Gazette*, 9 Jan 1839, quoted in *KCG*, 17 Jan 1839.
26. *KCG*, 5 Dec 1838.
27. *KCG*, 22 Dec 1838.
28. *KCG*, 8 Dec 1838.
29. *KCG*, 8 Dec 1838, letter "sinde and sealed" by J.W.H. and M.H.
30. NAC, CO 42, vol. 450, Arthur, 383, Griffin to Arthur, 20 Nov 1838.
31. Von Schoultz was correctly identified as a married Swede in the *KCG*, 29 Dec 1838.
32. Richardson, *Eight Years*, 67-68. On Richardson, see *DCB*.
33. *KCG*, 5 Dec 1838, quoting a Syracuse newspaper.
34. *KCG*, 5 Dec 1838.
35. *Toronto Patriot*, 1 Dec 1838.
36. *Onondaga Standard*, 12 Dec 1838, quoted in *KCG*, 19 Dec 1838.
37. *Montreal Herald* quoted in the *CO*, 20 Dec 1838.
38. *Niagara Chronicle*, quoted in *MG*, 31 Dec 1838.
39. *KCG*, 9 Jan 1839.
40. *KCG*, 8 Dec 1838.
41. *MG*, 29 Nov 1838, Van Buren's Proclamation, dated 21 Nov 1838.
42. *KCG*, 8 Dec 1838, quoting *New York Gazette*.
43. *KCG*, 8 Dec 1838, quoting *New York Gazette*; also Lindsey, 444.
44. *CO*, 17 Jan 1838. During the winter of 1838-1839, large public meetings were held at Oswego, Sackets Harbor, Watertown, Cape Vincent and Ogdensburg – and New York. For accounts of these meetings and the resolutions that sprang from them see *BR*, 6 Dec, *CO*, 10 Dec, *KCG*, 4, 22 Dec, *MG*, 13 Dec 1838.
45. *KCG*, 4 Dec 1838; *UCH*, 13 Dec 1838; Welch, *Recollections*, 292.
46. Douglas, "Windsor," 139-140; Theller, 260-262; *KCG*, 20

Dec 1838.

47. Guillet, *Lives and Times*, 145.

48. Douglas, "Battle of Windsor," 143.

49. McLeod, *Brief Review*, 263.

50. Henry Grant, quoted in Douglas, "The Battle of Windsor," 142.

51. Prince to Chichester, 19 Dec 1838, quoted in Douglas, "Windsor," 143. On Prince, see *DCB* entry and Douglas, *John Prince*.

52. NAC, RG A1, B39, evidence of Thebo.

53. Douglas, "Battle of Windsor," 145-146.

54. Brady to Scott, 8 Dec 1838, in Prucha, "Brady," 67. On Hunter casualties, see Guillet, *Lives and Times*, 145.

55. Prince diary, 4 Dec 1838, in Douglas, *John Prince*, 26.

56. On John Prince, see *DCB*.

57. Guillet, *Lives and Times*, 152. On Prince and the aftermath of the battle of Windsor, see Douglas, "Battle of Windsor," 146-152.

58. NAC, RG 5 A1, B40, trial of Daniel George.

59. *KCG*, 19 May, 1838, quoted in Creighton, *The Young Politician*, 54.

60. *KCG*, 19 Sep 1838, quoted in Creighton, *The Young Politician*, 58.

61. Creighton, *The Young Politician*, 63-64.

62. NAC, RG 5, B40, trial of Daniel George.

63. NAC, RG 5, B40, trial of von Schoultz; *KCG*, 12 Dec 1838.

64. NAC, RG 5 B40, trial of von Schoultz; Draper to Bullock, 30 Nov 1838.

65. *KCG*, 1 Dec 1838, statement of von Schoultz; NAC RG 5 B40, trial of von Schoultz.

66. NAC, RG 5, B40, trial of von Schoultz; Creighton, *Young Politician*, 67.

67. NAC, RG 5 A1, vol. 211, Draper to Arthur, 9 Dec 1838.

68. NAC, RG 5, B40, trial of von Schoultz, evidence of Gardner.

69. Guillet, *Lives and Times*, 283.

70. Guillet, *Lives and Times*, 283; RG 5 B41, vol. 2, Sentence passed on prisoners.

71. *KCG*, 20 Dec 1838, evidence of Lt. Smith.

72. NAC, RG B40 & 41, trials of Abbey and George.

73. AO, Pamph 1897 No. 88, Senter Memoir.

74. Lee, *Battle of the Windmill*, 156-157; NAC, RG 5 B40 and 41, trial records, 26 Nov 1838 - 3 Jan 1839.

75. Gates, *Recollections*, 47.

76. *KCG*, 20 Dec 1838.

77. For information on the Hunter prisoners and the sources from it was drawn, see Appendix D.

78. Heustis, *Narrative*, 78.

79. Heustis, *Narrative*, 78.

80. Wright, *Narrative*, 15.

81. Heustis, *Narrative*, 78.

82. *UCG*, Feb 1839, Militia General Order, 9 Feb 1839.

Chapter 11: "I smile through a tear:" Punishment

1. "The Maiden's Answer," a song supposedly composed and sung by Nils von Schoultz before his execution on 8 December 1838, see Wright, *Narrative*, 13.

2. Gowers, *Life for a Life*, 9-10.

3. Gowers, *Life for a Life*, 9-10; Lawrence, *Capital Punishment*, 95-105.

4. Gowers, *Life for a Life*, 9-11; Lawrence, *Capital Punishment*, 25-26, 47-48, 55, 99, 121-122.

5. Hangman Pierrepont testifying in 1956 before a parliamentary committee, quoted in Gowers, *Life for a Life*, 17.

6. Hangman Pierrepont testifying in 1956 before a parliamentary committee, quoted in Gowers, *Life for a Life*, 17.

7. *Quebec Gazette* quoted in Guillet, *Lives and Times*, 110.

8. McLeod, *Brief Review*, 159-160. The author has been unable to find this dramatic request for tenders from potential hangmen in the official records or the Canadian newspapers of the time. It is either a figment of McLeod's feverish imagination or the work of an American journalist who composed it to incite sympathy for the prisoners. For interest, the full text is as follows:

Office of the Provost Marshal,
Kingston, U.C. Nov. 24th, 1838
Sealed tenders will be received at this office, until 12 o'clock, noon, Dec. 6th, 1838, from persons who may be willing to contract for the hanging of such sympathisers, patriots, rebels, Yankees and other vagabonds, as have been, or may be taken in arms, during the present disturbances, the tenders to express the rate per dozen, *York currency*, at which due execution of the law will be performed. The contractor to be entitled to charge for all odd numbers of malefactors, under a dozen, as if the dozen had been fully completed. A gallows to accomodate the individuals, will be furnished by the Provost Marshal; but carts, ropes, ladders, &c., to be found by the contractor.

VIVAT REGINA.

On the dislike of tradesmen for constructing gallows, see NAC, RG 9 1A5, vol. 211, Macdonell to McCaulay, 5 Dec 1838. On the first person hanged in Upper Canada, see Firth, *Town of York*, 236, Willcocks to Willcocks, 3 Nov 1800.

9. NAC, RG 5 A1, vol. 211, Macdonell to McCauley, 5 Dec 1838.

10. NAC, RG 5 A1, vol. 211, Macdonell to McCauley, 5 Dec 1838.

11. On Hagerman, see NAC, RG 5 A1, vol. 211, Draper to Arthur, 9 Dec 1838; on Arthur's direction to the sheriff, see NAC, RG 5A1, Attorney General's Office to Macdonell, 7 Dec 1838.

12. Gates, *Recollections*, 43.

13. NAC, Joseph Pope Papers, vol. 98, Memorandum of a Conversation with Sir John A. Macdonald re von Schoultz, *DCB* entry for von Schoultz; Pipping, *Soldier of Fortune*, 166-167.

14. *UCH*, 11 Dec 1838, von Schoultz to Green.

15. *UCH*, 11 Dec 1838, von Schoultz to Green.

16. *UCH*, 11 Dec 1838.

17. *UCH*, 11 Dec 1838.

18. Heustis, *Narrative*, 71.

19. Heustis, *Narrative*, 73.

20. Heustis, *Narrative*, 73; also *UCH*, 18 Dec 1838; NAC, RG5 A1, vol. 211, Macdonell to Arthur, 14 Dec 1838.

21. *KS*, 14 Dec 1838.

22. *UCH*, 18 Dec 1838.

23. *UCH*, 18 Dec 1838; *BR*, 27 Dec 1838.

24. Gates, *Recollections*, 46.

25. *UCH*, 25 Dec 1838.

26. *KS*, 21 Dec 1838, quoted in Scott, *Battle of the Windmill*, 39.

27. *KS*, 21 Dec 1838, quoted in Scott, *Battle of the Windmill*, 39; also *KCG*, 19 Dec 1838.

28. *UCH*, 29 Dec 1838.

29. *KCG*, 22 Dec 1838, letter from "A Tory" dated 20 Dec 1838.

30. *CO*, 28 Dec 1838; also *UCH*, 29 Dec 1838.

31. On Swete and Peeler, see *CO*, 28 Dec 1838; and NAC, CO 42, vol. 452, 373, Deposition of Hely Chamberlain, 22 Dec 1838.

32. Heustis, *Narrative*, 74.

33. Heustis, *Narrative*, 72.

34. NAC, RG5 A1, vol. 211, McCauley, Jones and McLean to Arthur, 8 Dec 1838.

35. *Arthur*, I, 481, Arthur to Draper, 26 Dec 1838.

36. NAC, RG 5 A1, vol. 211, Sherwood to Arthur, 10 Dec 1838.

37. On Arthur in Australia, see *DCB*, entry for Arthur and Cahill, *Forgotten Patriots*, 254. On judges' advice, see NAC, RG 5 A1, vol. 211, McCauley, McLean and Jones to Arthur, 8 Dec 1838.

38. NAC, CO 42, vo. 456: Arthur to Glenelg, 1 Jan 1839; Report of Executive Council, 24 and 26 Dec 1838; Minutes of Executive Council, 26 Dec, 31 Dec 1838, and 1 Jan 1839.

39. NAC, RG 5 A1, vol. 214, Macdonell to Arthur, 3 Jan 1839; also NAC, CO 42, vo. 456: Arthur to Glenelg, 1 Jan 1839; Report of Executive Council, 26 Dec 1838; Minutes of Executive Council, 26 Dec 1838.

40. Gates, *Recollections*, 48-49.

41. *UCH*, 8 Jan 1839.

42. Heustis, *Narrative*, 74.

43. NAC, RG 5, B41, Draper to Arthur, 27 Dec 1838.
44. *KCG*, 29 Dec 1838; *UCH*, 11 Dec, 18 Dec 1838; Lee, *Battle of the Windmill*, 142.
45. *Arthur*, II, 26, Fox to Arthur, 31 Jan 1839.
46. NAC, CO 42, vol. 456, 7, Arthur to Glenelg, 1 Jan 1839.
47. Heustis, *Narrative*, 74.
48. Heustis, *Narrative*, 74. On Lewis, see NAC: CO 42, vol. 456, Arthur to Glenelg, 1 Jan 1839; RG 5 A1, vol. 212, Anonymous Note to Arthur, 22 Dec 1838.
49. *Arthur*, II, 38, Arthur to Colborne, 5 Feb 1838; NAC, CO 42, vol. 456, Minute of Executive Council, 2 Feb 1839; Arthur to Glenelg, 5 Feb 1839.
50. NAC, RG 5 A1, vol. 211, 214, Classification of the Prisoners … with reference to the Degree of Criminality, 29 Dec 1838.
51. NAC, RG 5 A1, vol. 211, 214, Classification of the Prisoners … with reference to the Degree of Criminality, 29 Dec 1838.
52. NAC, RG 5 A1, vol 214, Draper to Arthur, 1 Jan 1839; Macdonell to McCauley, 9 Jan 1839; MG 24, B98, vol. 1, Vaughan to Jones, 3 Dec 1838; Guillet, *Lives and Times*, 277-278; Lee, "Battle of the Windmill," 156; QUA, Memoir of Nelson Truax; FWP, Memoir of Justus Merriam; AO Pamph 1897, No. 88, Senter Memoir; Hough, *Jefferson County*, 527-528.
53. Hough, *Jefferson County*, 367.
54. Gates, *Recollections*, 49.
55. Heustis, *Narrative*, 81.
56. Heustis, *Narrative*, 81.
57. Gates, *Recollections*, 56.
58. Gates, *Recollections*, 57.
59. Scott, "Patriot Game," 287.
60. Burns, *Fort Wellington*, (1995), 46-48.
61. NAC, MG 24 B98, Account Books of Alpheus Jones.
62. NAC, RG 9 I B4: vol. 4, Militia Pension List, June 1843; vol. 6, 347, Petition of Edward Landers; 431, Petition of John Parlow; vol. 7, 613, Medical Certificate of John Gillespie.
63. *KCG*, 26 Oct 1839, Statement of sums paid … for the relief of the loyalists who suffered by the invasion of Brigands, etc. at the Windmill.
64. NAC, RG 9 I B4, vol. 7, 689, Wilson to Tucker, 10 Oct 1840.
65. Hough, *St. Lawrence*, 671, 673.
66. Hough, *St. Lawrence*, 671.
67. Hough, *St. Lawrence*, 672.
68. Hough, *St. Lawrence*, 671-672; Fryer, *Volunteers* and *Redcoats*, 121.
69. Scott, "Patriot Game," 287-288; Cahill, *Forgotten Patriots*, 81-96.
70. Scott, "Patriot Game," 288.
71. Cahill, *Forgotten Patriots*, 102, 109, 113.
72. Gates, *Recollections*, 81.
73. Gates, *Recollections*, 82.
74. Cahill, *Forgotten Patriots*, 119-120.
75. Gates, *Recollections*, 54.
76. Heustis, *Narrative*, 118. On Maria Wait, see Wait, *Letters*, and Cahill, *Forgotten Patriots*, 143-144.
77. Wright, *Narrative*, 28, 40.
78. Cahill, *Forgotten Patriots*, 169-170; Coke, *Recollections*, 169-172; Heustis, *Narrative*, 120-124; Wright, *Narrative*, 32-33.
79. Heustis, *Narrative*, 132.
80. Cahill, *Forgotten Patriots*, 205-206. For information on the Hunters captured at Prescott, their fate, and the sources from which this information was derived, see Appendix D.
81. On the later depredations of the Patriot Hunters, see Corey, *Crisis*, 120,122; Fryer, *Redcoats*, 124-134; Guillet, *Lives and Times*, 163-177; Hough, *Jefferson County*, 528; and Kinchen, *Hunters*, 103, 110-111.
82. Hough, *Jefferson County*, 529; Kinchen, *Hunters*, 111.
83. *New York Times* quoted in *CO*, 10 Jan 1839.

Epilogue: The fates of men and a windmill

1. "Prescott Volunteers" or "The Battle of the Windmill," sung to the tune of "The Girl I Left Behind Me," as recorded by Judson Polite of Domville in 1938. Note the references to Hamilton D. Jessup and Plomer Young, and the threat to "visit Ogdensburg." The equivalent verses in another common variant to this song (see Note 1 in Chapter 7 above) are as follows:

> If e'er they dare return again,
> They'll see what we can do;
> We'll show them British play, my boys,
> As we did at Waterloo.
> Under Captain Jessup we will fight,
> Let him go where he will;
> With powder and ball, they'll sure fall,
> As they did at the Windmill.

> If I were like great Vergil bright,
> I would employ my quill,
> I would write both day and night,
> Concerning the Windmill.
> Lest to intrude, I will conclude
> And finish off my song,
> We'll pay a visit to Ogdensburg –
> And that before too long.

2. *DAB*, Van Buren entry; Kinchen, *Hunters*, 104.
3. *DAB*, Scott entry.
4. Fredriksen, *Officers*, 70.
5. Fredriksen, *Officers*, 58; Wallace, *Worth*, 5.
6. On Bierce, see Kinchen, *Hunters*, 84; on Theller and McLeod, see their entries in the *DCB*.
7. Guillet, *Lives and Times*, 285.
8. Stanley, "Bill Johnston," 27.
9. Stanley, "Bill Johnston," 27-28; Guillet, *Lives and Times*, 161.
10. Pipping, *Soldier of Fortune*, 165-167.
11. Wright, *Narrative*, 35.
12. Heustis, *Narrative*, 153.
13. Guillet, *Lives and Times*, 229; Gates, *Recollections*, 181.
14. Guillet, *Lives and Times*, 229-230.
15. Hough, *Jefferson County*, 352-353.
16. Communication to author from Dr. Geoffrey Parnell, Keeper of Tower History, 7 Dec 2000.
17. *DNB*, Colborne entry.
18. *DCB*, Arthur entry.
19. *DNB*, Dundas entry.
20. Macbean to Colborne, 14 May 1839, copy in Grenville County Historical Society, Prescott.
21. PRO, Adm 1, vol 2565, Sandom to Paget, 14 May 1839.
22. *DCB*, Sandom entry.
23. *DCB*, Young entry.
24. Kane, *List of Officers*, 30.
25. *DCB*, Fowell entry.
26. Anderson, *Anglican Churches*, 35.
27. Field, *Britain's Sea Soldiers*, II, 334.
28. *DCB*, Mackenzie entry; Lindsey, *Mackenzie*, 452-454.
29. Guillet, *Lives and Times*, 235.
30. Douglas, *John Prince*, Prince diary, 28 Feb 1849.
31. *DCB*, Mackenzie entry; Kilbourn, *Firebrand*, 219-228.
32. *DCB*, Papineau entry.
33. *DCB*, Duncombe and Theller entries.
34. *DCB*, John Prince entry; Douglas, *John Prince*.
35. I am indebted to William Patterson of Kingston for information on the later life of Allan Macdonell.
36. *DCB*, Draper entry.
37. *DCB*, John A. Macdonald entry; Creighton, *The Young Politician*, 67-68.
38. *DCB*, Fraser entry; Halliday, *Murder Among Gentlemen*, 75.
39. *DCB*, Ogle Gowan entry.
40. *DCB*, Richardson entry.
41. Jesup, *Edward Jesup*; and information from Paul Fortier, Prescott.
42. FWP, Smith, "Recollections."
43. Information from Mr. Pember MacIntosh, Nepean.
44. Field, *Britain's Sea-Soldiers*, II, 234.
45. NAC, MG 26J, Mackenzie King diary, 1 July 1938.
46. Scott, *Battle of the Windmill*, 7.
47. Pipping, *Soldier of Fortune*.
48. Scott, "Patriot Game," 294. For information on the Hunters who were exiled to Van Diemen's Land, see Appendix D.

Bibliography

PRIMARY SOURCES

Archival
Archives of Ontario, Toronto
  MS 521, Hamilton Jessup, "Battle of the Windmill"
  Pamphlet 1897, No. 88, "The Patriot's War," translation of *Geschichte der Deutschen in Syracuse und Onondaga County*, 1897, Price Senter memoir
Cazenovia Public Library, Cazenovia, NY
  Scrapbook of Local History articles compiled by Jabez Abel
Friends of Windmill Point, Prescott
  Memoir of Private Allan MacIntosh, typescript
  Memoir of Hunter Justus Merriam, typescript
  Recollections of Colonel Thomas Bog, 1904, typescript
  Sergeant John Smith, "A Veteran's Recollections," newspaper clipping
  "Richard Dumbrill," newspaper clipping
Grenville County Historical Society, Prescott
  Letter, Major F. Macbean to Sir John Colborne, 13 May 1839
Marine Museum of the Great Lakes, Kingston
  Memoir of James Van Cleve
National Archives of Canada, Ottawa
  Manuscript Group 11, Colonial Office 42, correspondence
  Manuscript Group 19
    A 39, Duncan Clark papers
  Manuscript Group 24
    B97, Regulations and Pay of the North West Army
    B98, Account Books of Alpheus Jones, 1838-1839
  Manuscript Group 26 J, Diary of Mackenzie King
  Manuscript Group 27
    I E30, Ogle Gowan, "Memories of the Rebellion in Canada ..."
  Record Group 5 A1, Upper Canada Sundries
  Record Group 5, B40 and B41, State trials, 1838-1839
  Record Group 8 I, British military records
  Record Group 9 I B4, Militia Pension records
    Pope papers, vol. 98 Memorandum of a Conversation with John A. Macdonald
New York Historical Society, New York
  William J. Worth Papers
Public Record Office, Kew, Surrey
  Admiralty 1, Captains' Letters, Sandom, 1838-1840
  Admiralty 51, Captains' Logs
    vol. 3641, Log, HMS *Niagara*, November 1838
  War Office 17, Distribution and Returns of the Army
  War Office 25, Officers' Registers
Queen's University Archives, Kingston
  A. ARCH mc, Hiram Denio to wife, 14 Nov 1838
  A. ARCH mc, Reminiscences of Nelson Truax, 1838-1839

Published
American State Papers. Class V, Military Affairs. Vol. 6. Washington: Gales and Seaton, 1840.
Bonnycastle, Richard H. *Canada as it was, Is, and May Be.* London: Henry Colbourn, 1838, 2 vols.
Douglas, R. Alan, ed. *John Prince. A Collection of Documents.* Toronto: Champlain Society, 1980.
Durham Report. London: Methuen, 1922.
Gates, William. *Recollections of Life in Van Dieman's Land ...* Lockport: C.S. Crandal, 1850.
Heustis, Daniel D. *Narrative of the Adventures and Sufferings of Captain Daniel D. Heustis and His Companions in Canada and Van Dieman's Land ...* Boston: S.W. Wilder, 1848.
Mclean, Scott, ed. "The Battle of the Windmill Revisited: As Recounted by Lieutenant Andrew Agnew, 93rd Highland Regiment of Foot, 8 December 1838," *Canadian Military History*, vol. 9, no. 4, Autumn 2000, 65-72.
McLeod, Donald. *A Brief Review of the Settlement of Upper Canada ...* Cleveland: F.B. Penniman, 1841.
Ormsby, William, ed. *Crisis in the Canadas, 1838-1839.*

The Grey Journals and Letters. Toronto: Macmillan, 1964.
Preston, T.R. *Three Years' Residence in the Canadas, from 1837 to 1839.* London: Richard Bentley, 1840, 2 vols.
Prucha, Francis P., "Reports of General Brady on the Patriot War," *Canadian Historical Review*, 31 (Mar 1950), 56-68.
Richardson, John. *Eight Years in Canada.* Montreal: H.H. Cunningham, 1847.
Roach, Isaac, "Journal of Major Isaac Roach, 1812-1824," *Pennsylvania Magazine of History and Biography*, 17 (1893), 129-162.
Saunders, Charles, ed. *The Arthur Papers ...* Toronto: University of Toronto, 1957, 3 vols.
Scott, Winfield. *Memoirs of General Scott, Written by Himself.* New York: Sheldon, 1864, 2 vols.
Stacey, Charles P., ed., "An American Account of the Prescott Raid of 1838," *Canadian Defence Quarterly*, 9 (1932), 393-398.
——, ed., "A Private Report of General Winfield Scott on the Border Situation of 1839," *Canadian Historical Review*, 21 (1940), 407-414.
Theller, E.A. *Canada in 1837-1838, Showing by Historical Facts, the Causes of the Late Attempted Revolution, and of its Failure ...* New York: J. and H.G. Langley, 1841, 2 vols.
Wait, Benjamin. *Letters from Van Dieman's Land.* Buffalo: A.W. Wilgus, 1843.
Wright, Stephen. *Narrative and Recollections of Van Dieman's Land, During a Three Years' Captivity of Stephen S. Wright, together with an Account of the Battle of Prescott.* New York: J. Winchester, 1844.

Newspapers
Brockville Recorder, 1838-1839
Buffalo Commercial Advertizer, 1837
Buffalo Journal, 1837
Cornwall Observer, 1838-1839
The Jeffersonian, Watertown, 21 Dec 1838
Kingston Chronicle and Gazette, 1837-1840
Kingston Spectator, 1838-1839

Mackenzie's Gazette, 1838

Montreal Gazette, 1838-1839

New York Observer, 1837

New Yorker, 1838

Ogdensburg Times and Advertizer, 1838-1839

Ottawa Citizen, 1938

Prescott Journal, 1937-1938

Prescott Sentinel, 1838-1839

Toronto Patriot, 1838

Upper Canada Gazette, Toronto, 1838-1839

Upper Canada Herald, Kingston, 1838-1839

SECONDARY SOURCES

Books

Akenson, Don. *The Orangeman. The Life and Times of Ogle Gowan.* Toronto: Lorimer, 1986.

Anderson, Allen. *Anglican Churches of Kingston.* Kingston: Diocese of Ontario, 1964.

Anderson, Charles D. *Blue Bloods and Rednecks. Discord and Rebellion in the 1830s.* Burnstown: General Store Publishing, 1996.

Anderson, J. Carr. *Kemptville, Past and Present.* Kemptville, 1903, reprinted 1991.

Army List, The. A List of Officers of the Army and Royal Marines. London: War Office, 1838.

Blackmore, Howard. *British Military Firearms. 1650-1850.* London: Herbert Jenkins, 1961.

Britton Smith, Arthur, comp. *Kingston! Oh Kingston! An Anthology.* Kingston: Brown and Martin, 1987.

Burgoyne, Roderick H. *Historical Records of the 93rd Sutherland Highlanders.* London: Richard Bentley, 1883.

Burns, Robert. *Fort Wellington: A Narrative and Structural History, 1812-1838.* Ottawa: Parks Canada, 1979.

———. *Fort Wellington: A Narrative and Structural History, 1838-1870.* Ottawa: Parks Canada, 1983 and 1995.

Cahill, Jack. *Forgotten Patriots. Canadian Rebels on Australia's Convict Shores.* Toronto: Robin Brass Studio, 1998.

Cavendish, A.E.J. *An Reisimeid Chataich. The 93rd Sutherland Highlanders ... 1799-1927.* Author, 1928.

Chartrand, René. *Canadian Military Heritage, Vol. II, 1755-1871.* Ottawa: DND, 1995.

Corey, A.B. *The Crisis of 1830 to 1842 in Canadian-American Relations.* New Haven: Yale University Press, 1941.

Craig, Gerald M. *Upper Canada. The Formative Years, 1784-1841.* Toronto: McClelland and Stewart, 1963.

Creighton, Donald G. *The Young Politician. John A. Macdonald.* Toronto: Macmillan, 1952.

Current, R.N., Frederick Friedel and T. Harry Williams. *A History of the United States to 1877.* New York: Alfred Knopf, 1967.

Davis, William C. *Three Roads to the Alamo. The Lives and Fortunes of David Crockett, James Bowie and William Barret Travis.* New York: Harper, Collins, 1998.

Dictionary of American Biography. New York: Scribners, 1964, 22 vols.

Dictionary of Canadian Biography. Vols VI-IX, Toronto: University of Toronto, 1976-1988.

Dictionary of National Biography. 65 vols, London: 1885.

Facey-Crowthers, David. *The New Brunswick Militia, 1787-1867.* Fredericton: New Brunswick Museum, 1990.

Field, Cyril. *Britain's Sea-Soldiers. A History of the Royal Marines.* London: Lyceum Press, 1924, 2 vols.

Field Exercise and Evolutions of the Army, London: War Office, 1833.

Firth, Edith, ed. *The Town of York. A Collection of Documents of Early Toronto.* Toronto: Champlain Society, 1962.

Fredriksen, John C. *Officers of the Left Division with Portraits and Anecdotes.* Lewiston: Edgar Mellen, 1989

Fryer, Mary B. *Volunteers and Redcoats, Rebels and Raiders.* Toronto: Dundurn, 1987.

Gowers, Ernest A. *A Life for a Life. The Problem of Capital Punishment.* London: Chatto and Windus, 1956.

Graves, Donald E. *Field of Glory. The Battle of Crysler's Farm, 1813.* Toronto: Robin Brass Studio, 1999.

Guillet, Edwin C. *The Lives and Times of the Patriots.* Toronto: University of Toronto, 1963.

Halliday, Hugh M. *Murder among Gentlemen. A History of Duelling in Canada.* Toronto: Robin Brass Studio, 1999.

Harding, Marion, ed. *The Victorian Soldier. Studies in the History of the British Army, 1816-1914.* London: National Army Museum, 1993.

Historical Sketch, "D" Co., Buffalo City Guard. N.p. c. 1890.

History of the Founding and Growth of the St. Lawrence District. Prescott: *Prescott Journal*, 1938.

Hitsman, J. Mackay. *Safeguarding Canada, 1763-1871.* Toronto: University of Toronto, 1968.

Hough, Franklin B. *A History of Jefferson County in the State of New York.* Albany: Joel Munsell, 1854.

———. *A History of St. Lawrence and Franklin Counties ...* Albany: 1853, reprinted Baltimore, Regional Publishing, 1970.

Hughes, B.P. *British Smooth-Bore Artillery. The Muzzle-Loading Artillery of the 18th and 19th Centuries.* London: Lionel Leventhal, 1969.

Jesup, H.G. *Edward Jessup of West Farms, Westchester Co, New York.* Cambridge: author, 1887.

Johnson, Timothy D. *Winfield Scott. The Quest for Military Glory.* Lawrence: University of Kansas, 1988.

Kane, John. *List of Officers of the Royal Regiment of Artillery ...* Greenwich: Royal Artillery, c. 1850.

Ketchum, William. *An Authentic and Comprehensive History of Buffalo.* 2 vols, Buffalo: Rockwell, Baker, S. Hill, 1864, 2 vols.

Kilbourn, William. *The Firebrand. William Lyon Mackenzie and the Rebellion in Upper Canada.* Toronto: Clarke, Irwin, 1964.

Kinchen, Oscar A. *The Rise and Fall of the Patriot Hunters.* New York: Bookman Associates, 1956.

Laurence, John. *A History of Capital Punishment.* New York: Citadel Press, 1960.

Laws, M.E.S. *Battery Records of the Royal Artillery, 1716-1859.* Woolwich: Royal Artillery Institution, 1952.

Leavitt, Thaddeus. *A History of Leeds and Grenville, Ontario, from 1749 to 1879.* Brockville: Recorder Press, 1879.

Lee, David. *The Battle of the Windmill. November 1838.* Ottawa: Parks Canada, 1974.

Lindsey, Charles. *The Life and Times of William Lyon Mackenzie.* Toronto: Morang & Co., 1912.

Lizars, Robina, and Kathaleen Macfarlande. *Humours of '37.* Toronto: William Biggar, 1898.

Long, Jeff. *Duel of Eagles. The Mexican and U.S. Fight for the Almao.* New York: Morrow, 1990.

Lossing, Benson J. *The Pictorial Field-Book of the War of 1812 ...* New York: Harper, 1869.

Manual and Platoon Exercises, London: War Office, 1834.

McClellan, George B. *Manual of Bayonet Exercise Prepared for the Use of the Army of the United States.* Washington: J.B. Lippincott, 1862.

McConnell, David. *British Smooth-Bore Artillery. A Technological Study.* Ottawa: Parks Canada, 1988.

McKee, Christopher. *A Gentlemanly and Honorable Profession. The Creation of the U.S. Naval Officer Corps, 1794-1815.* Annapolis: United States Naval Institute Press, 1991.

Michalowski, Witold S. *Najemnicy Wolnosci.* Bialystok: Wydawnictwo Bialowieza, 1991.

Morris, John A., comp. *Prescott, 1810-1967.* Prescott: *Prescott Journal*, 1967.

Myatt, Frederick. *The British Infantry, 1660-1945*. Poole: Blandford, 1983.

Peterson, Harold. *Roundshot and Rammers*. Harrisburg: Stackpole, 1969.

Pipping, Ella. *Soldier of Fortune*. Toronto: Macmillan, 1971.

Porch, Douglas. *The French Foreign Legion. A Comprehensive History of the Legendary Fighting Force*. New York: Harper, Collins, 1991.

Prucha, Francis P. *The Sword of the Republic. The U.S. Army on the Frontier, 1783-1846*. Lincoln: University of Nebraska, 1969.

Read, Colin, and Ronald J. Stagg. *The Rebellion of 1837 in Upper Canada*. Toronto: Champlain Society, 1985.

Remini, Robert V. *Andrew Jackson and the Course of American Empire, 1767-1821*. New York: Harper, Row, 1977.

Robinson, Arthur J. *The Grenville Militia Regiments and Other Local Militia Regiments. November 1838*. Victoria, BC: Author, 2000.

Scott, K.F. *Prescott's Famous Battle of the Windmill. November 13-18, 1838*. Prescott: *Prescott Journal*, 1970.

Senior Elinor K. *Redcoats and Patriotes. The Rebellion in Lower Canada, 1837-1838*. Ottawa: Canadian War Museum, 1985.

St. Lawrence International Peace Centennial. June 30th–July 6th–1939. Prescott-Canada. [Programme] Prescott: *Prescott Journal*, 1938.

Stanley, George F. *Canada's Soldiers. The Military History of an Unmilitary People*. Toronto: Macmillan, 1974.

Strachan, Hew. *From Waterloo to Balaclava. Tactics, Technology, and the British Army, 1815-1854*. Cambridge: University Press, 1985.

Tait, George E. *One Dominion. The Story of Canada from 1800 to 1900*. Toronto: Ryerson, 1962.

Wallace, E.S. *William Jenkins Worth. Monterey's Forgotten Hero*. Dallas: Southern Methodist University Press, 1953.

Welch, Samuel. *Home History. Recollections of Buffalo, During the Decade from 1830 to 1840*. Buffalo: Peter, Paul and Brothers, 1891.

Articles

Angus, Margaret. "John Counter," *Historic Kingston*, 27, (1979) 16-25.

Bishop, Levi. "Recollections of the Patriot War of 1837-38," *Michigan Pioneer Collections*, 12, 416-418.

Cruikshank, Ernest A. "The Invasion of Navy Island," *Ontario Historical Society, Papers and Records*, 23 (1937), 7-84.

Douglas, R.A. "The Battle of Windsor," *Ontario History*, 61 (1959), 137-152.

Graves, Donald E. "American Ordnance of the War of 1812: A Preliminary Investigation," *Arms Collecting*, 31, No. 4 (1993), 111-120.

Green, Ernest, "The Battle of the Windmill," *Ontario Historical Society, Papers and Records*, vol. 34 (1942), 43-45.

Martyn, J.P. "The Patriot Invasion of Pelee Island," *Ontario History*, 66 (1964), 153-166.

Neale, Graham. "Colonel John Crysler of Crysler's Farm," *Journal of the Orders and Medals Records Society*, 21 (1982), 50-54.

Scott, Stuart. "The Patriot Game: New Yorkers and the Canadian Rebellions of 1837-1838," *New York History*, July, 1987, 281-295.

Stanley, George F. "William Johnston: Pirate or Patriot," *Historic Kingston*, 6 (1957), 13-28.

———. "The Battle of the Windmill," *Historic Kingston*, 3 (1953), 41-55.

Summers, Elsie G. "Activities of Canadian Patriots in the Rochester District, 1837-1838," *Ontario Historical Society, Papers and Records* (1944), 28-32.

Unpublished

Graves, Donald E. "Joseph Willcocks and the Canadian Volunteers: An Account of Political Disaffection in Upper Canada during the War of 1812," M.A. Thesis, Carleton University, 1982.

Index

About the author

DONALD E. GRAVES has been called "Canada's most reliable and readable military historian" and a "master of the battle-field narrative." A graduate in history of the University of Saskatchewan, he has written, co-written or edited nearly a dozen books and served as an historical consultant for the Canadian Broadcasting Corporation's *People's History of Canada.*

PHOTO BY DIANNE GRAVES

Donald Graves is perhaps best known for his popular series *Forgotten Soldiers: The War of 1812 in the North* (*Field of Glory: The Battle of Crysler's Farm, 1813,* and *Where Right and Glory Lead: The Battle of Lundy's Lane, 1814,* with a third volume forthcoming) but he is also the author of *South Albertas: A Canadian Regiment at War,* regarded by many as one of the best unit histories of the Canadian army in the Second World War, and the editor of *Fighting for Canada: Seven Battles, 1758-1945.* One of his current research projects is a study of the tactical battle to close the Falaise Gap in August 1944.

Donald Graves is the managing director of Ensign Heritage, a consulting firm with interest in historic sites, museums and publishing. He is in demand as a battlefield tour guide for both military units and commercial organizations. He resides with his author wife, Dianne, in a small community in Ontario.

Books by Donald E. Graves

ORIGINAL WORKS

FORGOTTEN SOLDIERS: THE WAR OF 1812 IN THE NORTH

> Vol. I: *Field of Glory: The Battle of Crysler's Farm, 1813*
> (Robin Brass Studio, 1999)

> Vol. II: *Where Right and Glory Lead! The Battle of Lundy's Lane, 1814*
> (Robin Brass Studio, 1997)

South Albertas: A Canadian Regiment at War
(Robin Brass Studio, 1998)

Redcoats and Grey Jackets: The Battle of Chippawa, 1814
(Dundurn Press, 1994)

(with Michael Whitby) *Normandy 1944: The Canadian Summer*
(Art Global, 1994)

EDITED WORKS

Fighting for Canada: Seven Battles, 1758-1945
(Robin Brass Studio, 2000)

The Incredible War of 1812: A Military History by J.M. Hitsman
(Updated by Donald E. Graves; Robin Brass Studio, 1999)

Soldiers of 1814: American Enlisted Men's Memoirs of the Niagara Campaign
(Old Fort Niagara Press, 1996)

Merry Hearts Make Light Days: The War of 1812 Memoirs of Lieutenant John Le Couteur, 104th Foot
(Carleton University Press, 1993, distributed by Robin Brass Studio)

1885. Experiences of the Halifax Battalion in the North-West
· (Museum Restoration Service, 1985)

MONOGRAPHS

Editor, *De Scheel's Treatise on Artillery, 1800*
(Museum Restoration Service, 1984)

Sir William Congreve and the Rocket's Red Glare
(Museum Restoration Service, 1989)